71
DAYS

THE MEDIA ASSAULT
ON OBAMA

MICHAEL JASON OVERSTREET

Visit www.booksurge.com to order additional copies.

For Cathy

CONTENTS

PROLOGUE

The corporate media is far too powerful in this country, and their power leaves most of us feeling helpless. The media has been called "The Fourth Branch of Government," an idea I endorse. Yet we do not elect them. They, more than any other entity, decide elections. I don't know whether they take an intentional position or if their sway is unintentional. But it's there. The present-day media makes mistakes, of course, primarily because they must react immediately and take their cues based on what is directly in front of them. Often, they soon realize their errors, try to self-correct, but fail to understand the damage they have already done—fail to realize that the die has already been cast. This is our media. They are affecting regular people's everyday lives but especially so during a Presidential election. It was one year ago that I decided to write this book. I remembered the effect the media had had on the Gore-Bush election of 2000; I'd seen them only get worse since then. Last year, it became apparent that Barack Obama was going to be a serious political player, and I decided that if he was able to win the Primary, I would write a journal covering the media's treatment of him from the beginning of the Democratic National Convention to Election Day. I had a hunch that he would be treated unfairly.

There are 71 days left until America elects its next President. To preface what I'm about to write over the next ten weeks, let me say that I intend to write what I see and feel as it happens. Once each day's events have been documented and my opinions, narratives, or quotes added, my work for that day will be permanent. For example, if CNN's Anderson Cooper says something that is not objective today and I lambaste him for it, but then he corrects the record next month and redeems himself, I will not go back and delete or edit my original comments about what he said. This is my way of ensuring authenticity, honesty, accuracy, and the feel of a live media feed. A history book, of course, lacks immediate emotional reaction to an event. For example, if I had written down what I was feeling on the day of 9/11, it would be quite different from what I would say about it today. My emotions wouldn't be involved now. I'm not as angry, raw or hurt anymore about 9/11.

I have no bone to pick with any specific members of the media. Does someone make journalists do what they do? Who exactly was in charge of deciding to run what seemed like endless footage on CNN of Jeremiah Wright during the Obama-Clinton Primary? I certainly don't know. Is there some wizard sitting in a dark room up high somewhere who says, *Yes, yes, yes—run that—say that—spin that?* And I'm sure that, in this book, there will be certain members of the media who take on a negative role, and others a positive one. There will probably be, as the days progress, a specific cast of good and bad characters. But my intention is to document exactly what they say and hold them to it. All of the specific times I use in this work will be Pacific, as I am writing from Los Angeles.

Pundits, commentators, and party spokespeople are expected to inject their viewpoints, but anchors and journalists—those tasked to provide reports and analyses but to refrain from opinion—will be my focus in this campaign. How journalists respond to false talking points and how they investigate stories that need to be magnified will be of utmost importance. Will they allow the candidates and their surrogates to blatantly lie? We shall see! My sources will be the network media, major newspapers, news magazines, radio, and Internet media outlets. Barack Obama, in his star-making convention speech of 2004, referred famously to the "Spin Masters". With the "Spin Masters" driving this General Election, it should be one hell of a ride.

DAY 1
"THESE PEOPLE"

Obama is campaigning in Davenport, Iowa, today—Monday, August 25—while McCain is in Sacramento, California. It is the first day of the 2008 Democratic National Convention in Denver, Colorado. The narrative for today, at least from a media perspective, is *How can Obama win over the disgruntled Hillary Clinton supporters?* This question, of course, is in reference to the Democratic primary voters who were staunch Clinton supporters throughout her campaign this year and remain so even after Barack Obama defeated her. All the major cable news networks—FOX News, CNN, and MSNBC—are choosing to run with this narrative. Whether or not this Clinton vs. Obama story it is rooted in fact does not appear to matter. If nothing else, it is a narrative that these three cable networks themselves are writing. Today, a CNN poll shows that 27% of Hillary Clinton backers say they support McCain. A Gallup poll shows that number at 30%. This number is newsworthy, but making it the headline issue at the Democratic National Convention does a disservice to the Obama campaign and provides an unfair advantage to John McCain. Obama perhaps needs the 18 million Clinton voters to help him in the General Election, but the millions who will vote in the upcoming General Election will dwarf the turnout of the Democratic Primary. Both Obama and Clinton received around 18 million votes, respectively, in the primary. But more than 120 million people will vote in the General Election. So why is the media focused on this Clinton demographic? They're giving it much weight. They're creating a perception. It's just the way of media politics as usual, I suppose.

No one can forget the hard-fought primary between Barack Obama and Hillary Clinton, and there is indeed some question about whether or not Obama can win over Clinton's supporters. Even Republican nominee John McCain is using this narrative to his advantage. Today, he launched an ad that specifically targets this Clinton constituency. The ad features a young woman, Debra Bartoshevich, talking forcefully about how she supported Hillary Clinton during the Democratic Primary. She speaks of how she is a "proud Hillary Clinton Democrat." The ad ends with Debra Bartoshevich holding up a "McCain for President" sign and saying that she now supports him for the Presidency. Whether Debra Bartoshevich is a true Clinton supporter or an actor can be left to speculation. But it is clear that McCain is trying to woo Clinton supporters.

Another McCain ad released today suggests Hillary Clinton should have been selected as Obama's running mate. Footage of Clinton making disparaging remarks about Obama during their primary is spliced into the ad to emphasize the narrator's comments. Mind-boggling! A Republican candidate is using Hillary Clinton—a woman whom the GOP has trashed like no other in history—to help him in his attempt to defeat Barack Obama. Here is a transcript of this ad:

Narrator: She won millions of votes. But isn't on his ticket. Why? For speaking the truth. On his plans...

Clinton: You never hear the specifics.

Narrator: On the Resco scandal...

Clinton: We still don't have a lot of answers about Senator Obama.

Narrator: On his attacks...

Clinton: Senator Obama's campaign has become increasingly negative.

Narrator: The truth hurt, and Obama didn't like it.

John McCain: I'm John McCain and I approve this message.

This ad was also played, in full, on CNN's *Larry King Live* at 9:25 pm. One would expect McCain to run such ads, but what I find disturbing is that the major networks continue to show the ads and use them as fodder for commentary. This is giving McCain free airtime. I have seen both McCain ads played several times as part of the news coverage itself throughout the day. It will be interesting to see if they do the same thing with the Obama ads during the Republican National Convention next week.

Today's *Gallup* poll shows the two candidates tied at 45%. With exactly 71 days left until America elects its 44th President, it should be fascinating to see how both campaigns strategize. One of the most glaring narratives coming out of the McCain campaign today is its defense of a blunder made last week regarding a question the candidate was asked about how many homes he owns. Today, McCain is trying to defend his inability to answer that question. We have since learned that McCain owns seven homes. He spoke to Katie Couric on CBS yesterday. Couric scolded, "This week you were roundly criticized for not being able to remember the number of homes you own. How is that possible? How could you not be able to recall that?" McCain responded by saying, "Well first of all let me say that I am grateful for the fact that I have a wonderful life. I spent some years without a kitchen table. Without a chair. And I know what it's like to be blessed by the opportunities of this great nation." It is becoming painfully clear that McCain has used, and will continue to use, his P.O.W. experience as a defense against everything. I recall Joe Biden, during one of the Democratic Primary debates saying, "The only thing you hear out of Rudy Giuliani is a noun, a verb, and 9/11." I am beginning to think the only thing we will hear out of John McCain is a noun, a verb, and P.O.W.

Today Barrack Obama spoke in Davenport, Iowa. The media is trying to make something of the fact that his newly-chosen running mate, Joe Biden, is in Denver and not with Obama in Iowa, even though Biden is scheduled to speak tomorrow night and Obama doesn't speak until Thursday night. His wife, Michelle Obama, is scheduled to be the keynote speaker tonight in Denver. Ted Kennedy is scheduled to speak before her. Members of the media are speculating about whether Ted Kennedy's last minute decision to attend the convention will somehow overshadow Michelle Obama's speech. He has been recovering for the past few months after undergoing surgery for brain cancer.

It had been thought that he wouldn't attend the convention, but he evidently changed his mind at the last minute.

In reference to the supposed rift between the Obama and Clinton camps, NBC's Brian Williams is calling this "The tale of two camps." Hillary Clinton spoke at a press conference in Denver today, answering questions about why she intends to go forward with a roll call for her nomination at the convention. She said, "We are following the conventional paths of conventions." She also answered questions about whether or not she is doing enough to help Obama get elected. She said, "I've been very focused on going wherever Senator Obama's campaign asks me to go. I am at their disposal. We have worked very hard together to make this convention as successful as possible. And I think it's going to be." When asked about the McCain camp's use of her likeness in their ads, she complained, "I don't appreciate having my words used or Senator Biden's words used." Biden's words from his Primary days have also been used against Obama in some McCain ads.

At a rally today in Denver, Clinton talked more about the McCain campaign using her in their ads. She clarified her position on McCain's tactic: "Let me be clear, I'm Hillary Clinton and I do not approve this message." This comment evoked laughter and cheers from the crowd, but she didn't go far enough here. I would like to have seen her denounce her past statements more forcefully, less frivolously. Today, her former campaign manager, Terry McAuliffe, spoke to *Hardball's* Chris Matthews about the McCain camp's use of Clinton's likeness in their ads. He said, "I hope they paid a lot of money for that ad because it's going nowhere."

Clinton also tried to clear up some of the question marks regarding whether or not she is giving Obama her full support. There are some questions as well regarding how her delegates will behave on the convention floor Wednesday. In reference to her delegates, Clinton revealed, "I will be formally releasing them on Wednesday." There was a tone to Clinton's voice on this issue that lacked authentic passion— not a tone that would inspire her supporters to change their minds and get on board with Obama.

There is also talk today about whom John McCain will choose as his Vice Presidential running mate. The media is predicting the types of people he will need to choose in order to counter Obama's recent pick of Joe Biden, who was selected two days ago. The two names mentioned most as McCain VP possibilities are Minnesota Gov. Tim Pawlenty and former Massachusetts Gov. Mitt Romney. Chuck Todd of MSNBC mentioned how the McCain camp may select Pawlenty in the belief that he can "aw shucks" his way through the debates against Joe Biden, much like many believe George Bush did against both Al Gore in 2000 and John Kerry in 2004. Many analysts believed that both Gore and Kerry won their respective debates against Bush but that it was Bush's "aw shucks" attitude that won over so many supporters and allowed him to defeat his more professorial-sounding opponents. On MSNBC, Luke Russert, son of the late Tim Russert, spoke about what his father would be saying today regarding Obama's selection of Joe Biden as his VP. He said that his father would be asking the question, "Will Joe Biden be gaff-free until the election?"

The issue of race! It's being batted around on the networks—all the networks, all the time, it seems. The question of whether or not America will elect a black president is front and center. Today, Valerie Jarrett, an Obama spokesperson, told MSNBC's David Gregory, "Race is not gonna be the issue that wins the day." *The Washington Post's* Eugene Robinson said he had spoken to someone previously who referred to Obama as "a person who had been born overseas." He said he had to correct that person by telling them, "It was McCain who was born overseas, and Obama was born in the United States." David Gregory's interview with Jarrett focused primarily on Obama's mixed heritage and the roll it will play in the election. Jarrett said, "Obama doesn't fit into a box." But it was the further commentary of Eugene Robinson that caught my attention: "The notion that America, which is a nation of immigrants, would in any way have a problem with a candidate who has lived overseas at some point during his life is silly." I echo that sentiment. In fact, in today's world, more real-life experience out and about in the world, interacting with various cultures could only add to a potential leader's capacity to navigate issues more deftly, it would seem.

When David Gregory later tried to give a theme to the week by saying that it will be important for Obama to pass a "threshold test," all I could ask myself was *What does any of this have to do with a threshold test and why the use of such dramatic-sounding language?* It's as if the media is creating the very threshold test that Obama will have to pass. If not creating it, then at the least amplifying it. Gregory went on to suggest that it will be important for people to be able to answer this question: "To know Barack Obama is to be comfortable with—what?" What the hell does that mean? A question comes to mind. *Will David Gregory ask: To know John McCain is to be comfortable with—what? —next week at the Republican National Convention?* And don't tell me that posing such a question about McCain won't be necessary because everyone already knows John McCain (Who knew he had all those houses?) but that, compared to McCain, Obama is young and unfamiliar—unfamiliar enough to make people uncomfortable.

The question David Gregory asked is one that is becoming a dominant theme for today on all the networks. I even saw Judy Woodruff of PBS talk about the importance of Barack Obama telling people "who he is." This type of language has racial undertones to it, whether intentionally or unintentionally. He went to Harvard for Christ's sake! He was the first Black editor of The Harvard Law Review. Harvard probably vets people more than the political parties do. Since when did the Harvard degree lose its credibility? Isn't Harvard the American gold standard? I always thought that if you graduated from Harvard, people were automatically expected to know "who you are." A very, very smart person!

For the past nineteen months, I have learned more about Barack Obama than any other person in history. So I pose this question to the media authors and peddlers of the *Who is Barack Obama?* narrative: *How can anyone who has a slight interest in government and has lived in the United States for the past two years not know who Barack Obama is?* And even if there are some voters who don't know him, how can posing such an extreme question like *Who is Barack Obama?* not sway people toward believing that, in some way, we might find out some egregious information about him—some awful secret we don't yet know. One must infer something foul from such a dramatic question, posed by the lead host of a show. This opinionated type of language is usually reserved for pundits and radio talking heads, not lead hosts, whom we depend on for having the professionalism and discipline to give us an unbiased reporting of the news.

The network that has mastered this art of political spin is FOX News, and they were at their best today. At 6:55 pm, FOX News' Sean Hannity talked about the upcoming speech due to be given by Michelle Obama. He said, "Whatever Michelle Obama says tonight, I have no doubt that it will have to be compared to her previous comments. Remember, this is a woman who has said that for the first time in my life I am proud of my country." His FOX News colleague, Karl Rove, then began speaking about both Michelle and Barack Obama. He added to the doubts: "The idea of how 'these people' are as a first couple matters a great deal. If we're gonna have 'these people' in our homes for the next four years, we're gonna need to know who 'these people' are." This commentary is quite racist and disturbing, but not surprising, considering what network that is spewing it. But it is this type of opinion-driven reporting that is too often finding its way onto other networks—networks that have historically been sources of reliable, unbiased coverage.

Today's convention events ended with Michelle Obama taking the stage at approximately 7:30 pm. She gave an effective and inspiring speech. Tasked to summon up words that would correct the false image that many Americans have of her—that she is an angry, unpatriotic woman—she nailed it. Largely the media helped paint this false image of her—most specifically FOX News. They did so by running, for months and months ad nauseam, footage of Michelle Obama giving a speech in which she states, "For the first time in my adult lifetime I am really proud of my country." Days after Michelle Obama made those comments, she clarified herself by saying that she was referring specifically to the political process. But her explanation didn't stop the media from continuing to play her original comments for months on end. Just today, as I previously mentioned, Sean Hannity reiterated, "This is a woman who has said that for the first time in my adult life I am proud of my country." Would you like to hear this sentence again? Stay tuned. It's Hannity's favorite sentence.

There is a specific way in which the broader media helped to perpetuate the false notion that Michelle Obama is unpatriotic. They have done so by asking loaded questions. I am paraphrasing here, but I have heard many questions like this on various networks: *Do you think Michelle Obama has done enough to convince people that she is patriotic and does love her country?* Questions like this imply that Michelle indeed didn't love her country at some point in the past. They give credence to an opinion about Michelle Obama that was originally framed by people like FOX News' Sean Hannity. He took her original comments and concluded that she didn't love her country—or at least tried (is trying) to sell this notion.

Today, just after Michelle Obama's speech, John King of CNN explained how her speech was important because people have questions. King said, "They don't know who *these people* are." Again, I'm not sure that saying "these people" is the best way to refer to the Obamas. David Gergen then followed by describing how tonight Michelle Obama did a good job of answering the question of *Who are these people?* During the Republican Convention next week, will the media feel compelled, as they endlessly are regarding the Obamas, to inquire *Who are Cindy and John McCain? Do we know these people?*

Gergen praised her speech, but again, his use of the phrase "these people" was more powerful than the point he was trying to make. Words matter, and these words are unacceptable. John King then explained how Michelle Obama had been tasked to beat back some of the Republican spin. King summed up her speech by claiming that the Obamas are in some way trying to say, "We may look different, but our lives have been like your lives." That was John King's actual quote. It surprised me. I myself didn't hear Michelle Obama say anything that even remotely implied the meaning "We may look different." I understand that King was trying to paint a picture, and that this was merely his interpretation, but if one reads the transcript of her speech, she never says a word about, nor implies, anything about looking different. And when John King says "your lives," to whom is he referring? Is the "your" in John King's "your lives" referring to white Americans, Hispanics, Asian Americans, Native Americans? Who? John King seemed to be trying to think for White viewers, ignoring every other demographic in his haste.

This is insensitive, narrow journalism, and, unfortunately, it affects voters. If the "your" in his comment was referring to blue collar workers, he should not have prefaced his comments by using the phrase "we may look different." This phrase implies race!

We need more neutrality here and less injected opinion. Michelle Obama's speech focused more on her father having MS and dying at a relatively young age. She spoke about Barack Obama's having been raised by a single parent. The theme of her speech centered on overcoming hardships in order to achieve greatness. It centered on her thankfulness to a country that allowed this triumph to happen, and it focused on her love for her husband. She said, "The Barack Obama I know today is the same man I fell in love with nineteen years ago. He's the same man who drove me and our new baby daughter home from the hospital ten years ago this summer, inching along at a snail's pace, peering anxiously at us in the rearview mirror, feeling the whole weight of her future in his hands." In no way did I ever hear her make any references to "looking different." John King is a very well respected journalist and I admire his work, but it is these types of subtle, perhaps even innocent, comments that serve to aid the politics of fear.

Another unsettling element of today's coverage centered on Anderson Cooper's coverage of the convention. I am finally convinced that I am to blame for thinking that he has ever been an unbiased journalist. He has redefined what it means to be a news reporter. I don't know what he is, but he works on a so-called serious network, not Comedy Central. I have studied broadcast journalism and was never taught any of the methods Mr. Cooper uses when tasked to cover serious news. His style seems better suited for shows like *E News Live, Entertainment Tonight, or Extra*—shows that thrive on tabloid-style journalism. During tonight's coverage, he stoked the fires of a media driven notion—a notion that the Democratic Party wasted the evening by not talking about anything substantive—by not attacking John McCain. James Carville made his sentiments clear regarding this issue. He felt that the night had indeed been wasted. But, as he is strictly a commentator, I expect hyperbole from him and the like. I don't, however, expect this from Anderson Cooper, who seems to jump on hyperbole and inflate it by asking one loaded question after another.

An interesting exchange between FOX News' Sean Hannity and former presidential candidate Howard Dean took place today. Hannity started by saying, "John Edwards and John Kerry both laid out the case about weapons of mass destruction the way the President did. Why do they get a pass from people like you?" Dean responded: "Well, there were other things that the President told us that were not so. There was no connection between Al Qaeda and Saddam Hussein. Even the 9/11 Commission just said so." Hannity immediately interrupted here and said, "The 9/11 Commission said, in fact, that there was friendly correspondence." Dean then cut him off forcefully: "No, that's not actually what they said, Sean. As a matter of fact, that's exactly what they didn't say, and if you think they did you should watch 'Out Foxed.' It's a great movie and it says why people like you say things like that on this television station." Sean Hannity then smirked and looked a bit like he wanted to change the subject immediately.

FOX News influences a large audience of voters, and too many of its hosts have obtained too much power. The higher ups at FOX would be wise to remember what George Bernard Shaw once said: "Power does not corrupt men; fools, however, if they get into a position of power, corrupt power."

Bill Maher, host of HBO's *Real Time*, provided one of the most poignant comments of the day. On MSNBC he talked about the media and its influence on Americans then suggested, "Americans need to look at themselves in the mirror. Too many of them believe that Barack Obama, who was raised by a single mother, is an elitist. Americans get the leaders they deserve, and they don't deserve a very good leader."

DAY 2
OBAMA VS CLINTON

Obama is campaigning in Kansas City, Missouri, today—Tuesday, August 26—while McCain is in Phoenix, Arizona. A story that is getting very little media attention is the arrest of four people allegedly involved in a plot to assassinate Obama during his speech Thursday night at INVESCO Field. It evidently was not a credible threat, or at least that's how the Obama campaign is choosing to portray it. Meanwhile, John McCain told the American Legion in Phoenix today that Obama could have expressed confidence in America's leadership when he spoke in Berlin during his recent trip to the Middle East and Europe. "[Obama] was the picture of confidence, in some ways," McCain said. "But confidence in oneself and confidence in one's country are not the same." McCain's believing that he can tell whether or not Obama is confident in America strikes me as quite remarkable.

The relationship between the Clinton and Obama camps at the convention is the leading story for today. MSNBC is calling it *The Clinton-Obama Drama*. Clinton is the keynote speaker at the convention tonight. Democratic Congresswoman Loretta Sanchez of California was more than willing to stoke the drama fires when speaking to Dan Abrams of MSNBC. She appeared upset that the Obama camp hadn't done enough to help Clinton pay off her debt. When asked if she will vote for Obama she said, "I haven't been asked. He needs to ask me. He can pick up the phone and ask." She appeared overwhelmingly petty in her inability to hide the obvious angst she still feels over the Primary results.

Referring to Obama's chances of getting elected, Bill Kristol of *The Weekly Standard* said on FOX News, "I don't know if Obama can simply say, 'I'm like you, please make me President.'" Who is Mr. Crystal referring to when he says "you"? Is he talking about class or race? He didn't expound on the word "you". His bazaar reference most certainly isn't clear. A vague mystery for us to ponder, I suppose. I don't recall witnessing a presidential election more wrapped in language that included references to being *like you* than this one. The media is obsessed with focusing on whether or not Barack Obama is *like you*. I still haven't figured out who the "you" is. Maybe I'll find out over the next 70 days. Past elections focused more on the candidate's competency, stance on issues, qualifications, etc. I don't recall the media pondering whether or not Ronald Reagan, George Bush, Bill Clinton, or George Bush Jr., were *like you*. Perhaps they should have. If any one of these former candidates was indeed sold as being just *like you* it was George W. Bush. Unfortunately, for the last eight years, we've seen how important it is for the candidate not to be like the proverbial "you" and why the proverbial "you" should never become President.

Barack Obama started the day in Kansas City. He responded to questions regarding a new ad being run by a "swift boat" operation, *The American Issues Project*. The Associated Press is reporting that the group spent $2.8 million on the ad in which they attempt to link Barack

Obama to a radical by the name of William Ayers. The ad isn't being run nationally, so I was surprised when I was online at *USAToday.com* and came across an article in their "On Politics" blogs section entitled **Obama Responds to Radical Ad.** Mark Memmott posted the article. Part of the article read "Why is Republican John McCain 'talking about the 60s?' Democrat Barack Obama's latest TV ad asks. It's a hard-hitting response to a conservative group's <u>hard-hitting ad</u>." *USA Today's* online article highlighted and underlined the words "hard-hitting ad" and allowed me to click on it. So I clicked on it and was led directly to *American Issues Project. Org.* There it was!—the slanderous ad against Obama. I was shocked that *USA Today* would provide a link to such a radical ad. I'm sure the *American Issues Project* is happy that their otherwise locally-run ad is being spread all over the world by a reputable media outlet like *USA Today.* Here is script of the egregious ad that McCain himself has not yet denounced:

> Beyond the speeches, how much do you know about Barack Obama? What does he really believe? Consider this: United 93 never hit the Capitol on 9/11. But the Capitol was bombed 30 years before by an American terrorist group called, 'Weather Underground' that declared war on the U.S., targeting the Capitol, the Pentagon, police stations, and more. One of the group's leaders, William Ayers, admits to the bombings, proudly saying later, 'We didn't do enough.' Some members of the group Ayers founded even went on to kill police. But Barack Obama

is a friend with Ayers, defending him as quote, 'respectable and mainstream.' Obama's political career was launched in Ayers' home and the two served together on a left-wing board. Why would Barack Obama be a friend with someone who bombed the Capitol and is proud of it? Do you know enough to elect Barack Obama?

I must reiterate: I was very surprised that *USA Today* would provide a link to this ad. It will be interesting to see if John McCain denounces the ad in the near future. It will also be fascinating to see what role the media will play regarding these attack ads over the next 70 days before the election. I have a sneaking suspicion that these "swift boat" outfits are beginning to think they can spend very little money on their cheap ads in the belief that some nationally recognized media outlet will jump on them—or do they slip certain members of the media some cash to jump on them? It's amazing what kinds of access lobbying can buy!

A political headline for an article written by Jodi Kantor in today's *New York Times* reads, **Michelle Obama, Now a Softer Presence, Takes Center Stage.** Who are the ones who originally defined her as not having a so-called "soft presence?" I don't believe she has ever had a hard presence. I don't believe that her mother, brother, children, or husband have ever described her as having a hard presence. FOX News and Republican spokespeople are the ones who've painted her as a woman with a hard presence. Did Kantor of the *New York Times* ever originally believe that Michelle Obama had a hard edge, or has she inadvertently taken her cues from FOX News and the GOP?

This is a classic example of how the media gets caught up in the muck, adopts a manufactured perception, having forgotten where it originated, then runs with it. At worst, Michelle Obama is perhaps guilty of political naivety. That's not a hard edge, that's the naivety of a political novice. When she said, "For the first time in my adult lifetime I am really proud of my country," she didn't say it with a hard edge or malice. It was said with introspection, sensitivity and softness. Just go back and listen to it! No one in that room gasped when she said it. If Michelle Obama did indeed become a "softer presence" last night, as Kantor suggests, I would expect this "softer presence" to serve as the standard from which to judge her over the next 70 days. If she has "adopted" this new persona, I expect the *New York Times* never again to reference anything regarding her implicit "harder presence."

To date, I have heard no one in the media mention The Keating Five. It will be interesting to see if this topic is raised over the next few weeks. Will the Obama campaign use this topic in any ads during the Republican Convention next week? I doubt it! So far they have been unwilling to engage in any kind of smear campaigning. But McCain is rolling out dirty attack ads by the minute. The following ad, which again includes excerpts of Hillary Clinton, has just become fodder for the media:

> **Narrator**: It's 3 am and your children are safe and asleep. Who do you want answering the phone?
> **Narrator**: Uncertainty! Dangerous aggression! Rogue nations! Radicalism!"
> **Hillary Clinton:** I know Senator McCain has a lifetime of experience that he will bring to the

White House and Senator Obama has a speech that he gave in 2002.
Narrator: Hillary's right! John McCain for President!
John McCain: I'm John McCain and I approve this message.

Now let's be clear! The reason I am acknowledging this ad is because the major news networks are running it. No other reason! On CNN, at 12:02 pm, *Headline News* ran the ad. Just after they showed it, a gentleman by the name of Paul Steinhauser commented, "The McCain campaign is not spending a lot of money on it. But the networks are picking it up." At 1:00 pm, Tom Brokaw was anchoring MSNBC's coverage of the convention. He showed this same ad. I don't know why I'm surprised, considering the fact that earlier this year, FOX and CNN ran looped feeds of Reverend Jeremiah Wright's inflammatory remarks for hours at a time, pausing only for commercials. Whether or not the media coverage of these McCain attack ads will affect Obama's chances for election remains to be seen.

Democrats are still pouncing on the McCain gaff regarding his inability to recall how many homes he owns. They are selling campaign buttons that say, "Ask me how many houses I own." Media members are also trying to claim that the Democrats aren't doing enough to paint McCain as a Bush clone—that they're not attacking him enough. MSNBC's Pat Buchanan shouted, "Where is Cheney? It's a free shot. Go after Cheney. Go after Bush."

But the more pressing topic dominating the press is the issue of Hillary Clinton's speech tonight. Will she throw her support convincingly behind Obama? Will she summon up the words to unite an obviously divided party? Will she respond to the McCain camp's use of her in their ads? MSNBC's Rachel Maddow spoke about how she thinks Hillary Clinton is allowing the McCain camp to use her. She stated emphatically, "They are using her! She is being used!"

The media is largely amplifying the issue of the rift, if one actually exists, between the Clinton and Obama camps. They are fueling this fire. It's as if the media is preparing to base their future coverage on what Clinton says tonight. If Clinton fully endorses Obama and ends the division within the party, will the media have to change their narrative? And if Clinton does manage to unite the party, what will the media latch onto next? I suspect that when this convention ends, the Clinton name is going to fade into the background and the media will be back to discussing issues like whether or not McCain is right when he accuses Obama of being more inclined to "lose a war rather than lose an election." Remember, the media is writing the narrative. They are the fourth branch of government, a dangerous fact in America. Why dangerous? Because we are dependent on their ethics to check their own power—no other checks and balances. Who's going to check the power of the press?

Hillary Clinton just finished her speech. The speech was powerful and appeared to be effective enough to help unite the party. You couldn't watch the speech without feeling the historical significance of it. The importance of the speech was palpable. One could feel a literal conversion happening as the cameras scanned the ever so loyal faces of the Clintonites—Clintonites that seemed to be slowly letting go of their past visions of certainty. Perhaps they had been too certain when visualizing their candidate, Senator Clinton, in the White House—so certain that they put themselves in the dangerous position of being loyal to a person instead of that person's issues. And now, as they absorb the words of their hero, they are being effectively convinced to let go of that vision. Tonight, it is abundantly clear: America is a democracy, not a monarchy.

Nevertheless, one could see the effect that Clinton has on her supporters. She convinced them to let go of that engrained dream and support Senator Obama. Clinton counseled her supporters, "I want you to ask yourselves *Were you in this campaign just for me*?" She then referenced a long list of issues and suggested that her supporters should be "in it" because of these major issues—not just for her. As Clinton spoke, Senator Obama was in Billings, Montana, where he watched the convention. According to several media outlets, he apparently liked it when Clinton said, "No way, no how, no McCain."

A line that has the media buzzing centers on Clinton's reference to the fact that McCain and the Republican National Convention will be in Minnesota next week. She joked, "It makes perfect sense that John McCain and George Bush will be in the Twin Cities next week…because these days Bush and McCain are awfully hard to tell apart." The line drew a huge cheer from the convention crowd.

Members of the media were more than willing to praise Clinton's speech. They did an about face. Suddenly they began speaking as if the Party was now magically united. CNN's James Carville said, "This is a bad night for all of the Hillary haters in the media. This was a bad night to be a Republican. What we saw tonight was a party coming together." Carl Bernstein added, "We've seen the ability of two movements to come together. Obama is getting what he wants out of this convention." David Gergen lauded the speech claiming, "This speech tonight puts pressure on Bill Clinton for his speech tomorrow night." A line from Clinton's speech that CNN left on the screen as a headline announced her message: *I am a proud supporter of Barack Obama.* With a large crowd gathered outside the convention and cheering, MSNBC's Rachel Maddow yelled over their noise, "Let the record show that many of the people shouting for Obama are holding Hillary Clinton signs. Let the record show!" Regarding McCain's future use of Clinton in his ads, CNN's Wolf Blitzer said, "It's unlikely they'll use anything she said tonight in their ads tomorrow?"

But of course the narrative was not entirely rosy after Clinton's speech, an observation that must mean I am about to refer to FOX News. Yes I am! FOX News' Greta Van Susteren asked Terry McAuliffe, "What is Senator Obama's sudden experience that Hillary mentioned in her speech—experience that she said he didn't have last spring? She said last spring that he didn't have any experience." McAuliffe responded by saying, "Look, that was Democrat against Democrat. Every Democrat was a better candidate than John McCain. They're not even in the same league."

DAY 3
KOOM BY YA

Obama is campaigning in Billings, Montana, today—Wednesday, August 27—while McCain is in Phoenix, Arizona. "None of us can afford to sit on the sidelines." This quote from Hillary Clinton's speech last night is spreading over the airwaves today. The media is fixated on whether or not Clinton's speech managed to convince her supporters to support Obama. Newspapers all over the country have similar political headlines today: *The Chicago Tribune*: "Did Hillary Clinton Sell it?" *The Boston Globe*: "An Impassioned Call for Unity"; *The San Francisco Chronicle*: "Clinton Hails Obama in Bid to Forge Unity"; *The New York Times*: "Clinton Rallies Her Troops to Fight for an Obama Victory"; *The Houston Chronicle*: "Ticket to Unity?" *The Miami Herald*: "Democrats Poised to Give Obama Historic Nomination"; *The Denver Post:* "Clinton: The Team Player"; *The Washington Post*: "Bill Clinton, Obama Distant"; *The Los Angeles Times:* "Hillary Clinton Calls on Democrats to End Their Rift." One outstanding exception, the paper that couldn't shift gears quite so quickly, *The Washington Post* remained stuck on the rift: "Bill Clinton, Obama Distant".

Referring to whether Hillary Clinton did enough to help Obama in her speech, Carl Bernstein of CNN said, "She's never going to like him. This is step one in Hillary

Clinton joining this ticket. I'm not sure she could have done everything last night." He went on to comment about Bill Clinton, who is scheduled to speak tonight. Bernstein added, " Bill Clinton does not have very warm feelings toward Barack Obama personally."

CNN's Amy Holmes tried to make the case that even though Clinton had delivered an effective speech, she never talked about the issue of leadership. Holmes said, "Hillary did not say that Barack Obama is ready to lead last night. The speech was pretty generic. Hillary had her chance to say *I believe that Barrack Obama is ready to lead.* And she did not!"

Celebrities are flocking to this year's convention. Soledad Obrien asked director Spike Lee, "What role will race play in this election moving forward?" Spike Lee believes it will play a significant role. Before he went off the air he said, "Can I ask you one last question? Can I say one last thing? I would really like CNN to do this. I would like CNN to contrast what the Democratic Convention looks like compared to what we're likely to see in Minnesota at the Republican Convention next week. Compare the faces. Compare the different races. Compare it! Compare it!"

I wonder if Spike Lee has stopped to consider the possibility that the very reason Barack Obama has become such a sensation—the very reason the media is covering this convention like no other in history—the very reason that more people voted for Obama in the primary than any other primary in history—is because Obama supporters are already aware of the very Republican portrait that Spike Lee is referring to. Obama supporters know that the Republican National Convention will consist largely of white faces. They know all of this already. Spike Lee is beating a dead horse. If he were truly as progressive thinking as he thinks he is, he would probably realize that, though he is a great director, his old school and divisive presence at the convention possibly hurts Obama. I like Spike Lee's films, but for him not to realize that Barack Obama's platform—his entire strategy—is based on being post-racial—is not very savvy. The reason he is the nominee at the convention where Spike Lee sits is because of awareness among Obama supporters that the Republican Party doesn't represent them. When he asks CNN to "look at the faces next week," he is stating the obvious. He is undermining the very goal he supposedly seeks. That said, we will probably all look more closely at those faces next week.

FOX News is making the issue of securing this country their narrative for the day. One of the main questions they are posing is *What is John McCain's plan for securing America's future?* But then they are rolling out one McCain crony after another to give their talking points on McCain's plan for securing America. The show must go on!

Rudolph Giuliani told NBC's Brian Williams, "We need John McCain's strength—not the kind of weakness that Barack Obama presents. Barack Obama will raise taxes. Barack Obama has never even been to Latin America. McCain has been all over the world. This is not the time to have someone who is a rookie. On the economy, McCain would be much stronger." I find Giuliani's comments insincere. He couldn't possibly believe his own words. I mean, think about it! All of this, coming from a Republican, whose party has claimed that Obama's worldly background is what makes him questionable. Now because he hasn't been to Latin America—Latin America! —he isn't qualified? That's a weak argument, Mr. Giuliani. Very weak!

Some media outlets are taking heat for running the William Ayers attack ad yesterday. And rightfully so! It is shameful that any reputable outlet would do so. The media is getting more irresponsible by the minute. It is getting to the point that if one wants to watch the convention without any spin or manufactured drama, C-SPAN is the only option. Why? Because the three major news networks—CNN, FOX News, and MSNBC—are spinning this election enough to make their viewers dizzy. I'm going to have to start calling them the "triplet networks."

Radio host Randi Rhodes agrees. She said, "I've got this disease. I think I'm going to have to call it 'mass madness.' That's why you have to watch C-SPAN. The three networks are all exactly the same. They pick the spin and they serve it up." She then accused the media of giving too much attention to the PUMAs, a small group of disgruntled Hillary Clinton supporters. "PUMA" actually stands for "Party Unity My Ass," and apparently is a legitimate group. But Rhodes has a point here. The media has turned a relatively unknown acronym into a media sensation. Rhodes went on:

> What the heck are Pumas? I am here at the convention, and I watched on the convention floor, Obama people and Clinton people reaching out and touching each other. But the media is spinning this Puma crap. I have not seen a Puma. According to the media, their natural

habitat is supposed to be here, but they're not here. The Pumas don't exist. I mean you watch tonight. Biden is gonna knock it out of the park tonight and the media is gonna spin it and say you should feel different about what you just saw. About what you just saw! But these media people are not real. They're not real! And I mean there is some resentment on the part of some members of the media for having to do this, but they have no control over it. They are over produced.

Both FOX News and MSNBC have shown an ad in which John McCain attacks Obama on foreign policy. Again, I didn't see the ad as a commercial; I saw it as news on these two networks:

> **Narrator:** Iran! Radical Islamic government. Known sponsors of terrorism. Developing nuclear capabilities to generate power. But threatening to eliminate Israel! Obama says Iran is a 'tiny' country. Doesn't pose a serious threat!' Terrorism! Destroying Israel! Those aren't serious threats? Obama! Dangerously unprepared to be President.
>
> **John McCain:** I'm John McCain and I approve this message.

FOX News' Bret Hume mentioned that he was impressed with how the McCain camp had been able to get out all of these attack ads during the convention. He did admit, however, that the networks were the ones getting these ads out. He was talking about this during today's nomination proceedings. During the nomination proceedings! Wow!

At 3:48 pm, Barack Obama was officially nominated as the Democratic candidate for President of the United States. *Quite a historic moment!* CNN showed the emotion that so many people on the floor of the convention were experiencing. Many people were crying—people that I have the feeling don't cry easily. Just a hunch! *I noticed because I too was crying.* The moment was a catharsis, not for Hillary supporters so much as for people who feel the sense of awe at history turning a page. All people who have known the depth of racism, and that includes some Americans of all stripes, know what that new page offers in terms of hope. For several minutes, the other major cable networks remained focused on the Obama-Clinton drama, C-SPAN remained focused on the platform, but CNN noticed the many tears and had the presence of mind to fall back into their professional roles as reporters and asked many of the emotional delegates why they were crying. The emotion of the moment was newsworthy.

Today's final headline should read *Tension Release,* because the tension between the Obama and Clinton camps has subsided. Even the media is acknowledging this change. But it remains to be seen if they will try to reignite an old or manufacture some new Clinton-Obama drama. Hillary Clinton herself has given a great endorsing speech and officially released her delegates to Obama. Her husband is currently giving a powerful speech of endorsement. So the facts on the ground suggest a unified party. It will be up to the media to decide whether or not to create a perception of disunity or join in the *koom by ya* moment.

"Bill Clinton was not a good foreign policy President." These were the words of *The Weekly Standard's* Fred Barnes after Bill Clinton's speech tonight. He said this on FOX News. I expected FOX News to pick Bill Clinton's speech apart and try to discredit it. Karl Rove, when asked if he believed that Bill Clinton had made the case for electing Obama, said, "I believe he made 'a' case, but I don't believe he made 'the' case." Very clever Mr. Rove! Actually, very pathetic! Bill Clinton, in no uncertain terms, said that Barack Obama was "ready to be President." He didn't equivocate. He didn't stutter. He didn't do it with a wry smile. He did it by comparing Obama to himself and talked about how he had come into the 1992 election with the same kinds of accusations of *too young and too inexperienced* being levied against him. He then reiterated how prosperous America had been during his Presidency, and that it could be again under Obama. So Karl Rove is wrong! Not surprising! The fact that FOX News even gives Rove a platform tells us everything about them. Rove is a man who is currently refusing a subpoena to appear before Congress. Justice for Valeria Plame can wait. Rove has other fish to fry, including appearing before a FOX News camera.

At some point in this country's future, the media is going to have to start analyzing what a person actually says, and not analyze what they believe the person was thinking. That is not honorable, credible journalism. It is spin. And of the three major news networks, FOX News does the most spinning. But at least the other networks have journalists who are able to make points on both sides of an issue. They are able to give credit where credit is due. But FOX News is 24-hour, Right Wing spin. It never ends. Someone needs to tell them and the Republican spokespeople who go on their network that you build credibility by analyzing both sides of an issue. That's journalism!

It's amazing that FOX News even exists. FOX News abuses their First Amendment rights. Daily! But they may actually hang themselves over the next 69 days. They want to win the election too much, so their competitiveness is getting worse by the day as they see the Republican Party slipping into defeat. They are getting sloppy. And the power that they managed to gain over the past several years is going to be in jeopardy if Obama wins and Congress gets a majority. FOX News and the GOP have a lot to lose, so I expect to see them reach an all-time low in the coming weeks. Or! And I say "or" skeptically! If they sense that Obama is going to win, they might move toward fairness. Let's just say that if that happens, I will be shocked. At least MSNBC seems to value logic. I'll admit that they do lean heavily to the Left, but even if their Right Winger, Pat Buchanan, makes a point, the other commentators acknowledge his perspective. FOX News, on the other hand, always has talking points and seems to go with the Republican Party line. And I will not accept Alan Colmes as a defense against any of this because he rarely gets the final word on anything.

Joe Biden was the final speaker at tonight's convention. He really hit John McCain hard, saying that he is "a friend, but his judgment has been wrong." He accused him of voting with George Bush 95% of the time. After he spoke, Fred Barnes of *The Weekly Standard* said on FOX News, "Biden said

Obama's basic judgment was better. I think Biden violated his friendship with McCain." Chris Wallace of FOX News claimed that Obama's "change message" is now becoming strictly like the Democratic Party's. He mumbled, "What struck me tonight was the redefinition of the word 'change.'" He believes that Obama is adopting the traditional Democratic policies and no longer focusing on his own rhetoric. He claimed that this election would now be about Democratic policies vs. Republican policies.

Wallace knows that the Republicans stand a chance against typical Democratic policies but have no chance if Obama can hold onto his unique individuality and powerful message. They don't know how to defeat it because they've never seen it. Wallace is obviously trying to tell people that Obama isn't going to deliver any kind of real change—that he isn't a new kind of politician. I think he realizes how powerful Obama's "change message" has been and is now trying to paint him as someone who isn't fresh and progressive. Actually, Obama has successfully demonstrated over the past nineteen months that he is all of these things. Wallace is trying to tell us that Obama will be more of the same old, same old. Wallace's subtlety doesn't escape me. The Right Wing fears Obama's powerfully innovative and real "change message" and they are going to do everything in their power to diminish it.

So far, McCain hasn't succumbed to the temptation of using Jeremiah Wright, Obama's former pastor, who said some inflammatory things in the past that hurt Obama during the Democratic Primary. But will McCain decide to use Wright in the coming days? Will he allow his supporters to paint Obama as a Muslim, which he isn't? What will the coming days show us about McCain's tactics? Obama hasn't been willing to engage in dirty politics. McCain has! But I'm interested to see if McCain's tactics will get even more ugly as the election heats up. After all, it was Thomas Jefferson who said, "Whenever a man has cast a longing eye on offices, a rottenness begins in his conduct." This is not the first time the 72-year-old McCain has run for President. And how will the media participate? It should be absolutely fascinating.

DAY 4
"ENOUGH!"

Obama is in Denver, Colorado, today—Thursday, August 28—while McCain is in Phoenix, Arizona. Obama's big speech tonight is the headline for today. Obama is scheduled to give his acceptance speech at INVESCO field in front of an estimated 75,000 people. The media is trying to set the bar high for Obama by running endless clips of Bill Clinton's speech last night. "Barack Obama is on the right side of history." Those were the words of Clinton. *Will Obama be able to match the greatness of the Clinton speech?* This is the question the media is feeding us today. "Can Obama surpass his own last great convention speech?" This was the question MSNBC's Chuck Todd posed this morning at 9:09 am. The media is putting up one hurdle after another for Obama to prove he can clear. He is tasked to prove something different by the minute. "Obama has somewhat of a problem of being considered formidable." This is the opinion stated by Carl Bernstein.

As I mentioned, there appears to be a consensus regarding Bill Clinton's speech last night—that it was very effective. Analysts seem to believe that Clinton did a good job of comparing his own nomination in 1992 to Obama's current one—that he was able to effectively compare Obama to himself by mentioning how people thought that he too was too young and didn't have any foreign policy experience, etc.

A headline in *The Washington Post* reads **Clinton Links His Presidency to Obama.** But today on FOX News, Byron York said, "Actually, the first two years of the Clinton Presidency was a pretty whacky ride." *Actually, the whacky ride has been the last eight years under the Bush Administration!*

There is some media spin going on regarding Obama's decision to speak at INVESCO field tonight instead of the much smaller Pepsi Center. INVESCO is a huge outdoor stadium. Obama will be speaking on a stage with large Roman-looking columns. The idea was to create a setting that looks important and stately. But the media is debating whether Obama's decision to have this type of setting gives merit to McCain's accusation that Obama is a celebrity like Paris Hilton and Brittney Spears. McCain has an ad in which he compares Obama to these two. Dana Bash reported, "Many believe his challenge is to bring his soaring rhetoric down to earth." She went on to say that the Republican Party is accusing Obama of being "out of touch," and they are labeling tonight's speech "Barackopolis." Jay Carney of *Time* said on MSNBC at 3:55 pm: "With the Greek temple behind Obama, maybe he's Zeus." Not funny!

I was surprised to hear CNN anchor Soledad O'Brien—whose job, remember, is supposed to be to ask questions and report facts—inject this opinion: "There is some truth to this GOP celebrity accusation." She actually said this today! Go to CNN headquarters—ask to see the tape for today's date—and roll the 24-hour coverage. She said it! Is this her job? She is not a commentator. Carl Bernstein feels that the media has been focusing too much on this Obama celebrity talk and missing the real story. He feels that "The real story is about the Democratic Party coming together." Amy Holmes disagreed, saying, "Actually, Obama had the same people who designed Brittney Spears' stages design this stage at INVESCO, so there is some merit to Obama being compared to Brittney Spears and Paris Hilton." Bernstein immediately injected, "So! So! Who designed this CNN stage?"

I don't expect CNN reporters to rush out and research who actually designed their own set. They, being celebrities themselves, don't really have as much contempt for celebrities as they pretend. I expect to hear more of this spin today, as Amy Holmes is notorious for doing nothing more than spouting Republican talking points. When asked, at 10:38 am, if she thinks this McCain-created celebrity theme against Obama has wings, Gloria Borger said, "I think it does." One question here—*Does Gloria Borger work for CNN or does she work for John McCain?* I can't tell. The theme about Obama being a celebrity just won't go away. As Major Garrett was reporting from INVESCO in front of the stage, his FOX News colleague Neil Cavuto told him, "You know Major Garrett, you look very God-like with those pillars behind you."

Where the hell do we turn for journalistic integrity anymore? Think about it! It was not the media who manufactured this "celebrity" label. As a matter of fact, the first time America heard the word "celebrity" used to describe Obama was when McCain ran the Paris Hilton/ Brittney Spears ad. McCain created the illusion and the media swallowed it hook, line, and sinker.

The reason Obama decided to speak at INVESCO is because his message all along has been based around the theme *Change does not happen from the top down, but from the bottom up*—not because he thinks he's a celebrity. What better way is there to show this philosophy than by letting 75,000 people in to hear you speak for free? This is a gift to the people. He has said all along that the people have the power, not him. I find it ironic that the GOP is criticizing him for being nothing more than a celebrity, when the exact same failing ploy was used against their most hailed hero, Ronald Reagan, back in 1980.

Today is the 45th anniversary of Martin Luther King's "I Have a Dream" speech. That speech is, to say the least, difficult for Obama to measure up to, but the anticipation of tonight's speech is palpable. I don't expect to see any attack ads today, considering the historical significance of the day. Senator McCain is actually running a congratulatory ad:

> **McCain:** Senator Obama! This is truly a good day for America. You know, too often the achievements of our opponents go unnoticed. So I wanted to stop and say—congratulations. How perfect that your nomination would come on this historic day. Tomorrow we'll be back at it. But tonight, Senator—a job well done!

Frederick Douglas was the first African American to receive a vote for President. He received one vote. That was 120 years ago. Now Obama seeks to take the first step at becoming the first African American to win a general election. He will need to get votes from every demographic—especially women. A new poll out today shows Obama leading McCain among women 50% to 36%.

The Weekly Standard allowed Karl Rove to write this about Obama today in an article entitled **Biden's Exaggerations:** "The American people are particular about who they elect as President. And voters do not tolerate candidates whose opinion of ordinary citizens is so low they think they can get away with misleading them." Really? Karl Rove thinks that Barack Obama has a low opinion of ordinary citizens? I will leave this audacious comment for you to try to digest. Or maybe I should leave it to the 75,000 ordinary citizens that Obama let in to Mile High Stadium for free to hear him speak.

And what a speech it was! Barack Obama has just delivered one of the most powerful speeches I have ever heard. It was unquestionably moving and specific. It could go down as one of our nation's greatest speeches. It included all of the inspiring elements of his past speeches, but he took McCain on more directly. He said, "John McCain likes to say he'll follow Bin Laden to the gates of Hell. But he won't even go to the cave where he lives." The crowd erupted. This remark will certainly draw a response from McCain next week. After the speech, the media was gushing. It was praise! Praise! Praise!

Michelle Bernard of MSNBC said, "During the speech I went into the green room and wept. This is the most amazing evening of my entire life." David Gergen praised him saying: "Anderson we're sharing the Kool-aid tonight. He seemed to be bigger tonight. He's growing into the job. I mean to come out swinging! There was a sense of moral outrage. I was deeply impressed. It was a symphony. As a political speech, it was a masterpiece."

Obama had been expected to speak in front of 75,000 but the number ended up being about 85,000. The people in the football stadium were transfixed throughout. As the cameras panned the crowd, people were hanging on his every word. That rapt attention in itself is an amazing feat on Obama's part. Even during a Super Bowl, people in the crowd can always be seen paying attention to things other than the game itself. But not this crowd! Obama had them in the palm of his hand. He told John McCain, "So I've got news for you, John McCain! We all put our country first!" McCain is known for saying he will always put his country first. But he says so in a way that almost seems to suggest that others don't.

The media's fickleness has never been so magnified. Looks like the falsely-labeled "celebrity" is now someone every person in the media wants to marry. Even the Right Wing voices are getting into the praising act. *The Weekly Standard's* Fred Barnes said on FOX News, "No other politician in America could have gotten 85,000 people to come hear them speak at a stadium. No other!" Who would have thought that the usually reliable CNN conservative talking head, Alex Castellanos, would acknowledge the greatness of the speech with this comment? "Whoever didn't get picked for a Republican VP today may be a lucky Republican."

Chuck Todd got it right: "The toughness of the speech is probably what's gonna stand out. And there has been no response from the McCain camp so far. They don't know how to respond yet." I guess Obama must now be considered formidable because Carl Bernstein claimed, "This was the greatest speech I've heard since Kennedy." John King referred to Obama's ability to really connect with people and the issues they are concerned with by saying: "About two-thirds of the way through his speech Barack Obama said 'I get it' and he clearly does." I thought it was poignant when Obama said, "It's not that John McCain doesn't care—it's that John McCain doesn't know." Unfortunately, I think that too many members of the media don't know what it's all about and perhaps won't even care after this night is over.

Just after Obama's historic speech, Keith Olbermann said one of the most intelligent and profound things regarding how members of the press can cause damage. Mr. Olbermann appeared quite emphatic and a bit incensed during his remarks—and rightfully so:

> I feel impelled to read something from the Associated Press—which is a service that is distributed to thousands of newspapers around the continent mostly—our continent. This is called 'Convention Analysis.' I'm not familiar with the writer. He's identified as Charles Babington. But let me read part of this in full. 'Barack Obama, whose campaign theme is 'change we can believe in,' promised Thursday to spell out exactly what that 'change' would mean. But instead of dwelling on specifics, he laced the crowning speech of his long campaign with the type of rhetorical flourishes that Republicans mock and the attacks on John McCain that Democrats cheer. The country saw a candidate, confident in his existing campaign formula, tie McCain tightly

to President Bush, and remind voters why they are unhappy with the incumbent. Of course,' he went on to write, 'no candidate can outline every initiative in a 35-minute speech, especially one that must also inspire voters.' Mr. Babington got the length of the speech wrong by at least seven minutes. And this is analysis that will be printed in many, many newspapers—hundreds of them around the country. It is analysis that strikes me as having done—of having born—no resemblance to the speech that you and I just watched. None whatsoever! And for it to be distributed by the lone, national news organization—in terms of wire copy—to newspapers around the country, and websites—is a remarkable failure of that news organization. Charles Babington! ... Find new work!

History was made today, but the next 67 days will determine whether or not the media will stay in this *praise Obama* mode. I have seen no indication that the media has the capability of staying in a consistent mode. Tomorrow will bring a new narrative, and Obama will likely be back to dodging arrows, many of which will be slung by the media. Or maybe I should hold out hope that the media too can be changed. Then again, outside forces like the FCC or Congress haven't shown willingness to pressure the media. So maybe *We the People* need to put pressure on the FCC and Congress. After all, my favorite line of Obama's speech tonight was a powerful one: "Change doesn't come from Washington.

Change comes to Washington." When Obama uttered the word "enough" I heard a small amount of anger in his voice that I've never detected before. He was, of course, referring to the failed policies of the past eight years because he then said, "Eight is enough!" But he said the word "enough" with a power that rocked the crowd. I'd like to say "enough" also, but my "enough" is directed squarely at the media. Enough!

DAY 5
HELLO, MRS. PALIN

Obama is campaigning in Beaver, Pennsylvania, today—Friday, August 29—while McCain is in Dayton, Ohio. Obama's speech last night was hugely inspiring. My gut feeling, after digesting this speech, is that the race is over. The speech was that powerful. I feel like even McCain probably wants to throw in the towel—that he must know that there is probably no one else in the world who could have brought out and performed that well in front of 85 thousand people. But this fact remains: Obama cannot get elected if the media decides to beat him up. They are the fourth branch of government. They decide! He can't win if they decide not to play fair. Even if he continues to propose the best policies and deliver the best speeches ever, it's possible that the media could tear his campaign down to the ground. They're relentless. When Obama said last night, "I know I don't fit the typical pedigree," I was hoping that the media would take heed and decide not to be so typically embroiled in spin.

Today, Obama is in Beaver, Pennsylvania, but the news of the day is John McCain's selection of a VP running mate. Forty-four year old Alaska Gov. Sarah Palin was his choice. The immediate response of the media has been one of shock. Palin has been governor for twenty months and before that was mayor of Wasilla, a small town in Alaska, for six years. McCain, who turned 72 today, is taking heat for choosing someone so inexperienced to be the person who is a heartbeat away from the Presidency. The media is also claiming that this pick was made in order to quell some of the excitement surrounding last night's Obama speech. The GOP is touting the fact that they've made history too by selecting a female VP running mate for the first time in their party's history.

My question to the media is this: *Was there an Obama speech last night?* It was obviously one of the most amazing days in American political history, and the media is barely even covering it. The fact that they're not flooding the airwaves with that historic, undeniably monumental day is mind-boggling. It's going to be interesting someday to see how such a petty selection for Vice President could knock off an amazing, historical event. Here are some facts about last night: 40 million people watched Obama's speech on television. More people watched it than watched this year's opening ceremony for the Olympics, this year's finale of *American Idol,* or this year's Academy Awards. But the media has managed to kill Obama's momentum. Governor Mike Huckabee even noted this fact today on FOX News. He said, "McCain did a good job with this pick by taking that Obama speech off of the news cycle. Thirty eight million people watched that speech last night and today nobody's talking about it."

Meanwhile, I believe that most Americans, whether Republican or Democrat, woke up this morning saying, *Wow! That was history in the making last night, and I was alive to see it.* I mean, think about it! One of the most right wing, obstinate talking heads in America—Pat Buchanan—called Obama's speech "the greatest convention speech of all time." But it won't be long before he's telling us that Obama is the worst speaker he's ever heard. Most things he says are designed to set people up for some kind of killer blow. It's always reverse psychology from Buchanan.

Last night also marked the end of the convention. The media did a terrible job of covering the actual speaking that went on each day in the Pepsi Center. We missed speaker after speaker talk about issues like Global Warming, poverty, health care, impeachment, etc. I had to tivo C-SPAN in order to see the great speeches delivered by Dennis Kucinich and Montana Gov. Brian Schweitzer. Instead they fed us four days of political babble.

The media had an opportunity to let Americans hear leaders talk about the issues that affect their lives but chose instead to let their talking heads do a free-for-all. I guess they didn't feel like 300 million Americans needed to hear from Kucinich. I think what he had to say was critical for any voter to hear. Hearing from elected officials is the entire point of the convention. The media had to know that his words were, at the very least, newsworthy. They certainly were important enough to make the entire Pepsi Center stand up and cheer loudly. History will show that his words were important. And I believe they're important enough to put in this journal. Here is part of what the national media didn't show him say:

> Millions of Americans have lost their jobs, their homes, their health care, their pensions. Trillions of dollars for an unnecessary war paid with borrowed money. Tens of billions of dollars in cash and weapons disappeared into thin air, at the

cost of the lives of our troops and innocent Iraqis, while all the President's oilmen are maneuvering to grab Iraq's oil. ⊠Borrowed money to bomb bridges in Iraq, Afghanistan, and Pakistan. No money to rebuild bridges in America. Money to start a hot war with Iran. Now we have another cold war with Russia, while the American economy has become a game of Russian roulette…. Wake up, America! Wake up, America! Wake up, America! Wake up, America!

Today's national *Gallup* daily tracking poll shows Obama at 49% and McCain at 41%. Back and forth go the polls! I heard former Senator Tom Daschle on MSNBC mention how he considers John McCain a "friend." This reminded me of how, too often, I hear politicians mention how they completely disagree with their colleagues, yet consider them friends. They then proceed to completely undress them verbally. I want to ask these politicians what their definition of "friend" is. When a politician fundamentally disagrees with someone on issues that often negatively affect the lives of millions but then says they consider them a "friend," they lose all credibility with me. Senate pleasantries should stay in the Senate.

One of the funniest things I've heard today came out of the mouth of FOX News' Bill O'Reilly. I never have watched FOX News much until deciding to write this book, so I found it astonishingly laughable to hear this O'Reilly slogan: "Remember, the spin stops right here because we're looking out for you." Are you kidding me? Actually, Mr. O'Reilly, the spin "starts" right there on your show. Former Clinton advisor, Dick Morris, said this on FOX News today: "Palin walks on water in Alaska." Trying to top Morris with the Palin-gushing was CNN's Amy Holmes. She claimed, "This is what real authenticity looks like."

I just wonder what the media would have done to Obama had he picked such an inexperienced VP. No, I don't wonder—they would have destroyed him. And I'm sure they would justify their bias by claiming that McCain's wealth of experience justifies such a pick, whereas Obama's thin resume required an experience pick like Biden. But that is all spin. Obama was editor of the Harvard Law Review. He was a Constitutional Law Professor. He was an Illinois state legislator for eight years. He was a civil rights attorney. And he's been a U.S. senator for four years. But the media has allowed him to be compared to Palin all day today. Of course, this comparison is coming from the GOP, but the media is buying in. They're letting the GOP get their talking points out.

David Brody of *The Christian Broadcasting Network* commented on how much Palin will help McCain. He said, "We've seen a dramatic shift amongst evangelicals today because of this. She has loads of personality." Now I have no problem with Mr. Brody saying this on his own network, but he said it on CNN. And they just let him say it without challenging him on it. I would have asked him this: *How in the hell can you make such a profound statement about a VP choice's affect on an entire demographic in such a short period of time? How many evangelicals have you heard from since she was selected?* Instead, CNN gives these otherwise small voices a huge audience by allowing them to spew talking points on national television. I'm sure that Mr. Brody's comment on CNN was effective at recruiting a slew of new, formerly uninspired evangelicals—ones who may otherwise not have voted this year. Thank you CNN!

CNN's Campbell Brown opened her show with, "We've got the facts for you today—no bull!" I laughed out loud at that. Andrea Mitchell said the Palin pick "could be a game changer." Did she mean the media game? According to Barack Obama, politics is not a game. But the media thinks it is. Today, when *Newsweek's* Howard Fineman said on MSNBC, "This pick makes it fun—it makes it interesting," was he referring to the same game Andrea Mitchell mentioned? Who we elect as our next President is serious business. The political process warrants more than references to VP choices being "fun" or "game changers." We saw how George W. Bush's smirk and folksy way made him a media favorite back in 2000. I recall Bush getting lambasted by Gore in those 2000 debates, only to have the media say he was funny and able to make the audience laugh. They accused Gore of being too serious and intelligent sounding. I hope to God we're not going down that same path here with this Palin pick. The media is going very soft on her.

I am still perplexed by the media's quick change on this Obama speech coverage. They have allowed an unknown governor of a state with a population of 683,478 people to upstage a man who just got back from Germany where he spoke in front of 200 thousand people. James Carville proved my point about this relatively unknown governor. He stated on CNN, "I'm completely befuddled by this choice.

I am completely floored by this choice." David Gergen said, "This is the biggest political gamble I've ever seen in a VP choice." But even though the media is allowing people to criticize the pick, the coverage is playing into the GOP's hands because the topic is dominating the news cycle. The media is especially surprised by McCain's pick because of a report claiming that he has met with Palin only one time in the past.

Anderson Cooper said, "Up next, the pick that is rocking the political world." Does he mean the real political world or the political media world that he is partly responsible for creating? The real political world finds the pick a curiosity. The political media world, however, is building Palin up by the minute. She is already a star, though she has neither done nor said anything to warrant such star status. Nothing! Obama became a star for actually saying something profound at the 2004 Democratic National Convention, then following those words with a resounding Senate victory and a year-long run for the Presidency. Anderson Cooper should go back and look at that 2004 speech. He would then see that saying things like "rocking the political world" should be reserved for moments like that moving Obama speech in 2004. He earned his fame. *Newsweek's* Howard Fineman helped make my point when he said, "Sarah Palin makes Barack Obama look like John Adams." This is a funny comment, but he's wrong here again. And it's subtle. The fact is that Barack Obama makes Barack Obama look like John Adams. Fineman's comment feeds into this fabrication that Obama has very little experience.

CNN's Glenn Beck said, "If Palin is who I think she is, I may pull the lever for John McCain." I'm glad that CNN allows its employees to endorse candidates on national television. How does such an endorsement affect the integrity of our country's electoral process? It's the subtlety of the media that often irks me. It's truly as if they don't understand, or care, how the subtle things they utter casually literally change the dynamic of an election. For example, Larry King had Republican spokesman Kevin Madden on his program today. King specifically asked him this: "Is Sarah Palin the most qualified person available in the Republican Party to be Vice President?" This is a very direct question—one that our media members should demand a direct answer to. But they often don't. They let spokespeople waffle and change the subject. Kevin Madden never answered King's question. Yet he's asked to go on his show regularly. King should have demanded an answer. Instead he allowed Madden to utter this outlandish comment: "Barack Obama has never done anything in his political career." King never called him on this deplorable lie. I wanted to take King's place and say, *Look—you're not going to come on my program and blatantly lie.* But I guess I'm living in a fantasy world.

The weather forecast is showing a hurricane heading toward New Orleans. This is ironic considering the fact that a Republican-loving, Right Wing conservative member of Pastor James Dobson's *Focus on The Family* prayed to have rain destroy the Obama speech last night. We'll see if the hurricane instead knocks their Republican National Convention's news coverage off the air next week.

DAY 6
GUSTAV

Obama is campaigning in Dublin, Ohio, today—Saturday, August 30—while McCain is in Washington, Pennsylvania. Sarah Palin is still front and center today. A headline in this morning's *USA Today* online page reads, **Friends: VP Choice Has 'Very Strong' Values.** Granted, *USA Today* is using a partial quote in their chosen headline, but it's funny how they chose to make this the title of the article. Is this *USA Today's* opinion of Palin or Curt Menard's, a mayor in Alaska who said, "She's very, very strong in her values?" Menard is actually the only one in the entire article who specifically says the words "very strong ...values." It would have been no less egregious, but at least accurate, if the title had read: "One Friend Says 'VP Choice Has Very Strong Values.'" Why? Because to the casual, less savvy reader, the *USA Today* headline could certainly be construed as fact. Since when is something a friend or buddy says about a Vice Presidential candidate worthy of being headline news? Headline news! We're electing a VP, not a scout leader. And as I previously mentioned, only one person used the words "very strong... values." Others in the article said positive things about her, but the article's title suggests that each person said those exact words. The headline is an outrageous error. Bias is too weak a word for this kind of pro Republican campaigning on the part of *USA Today*.

Obama is in Cleveland, Ohio, today to attend the memorial for Congresswoman Stephanie Tubbs Jones. He will also be campaigning in the state. The media question for the day is *Who is Sarah Palin?* The media is telling America what they deem important for us to know. I wonder if they will give us the facts. One thing the GOP is selling the media is this idea that Palin is the most popular governor in the country. Talk about a subjective bit of information, given the population of Alaska! But the media seems to be allowing this talking point to go unchallenged.

However, some hard news stories regarding Sarah Palin are surfacing. One comes via *Time* magazine in an article written by Tiffany Sharples today, entitled **10 Facts About Sarah Palin**:

> Earlier this month, a legislative panel launched a $100,000 investigation to determine whether Palin abused her influence by attempting to get her former brother-in-law fired as a state trooper. The panel is currently questioning whether Palin dismissed the state's safety commissioner, Walt Monegan, because he refused to fire her ex-brother-in-law, Mike Wooten, whose marriage to Palin's sister ended in a bitter divorce—and custody battle—in 2005. Palin has denied the charges, and says she did not coordinate the reported dozens of telephone calls placed by her husband and administration to Wooten's bosses. Before Palin ran for governor, she and her husband accused Wooten of drinking alcohol on the job and illegal

hunting. Wooten was briefly suspended over the allegations in 2006 but never dismissed.

We should all be curious to see if the media even bothers to spend much time on this fact. They certainly haven't spent any time on the "Keating Five" scandal. Sarah Palin also believes in teaching both evolution and creationism. The definition of creationism according to the *Britannica Concise Encyclopedia* is "The belief that matter, the various forms of life, and the world were created by God out of nothing. Biblical creationists believe that the story told in Genesis of God's six-day creation of the universe and all living things is literal." Creationists don't believe in scientific evidence to the contrary. Does Palin have a pastor who preaches about this? Maybe not! But if she does, will the media show us clips of Palin's pastor yelling from the pulpit? What exactly is said in that church? Quick, Anderson Cooper! Run the loop of her pastor for an hour straight like you did with Jeremiah Wright. Run it! Run it! Run it! Or, better yet, run an endless loop of Palin saying this on CNBC a few months back: "What is it exactly that the VP does everyday?" She actually said this. Go ahead Anderson! Run the loop!

During her concession speech earlier this year, Hillary Clinton talked about how she wasn't quite able to break that "glass ceiling" but claimed to have "put about 18 million cracks in it." This was a good line. She was referring to how women hadn't been able to break through the glass ceiling and actually win the Presidency. When I heard Sarah Palin say, "It turns out the women of America aren't finished yet and we can shatter that glass ceiling once and for all,"

I immediately wondered what Hillary was thinking. She had to be a little peeved. How can a woman, whom no one even knows, compare herself immediately to a woman who received 18 million votes? Hear me out! This would be the equivalent of Lance Armstrong coming within a hundred yards of the finish line in the Tour de France, but stopping due to an injury, only to have an unknown cyclist pick up his bike, cross the finish line, and proceed to tell us how proud he is to be the American who, thanks to Lance Armstrong, was finally able to be the one to actually win the biggest race in the world. Besides, becoming a VP is not what Hillary was referring to. She was talking about the big office. I kept waiting for the media to pounce on Palin for this, but to no avail.

The media is forced to give a lot of its attention to Hurricane Gustav, a huge storm in the Gulf of Mexico heading toward New Orleans. But they are still trying to suggest that Palin represents the same change as Obama. On MSNBC, *The Financial Times'* Chrystia Freeman claimed that regarding the issue of change, "Sarah Palin's past track record actually speaks to that." *The Chicago Sun Times'* Lynn Sweet added, "She's got a terrific story to tell from top to bottom." I don't think the American people are buying this—yet!

At 3:38 pm, MSNBC's Peter Alexander was anchoring the news. He appeared very professional. He was uttering no opinions—just giving us the hard facts. But suddenly, he said, very innocently, and in passing: "McCain still owns the issue of experience." I just shook my head. An anchor giving his opinion—a damaging one at that. I just have to ask— *What is a news anchor?* Americans used to know. *The Museum of Broadcast Communications* (See *www.museum.tv/archives/etv/*

A/htmlA/anchor/anchor.htm) describes what the role of a news anchor should be: "…the anchor is a television host at the top of a hierarchical chain of command with special reportorial credentials and responsibilities centered around 'hard' or serious news of the day; celebrity interview and tabloid news shows have hosts, not anchors…"

Every now and then we have to stop in our tracks and say, *Wow, that was something special and history in the making.* That is what Obama's speech has done to the nation. I believe the nation is in a state of shock. And that includes Republicans. What we saw the other night was so completely, undeniably, historic, that Americans are having a difficult time coming to terms with it. When Bill Clinton said, "Barack Obama is on the right side of history," he was correct. And what that means, more literally, is that Obama has done the right things. He has previously earned ethical capital, and as a result, has a great deal of confidence in going forward.

When the Republicans saw 85 thousand people cram into that stadium, and the entire event come off without a hitch, they must have begun to realize the phenomenon they are dealing with. They had to be shocked at how organized this man is. And that must have scared them. I believe the media itself was stunned at the enormity of the spectacle. They knew they were going to show up and see a man speak to a large audience, but they themselves had never witnessed anything like it—because it hadn't ever happened. So they didn't truly know how to report on it afterwards. America has huge celebrities—actors, musicians, athletes, etc. This speech moved Obama beyond celebrity. He makes the word seem petty. This country has plenty of those. But in my

36-year lifetime, I have never witnessed an event that awe inspiring, and I'm glad I'm alive to cover it. All I can think is *What will come next?*

I didn't have to wait long. An article by *The Weekly Standard's* William Kristol came out today entitled **Why The Left is Scared to Death of McCain's Running Mate.** For Kristol, evidently, seeing Sarah Palin was love at first sight:

> A specter is haunting the liberal elites of New York and Washington—the specter of a young, attractive, unapologetic conservatism, rising out of the American countryside, free of the taint (fair or unfair) of the Bush administration and the recent Republican Congress, able to invigorate a McCain administration and to govern beyond it. That specter has a name—Sarah Palin, the 44-year-old governor of Alaska chosen by John McCain on Friday to be his running mate. There she is: a working woman who's a proud wife and mother; a traditionalist in important matters who's broken through all kinds of barriers; a reformer who's a Republican; a challenger of a corrupt good-old-boy establishment who's a conservative; a successful woman whose life is unapologetically grounded in religious belief; a lady who's a leader.

I can't imagine being such an ideologue! The political people I know and respect are critical, even of someone who claims to be of the same political affiliation. All it takes for a mouthpiece like Kristol to know that he is all in for Palin is to hear a few ideological buzzwords. I hope he has met her more than the one time McCain had before he named her as his running mate. Kristol writes as if he's one of her closest friends. Of course, he leans to the Right, but as a journalist, he still owes the reader a more balanced analysis of the political landscape. Joseph Joubert once said, "Those who never retract their opinions love themselves more than they love the truth." We'll see if Kristol will feel the need someday to retract his opinion that was formed on the spur of the moment.

DAY 7
BEER BUDDY

Obama is campaigning in Toledo, Ohio, today—Sunday, August 31—while McCain is in Jackson, Mississippi. "The Vice President has two duties: one is to inquire daily as to the health of the President, and the other is to attend the funerals of third world dictators." That is what John McCain said in 2000. Today, on *Meet the Press*, Tom Brokaw failed miserably at hiding what I believe is his very influential opinion.

Brokaw claimed that he had talked to a person in a Montana airport about Obama's speech who said, "My god he promised everything." People on the *Meet the Press* panel laughed at that zinger. This is Brokaw's own opinion. The problem here is that he's famous and probably gets told things by people in airports all the time. How does Mr. Brokaw decide what's important to share with us on *Meet the Press* about his day to day life? Why did he choose to tell this stupid little story that in no way serves any purpose except denigrating Obama? He most certainly didn't have to share it, and if there is an uncertain voter out there who admires Mr. Brokaw, I'm sure this subtle little anecdote served to make them question Obama's ability to make good on his promises. Mr. Brokaw's story hurts Obama. Did Brokaw forget the basic tenants of being an unbiased moderator?

One of Brokaw's guests was Gov. Tim Pawlenty. His mission was to diminish the accomplishments of Obama.

He offered up this abysmal talking point regarding Sarah Palin: "She has as much or more experience as Barack Obama." The only person on the program with a reasoned, expert, and responsible take on the election was Doris Kearns Goodwin. "I think the idea that the Vice President's main role is to simply inquire after the health of the President is an old, whack idea that's no longer relevant. First of all, when you look at history, nearly one out of three Vice Presidents has actually become President." Goodwin went on to say that this pick "really does provide a window, I think, into the first major decision that Mr. McCain made. Even last spring he said 'I know I'm older and I'm gonna choose somebody—the first important thing is that they be ready to be President.'" Goodwin's perspective is based on solid ground. She expounded further on Palin: "How much time do they have to really vet her? ….You could be Einstein and not be able to answer the questions that you guys are going to put at her…. I think it's a very strange choice." We'll see if the media actually decides to ask her the tough questions that Goodwin suggested.

Maria Bartiromo of CNBC felt compelled to add this: "I think it was a very savvy pick actually." Brokaw got back to injecting his subtle take on things. "She has that Alaska candor… She does have a very winning way about her." Of McCain, Brokaw claimed, "He has the constitution of a bull elephant." I do recall Tim Russert personalizing things sometimes, but I never got the feeling that he was trying to persuade me in any way. I can't say the same for Mr. Brokaw.

David Gregory was also a guest today. He wasted no time building the case for Palin. He professed, "I just want to make one point here about the potential outreach to independent voters who, with this pick, have the opportunity, if they're Republican leaning, to vote for history without voting for Barack Obama. And I think that's significant." In other words, Mr. Gregory is letting people know that they don't have to vote for a Black Person to make history. Thanks for educating people on this obvious fact. Way to assuage people's guilt. Gregory went on with, "I think there's also an overstatement of the importance of social issues like abortion in this debate." What does that mean? He then gushed over the fact that she had four children and still managed to be in charge of Alaska when she went into labor. He said, "She's figured out the work-life balance that a lot of women struggle with. She went into labor and got on an airplane to go back to Alaska. That's pretty cool! I think there's a lot of people, men and women, who are going to look at this story and say 'This is a compelling person; I wanna take a new look at this ticket.'"

How is this an example of figuring out the "work-life balance?" The logic escapes me. What woman in the world wouldn't get back to her home-doctor if she was going into labor? David Gregory is a well-respected journalist. I just can't figure out why he hasn't committed himself to avoiding what sound like talking points. He needs to stick to quoting people and analyzing what they actually said. Then let us decide what to think about what he's reported to us. He has access to information that none of us do, and he should report it to us and then allow us to digest it.

Hurricane Gustav is largely overshadowing the day's political news. The heads of The Republican Party have decided to cancel most of tomorrow's speeches at the convention. Bush and Cheney will not speak. I'm sure the Party is happy about that. I get the sneaking suspicion that the GOP is going to use this hurricane to their political advantage any way they can. I won't be surprised to hear them say, "This isn't the time for gigantic crowds and speeches. This is the time for gritty leadership and 'straight talk.' We'll leave the big speeches to the Democrats."

I hope the hurricane doesn't cost America any lives. But politically, I think John McCain and George Bush lucked out that something has changed the dynamics of the media buzz over Obama's speech. They were shaking in their boots at the thought of having to directly follow that amazing spectacle. This weather news has taken some of the pressure off the two. McCain's campaign manager, Rick Davis, said this regarding the responsibility that fellow Republicans need to take concerning the imminent hurricane: "We need to take our Republican hats off and put our American hats on." Actually, Mr. Davis, you need to take the Republican hats off and "keep" your American hats on. Shouldn't your American hat always be on?

For all the criticism that John McCain has leveled against Obama for being a so-called celebrity, it's surprising that he and the press have spent this entire weekend trying to create a celebrity for McCain's ticket. Instead of Paris Hilton and Brittney Spears—mere celebrities—they have Sarah Palin, who is turning out to be their Wonder Woman. She can do everything. Elisabeth Bumiller of the *New York Times* said on NBC earlier, "She's extremely personal and charismatic." Howard Fineman suggested, on *The Chris Matthews Show*, that Karl Rove had been responsible for the Palin pick. At least he found a way to mix in something positive about Obama.

Regarding the speech he stated, "One word—strength." Fineman found out why the Obama team created such an elaborate staging of the speech. He mentioned that David Axelrod told him, "That was our prebuttal." Axelrod was referring to the dramatic staging being a "prebuttal in defense of next weeks Republican National Convention."

Obama spoke to *60 Minutes* correspondent Steve Kroft today—a very well respected journalist. One of the purposes of this journal revolves around a prediction that I made before I started writing it: that the media would continue doing damage to Obama in a very subtle way. It's the subtleties that escape the casual voter. Here is an exchange between Kroft and Obama that took place today, and it exemplifies this subtlety:

> **Kroft:** But you tried really hard to reach these people [Blue Collar Workers]. You went and sipped beer, which I know you don't particularly like - I mean you even...
> **Obama:** Steve, I had a beer last night. I mean, where do these stories come from, man? Where does the story come from that...I don't like beer? ...C'mon, man.

Kroft didn't mean any harm, but still, those off-the-cuff remarks have legs. There are probably millions of people out there who now think that Obama doesn't drink beer. Sounds like no big deal, but to the guy who loves his brewsky and wants to vote for "one of the guys," it could very well be a big deal.

The coming weeks are going to be historic. As Hurricane Gustav makes its way toward the Gulf, McCain is jockeying for the politically correct position to take on its potential devastation. He, along with Palin, actually went to Mississippi during the evacuation today. Both candidates need to come across as leaders who know how to respond to a crisis, but visiting during an actual evacuation strikes me as pandering. And it's distracting! But both candidates do need to display strength, especially after the debacle surrounding Bush's handling of Hurricane Katrina.

Obama said he would tap his huge political network of donors and volunteers to help U.S. victims of Hurricane Gustav after it comes inland. "I think we can get tons of volunteers to travel down there, if it becomes necessary," Obama told reporters after attending St. Luke's Lutheran Church in Lima, Ohio. "I think we can activate an e-mail list of a couple of million people who want to give back," he said. He added that donations could include cash, goods, and individual labor. Obama said he first would ask officials in the affected areas what is most needed, which may not be known for a few days. He might visit storm-damaged areas once "…things have settled down."

John McCain told NBC that he can give his acceptance speech via satellite from the Gulf Cost, if need be, and not from the Convention in St. Paul. Both candidates are responding quite differently to the storm. But even during and beyond the coming hurricane, the campaign for Presidency is going to heat up. Clarence Page of the *Chicago Tribune* put it best today on NBC: "It's gonna be a blood bath."

DAY 8
OUT OF WEDLOCK

Obama is campaigning in Detroit, Michigan, today—Monday, September 1—while McCain is in Toledo, Ohio. *I am 17 years old. I am pregnant. I am not married. And my mother has just been chosen as John McCain's Vice Presidential running mate.* No one has actually said these words, but it has just been reported that Sarah Palin's 17-year-old daughter is pregnant. She is also unmarried. Yikes! Not the headline the McCain camp was hoping for, I'm sure. There's an old saying: *You couldn't write this stuff—it's too unbelievable—no one would buy it.* We'll have to wait and see how the media decides to run with this. Barack Obama is in Milwaukee, Wisconsin, and will be in Detroit later today to speak briefly. He is expected to cancel his normal campaign stump speech in order to honor those dealing with Hurricane Gustav.

I find it interesting that as Hurricane Gustav is hammering down on Mississippi and Louisiana, there has been absolutely no coverage of the James Dobson crony, Stuart Shepard, who previously prayed for rain. His prayers weren't answered when it came to his desire to have Obama's speech rained out, but how ironic that this storm is now dominating the news cycle and completely disrupting the Party's Convention that Dr. Dobson endorses. Dobson has just come out and completely endorsed the choice of Sarah Palin. If Reverend Jeremiah Wright had prayed for rain to somehow disrupt John

McCain's acceptance speech, but instead a massive storm came smashing down during Obama's potential speech, the media would have been all over the story.

Breaking news: Sarah Palin has hired an attorney for what the media is calling "Troopergate." I referred to this case before. It involves Palin supposedly having a public safety commissioner fired. How much press this will actually get remains to be seen. McCain visited a disaster relief center in Toledo, Ohio today, continuing his effort to get out in front of Hurricane Gustav politically. "This is what it's all about ..." McCain said. He also told a group of volunteers, "This epitomizes the millions of Americans who are serving on behalf of causes greater than their own self-interest and putting their country first."

Arriana Huffington, Peggy Noonan, John Harris, Tucker Carlson, and Mark Halprin spoke at a forum in St. Paul earlier today. The topic: "New Media vs. Old Media." They represented *The Huffington Post.com, The Wall Street Journal, The Politico, MSNBC,* and *Time,* respectively. They talked about the role of the media. The panel was in agreement over the idea that New Media is influenced by the blogosphere. All agreed that a journalist today is less likely to get away with writing or saying something inaccurate because bloggers are able to instantly fact-check them and force an immediate correction from said journalist.

Mark Halprin commented on how New Media is operating: "What's happening now is great." Halprin feels that there is "more minute-to-minute engagement from the Left to the Right." He's correct, but he's talking about the blogosphere, and according to *ZDNet Research,* only 3 % of

Americans read blogs daily. *ZDNet Research* also says, "The percentage of Americans getting their news on a daily basis from the mainstream media is 51% for local television news, 44% for local newspapers, 39% for cable news networks, 36% for the nightly broadcast network news, and 21% for radio talk shows." If ABC's Charles Gibson says something incorrect on the nightly news, only a tiny percentage of people are going to get the corrected information that some fact-checking blogger decides to post. Gibson's influence is enormous.

During the Democratic Primary, I spent many days upset about something I had heard the day before. I was consistently irked by the media coverage of, for example, an underhanded attack that Hillary Clinton made and got away with. I was in a constant state of frustration for a year and often didn't know exactly why. John Harris said something that is at the crux of why I decided to document the day-to-day activities of the media during this campaign. He referred to what is often said in the media that angers us and how easily we forget it. "I can never remember what I was all up in arms about two months ago....Why was I upset?" said Harris. Harris had nailed the feelings I too had experienced. The electronic media is so fleeting, leaving nothing to refer back to, to ponder. So many sound bites in a day with so few facts to hang our hats on!

The most entertaining moment of the forum came when Arriana Huffington and Tucker Carlson got into a bit of a heated disagreement over the role of a news anchor. Carlson first said, "The traditional model news anchor holds the news cast in place." He went on to emphasize the importance of having a neutral anchor. He had me there but then lost me when he claimed that more than one thing can be true at the same time and that the anchor should at least pretend to be neutral. Huffington said, "The truth is not to be formed by splitting the difference between two sides." I agree! One side may be completely wrong. Huffington also said, "It is the job of the anchor to be on the side of the truth." I have already expressed how important I think it is for anchors to be neutral, but Huffington made an excellent point when she said that an anchor shouldn't allow a person to claim that the world is flat without correcting them. I have emphasized the importance of anchors refraining from injecting their opinions, but telling an obstinate person that the world is indeed round would be all right with me—even if it came from Tom Brokaw. Tucker Carlson never seemed to grasp the simplicity of Huffington's point—that ignoring falsehoods is not the role of an anchor. On the other hand, if Katie Couric decided to tell us that she ran into a woman at the post office who told her that Obama's speech was terrible and that she would never vote for him in a million years or that "McCain still owns the issue of experience," as NBC's Peter Alexander put it, I would find it unacceptable.

A new Gallup poll has Obama maintaining a 6-point lead, up 49% to 43%. But Hurricane Gustav continues to dominate the news. One story that is popping up from to time to time, and could likely explode tomorrow, is the pregnant daughter of Palin story. Sean Hannity made one of the most inaccurate comments regarding this story. Newt Gingrich was on FOX News and told Hannity that Obama had done a good job of putting the story in perspective. Gingrich praised Obama for saying that the story shouldn't be part of our politics.

Hannity then said, "Especially considering that Obama has a similar background." Hannity was referring to the fact that Obama's mother had gotten pregnant with him before she had married his father. As if Obama had anything to do with the fact that his mother got pregnant out of wedlock! Earth to Hannity! Obama wasn't the one who got pregnant. It wasn't his decision, idiot. It wasn't his daughter either! Bad comparison! Besides, Palin is against teaching sex education and is for abstinence only. And it's the Right Wing that makes out-of-wedlock pregnancy such a huge political topic. The FCC should investigate Sean Hannity for failure to appreciate irony or at least for making atrocious analogies. How about for a child worker impersonating an adult?

Breaking News: In July of 2008, Palin replaced the Public Safety Commissioner, whom she had fired, with a high school friend of hers, Chuck Kopp. Kopp had to instantly resign because of a previous sexual harassment charge. Looks like cronyism and more! And it doesn't look like we are going to have to wait until tomorrow to see the media jump all over this Palin story regarding her daughter. CNN is covering the story full time, as Hurricane Gustav has just been downgraded to a tropical storm. But three new hurricanes are on their way— Hurricanes Hannah, Ike, and Josephine. But the networks are on this Palin story like hawks. Reporters are flooding into Alaska by the minute. Apparently, they are uncovering e-mails that went back and forth from the governor's office and those officials involved in ultimately removing the Public Safety Commissioner.

My gut feeling is that McCain is going to have to remove Palin as his VP running mate immediately. Why? Because the coverage of both stories—"Troopergate" and "pregnant daughter"—is so negative and likely to dominate the next few days. The Republican National Convention held only a few activities today and there were no speeches, other than brief statements given by Cindy McCain and Laura Bush regarding the outreach that is going on to help storm victims.

I am curious to see if Palin can survive until the acceptance speech she is due to deliver on Thursday night— today is Monday. Barack Obama told reporters today that a candidate's family life is "off limits." Republican talkies are praising Obama's ability to "take the high rode." I'm not quite sure they would offer the same courtesy if the shoe were on the other foot and Biden had a 17 year old daughter in the same situation. Obama has just said that he would fire anyone in his camp that talked about Palin's daughter. Now that's tough! I hope the Republicans don't think that Obama intends to offer them the same pass on this potential "Troopergate" scandal. That is not a family issue and speaks directly to abuse of power. If the media does its job and uncovers that Palin took advantage of her powers as both a mayor and governor, it will then be frightening to imagine how she will conduct herself as the Vice President. Right now she is showing an ability to shrug off adversity, but if she did abuse her power and manages to get away with it, only to find herself perched behind a desk belonging to the very powerful Office of theVice President, what lesson will she have learned? It was Abraham Lincoln who said, "Nearly all men can stand adversity, but if you want to test a man's character, give him power." Unlike being mayor of a tiny town and governor of the sparsely-populated Alaska, the Vice Presidency will test Palin's character as it has never been tested before.

DAY 9
TUCKER WAY OUT OF BOUNDS

Obama is in Chicago, Illinois, today—Tuesday, September 2—while McCain is in Philadelphia, Pennsylvania. "We're proud of Bristol's decision to have her baby and even prouder to become grandparents. As Bristol faces the responsibilities of adulthood, she knows she has our unconditional love and support." This statement came from Sarah Palin regarding the news of her daughter's pregnancy. The story is gaining momentum. Three questions for the media: Will you find out how old the boy who got her pregnant is? Was Bristol 16 when she got pregnant? What are the laws in Alaska regarding teen-sex age limits? Is Palin proud of her daughter's "decision?" How could it have been a decision? She doesn't believe there is such a thing as choice. Funny how the very people who shun and condemn those who are gay, have sex out of wedlock, etc., are now praising a 17-year-old girl whom they would have raked over the coals had she been one of the Democrats' daughters. What happened to their family values platform that they've been shoving down our throats for my 36-year lifetime?

Foreign policy experience is the issue that John McCain has tried to hammer Obama with. The media has definitely helped the Republicans make their case against Obama. Does McCain actually have more foreign policy experience? Truthfully, only a sitting President can actually gain the kind of foreign policy experience needed by the President. The only constitutional power a U.S. Senator has over foreign policy is one vote in ratifying a treaty and one vote in declaring war. Congressional committee work is educational, but of the four people on the tickets, none has true Presidential foreign policy experience. Joe Biden's chairmanship of the Senate Foreign Relations Committee is the closest any of them have to foreign policy experience, but even that experience in only an advice role. The President of the United States sets and enforces foreign policy. Today, Joe Biden talked about his foreign "relations" experience and how he knows all these heads of state, but that's quite different. He never claimed to have foreign "policy" experience, which, in the end, is the only resume item we can render judgment on in hiring our next President.

CNN's Campbell Brown recently spoke to Tucker Bounds, McCain's campaign spokesperson. She went after him hard and did a good job of making him defend his party's recent choice of Palin, a person with no foreign policy knowledge. This was Brown's first statement: "Tucker, foreign policy experience has been a huge issue in this campaign because you guys made it a big issue in this campaign—pointing out time and time again as you did that John McCain had far more experience than Barack Obama, and that nothing, in your view, was more important in the campaign." She set the table with this statement and said that McCain's camp wasn't holding Palin to their own original standard against Obama. Bounds tried to make his case that it was McCain who had more experience than Obama and that because Palin was on the ticket with him, the issue was less important. But in her haste, Brown said this: "No one's arguing with you that McCain has much more [foreign policy] experience than Barack Obama." Actually, Campbell Brown, I myself am arguing with him. So how could you say, "no one is?"

Bounds also went on to claim that Palin had foreign policy experience. Bounds said, "She's been the commander of the National Guard... of the Alaska National Guard that's been deployed overseas. That's foreign policy experience.... Any decision she has made as the commander of the National Guard that's deployed overseas is more of a decision than Barack Obama has been making as he's been running for President for the last two years." Brown cut him off and asked him to give her one example of a time when Palin had deployed the National Guard. Bounds could not do so. She nailed him.

But later when speaking to Wolf Blitzer today about the interview, Brown said that she had since found out, with the help of a colleague, that Palin had indeed deployed the Alaska National Guard. She said that Palin had deployed them to help with a forest fire. Brown said that if Bounds had simply known this fact, he could have used it and won the debate she was having with him. Wrong! Bounds originally claimed that Palin had foreign policy experience. Campbell Brown forgot her original point. She had been able to pin Bounds down with this specific statement: "Tucker... no governor makes decisions about how to equip or deploy the National Guard. When they go to Iraq, those decisions, as you well know, are made by the Pentagon."

Brown is wrong to say that Bounds needed only to point out the fact that Palin had deployed the National Guard to a forest fire in order to end the debate. And again, this inaccuracy hurts Obama. Palin has zero foreign policy knowledge. Zero! Stop letting these people off the hook! Who cares if she deployed them to a forest fire! Was this what Brown was originally trying to get Bounds to say? Brown didn't start off by saying that the major issue was executive experience—the topic was foreign policy experience, Campbell Brown. And even though Brown did a good job at first, in the end she bailed McCain out and left the nation thinking that Palin has more foreign policy experience than Obama. Maybe the forest fire she sent her National Guard to put out was in Russia.

The *Politico's* Charles Mahtesian wrote this online in defense of Palin today: "Even the governor's own Trooper-gate scandal, in which Palin is alleged to have exerted undue pressure to fire a state trooper, is suffused with an element that many families can identify with: one sister stepping in on behalf of another in an acrimonious dispute with a brother-in-law." Is Mr. Mahtesian serious? Is it his job to help build a defense for Palin? She's hired a lawyer! Let the lawyer defend her. And let the McCain camp defend McCain's choice. Is Mahtesian analyzing the news or is he creating the news? Besides, if a governor brings the power of her office to the defense of her family, that's called "abuse of power." And enough with the stories about how "many families" can relate to this. "Many families" can't relate to being an "actual" governor. That is the reality. That is the focus here. "Many families" have no idea what it's like to have that type of power. Note to the media: We the people do not want an average, everyday American, one we can relate to, hang out with, have a beer with, or hunt with, running the country. We have friends for that. We want someone that none of us can relate to because they are off-the-scales-smart, wise, worldly, educated, and dignified.

At 1:32 pm, Wolf Blitzer said that CNN was committed to fair coverage on both sides. This comment came in response to John McCain's decision to cancel an interview with Larry King due to the heated exchange that took place between Campbell Brown and Tucker Bounds. McCain claimed that CNN crossed the line. Glenn Beck spoke to Wolf Blitzer later and tried to defend Palin. He said a few things in her defense before then offering this less than flattering piece of information: "I'm white trash." Beck then tried to explain how those like him were looking for someone indeed like them. Blitzer then told Beck that he doesn't consider him "white trash." The two then laughed.

Obama is at home in Chicago today. I wonder what he is making of this media spectacle? He isn't campaigning, so he may be sitting back and wondering—wondering what would have happened had this been his seventeen-year-old daughter who had gotten pregnant out of wedlock. (His oldest daughter is only 11, but pretend with me for a second.) I have an opinion: A story like this would end his candidacy. Republicans would talk endlessly about the moral issues involved and how abstinence is the only choice. They would say things like, *This speaks to the issue of parenting. It speaks to the type of mother Michelle Obama is. It speaks to whether or not Mr. Obama spends enough time with his daughter or is more focused on being a celebrity. It speaks to the issue of judgment. It speaks to the kind of values Americans demand of their First Family.* Republicans would pounce on this. They would formulate a laundry list of talking points on parental responsibility. They'd say things like, *It speaks to the issue of who Barack Obama is—I mean think about it—his own mother was a teenager who got pregnant out of wedlock. Our Republican platform speaks to these very issues. It also shows how abstinence works better than sex education.*

And then, of course, there would be the racial element that would come up. They would likely refer to the percentage of black teenage pregnancies per capita versus white teenage pregnancies. Republicans would see this as their big chance to beat Obama, and they would take full advantage of it. They wouldn't suggest that candidate's children are "off limits," as Obama did yesterday. And the media would allow Republicans to make these talking points. I cannot say that the media would actually drive the fracas, but they would allow the Republicans to make a huge spectacle out of it. And I think the media itself would at least put Obama through the ringer for days on end. They would not allow the story to go away anytime soon.

If we assume that the manufactured premise I just outlined is probably true, then we must analyze what is happening with the Palin scandal with this manufactured premise in mind. Is Obama's camp giving the media any talking points that could be used to destroy Palin? The answer is no. Is the media going to make this story last as long as they would if Obama were the subject? We'll have to wait and see.

Fred Thompson is scheduled to speak today at the convention. Referring to Thompson, Tom Brokaw said that we all know he has "great thespian skills." Personally, Mr. Brokaw, I have never considered Fred Thompson a great actor. At all! Acting references aside, the media should be completely focused on McCain's judgment. Yes, they are talking about it, but not enough. The first major decision of McCain's candidacy has seen him make a bad choice. Here is a fact: John McCain met Sarah Palin one time before selecting her to be his running mate. This should be the focus of the media. They should not allow McCain to squirm out of this one. This goes directly to the issue of judgment and making hasty decisions. He left the vetting of the Vice Presidential nominee to the press, and they should be letting the world know, without apology, that they intend to do their job thoroughly.

There is a story brewing involving Palin's possible connection to a political party that at one point had designs on seceding from the United States. *The New York Times'* Elisabeth Bumiller writes today: "Among other less attention-grabbing news of the day: it was learned that Ms. Palin now has a private lawyer in a legislative ethics investigation in Alaska into whether she abused her power in dismissing the state's public safety commissioner; that she was a member for two years in the 1990s of the Alaska Independence Party, which has at times sought a vote on whether the state should secede; and that Mr. Palin was arrested 22 years ago on a drunken-driving charge." If this story about Palin being a part of said Party is true, it could be the end of her. At 2:10 pm, Howard Fineman said that Palin was not a secessionist, but that she had simply said some positive things about the party in the past. To Mr. Fineman I say, "Really? Are you sure about that?" Sounds like the guy who says, "I'm not a Klansman—I've just said some positive things about the KKK in the past." Sorry! That doesn't pass the smell test. Why did Palin *ever* say anything positive about that party?

FOX News' Dick Morris felt compelled to tell America that "a man would have never had to go through this." He was referring, of course, to the supposed scrutiny that Palin has come under. Sean Hannity then took the cake when he proclaimed, "Journalism is dead in this country." I literally fell out of my chair. Morris then took the opportunity to slam Obama for supposedly being behind any attacks that have been levied at Palin. He professed, "His negative research group is working overtime." He happened to be talking to Alan Colmes who responded by saying, "They all do that." Colmes should have reminded Morris that Obama had told his camp that anyone involved in attacking Palin would be fired. Morris said that Obama was acting like he is "all holier than thou" when he claimed that he didn't want any negative talk coming from his campaign staff. Listen Mr. Dick! If you are the "thou" that you are talking about, then Obama is indeed "holier than thou." From now on I will refer to Dick Morris as "Thou." I mean, think about it! This coming from Dick Morris, a man who in 1996 resigned from the Clinton campaign after reports surfaced that he had been involved with a prostitute. I'm sure anyone who hasn't been would be considered "all holier than thou" by Morris. And FOX News just lets him ramble and spew and it goes on and on and on.

Tonight's convention coverage is centered on George Bush's speech. Before he speaks, they are paying tribute to his father. At 6:25, Wolf Blitzer felt obligated to praise Bush Sr. after the convention crowd gave him a standing ovation. "They love him here, as they certainly should," said Blitzer.

I kept waiting for Wolf to tell me why they should "certainly" love him. Meanwhile, Bush Jr. is speaking from Washington, D.C., because of the hurricane—at least that's what the GOP is selling. One glaring remark from Bush was this: "If the Hanoi Hilton could not break John McCain's resolve to do what's best for his country, you can be sure that the angry Left never will." I'm not sure this statement coming from this person is exactly what John McCain needs right now.

As I scan the convention delegates, it is stunning how different they look from the Democratic delegates. America is becoming two countries in appearance. The audience at the Republican National Convention is largely made up of older, grey-haired, white men. There are very few women that look independent—most of them appear to be loyal wives, literally and righteously standing by their man. Not that there's anything wrong with that! It just seems like a really big divide is widening in this country by the minute. This partisan battle is going to get very ugly. The Republicans are doing everything they can tonight to try to make this a referendum on militarism—suggesting that Democrats are unfit to protect the country. As George Bush spoke tonight, I couldn't help but feel the entire country taking one huge collective anxious deep breath and saying to themselves, *Can you believe this is our President?* Fred Thompson has been tasked to explain to America how heroic John McCain is. He is telling a detailed story of McCain's P.O.W. experience. The GOP also acknowledged other prisoners of war at the convention by having them all stand up. I kept thinking to myself, *Wow—all those prisoners of war, and none of them claiming they are qualified to be President as a result of having been held in captivity.*

DAY 10
"DRILL, BABY, DRILL"

Obama is campaigning in New Philadelphia, Ohio, today—Wednesday, September 3—while McCain is in St. Paul, Minnesota. John McCain, as mentioned earlier, canceled an interview with Larry King last night because he was offended that Campbell Brown had been so hard on Tucker Bounds. The media should be going after McCain on his no show for being absolutely childish. If Obama had done the same thing, they would be raking him over he coals. They would be claiming that he can't handle pressure—that he will certainly have a difficult time dealing with foreign dictators if he can't take the heat of an aggressive reporter. McCain is using this ploy to pressure the media into moving to the Right.

One Republican after another has been going on news programs and claiming that Barack Obama has never reached across the aisle and gotten anything accomplished. They have been peddling this lie for two years. It is time for the media to start asking these talking heads not to come on their programs anymore if they are going to continue stating this absolute lie. Here is a fact for Chris Matthews, Tom Brokaw, Larry King, Katie Couric, Charles Gibson, Campbell Brown, Lou Dobbs, Sean Hannity, Bill O'Reilly, David Gregory, Brian Williams, Joe Scarborough, Rush Limbaugh, Anderson Cooper, Wolf Blitzer, Chuck Todd, Greta Van Susteren, Bret

Hume, and George Stephanopoulos: On January 11, 2007, the "Lugar-Obama Nonproliferation Legislation" was signed into law by the President of the United States. Lugar is a Republican. Obama is a Democrat. Getting this legislation signed together is called "reaching across the aisle." Period! End of discussion! If one more of these anchors allows a talkie to come on their program and tell this lie, they themselves should be accused of endorsing the lie. And just how important is the news about nonproliferation? I'm sure the world considers it newsworthy—an endeavor worth reiterating during the campaign.

I am completely dumbfounded by the media's inability to evenhandedly and authentically deal with this issue of experience that the Republicans are raising. The GOP is insistent on trying to claim that Palin has more experience than Barack Obama. The media is giving validity to this weak debate by allowing the issue to dominate the airwaves. It is important to note that Obama himself is not commenting on Palin's experience. Yet the GOP is claiming that his campaign is the one belittling Palin. This claim is false, yet the media is doing a poor job of debunking it. They, in fact, are the ones proliferating it. If the Republicans go on television and decide to claim that Obama is responsible for leaking the story about Palin's daughter, is the media going to give it legs? Will they allow the McCain camp to claim anything, then report it as news?

"You can't ignore the fact that she's a pretty remarkable woman." This statement came from CNN's Kyra Phillips, who is on location in Anchorage, Alaska, today. How can she tell us that we can't ignore the "fact"? Really? This is a "fact"?

Phillips went on to say that Palin was a "renaissance woman". What? Kyra Phillips needs to be told that the definition of a renaissance woman, according to *Dictionary.com* is: "a woman who has broad intellectual interests and is accomplished in areas of both the arts and the sciences." Careful how you throw praise Palin's way, Kyra Phillips! I haven't seen Phillips describe Obama as a "renaissance man". And Palin's ability to fish, hunt, and ski—all of which she can indeed do—does not put her in the renaissance category. Was George Bush ever described as a renaissance man? He is notorious, for chopping wood, cycling, jogging, and golfing. Palin had never been out of the country before 2007. Never! She didn't even have a passport until then. Stop praising this person without real facts to back up the praise.

Is the *Financial Times* committed to electing John McCain? One of their writers, Chrystia Freeland, surely seems to be. Today, in **Sarah Palin is a True Feminist Role Model**, Freeland writes, "Governor Palin, who took on her own party's good ole boys and won, has as much of a record of political achievement as does Senator Obama: running a state, no matter how sparsely populated, is a bigger executive job than being a senator." I'm already pissed! But Freeland isn't finished. "What Democrats, and progressives generally, will have a harder time accepting is that Governor Palin's nomination could be a milestone for American women: in many ways she is an even better feminist icon than America's reigning top gal Hillary Clinton." *Top gal?* Freeland is obviously not a feminist. What feminist worth her salt would refer to any woman as a "gal"? The last time I checked, Hillary Clinton had put herself through law school, something that defines "self made", but Freeland is not impressed. She goes on, "In contrast with Mrs. Clinton, whose most important political decision was whom she married, Mrs. Palin is a genuinely self-made woman, who broke into politics without the head start of a powerful husband or father. Moreover, like Senator Clinton, Governor Palin is a working mother role model, giving birth to her fifth child less than five months ago, going back to work three days later." Too soon, I should think, if she wants to bond with her baby.

Dominating today's news cycle is Palin's speech tonight. The media appears to be teetering on caving in to the backlash coming from the GOP. Republicans are lambasting the media for being unfair to Palin. They're calling them the elite media. They are accusing the media of being insensitive by talking about Palin's daughter. They are accusing the overall media of being all in for Obama. They've got to be kidding with this pathetic attempt to stymie the press' obligation to vet Palin. But, then again, the press may just fall for it and decide not to do their jobs. And that would include continuing to uncover anything whatsoever that might disqualify Palin from being a viable candidate for high office. I keep waiting for a major reporter to reveal the fact that Palin managed to run up a $22 million debt while she was a mayor in Alaska—this after taking the job with a surplus to work with. And that all this debt was as mayor of that little Alaskan town that had a population of just 6,000.

Pat Buchanan helped fuel Republican fire by saying, "The press has been savage on her.... It has been a disgraceful performance by the press." Sean Hannity went on record with, "The media has set out to destroy an innocent woman."

The GOP knows that their only hope is to get the media to stop investigating Palin. If they continue to do their jobs, there is some evidence that they will find enough wrongdoing to end her candidacy. Just a hunch, but I think the media is caving in.

Rudy Giuliani just delivered one of the most low-life, mean spirited speeches I have ever heard, and a large portion was directed toward Barack Obama. He talked about Obama as if he wasn't qualified to take out the trash. I was embarrassed for the Republican Party. Giuliani wasn't able to give any credit whatsoever to Obama. The speech was filled with venom. At one point during his speech, the convention crowd started chanting, "Drill, baby, drill". What a stupid chant! Especially during a time of global warming. But, Giuliani seemed to enjoy it. I can't wait to see how the media responds to his below- the-belt, sarcastic, arrogant, childish, unstatesman-like, excoriating, divisive, pompous, petty, fear-mongering, inaccuracy-laden, and downright hateful speech.

Perhaps if one were to read only the transcript of Giuliani's speech, they would not pick up on the tone of it. It was the sarcastic laughter—the facial expressions—the over-the-top grinning—that made the speech unworthy. He was reveling in the fact that he had punctured Obama, even though, in fact, he hadn't. He had inflicted nothing, yet stuck his chest out with a certainty that was laughable—the certainty of a fool. The speech lacked anything resembling what America is about. There was no trace of bi-partisanship. Most of the truth was replaced with jokes. And Giuliani bathed in the laughter bestowed upon him by the partisan, transfixed, and jubilant crowd. He sold fear—assuming his audience was ignorant—and they, as he expected, oohed and aahed like puppets on a string. He said, "Hope is not a strategy." Yet it was the strategy he was banking on in Florida to save his own campaign. He then proclaimed, "Barack Obama has never led anything—nothing—nada!" You mean he's never "led" us into a war that caused thousands of American troops to be killed? Giuliani also laughingly said, "On the other hand, you have a resume from a gifted man with an Ivy League education. He worked as a community organizer, and immersed himself in Chicago machine politics." It was the way in which Giuliani said community organizer that was off-putting. He mocked the profession. One question for Mr. Giuliani! Where is the line? Do you have one? Is there anything to you that is not worthy of saying, even if not saying it means the end of your political career? Have you no decency? You spoke of Obama as if he were not a fellow American. Shame on you!

Palin just gave her convention speech. It looked a bit like a carbon copy of Giuliani's, only it lacked the same venom. Hers was more wrapped in ignorance. Remember, this is a woman who asked what the VP slot was all about just a few months ago. In the speech, she did not mention the economy one time. She spent a great deal of her time attacking Obama. She was sarcastic. She told jokes. She made sweeping, tactless comments. She played overbearingly to the crowd, desperately seeking their approval. It was the *anything I can say to get you to like me speech*. A true insult to any American with a modicum of intelligence. She won over the crowd with sarcasm: "I guess a small-town mayor is sort of like a 'community organizer', except that you have actual responsibilities…. I've noticed a pattern with our opponent. Maybe you have, too. We've all heard his dramatic speeches before devoted followers. Listening to him speak, it's easy to forget that this is a man who has authored two memoirs but not a single major law or reform—not even in the state senate." Excuse me, Mrs. Palin! Not a single major law? I am not going to go into detail on this, but telling this type of bald-faced lie, during a major VP speech to the entire nation, should lead to civil court. She is blatantly lying to the American people. I will be waiting for the media to call her out on this big fat lie, but I'm betting they won't.

Palin had more high school-level rhetoric to mouth. She said, "This is a man [Obama] who can give an entire speech about the wars America is fighting, and never use the word 'victory' except when he's talking about his own campaign. But when the cloud of rhetoric has passed … when the roar of the crowd fades away … when the stadium lights go out, and those Styrofoam Greek columns are hauled back to some studio lot - what exactly is our opponent's plan?" Bravo Mrs. Palin! We can thank the media for creating the "Greek Column" theme that Palin referred to. Thank you for giving Palin this zinger. She drew huge applause when she mocked Obama:

> What does he actually seek to accomplish, after he's done turning back the waters and healing the planet? The answer is to make government bigger… take more of your money…give you more orders from Washington…and to reduce the strength of America in a dangerous world.

America needs more energy … our opponent is against producing it. Victory in Iraq is finally in sight…he wants to forfeit. Terrorist states are seeking new-clear weapons without delay…he wants to meet them without preconditions. Al-Qaeda terrorists still plot to inflict catastrophic harm on America…he's worried that someone won't read them their rights? Government is too big…he wants to grow it…. My fellow citizens, the American presidency is not supposed to be a journey of 'personal discovery.' This world of threats and dangers is not just a community, and it doesn't just need an organizer.

The speech is laughable and I'm surprised the press is giving her a pass. The only people I've heard analyze the speech correctly are a few Democrats. Congresswoman Debbie Wasserman-Schultz referred to it as a "tirade of attacks". Radio host Stephanie Miller labeled it a "nasty string of attacks." Ed Schultz said, "This speech tonight was lacking in detail…Ok she can read a teleprompter—big deal!" But the media itself is doing nothing but saying how effective her speech was. How she really had the crowd going, etc. If you had told me last week in Denver, after the wonderful Obama speech was being praised by the media, that they would then turn around and praise a simple-minded, high school-level speech like this, I may not have believed it. Yes, unfortunately, I would have!

The Republicans, with help from the media, are claiming that what the country now desperately needs is a person from outside of Washington—like Palin? This is the new talking point. Note to the media! John McCain has been in Washington for almost three decades, and he's on the top of the ticket. Hello! Call them out on this weak-ass talking point. They've been telling us for the last six months that the country could not afford someone like Obama who has only been in Washington for three years, unlike their main man John McCain. And now they're saying that we need someone like Palin who hasn't been in Washington at all. The swirling, spinning hypocrisy is making me dizzy.

I still haven't heard David Gregory ask: "To know John McCain is to be comfortable with what?" I still haven't heard John King say that America is asking themselves, who are "these people," in reference to the Palins. I haven't heard King praise Palin's speech and then claim that Palin is trying to say, "We may look different, but our lives have been like yours." I haven't heard anyone bring up the "seven homes" issue regarding regular American McCain. Where is that story? I haven't heard them question McCain on his decision not to denounce the horrible William Ayers ad that was run against Obama. The "Keating Five" hasn't come up this week. No one has asked McCain why he had made light of the serious subject of bombing Iran by singing "Bomb, bomb, bomb, bomb, bomb Iran!" to the tune of "Barbara Ann". No one has questioned him for pathetically cancelling an interview with Larry King because his feelings were hurt. No reporter has demanded an answer from McCain regarding how he could meet Palin once and put her one heartbeat away from the Presidency. Why has Cindy McCain's questionable past been virtually ignored by the press? *Who is she?* Why isn't the media outlining— specifically—the Bush horrors of the past eight years and pointing out the fact that McCain voted with him over 90% of the time? It's the media's job to be pointing out this voting record and magnifying it—not just the Obama campaign's job.

Has the media forgotten suddenly that these have been arguably the worst eight years in modern American history? We're at the Republican National Convention and the media has brought none of this up. The past eight years have been completely ignored. This will be a scar on the mainstream media for years to come. Instead, they are marching in unison behind this sensationalized, *US Magazine*-driven Palin drama—practically salivating over the fact that she's a proud hockey mom for Christ's sake! If they decided to focus on the Bush record of the past eight years, I would gladly let this Palin investigation go. Palin is small potatoes, and serves to do nothing more than get the media to take their eyes off of the ball. And they have! The ball is George W. Bush. Home foreclosures! A trillion dollars in Iraq! Blithely ignoring a fundamental American right—*habeas corpus*! Leaking Valerie Plame's identity! An endless list of lies! Stop! Stop! Stop talking about Sarah Freaking Palin! She has nothing to do with the Mount Kilimanjaro-sized mess that Bush and McCain have left us. Set the agenda, media! Report the facts! Do your jobs! I'm waiting!

DAY 11
O'REILLY MEETS THE OBAMA FACTOR

Obama is campaigning in York, Pennsylvania, today—Thursday, September 4—while McCain is in St. Paul, Minnesota. "With all due respect again to Governor Kaine, he's been a governor for three years. He's been able but undistinguished. I don't think people could really name a big important thing that he's done. He was mayor of the 105th largest city in America and again, with all due respect to Richmond, Virginia—small as in Chula Vista, California; Aurora, Colorado; Mesa or Gilbert, Arizona; North Las Vegas or Henderson, Nevada. It's not a big town." This came directly from the mouth of Karl Rove. I haven't seen the media throw this quote in the face of a single Republican talking head. How can the GOP tout Sarah Palin, when their leading spokesman, Karl Rove, has undressed former Democratic potential VP nominee, Gov. Tim Kaine, for having the small-town mayor experience as his own new VP pick? Rove is now praising Palin, ignoring everything he previously said about Kaine. He's acting as if he never even made those comments on CBS. The media should be running this Rove comment every time they reference Palin's small-town mayor experience.

Instead of criticizing last night's speeches for being nothing more than a laundry list of lies, the media is focused on how effective Palin's words were—how she has managed to change the narrative and put the Obama camp on unstable ground, unsure of how to deal with Palin. Please! CNN's Carl Bernstein took the opportunity this morning to slam a new Obama ad. The ad was actually an effective response to the lying parade that took place last night, but Bernstein said that he "thought the ad was lame."

The media is spending most of today talking about Palin. Nearly one hundred percent! The GOP has successfully managed to play the media like a flute. No coverage of Obama! No issues! Just Palin! The GOP knew that they could take over the airwaves if they simply put an unknown governor on their ticket. To the GOP, I say, "Dirty job well done." To the media I say, "Shame on you."

Vanity Fair just uncovered an interesting fact about the outfit that Cindy McCain was wearing the other night at the convention. Their article entitled **Cindy McCain's $300,000 Outfit** should become a huge story. Remind me who the elitists are here. Anyone who wears an outfit worth that much defines the word elitist, even if they don't intend to. And I actually don't care how expensive her outfit is—it's just that the McCain camp has been reveling in their ability to paint the Obamas as elitists.

One of the main themes in last night's speeches was making fun of Obama's community organizing experience. Since when did being a 22-year-old young man who decides to give back to the community become a subject to be made fun of in our country? The media should be interviewing young college-level community organizers from all over the country, White and Black, and asking them why they decided to take on such meaningless work. Americans deserve to know. Is this a meaningless job? According to the Republican Party, it is. Do your jobs, media members. Go interview a few of the legions of Black, White, Asian, Hispanic, and Native American community organizers. They come from all over the country and work in many areas of need—in agricultural areas, inner cities, reservations, etc. Ask them why Sarah Palin and Rudy Giuliani think their jobs are laughable.

Chris Matthews of MSNBC must think that all of these mean -spirited lies coming from the Republicans are funny. He laughed like a goon as he spoke to Rudolph Giuliani today. At 2:30 pm, Matthews told Giuliani, "I thought your speech was one of the great, fun speeches of my life." If you admire that kind of cynicism, your life has been one that I'm glad I haven't had to live. And you need to go hear a lot more speeches. Does Mr. Matthews think that it was great fun to hear Giuliani demean the thousands of teenagers who are helping disabled homeless people all over the country? Many community organizers are indeed teenagers. I have never been so utterly disappointed in an MSNBC host. Mr. Matthews needs to stop yucking it up with these guys and hold them accountable—100% of the time! Stop being a buddy and pretending you're at a Washington cocktail party. Giuliani deserved to be excoriated, not lauded.

There is a strong suggestion on the part of the Republican spokespeople that Obama went directly from being a community organizer to running for President. The narrative is getting some traction. CNN's Tara Wall was asked if the GOP had been too unfair last night by attacking Obama's community organizing experience. She said that they were only trying to point out that community organizing experience is fine but it doesn't prepare you for going straight to the Presidency. John King, Wolf Blitzer, and Gloria Borger just let her throw that talking point out and none of them challenged her on that specific inaccuracy. Who thinks that Obama is trying to go directly from community organizing to being President?

Evidently the media does because it's is allowing this talking point to dominate today. It's a talking point that the GOP has quickly come up with because they understand the mistake they made last night. They know that, in their haste, they offended thousands of Americans who work with poverty-stricken citizens. Let me help King, Blitzer and Borger out. Let me help them figure out how to never, ever, ever let weak, fly-by-the-seat-of-your-pants talking points get blurted out without any rebuttal whatsoever. One of you could have said, "Listen, Tara Wall, community organizing was the job Obama took at the age of 22. Twenty-two! Working in a family commercial fishing business is the job Sarah Palin took at around that same age. Based on your own logic and standard, I must ask you to tell our viewers how being a commercial fishing business employee is a solid qualification to go directly to becoming Vice President of the United States?"

Cindy McCain spoke at the convention tonight. The speech was less than substantial. But what struck me the most about the pre-analysis of her speech was the lack of pressure the media put on her. When Michelle Obama spoke, the media put as much pressure on her to deliver a great speech as they did Barack himself. They expected Michelle—a potential First Lady—to speak as though she were running for President herself. But tonight there has been absolutely no expectations placed on Cindy McCain. The media has given her a pass. They've given her nothing to prove. They've said nothing about her past prescription drug abuse. Her speech was actually quite terrible. And the media did no real critiquing of her at all. She got a complete pass.

At 6:58 pm, instead of telling America how poorly read Mrs. McCain's speech was, John King chose to remind us all that "Michelle Obama has been both a compelling and a somewhat controversial figure." He seemed to be suggesting that unlike Cindy McCain, Michelle had needed to do some serious explaining because of that unique, controversial image. On a night when Michelle Obama wasn't even there to defend herself, King chose to bring her name up again. Why even bring her up? After Michelle Obama gave her speech last week, John King and others made it sound as if she had shaken the controversial image once and for all. I guess the media isn't going to let Mrs. Obama ever rid herself of that label they pinned on her.

Barack Obama shocked the Right Wing by appearing on FOX News' *O'Reilly Factor*. He did very well, even though O'Reilly tried to speed up the interview and never allowed Obama to expound on a single thing. He tried to bring Obama down to his simple-minded level. Obama explained the complexities of the "surge" that recently took place in Iraq. Obama admitted that the "surge" had succeeded "beyond our wildest dreams". But, O'Reilly wouldn't accept Obama's explanation that even though the "surge" had indeed reduced violence, it hadn't changed the fact that the Iraqi government still needed to take political responsibility.

O'Reilly simplified everyting by saying that the "surge" worked. He couldn't understand why Obama wouldn't specifically say that he was "wrong on the surge". Again, Obama said that the "surge" had indeed played a role in reducing violence, but that it hadn't changed the fact that the Iraqi government needed to take political responsibility and that we were still spending tremendous amounts of money there. Obama pretty much agreed that the "surge" itself—the adding of extra troops to quell violence—had indeed been partly responsible for the success. But he added, "Al Qaeda, the Taliban, a whole host of networks that are bent on attacking America, who have perverted the faith of Islam…we have to go after them." O'Reilly said, "I think you were desperately wrong on the 'surge,' and I think you should admit it to the nation." Obama rightfully declined to do that because the situation in Iraq required a more intelligent and nuanced evaluation. If it worked, Mr. O'Reilly, why are we still there?

Bill O'Reilly is the only person I've seen who, while interviewing Obama, talked to him in such a condescending way. He showed no respect for Obama as a human being, as a person who has unique accomplishments, as a potential next President of the United States of America. Not one shred of respect—the kind of respect people need in order to maintain a semblance of dignity—did Obama get from O'Reilly. His rudeness is an embarrassment. Yet to reach a segment of the American population, Obama needed to get in the pen with O'Reilly. How sad!

John McCain's acceptance speech tonight lacked specificity. He tried to make the case that he would be a change candidate. How can a man who voted 90% of the time with George Bush be a candidate of change? Obama has been accusing the GOP of refusing to talk about bread and butter issues this week at their convention. Someone must have given McCain that memo because he threw in everything but the kitchen sink tonight. He mentioned several plans but never said how he would accomplish them. He shied away from attacking Obama personally, but it appears he took this tone simply to imitate Obama's bi-partisan approach. Either that or he is embarrassed by the tirades that have taken place the two previous nights. Perhaps his campaign informed him that his job is to play the good guy role to offset the roles of his bad guy surragates.

One of the funniest lines happened when McCain was struggling to read his teleprompter. He was asking young Americans to give back and become teachers, nurses, etc. But he was having difficulty reading. It was ironic that the line he fumbled was this one: "Teach an illiterate adult to read." But the speech itself was poor. That didn't stop John King from saying, "He's a pretty tough, remarkable guy." At 8:10 pm, Anderson Cooper got in on the praise by claiming that we've heard "perhaps more specifics in this speech than we did in Barack Obama's speech."

I would like every red-blooded American to get the transcripts of both the McCain and Obama speeches and read them side-by-side. Outline all the "specifics." There is not an honest human being in the country, Republican or Democrat, who could then repeat Anderson Cooper's jaw dropping assessment with a straight face. It is becoming difficult to hear these incorrect assessments. What was Anderson Cooper watching? Good luck, Barack! You're going to need it.

Protestors disrupted McCain's speech only to be met by comedic response lines from McCain. I had to wonder if the protestors were planted there, because McCain had these instant funny lines that evoked laughter from the crowd. The biggest applause came when Palin joined him on the stage afterwards. The media has managed to take the Republican bate and have turned Palin into a rock star. The same individuals that were berating Obama for his so-called celebrity persona are now in awe of Palin for her extraordinary ability to become a huge star overnight. Republicans are gushing and saying, *Now we have our own star on the ticket.* It's their narrative now. How long can they run with it?

DAY 12
IT DIDN'T SELL ON EBAY

Obama is campaigning in Middletown, New Jersey, today—Friday, September 5—while McCain is in Cedarburg, Wisconsin. Now that Obama has explained to Bill O'Reilly that the "surge" itself has played a role in reducing violence, what will the Republicans use as their major talking point? Obama has now taken that tired old rhetoric off of the table. What will McCain now use to paint Obama as a man who can't admit when he's wrong? They're going to have to come up with something new. They have treated this "surge" issue as Rudy Giuliani treated 9/11. It's all they have talked about. Now what? How will they attack Obama's patriotism from this point forward? Obama probably made this move so that he won't have to deal with it during the debates. I have been waiting for McCain to trot that "surge" line out in Mississippi at the first Presidential debate. I imagine him saying, *Senator Obama was against the 'surge.' I was the one who demanded it. Senator Obama was wrong. He was wrong. I was right. The 'surge' has worked, my friends. The 'surge' has worked. Let's have a little straight talk. The 'surge' has worked. And Senator Obama will not admit it. Surge! Surge! Surge!"*

Stars Flock to GOP's New Celebrity—this was a headline in today's *Los Angeles Times*. I canceled my subscription immediately. Just kidding! First of all, the "stars" the *LA Times* was referring to were Pat Boone, Harry Sloan, and Jon Voight.

These are the only people mentioned in the entire article. The headline makes it sound as if Brad Pitt, Angelina Jolie, George Clooney, and a host of other big names were there. Making a big deal about Pat Boone being at a Republican convention is like going coo-coo over Sonny Bono being at a convention back in the early 90's. And if you're going to use the word "flock," you might want to mention more than three people. The headline made me think that hundreds of stars were cramming into the convention. Talk about misleading!

A new *Gallup* poll shows Obama leading 49% to 42%. A CBS poll has the two candidates tied at 42%. Sarah Palin is pouncing on Obama for not completely admitting that the "surge" worked. Yes, we're back to the ubiquitous "surge" today. If Obama agrees to admit that the "surge" was the right thing to do, I wonder if McCain will then be willing to admit that his voting for the war itself was wrong? Why do a good job of the wrong thing? Is this a deal McCain will make with Obama? Of course not!

McCain's bragging about how he was right on the "surge" makes no sense. Let's pretend that McCain, Bush, and Obama had been driving in a van full of people and Obama decided to make them stop because he felt danger ahead and was certain of it. Suppose they let Obama get out, but the two continued on the road, only to drive over a cliff into a huge lake, killing everyone except the two of them. Suppose Obama then tried to suggest a way to successfully pull them from the van and get them out of the lake, but McCain instead figured out his own way of saving their lives. Then suppose McCain began demanding that the entire world tell him how he was right on figuring out how to save his and Bush's life—and that Senator Obama way would have been absolutely wrong. This is the same logic that McCain is using about the "surge".

At about 3:50 pm on FOX News, Fred Barnes analyzed McCain's acceptance speech. He said, "[McCain] did about as well as Obama did. McCain broadened his appeal." Barnes then spoke of what was lacking in Obama's speech. Barnes said, "Obama narrowed his appeal…. In that case, I think McCain's speech was better." At what point did FOX News actually decide to be a network of idiots? Aside from Alan Colmes and maybe a few others, they must have made a calculated decision to make an appeal to the completely ignorant demographic, perhaps greedily suspecting that that demographic in America is huge. If Barack Obama went to Afghanistan and killed Bin Laden with his own bare hands then described his actions in a speech, FOX News would claim that Obama was in Afghanistan for nefarious reasons and that his speech lacked action. On FOX News, the truth has been asked to go to the back of the bus and keep quiet permanently. Almost all of their talking heads are too far gone to save.

The media is up in arms about the fact that Sarah Palin hasn't sat down to do a real one-on-one interview. Instead she's been running around giving canned speeches and mastering the teleprompter. When she finally does sit down to do a hard interview, will the media hammer her hard as they should? Or will they throw cupcake questions at her? So far she's managed to insult Obama consistently but has yet to answer a single question about why she suggested, in her acceptance speech, that she had sold her office's corporate jet on eBay. Today McCain said, "You know what I enjoyed the most, [Palin] took the luxury jet bought by her predecessor and sold it on eBay. And made a profit." There is only one problem here. The jet never sold on eBay. She did manage to sell it, however, but not on eBay. And she ended up losing the state about $600 thousand in the process. Why is this not a huge story? It should be. She presented what appears to be a lie in her acceptance speech. Palin also inquired about what books were being distributed in a Wasilla library. This story should be all over the front pages.

Today, the *Anchorage Daily News'* Rindi White writes, "Back in 1996, when she first became mayor, Sarah Palin asked the city librarian if she would be all right with censoring library books should she be asked to do so. According to news coverage at the time, the librarian said she would definitely not be all right with it. A few months later, the librarian, Mary Ellen Emmons, got a letter from Palin telling her she was going to be fired. The censorship issue was not mentioned as a reason for the firing. The letter just said the new mayor felt Emmons didn't fully support her and had to go." I am waiting for NBC, CBS, and ABC to cover this issue.

A *Newsweek* web exclusive article came out today entitled **Friends Like These: How the Detroit Mayor's Fall Hurts Obama.** The Detroit mayor is Kwame Kilpatrick. He resigned yesterday after pleading guilty to lying under oath. How dare *Newsweek* run this article! As if Obama is automatically connected to every black politician in the country. The list of disgraced white politicians is endless, and no one is automatically linking McCain to them because of his skin color. Shame on *Newsweek!* This is disgusting journalism!

Obama has said positive things about mayor Kilpatrick in the past—before any of the charges were brought against the mayor—almost two years ago. Does *Newsweek* understand that Obama has probably said something positive about every single Democratic, large-city mayor, every Democratic governor, every Democratic senator, and every Democratic member of the House of Representatives, in this country? Part of political campaigning is saying nice things about fellow party members. I find it astounding that *Newsweek* is doing this, considering the fact that there is a laundry list of occasions where McCain has said very kind things about George W. Bush and other Republicans mentioned as operating outside the law. Who has affected America more negatively, Kwami Kilpatrick or George W. Bush?

When *Newsweek's* Keith Naughton writes, "Even with Kwami Kilpatrick in the slammer, Barack Obama will be dogged by the scandal that brought down Detroit's mayor," is he suggesting that he can predict the future? Naughton ought to be ashamed of himself. Did *Newsweek* ever write an article with the headline: *How Los Angeles Mayor's Sex Scandal Hurts Hillary Clinton?* After all, Mayor Antonio Villaraigosa was one of Clinton's major campaign supporters. For the hurried casual reader, it is article headlines like this one from *Newsweek* that kill candidates, even more than the content of the article itself.

Does *Newsweek* intend to dig up the cordial comments that McCain has made about disgraced Idaho Sen. Larry Craig or shamed Louisiana Sen. David Vitter? After all, they are all Republicans and I'm sure they've had to say politically helpful things about each other. And if *Newsweek* has run a past article connecting McCain to either of them, it won't hurt McCain. Unless they run an article during the presidential campaign, it won't affect him. But they shouldn't run an article like this on either candidate. If *Newsweek* could prove that McCain had made a nice comment about a convicted Republican mayor in Timbuktu, Arizona, I wouldn't care. McCain probably knows the mayor of Scottsdale. If the Scottsdale mayor gets convicted next month of lying about having sex, why should this derail McCain's campaign? I would not expect *Newsweek* to run an over the top, suggestive headline about it. But they've managed to do this to Obama, and I'm not letting it go easily.

In this case regarding Obama being friends with Kilpatrick, the potential damage the article could do to his Presidential campaign is enormous. If Obama's crime was saying that Kilpatrick was a good mayor and his punishment is losing the Presidency as a result, it's an understatement to say that the punishment doesn't fit the crime. Detroit is 81% Black. I would have thought that Barack Obama was an absolute idiot if he hadn't gone into Detroit to try and woo voters by developing a relationship with Kilpatrick. He's running for President. He can't win Michigan without getting the majority of the black vote in Detroit. A Presidential candidate is introduced by the mayor of every town he campaigns in. Is there a black politician in America who wouldn't have sought to befriend Kilpatrick if given the same circumstances? Back in 2000, McCain apologized for suggesting that South Carolina remove the Confederate flag. The Confederate flag! A symbol of racism! Why did McCain do it? To get Southern votes! I'm waiting for a *Newsweek* headline on that disgraceful story. Bring that back up during the campaign. The headline could read: *Friends Like These: How Pandering to Racist Southerners Hurts McCain.* Whoever wrote this Obama-Kilpatrick headline is not off the hook with me yet!

Newsweek's headline didn't say that Kilpatrick's fall *could* hurt Obama. They left the word "could" out. *Newsweek* is certain that it will hurt Obama—either that or they're reminding their readers not to forget to *make* it hurt Obama. The problem with *Newsweek* is that they fail to realize something: the only time they can legitimately use the word "hurt" without using the word "could" before it, is the day after Obama loses in the state of Michigan. And that is unlikely. *Newsweek* would need to prove in the exit polls that Obama's kind words for Kilpatrick were the reason people didn't vote for him. A non-vote is the only thing that will "hurt" Obama. Enough said? Perhaps, but I'm still mad!

DAY 13
MAVERICKS OR CLONES?

Obama is campaigning in Terre Haute, Indiana, today—Saturday, September 6—while McCain is in Colorado Springs, Colorado. With 59 days left until we elect our next President, the candidates are positioning themselves for the upcoming debates. The media is building up the first debate, and it has the feel of a showdown that could very well decide the election. It should be fascinating to see how the media pre-analyzes the debate and how they do the post-analysis. Given what we've seen so far regarding speaking ability, the debate should be no contest. McCain struggles to speak unless he's in a town hall meeting, whereas Obama was able to stand toe to toe with Hillary Clinton, who showed a great mastery of the issues. If McCain performs as I suspect, the media will have ammunition to go after him afterwards. But, as I also suspect, they won't!

The media is actually running with a story about flags today. Apparently there were several flags left behind at INVESCO Field in Denver after Obama spoke. An INVESCO cleaning-crew member gathered up all the flags and brought them to a rally for McCain today in Colorado Springs. For the media to give such a silly story any airtime at all is baffling. If this becomes an even bigger story, I'll be certain that Obama's chances of winning are slipping away by the minute. A headline on CNN reads, "Flag Flop." Talk about making a mountain out of a molehill! Stories like this one surface when the media gets bored. Their boredom tends to affect Obama negatively. Besides, the flag story is unsubstantiated. Some cleaning crew guy told CNN a story and they ran with it. In the same vein, there's also an unsubstantiated story going around the Internet about a waitress who claims that she overheard Sarah Palin using the word "Sambo" in reference to Obama. Of course, I don't necessarily believe that, but if CNN decides to run it, I just might give it the same respect I give the flag story.

Perhaps the media could focus on the fact that the McCain camp is being hypocritical. They have been spending the past few days complaining about how Democrats are being sexist in their approach to talking about Palin. Huh? This talking point is, of course, false. The GOP is actually trying to sell this line. But the media should be running a story about how Republican delegates wore buttons at their convention with Palin's face on them that said "The Hottest VP From the Coolest State." If that isn't sexism, I don't know what is. Instead the media is focused on a flag flop story.

The Mavericks. These are the words that appeared on the online advertisement cover for *Newsweek* magazine today. A photo of McCain and Palin accompanies the online cover. Of course, when I went to buy the actual magazine, these words were not on the cover. I guess *Newsweek* chose to write "The Mavericks" on the online ad cover simply to entice buyers. A Maverick is defined as "a politician who takes an independent stand apart from his or her associate." *Newsweek* is obviously endorsing McCain as a politician who has taken an independent stand apart from George W. Bush. Is *Newsweek* kidding? The cover should read, **The Clones.** The definition of a clone is "a person or thing that duplicates, imitates, or closely resembles another in appearance, function, performance, or style." *Newsweek* forgot that McCain voted over 90% of the time with Bush—very close to the definition of a clone—the complete opposite of a maverick. Have we reached the point in America where we can simply name ourselves whatever we want and the media will endorse it? In that case, I would like to refer to myself as a genius from now on. Do you hear me *Newsweek*? I want to be on your cover with the hockey mom of my choosing. And I want **The Geniuses** to grace the cover. For crying out loud *Newsweek*, check yourselves! You are a globally-read magazine. Grow up and behave yourselves. You are leaking credibility by the minute. And it doesn't matter if you've written objective articles about Obama in the past. You're just killing him softly.

An article in today's *The New Republic* uses a very misleading title in referencing Obama's community organizing experience. The title reads: **Creation Myth: What Barack Obama Won't Tell You About His Community Organizing.** This article by John B. Judis goes in depth about Obama's community organizing experience, but in no way does the article parallel the implications of the title itself. When I saw the title, I assumed that there was some deep dark secret about him, like drug selling, stealing money, or some other kind of egregious act. But the only thing the article reveals is a young man who had questioned whether or not he should continue his career in community organizing. The reader learns that Obama perhaps questioned some of the methods that community organizing required of him.

All we learn in the article is that Obama evolved—perhaps grew beyond some of the specific philosophies of community organizing—wanted to better himself by going to Harvard, and that he chose to go into politics. Judis writes:

> In truth, however, if you examine carefully how Obama conducted himself as an organizer and how he has conducted himself as a politician, if you consider what he said about organizing to his fellow organizers, and if you look at the reasons he gave friends and colleagues for abandoning organizing, then a very different picture emerges: that of a disillusioned activist who fashioned his political identity not as an extension of community organizing but as a wholesale rejection of it. Indeed, the most important thing to know about Barack Obama's time as a community organizer in Chicago may not be what he gained from the experience—but rather why, in late 1987, he decided to quit.

"Why... he decided to quit." Sounds so dramatic! But in truth, it wasn't that dramatic. Reading the article, I found nothing that would lead me to believe that Obama "abandoned" organizing. That is so extreme. I also never felt like Obama decided on a "wholesale rejection" of community organizing. A wholesale rejection would suggest that one might find a book or article Obama has written entitled "Why Community Organizing is Evil." But there is no such indictment in Obama's writings. I also question the idea that Obama "quit" organizing. He left it to attend Harvard, a move that can hardly be called quitting. Quitting implies that he gave up in pursuit of a totally different career path, not a path, as the facts suggest, that would afford him more leverage in pursuing the same kinds of goals a community organizer has. If there is a community-organizing boss in the entire country that would advise one of his young employees to turn down an acceptance letter to Harvard and call him a quitter, arrest him immediately. Judis writes further:

> And so, Obama told Kellman, he had decided to leave community organizing and go to law school. Kellman, who was already thinking of leaving organizing himself, found no reason to argue with him. 'Organizing,' Kellman tells me, as we sit in a Chicago restaurant down the street from the Catholic Church where he now works as a lay minister, 'is always a lost cause.' Obama, circa late 1987, might or might not have put it quite that strongly. But he had clearly developed serious doubts about the career he was pursuing.

Judis draws a lot of conclusions based on some very limited information. Earlier Judis wrote that he quit, yet above he writes, "Obama told Kellman, he had decided to leave community organizing and go to law school." So make up your mind, Judis. Did he quit on a career or did he leave to further that career? Those are two distinctively different words that imply something quite different. Quitting implies giving up. Leaving does not. We've all left something for good reason. Did Obama ever tell anyone that he intended to be an entry-level organizer his entire life?

When Judis writes "He had developed serious doubts about the career he was pursuing," does he know something we don't know—something he didn't write? Does he know that Obama had chosen street-level organizing as a lifelong career? Did Obama tell him that? It was a job! A path! We have all developed doubts about our path in life. Is there a politician alive who loved every element of the job he had before entering political life? Of course not! I would think most enter politics to make changes in business as usual. Judis writes, "Yet, two decades later, to hear Obama the Presidential candidate tell it, those years in Chicago as a community organizer shaped the person—and the politician—he has become." Mr. Judis, how could Obama have worked as an organizer and now claim that it had no affect on who he is today? Of course there were bad parts of the job. What idiot would believe otherwise? I don't recall Obama claiming that his organizing years were all roses and candy.

Judis went on: "Still, one has to wonder: In making the transition from organizer to politician, did Obama go too far in rejecting one of the cardinal principles of community organizing?" This question seems too hypothetical. Does one really have to wonder this? Or can't we just accept that there is no such thing as going "too far in rejecting the cardinal principal of organizing?" Obama became a politician. So what! Yes, the cardinal principle is to reject politics, but Obama saw otherwise. As President, with a loyalty to community organizing and a deep understanding of its founding principles, Obama will be able to do more for that field than anyone in history. And if this turns out to be true, every community organizer in the country will be happy that he went "too far in rejecting one of the cardinal principles."

If Judis had decided to make his following comments the crux of the article's title, it would have been more accurate: "None of this is to say that Obama was wrong to abandon community organizing for politics. Or that his critique of organizing was incorrect. In fact, many of today's community organizers would acknowledge that Obama was absolutely right to question the limitations of Alinsky-style organizing." The word "abandon" has an implicitly negative connotation, and if Judis is not trying to say that Obama is ashamed of having to "abandon" it, then why write the article? Based on what he wrote, his article title could have been *Obama Was Right to Leave Organizing.* If what Judis wrote in the article is true, why imply in the title that he has some shameful dark secret? All he can truthfully say based on evidence he accumulated is that Obama critiqued some of the organizing methods used by his predecessors. He simply grew. He still sees himself as a community organizer. He has simply redefined what it means to be one. Community organizing has evolved as a result of Obama's own evolution, and evidently he remains committed to the possibilities of community organizing—just on a much grander scale.

I guess Mr. Judis will now write an article describing Obama's disgruntled Harvard days. I'm sure there were times when he wanted to leave—thought they were being unfair to him because he was Black, missed home, didn't know if he really wanted to be editor of the Harvard Law Review, didn't like his professors, began to believe that lawyers were dishonest, had strong philosophical disagreements with how his mentors believed the law should be interpreted, grew weary of the idea of practicing law, wanted instead to be a professor—and on and on and on. After reading your article, John B. Judi's, I am certain that your title, **Creation Myth: What Barack Obama Won't Tell You About His Community Organizing,** is intentionally misleading to hurried readers, cunningly damaging on its face, and a tremendous reach when compared to the body of the text. It was clever, but it was once said that clever liars give details, but the cleverest don't.

DAY 14
PIT BULL

Obama is at home in Chicago, Illinois, today—Sunday, September 7—while McCain is in Washington, D.C. The narrative today is being written by the media for the McCain camp. It's the first time I've heard them make this point a real issue. They are posing the idea that there is going to be a divided government if McCain is elected and that Americans tend to like this scenario. They are suggesting that because there will definitely be a majority Democratic Congress, the American people may want a Republican in office. Let the American people figure this out on their own. Don't remind us of it, as if we need to really think long and hard about what a vote for Obama could actually mean. The problem with this opinion is that the media has authored it. Come to think of it, now that they have brought it to our attention, maybe millions of Americans will say, *Yeah, I don't like the idea of Congress being Democratic and the President being a Democrat. I think I'll vote for McCain for that reason alone.*

By creating and disseminating this hypothesis, the media could very well be manufacturing a self-fulfilling prophecy. They have brought an obvious situation to the forefront and given it extreme importance. If Americans decide to embrace this narrative, it can only hurt Obama. On ABC this morning, Jonathan Capehart co-authored this media-created narrative by claiming, "It's also what [George Will] just pointed out. Democrats have to be very mindful of the fact that yes the American people do like divided government and to have John McCain there to temper the Democrats is something that could be very appealing, and it's probably the only thing that Senator McCain has to go up against the tidal wave that's out there."

On ABC's *This Week* today, George Will said, "In winning the Republican nomination McCain did something that hasn't been done probably since 1948, that is he won the Republican nomination losing the Republican base.... He had to expand his appeal while appealing to his base. Their gamble is that [Palin} does that." George Stephanopoulos threw in his unwarranted, Republican-helping response with: "And Sarah Palin was probably the one person in the country who can do that." Really George! She is the "one" person in the entire country? One? I mean talk about exaggeration! I had to rewind that statement and listen to it over and over just to make sure I heard it right. I thought, *When did George Stephanopoulos become a Palin advocate?*

But the roundtable on ABC's *This Week*, a supposed non-partisan panel, made up of hard-core journalists, wasn't finished throwing praise Palin's way. Martha Raddatz could barely contain herself when describing how great Palin was at the convention. Raddatz said the Palin's speech "was the kind of thing you couldn't not watch. When she started talking, you were riveted." Really Mrs. Raddatz? "The kind of thing you couldn't NOT watch?" Are you kidding? I think you are way off your rocker on this one. Riveted? Riveted? Take that over-zealous commentary behind closed doors please. It's embarrassing. Stop flashing your Republican

Party membership card. Contain yourself! Raddatz is an ABC reporter. She went on. "Sarah Palin energized that party and I know we say that again and again but what that means is that people will not only go and vote, they will tell their neighbors to vote, they will want to volunteer. And that really matters. She's done that. The enthusiasm is huge." I have nothing left to say about Martha Raddatz. I think her drool speaks for itself.

Palin the Pit Bull—These were the words on the screen in big white letters at 9:43 am this morning. CNN has taken Palin's self-given nickname and put it in big bright national lights. Think about it! Palin the "Pit Bull!" As if there is no question to the contrary. Endorsed by CNN! CNN at least owes us a big question mark after the nickname. Can we get a *Palin The Self Described Pit Bull* from you CNN? Put that question in big white letters. Is that too much to ask? Instead they have chosen to give us a litany of reasons why she is indeed a good old-fashioned, rootin' tootin' pit bull. What are pit bulls known for? Their propensity for locking on to something and never letting go, like George Bush reminding us for years to "stay the course" in Iraq regardless of evidence to the contrary. Evidence didn't unlock his pit bull jaws. Only public outcry at 3,000 plus American deaths did. So now, according to CNN, we have a new pit bull pig-headedly heading to high power in Washington.

The media has finally seen the fruits of their labor: John McCain has overtaken Barack Obama in the Gallup daily tracking poll and has his highest level of support in that poll since early May. McCain leads Obama 48 percent to 45 percent among registered voters, by Gallup's measure. One of the big reasons for this surge may have something to do with the influx of media soldiers in their army, or could it be the rampant postings of article headlines such as this one on the front page of the *Los Angeles Times?* **The Palin Charm is a Tough Sell Here.** The article was written on location in Uniontown, Pennsylvania. It actually does an effective job of showing how women are not taking the bait and lining up in unison behind Palin in Uniontown, but before allowing this article to go to print, the editor should have edited the title. The title implies that Palin does indeed have charm but is merely having difficulty selling it.

Does Sarah Palin have charm? I'm sure that at least 50 percent of the nation would say no. I don't think she has charm. I most certainly don't believe that we should all concede that she has charm by including it as fact in our news headlines. Anybody who uses that much sarcasm, which she certainly does, is not charming. She made fun of Obama for having been a community organizer. Does that fit into the charming category? Insulting—yes! Charming—no! The reason Palin is having a difficult time selling herself in Uniontown, as the article suggests, is because she lacks the very charm the *LA Times* headline gives her credit for having. Most people glance through the newspaper for headlines that pique their interest. In that case, the only thing a majority of people got out of this article is that Palin must be charming. Is there a pattern developing here? Are hard news stories being undermined by deceptive headlines? If so, the effect of these newspaper and television headlines is almost subliminal. I'll be waiting for next week's *LA Times* FrontPage headline: ***The Obama Brilliance is a Tough Sell Here.***

DAY 15
"YOU CAN'T JUST MAKE STUFF UP"

Obama is campaigning in Flint, Michigan, today—Monday, September 8—while McCain is in Lee's Summit, Missouri. *The Big Tilt!* These three words best describe what is taking place in this Presidential race. The addition of Palin has obviously tilted the race in McCain's favor. Obama and Biden need to find a way to neutralize Palin. It's almost as if they haven't quite figured out exactly how to deal with her. Although Obama may know exactly what he's doing, he hasn't shared it with the rest of us. Part two of his interview with Bill O'Reilly is airing today. Maybe this is part of Obama's game plan. Is this an effort on his part to regain some traction in the polls after the Palin bump? Perhaps the millions of O'Reilly viewers will come to realize that Obama doesn't have horns growing out of his head. They'll see that he is actually quite normal and not the monster that far too many hateful e-mails and FOX News have suggested. But, regarding Palin—can her popularity last for the next 57 days? Maybe a more important question is *When will the McCain camp allow Sarah Palin to do a one-on-one interview with the press?* This is the question that is dominating the political world, and networks are muscling each other for position to get that elusive first interview. McCain has already shown a willingness to retaliate against the press for any hard questions by canceling an interview with Larry King. Not enough was made of that crying fit. As Jeffrey Toobin so correctly put it, this is a man who claims that he is the one who should sit down face to face with Russia's Putin, yet he thinks that Campbell Brown was too tough on one of his surrogates. I'm sure McCain has the media scared to ask Palin even one tough question. God forbid they actually ask her something that will prove how unprepared she is—which she obviously is.

The Republicans are winning the media battle right now, and many Americans probably won't wake up and recognize how they are being duped until the first Presidential debate on September 26 in Oxford, Mississippi. Obama will probably pummel McCain in that debate. He should start by calling out the media for the terrible job they did in analyzing the Gore-Bush debate back in 2000. I have the feeling that Obama is more of a fighter and will not allow the media to paint a very different picture from what he actually says in the upcoming debate. He has all of the issues on his side and probably won't let McCain squirm his way out of answering the specific questions on healthcare, education, taxes etc.

Obama's Antidote to Palin: Deploys Hillary Clinton to Florida. This was the headline on CNN at 1:01 pm. The only problem with this headline is that it's not true. Clinton has been scheduled to speak in Florida for weeks. Why is the media acting as if every move that Obama now makes is in reaction to Palin? CNN is spinning this. They're creating this myth—this myth that Obama is scrambling and somehow reeling because of this new phenomenon named Palin. If the media instead decided, right this minute, to cover Obama's rally in Michigan and to build it up with a lot of hype and say things like, *Obama's base is fired up and ready to go,* the country would feel that Obama is still in the driver's seat. But instead they are covering McCain and Palin, showing their rallies, and creating the perception of a juggernaut. All that America knows is what the press shows us, and right now that happens to be McCain-Palin rallies, talking points that are blatant lies, jokes, lying surrogates, inflated poll numbers, and zero interviews with Palin. This is what Obama is up against right now. But he appears to have more stamina than either McCain or Palin.

"Is this the new welfare queen?" Chris Matthews asked this question about the Republican's characterization of community organizing at 2:09 pm. I seriously can't understand where Matthews is coming from half of the time. Why even bring up welfare? If the Republicans do indeed believe that community organizing is the "new welfare queen," why not let them be the ones to introduce it as such? Don't write their creative one-liners for them, Matthews. The GOP probably heard you utter that and are sitting back right now saying, *Hey! That sounds pretty clever—new welfare queen! Let's use that.* Matthews has a way of building Obama up and then offering the potentially most politically damaging narratives possible. Thanks for putting the welfare image card on the table. I'm sure 90 percent of the country hadn't connected those dots yet but are now researching the commonalities between community organizing and welfare recipients. Chuck Todd suggested that perhaps the Obama camp is wishing they hadn't made this community organizing term a part of their campaign. Todd and Matthews are missing the boat on this one. One would think that these two would know and promote the case for community organizing rather than practically cosigning the Republican's demeaning characterization of it. Matthews wasn't finished hammering community organizing. At 2:11 pm, he said, "I think it has Al Sharpton connotations." He suggested that people in Scranton, Pennsylvania, have a less than positive image of community organizing. Wait a minute! So Matthews is now trying to help Obama appeal to America's Scrantons by doing word associations—like welfare queen and Sharpton—that can only do damage to the Obama campaign? Unbelievable! Matthews needed to be talking about how pathetic it is for the GOP to be belittling young hard-working Americans.

The Financial Times' Chrystia Freeland chose today to link the Republican's usage of community organizing to racism. She did so on MSNBC. Yes, I heard Giuliani make fun of community organizing. Yes, I heard Palin put it down. But I never thought that either of them was using it with racial undertones. But now that Chrystia Freeland has offered a completely hypothetical narrative, we'll see if there's any validity to it. Freeland also feels that McCain and Palin are offering up other subliminal racial messages. She referred to it as "dog whistle politics." Are they using coded language that only true racists can understand, as Freeland suggests? Or has Freeland gone entirely too far, and in so doing, created this very reality herself? Freeland went on to say that McCain and Palin are saying, "Remember me? Wink-wink! [Obama] is actually African American!" I believe that Freeland may possibly be correct, but I can't tell whom she is trying to help by offering this unnecessary commentary. At 2:51 pm, Freeland said that McCain and Palin also seemed to be asking, "Aren't we a little more like you than these two [Obamas]? Wouldn't you rather hang out with us?" It is sad that Freeland would take an unprovable theory and expound on it on national television. It goes beyond the pale. Freeland introduced this theory—whether it has weight or not—and she will ultimately have to take responsibility for introducing it—not McCain and Palin. On the other hand, some people may need to have such potential insidious racism pointed out to them.

"The national media is liberal and biased." This from the mouth of "Mr. Independent," Lou Dobbs, at 4:32 pm! Dobbs also had a caption that read, "McCain Aide: Media on Mission to Destroy Palin." Dobbs has a difficult time not showing his true colors. He claims to be an Independent, but his captions, words, and cowering guests suggest otherwise. I, for one, think of only two words when listening to Dobbs: *anti-immigrant* and *biased.*

Barack Obama himself told Keith Olbermann today that he was a bit surprised that the media hadn't been more vigilant in calling out the McCain camp for the false claims they've been making. He is right. Palin herself has been more than wiling to offer up statements that are completely inaccurate. The media should have been focused on picking the following ad apart bit by bit. The title of the ad is "The Original Mavericks." The ad uses blurbs but makes them look like front page newspaper headlines. It's very misleading. This is what hit the air today:

> **Narrator:** The original Mavericks.
> **San Jose Mercury News Blurb:** McCain Faults Bush For Pork Barrel Spending
> **Narrator:** He fights pork barrel spending.

Anchorage Daily News Blurb: Palin Flies High as Reformer

Narrator: She stopped the bridge to nowhere.

Associated Press Blurb: McCain Calls For Permitting the Importation of Prescription Drugs From Canada

Narrator: He took on the drug industry.

Associated Press Blurb: Palin Takes on Oil Industry, Republicans

Narrator: She took on big oil.

Boston Herald Blurb: Maverick McCain Rips GOP

Narrator: He battled Republicans and reformed Washington.

The Wall Street Journal Blurb: Palin Fought for Reform in Alaska

Narrator: She battled Republicans and reformed Alaska. —They'll make history. They'll change Washington. McCain-Palin! Real change!

John McCain: I'm John McCain and I approve this message.

The press would be well within their rights to go through this ad issue by issue and discredit each and every one of them. The media certainly has been more than willing to show the ad—much, I'm sure, to the delight of the McCain folks. The media's willingness to turn a blind eye to what amounts to a series of inaccuracies, is a disturbing trend. Yes, CNN's Anderson Cooper ran his segment today called "Keeping Them Honest," in which he claimed to be setting the record straight on Palin. He put up some numbers comparing Obama's earmark spending vs. Palin's earmark spending. He went on to talk about how Palin originally supported the "Bridge to Nowhere" in Alaska but then claimed to be against it. Cooper gets points for these facts, but the segment failed to point out that Obama has never claimed to be completely opposed to earmarks. He's not running on this talking point as McCain and Palin are.

It is Palin who said today that she had been an earmark reformer. "We've reformed the abuse of earmarks in our state," she proclaimed. She was lying. Her state was one of the biggest earmark spenders in the country. Cooper's segment also showed Obama's earmark spending from 2004 through 2007. But he put up Palin's earmark spending for this year alone, and this is only September. CNN tried to compare those two numbers by placing them side-by-side. Obama's earmark spending was higher, but covered three entire years. The segment mentioned—but failed to emphasize—this vital fact. The way they presented the numbers was misleading. I keep repeating that the McCain campaign is lying, but the facts are the facts—they are getting away with selling America a bill of goods the same way George W. Bush did to get us into Iraq. Has lying become the norm?

This is a pivotal moment in the election because the McCain campaign is showing an ability to lie and get away with it, allowing them to take the lead in the polls. If McCain thinks he can continue to get away with creating this mass confusion—never having to explain what amounts to a series of lies regarding his own record—never being asked to tell Americans how he will pay for his proposals—constantly being allowed to distort Obama's words—hiding his VP from the press—making the overwhelmingly laughable claim that Palin is more prepared than Obama—suddenly claiming that he is the change candidate, forgetting that his mantra has always been experience. It is the media's job to point out, until America is dizzied by it, the fact that McCain's new claim of being the change agent doesn't match the facts— particularly the fact that he has voted in lock step with Bush 90 percent of the time. Obama said today at a rally, "You just can't make stuff up!" He's correct, but he's doing your job, journalists of America! Pound the facts home or this will amount to an undeserving, unearned gift that you have given John McCain.

This is actually the saddest day of the election. There is just a palpable sadness that exists—based largely on the GOP's effective distortions of various truths—distortions that are permeating the airwaves—distortions that the media has allowed to get completely out of control—distortions that are winning over too many Americans who are failing to realize that they can't afford to be fooled again. Americans need to remember what George Herbert once said: "Show me a liar, and I'll show thee a thief." We can't afford another thief. Will the truth resurface? Remember this day—a day when lies trumped the truth.

DAY 16
SEX ED

Obama is campaigning in Lebanon, Virginia, today—Tuesday, September 9—while McCain is in Lancaster, Pennsylvania. *What is the significance of the "Alaska Pipeline?" What is the significance of the "Bridge to Nowhere?"* These are questions for the press to answer. They then need to hold Sarah Palin accountable for her role in each. She acts as if she's always been against big oil and has always stood up to the "good ol' boys network," yet she was for the pipeline. She was originally for, but now claims she was against, the bridge. We have not heard one word out of her that wasn't part of her prepared stump speech. She is using this "Bridge to Nowhere" line at every rally and drawing huge applause.

A *Washington Post*/ABC Poll shows McCain leading 49% to 48% today. One gets the feeling that the only thing that can get the media to stop salivating over an unproven figure like Palin is Hurricane Ike, which is making its way toward the Gulf of Mexico right now. On FOX News, Monica Crowley joked about the boost Palin has given McCain. She said, "She's like McCain's political Viagra." I guess these are the kinds of sleazy one-liners that FOX News feels will appeal to their base. After all, it was McCain's campaign manager, Rick Davis, who said that this campaign was not going to be about the issues. Monica Crowley understands this better than most, and knows that distracting people from the serious issues will help McCain better than anything else. If they can make this a soap opera, it serves them well.

Paul Begala was angry this morning with the media's failure to correct the Palin record. Begala said, "This is the problem—we're having this false debate—we should at least have agreed upon facts." He then frustratingly took off his microphone and shook his head in disgust. He is frustrated that the truth is being ignored and Republicans are sticking to these talking points that are based on complete lies. He's correct.

Palin has taken taxpayer money, a per diem, while living at her own home, instead of the governor's mansion. This is a story that is grabbing some headlines, but it isn't catching on. Had this been Obama who had used taxpayer money while at home in Chicago, the press would be excoriating him. Is this becoming a "culture war?" Are issues like global warming and the wars being trumped by issues like pro-life, guns, and Christianity? It is startling that Palin is getting pass after pass on critical issues. Is this because of race or desire of the corporate media to keep the status quo? What is the press afraid of? This cycle of the press' daily fascination with Palin is beginning to snowball.

By 2:00 pm today, the Randi Rhodes radio talk show had run a fiery speech by Joe Biden lambasting Bush for the "harm" he has done to our country and calling out John McCain for calling himself courageous but not having the courage to stand up against the abuses of the Bush administration. It was the most aggressive speech since the Democratic convention, yet the mainstream media has not run any of it so far. They have, however, run and rerun Sarah Palin's tough-talk stump speech. They're ramming it down our throats. Obama put it best when he said, "She's had the attention of you folks," referring to the press. Obama is hoping to get the attention of Bill O'Reilly's folks as part three of their interview airs tonight.

David Gregory's headline was "Obama On the Ropes." This tells you all you need to know about the choice the media has made. Of course Obama is not on the ropes, but they are going to create the illusion that he is. Will the media keep her unwarranted star status going? Jay Carney of *Time* asked rhetorically if Palin is like an opening weekend box office hit that will fade or will she go on to become a blockbuster? The answer to this question is up to the press.

A new McCain ad came out today which unfairly paints Obama as someone who is pushing sex education in schools. This ad came as a response to Obama's multi-layered speech today on education. Obama is trying to talk about the issues and McCain is trying to distract. The attack ad is completely suggestive. It has music in it that sounds like children's bedtime music. The music sounds like a child playing a xylophone. It's sick! The pictures they use of Obama are very unflattering, to say the least. It ends by showing a large photo of Obama, apparently leering, with little children in the background. It is a new low for McCain. The media is not focused on the Obama speech. At 3:38 pm, David Gregory gave the McCain camp an assist by showing this entire below-the-belt McCain ad:

Narrator: *Education Week* says Obama hasn't made a significant mark on Education. That he's elusive on accountability. A staunch defender of the existing public school monopoly. Obama's one accomplishment? Legislation to teach comprehensive sex education to kindergartners. Learning about SEX before learning to READ? Barack Obama! Wrong on Education! Wrong for your family!

John McCain: I'm John McCain and I approve this message.

Again, I include these ads only if they are shown to me on the mainstream news. It shows how the media is completely helping John McCain do his dirty work. Obama has not run such ads, so we don't know if the media would offer him the same benefit. I doubt it. I know that it is late in the day now and we still have seen no signs of Joe Biden's powerful speech against the Bush Administration. I heard it on a liberal radio station but not a peep about it on the main networks. Very disappointing! It is a powerful speech that would definitely help Obama and enlighten the public. And it would have a tremendous effect on stemming the tide that Palin has brought on.

Anderson Cooper showed the pathetic McCain Sex-Education ad against Obama at 7:04 pm. One Obama spokesman has accused the McCain campaign of stooping to a new low with this ad—saying that it was "perverse." The Obama spokesman said that he now understood why McCain had difficulty explaining what honor is—because he has none. The media is focusing more on the harsh words of the Obama spokesman than they are on the actual ad that evoked the comments. Candy Crowley said that the Obama camp is struggling to get the headlines back. Does she understand that Obama has nothing to do with that? That she and her colleagues are the ones who control the headlines?

Obama accused Palin of flip-flopping on the bridge issue, and all the press can do is focus on the notion that he shouldn't be taking her on because she is a VP—that somehow he is bringing her up to his level—and doesn't he know better than to go one-on-one with a lowly VP? The press should be focusing on the accurate comments Obama made about Palin—not on why he shouldn't be taking her on. If Palin is lying, I expect a Presidential candidate to call her out. Mark Halperin of *Time* suggested that Obama is struggling lately—just as Hillary Clinton had predicted he would during the primary. Halperin said, "Boy are they off their game." He's wrong and he forgot that months ago Obama said that electing a President is not a game! Halperin and the rest of the media are the ones who are hot on their game. They are on their game but way off their job description. Obama is doing their jobs for them. Of course he's taking Palin on. He's finally realized that the media won't. All the press has done so far is assist McCain's claim that Obama is being unfair to her. I have two words for the so-called diligent press: Twelve days! That's how long McCain has kept Palin hidden from you. She hasn't done a single interview. And when she finally does, I expect the press to throw her softballs right down the middle of the plate.

DAY 17
LIPSTICK ON A PIG

Obama is campaigning in Norfolk, Virginia, today—Wednesday, September 10—while McCain is in Fairfax, Virginia. "You can put lipstick on a pig, but it's still a pig." Obama said this while campaigning yesterday. It is one of the most commonly used lines in the world of politics. But now that Obama has used it to describe John McCain's recent decision to label himself the change candidate, he is taking some heat from the press. Obama was referring to McCain's economic policy—that it was the same as Bush's, just dressed up differently. McCain has somehow managed to accuse Obama of using the line to insult Palin, who has used the word lipstick during her speeches. She has said that the only difference between herself and a pit bull is lipstick. So naturally, McCain has managed to say that Obama was going after his VP. Instead of the media completely defending Obama, based on their absolute understanding of what he meant by his words, they are leaving it up to the American people to decide. The media must know that a lot of people probably aren't aware that the funny line is used regularly in the political arena. So for them not to defend Obama on this no-brainer is typical. Obama said it best: "Spare me the phony outrage."

This morning, Obama just repeated the famous word from his speech in Denver. He said, "Enough!" Will the media listen or will they continue to inflate this lipstick non-issue? Obama proceeded to talk in great depth about his education policies. The speech was impressive, but the media decided to cut to the mud. They went right into the lipstick issue again. They are not going to let it go.

Obama wants to move on. He knows that Americans want to know more about education. He knows that McCain has no policies that will change our education system. He knows that McCain would rather stay in the mud on this lipstick issue. But Obama has moved on to issues that matter to people. It's the media who is going to keep this lipstick drama moving. They're sick! It's their responsibility to show, in it's entirety, Obama's detailed lecture on education. He is delivering it right now and we can't even watch it.

As we, the media's audience, search for the remainder of Obama's powerful education speech somewhere on the satellite channels, we are denied access! I would even like to see a McCain education speech. This morning, Obama scolded the media for running with the lipstick story. He said, "Of course, the news media—ya'll decided that was the lead story yesterday. You know who ends up losing at the end of the day? Not the Democratic candidate—not the Republican candidate. You, the American people." These are Obama's words in describing the media circus.

No Child Left Behind, extra money for charter schools to give parents more public school choice, Pell Grants, technology in the classroom to help our students compete on the world market—these all take a back seat to "lipstick on a pig". McCain, Palin, and the media evidently think this everyday expression and analysis of it is more important than education. This tack is abusive. I feel abused by the media. Show us Obama's education speech. I'm sure tonight the media will be saying, *Obama needs to get back to talking about bread and butter issues. He is off his game. He needs to get off this lipstick talk and stop attacking the VP.* They will completely ignore what Obama has really been doing today—giving specifics on education.

John McCain and Sarah Palin spoke at a rally in Fairfax, Virginia, this morning. It was the same canned speech they've been delivering for ten days, with the same lies in it. Bridge to nowhere, standing up to the good ol' boys, gas pipeline, and on and on and on! Will the media point this fact out? The only observable difference between the Palin I see today and the Palin I've observed over the past thirteen days is lipstick. Palin is noticeably not wearing any lipstick this morning. Hmmm!

Today, Andrea Mitchell said, "She's obviously smart," in reference to how Palin will do in her upcoming interviews. She's not obviously smart! This is not obvious. She has not given one single solitary interview. How do you know she is smart? Is it because she has been a governor for twenty months? Is George Bush smart? He was a governor. What are you basing her supposed smartness on? Just tell the rest of us. I want to be as certain of her smartness as you are, Andrea Mitchell.

Andrea Mitchell just showed the McCain Sex Education ad on MSNBC at 11:53 am. Why are they helping McCain defeat Obama? Do they understand that they are doing this? Do they care? Does McCain even have to spend any money on getting his ads out anymore? When Obama said that the

McCain campaign knows this lipstick stuff can be "catnip for the news media," he is absolutely correct. This entire lipstick commentary is bringing out the worst in the media. They will not stop talking about it. They are showing their true colors. As MSNBC opened their 1:00 pm hour, one of their lead-in lines was, "Coming up we will play the Obama [lipstick] comments in their entirety so you can judge for yourselves." Like we have to judge! Please! We've already judged, but you media folks won't stop until we all say, *Obama is being sexist.* I say, if Obama managed with one clever stroke to point out the Bushness of McCain's policies and at the same time cunningly lambast Palin for making a school-girl, e-mail circulated joke at the Republican Convention, more power to him. He's smart. Get over it.

CNN's Ed Henry did a report at 1:04 pm that covered McCain's rally today. Henry seemed to suggest that McCain and Palin were focused only on the issues. He said, "The McCain campaign almost focused entirely on policy" earlier today at the rally. Henry failed to mention that McCain's campaign is feeding the press lines on this lipstick issue by the hour. Henry failed to mention how McCain has an ad out right now attacking Obama on the lipstick comment—an ad that completely suggests that Obama was calling Palin a pig. The ad even uses Katie Couric at the end. Earlier this year Couric said something about the Obama campaign being sexist, so McCain used her comment in the ad. Couric's comments came during the Clinton-Obama primary, but McCain's ad makes it look as if she is talking about the lipstick comment. The news media is running the ad all day today.

Barbara Boxer said the McCain camp wanted to distract the American people. She's right. But they need the media to help them in order to do this. Boxer needed to be going after Chris Matthews, who was interviewing her. She needed to be excoriating the entire press. The entire time Matthews was interviewing Boxer, this was the headline just below her face: **Lipstick on a Pig and the Politics of Distraction.** The folks at MSNBC are obviously letting it "distract" them.

Wolf Blitzer played the McCain sex education attack ad at 2:36 pm in its entirety. After showing the ad, he, like everyone else who shows it, tried to act as if he didn't know whether or not the ad is unfair. Wolf never came right out and called the ad a lie. He knows it's a lie. Instead he asked the guests on his program what they thought about the ad. For the life of me, I can't understand why he doesn't just have his research staff point out some of the positive legislation Obama has passed on education. Wolf Blitzer is a smart man. He knows the ad has pedophilia undertones to it. Yet Blitzer allows the circus to continue.

Shame on David Gregory! He showed a new attack ad at 3:09 pm that was completely out of line. It was an ad that wasn't even approved by John McCain. The sleazy Freedom's Defense Fund.org put it out. The ad tries to link Obama to ex-mayor, Kwame Kilpatrick. Obama introduced Kilpatrick at an event almost two years ago. No one! No one! No one outside of Michigan would have seen this ad had David Gregory not shown it. But this is what Gregory chose to show at 3:09 pm:

Video of Obama introducing Kilpatrick starts ad; then photo of the two together.

Dark mug shot of Kwame Kilpatrick remains throughout ad with a sign under his face reading: WAYNE CO. JAIL – KILPATRICK, K

Obama's voice heard throughout ad saying: I want to first of all acknowledge your great mayor, Kwame Kilpatrick, and he is a leader not just here in Detroit, not just in Michigan, but all across the country—people look to him. We know that he is going to be doing astounding things for many years to come. I'm grateful to call him a friend and a colleague and I'm looking forward to a lengthy collaboration.

These Blurbs Scroll Over Kilpatrick's Very Dark Mug Shot Throughout Ad:

- Perjury (Count # 1)
- Conspiracy to Commit Obstruction of Justice
- Assaulting a Law Officer
- Misconduct in Office (Count #1)
- Perjury (Count # 2)
- Obstruction of Justice
- Perjury (Count # 3)
- Misconduct in Office (Count # 2)
- Perjury (Count # 4)

Final Blurb: You Should Know Who Barack Obama's Friends Are.

David Gregory then added, "A lot of people say, 'Does Obama really connect with people?'" Tell us who your "a lot of people" are Mr. Gregory. And by the way, Gregory failed to mention the very important speech Obama gave this morning on education. As a matter of fact, other than perhaps C-SPAN, the major networks have completely ignored his speech. It didn't have enough dirt in it. For the past thirteen days, all we've had is Palin-gushing from the press. I guess Obama realized this trend and decided to make the lipstick comment in order to get Palin off of the news cycle. He read the press like a book. He is all they are talking about now. He knew that the media would bite, and he's playing them like a drum. He probably doesn't want to do this. He just realizes what he's up against. The media will not cover his very detailed, critically-important speeches on real issues. Obama's topic this entire week has been education. The people have only been educated on what lipstick on a pig means. And there has been zero coverage of Joe Biden. Does the media even know he exists?

Rachel Maddow showed the perverted McCain sex education ad at 6:41 pm. She is trying to show how the ad is unfair. To her credit she pointed out that Obama didn't even sponsor the legislation; he voted for it. It was designed to protect young kids from sexual predators—to teach them when to recognize inappropriate touching. McCain is grossly distorting Obama's record on this bill. At 6:55 pm Larry King got in on the feeding frenzy and showed the perverted McCain sex education ad. If Obama can win this election despite this onslaught by the media, he will go down as the toughest politician in history.

Candy Crowley, David Gergen, and John King spoke about the day's events at about 7:18 pm on CNN. It was a terribly biased segment in McCain's favor. John King said that the people he is talking to in Michigan are telling him they used to see Obama as the new kind of politics guy but now see Palin and McCain as that new brand. To John King I say, *Prove it! Who did you talk to, King? Let us see their damn faces. That just sounds like gossip. Go talk to some people who haven't bought that Palin brand yet. For all we know, you made these conversations up. How many people did you talk to and what percent said they have changed from Obama to the McCain brand? You're losing credibility by the minute, and your comment did nothing but serve to hurt Obama.* Crowley said that she had talked to several Democrats today that said that they just wanted Obama to talk about the issues and not expound on the lipstick comment. Crowley failed to mention that Obama had done just that today by talking about education. Gergen said that Obama had done a good job of pivoting off the lipstick issue this morning, but needed to move on to real issues. Earth to Gergen! He gave a detailed speech today. Gergen then said, "Where is Joe Biden?" Why doesn't Gergen tell CNN to point one of their lipstick-smeared cameras toward Biden? Biden's been talking. The media only has ears and eyes for Sarah. I have seen portions of McCain and Palin's canned speech at least ten times today. And every time they've shown it, it was presented as brand new news. The entire day passed without a snippet of Obama's education speech. Where do we turn for the truth?

DAY 18
THE BUSH DOCTRINE

Obama and McCain are both in New York City today and have agreed not to campaign in honor of September 11. They will attend a 9/11 ceremony during the day and speak at a forum tonight. This show of respect isn't stopping the media from stirring the pot. The press is claiming that both candidates have agreed to take down their attack ads today. They failed to mention that Obama doesn't have any attack ads—at least not any that the media has played for us. It's McCain who has thrown up one disgusting ad after another. One couldn't help but wake up this morning with a sick feeling after seeing that McCain ad that was suggestive of pedophilia. Shame on John McCain! And shame on every major news outlet that ran it over and over and over yesterday. John McCain is no longer an honorable man. He has drawn first blood, and it is time for Obama to respond in kind. He should release his 527s and let them go hog wild on McCain. All they would have to do is show some of the horrible remarks he has made in the past. It's time for Obama to let the 527s have at it. Like Obama, I believe in talking to the enemy, but also like Obama, I believe that when talking and reasoning together result in nothing but attacks from the enemy, it's time to fight.

Today's *Forum on Service* at Columbia University presented both McCain and Obama answering questions about public service. Obama presented specific ideas for getting people of all ages involved in service to the country. Veteran support workers, senior citizen community workers, environmental volunteers, and various other civilian service jobs—these are just some of the examples Obama suggested that have potential to bring the country out of the "me first" mentality sold to us by the self-interest oligarchs. The spin by Chris Matthews and David Gregory, however, made it seem like each candidate equally advocated government- sponsored service. They failed to mention that McCain had a caveat in every reference—that service is better performed by non-governmental agencies. Obama's vision of government inspiring these efforts was ignored. The spin masters left the viewers thinking both McCain and Obama were equally adamant about community service as a patriotic duty.

On a day when the candidates decided not to campaign, Gregory and Matthews showed that they could still find a way to inaccurately analyze Obama's performance at the forum. Matthews said that McCain's vision for national service was more national oriented whereas Obama's was more about community. Wrong! Obama never presented a philosophy that was any less focused on national service than McCain's. In fact Obama's presentation provided many more examples and specifics about how to do national service. For some reason, and I can't put my finger on it, Gregory and Matthews couldn't just give it up to Obama. His presentation appeared flawless to me, yet in hearing them analyze it, it seemed that Obama's nuanced message went over their heads. They just completely got it wrong. And again, this hurts Obama. I am finding it difficult to listen to very detailed, intelligent presentations given by Obama, only to have analysts show that they either lack the capacity to grasp his message or are unable to put their axes down. They take any opportunity available to grind Obama. Tonight's forum showed that Obama had a specific plan for national service and McCain did not. It was obvious to everyone watching. It is also obvious that the media's job is to provide fair and balanced coverage. They are obviously not. I know what I saw. Don't try to spin the news every single day, media.

What's frustrating, and I'm even going to give it up for McCain on this point, is that for two hours we lost ourselves. We were able to escape from the sickness that comes from a campaign. Even during McCain's presentation, I felt good. There was just an overall feeling of goodness. Both candidates were talking about something that the nation wanted to hear, and it's almost as if we were cleansing ourselves. So to finish watching this and then immediately hear the analysts talk about it was shocking. The feeling was *Where have these people been*? Have they been in the sewer? It was like entering into a different world, and it took me about five minutes before the goodness of what had actually taken place was scrubbed off of me by the smarmy, agenda-driven press. It became a metaphor for what happened after 9/11. After the devastation, we waited with baited breath to hear our President give us a mission of service to our country. Tonight, after these two senators outlined ways in which we could serve our nation, we readied ourselves to go forward in unity. But instead, our corporate media didn't tell us to go shopping, as Bush did, but steered our focus back on the sensationalized message they want us to consume.

The other major political event that took place today was Sarah Palin's first sit-down interview with ABC's Charles Gibson. There was a mixed response from the media as to how she did. She was asked one specific question that has the talking heads abuzz. Gibson asked, "Do you agree with the Bush Doctrine?" She obviously didn't know what that meant. She responded by asking, "In what respect, Charley?" She was struggling. Gibson then asked her what her interpretation of it was. She hesitated again before asking, "His world view?" Gibson then said, "No, the Bush Doctrine, annunciated September, 2002, before the Iraq War." Palin was clueless and gave an answer that only further proved her unfamiliarity with the doctrine. David Gergen of CNN said afterward that he thought Palin didn't know what the Bush Doctrine was. But he went on to say, "I don't think most people know what the Bush Doctrine is or was." Most people aren't running for Vice President, Mr. Gergen. Even the usually reliable Candy Crowley said that most voters in Missouri, where she is from, don't care whether or not Palin knows what the Bush Doctrine is. I'm starting to wonder if there is any hurdle the media won't help Palin clear. Most people in Missouri may not care if Palin knows what the Bush Doctrine is, but those of us who truly put "Country First" certainly do. We want to know whether she's informed and has positions on issues our top leaders confront. And remember, McCain didn't vet Palin, she hasn't been allowed to answer questions from the press, so Gibson is not trying to stump her, but rather to use this rare opportunity to help the public assess her readiness to be Vice President. Gibson continued by asking Palin if she had ever met a foreign head of state. Palin said she had not and added, "And I think, if you go back in history, and if you ask that question of many Vice Presidents, they may have the same answer that I just gave you." Actually, over the last 30 years, all Vice Presidents had met a foreign head of state prior to being picked as a running mate. Anderson Cooper asked Bay Buchanan, a person who has no objectivity at all, if it mattered that Palin hadn't met a foreign head of state. Buchanan answered, "No, it doesn't at all. Her answer was excellent, Anderson, because it will make Americans feel that much closer to her. She's very real. Sure, she hasn't traveled overseas to meet these foreign leaders, but that's not what Americans are looking for." Wow! I'm sure Americans across the country are comforted by Bay Buchanan's even-handedness. It's so reassuring. Talk about a spin master! Nice hire, CNN.

DAY 19
WOMEN OF "THE VIEW" TO THE RESCUE

Obama is campaigning in Concord, New Hampshire, today—Friday, September 12—while McCain is in New York City. Hurricane Ike is hitting the Gulf Coast of Texas this morning and is dominating the news cycle. Ike is probably the only thing that could have upstaged Sarah Palin, but I still expect the press to hammer her today for her less than stellar performance last night with Charles Gibson. Some of today's headlines are already providing the misleading images of her performance. If one were to wake up this morning having not seen the ABC interview and read this morning's *LA Times* front page headline, he would surely get the wrong impression. The headline reads, **Palin Talks Tough on Russia, Iran.** This provides positive imagery. Her answers were at best lacking breadth and nuance. But at worst her answers were painfully uneducated. She didn't talk tough on Russia and Iran. Talking tough implies that she was effective. She talked weak on Russia and Iran. She simply gave studied answers that often ignored the specificity of the questions themselves. The *LA Times* may simply be trying to say that Palin talked tough and that's all it was—all talk and no action. They may be trying to imply that anyone can talk tough. I get that! But the *LA Times* assumes too much if that was their intention. Only those who read the article would get that point. Others—well, they might walk away saying *Boy,* *that Palin's ready to lead—she's tough!* It's all in the headlines, and the *LA Times* needs to figure this out.

Another headline this morning on MSNBC reads, **Sarah Palin Says She's Ready.** Again, those who did not see her performance would be mislead by this headline. The headline just as easily could have read, ***Palin Has Difficulty Answering Question on Bush Doctrine.*** The media is cheating to help Palin pass her first test.

Gerard Baker of the *Times of London* has obviously read the latest polls and decided to jump on the "Obama will lose" bandwagon today. He wants to be on record as having been one of those Nostradamuses who pointed out Obama's flaws before he actually loses. I'm sure a month ago, Mr. Baker, was firmly behind Obama. He just sounds like one of those types—with you when you're winning—never knew ya' when you're losing! He starts off his article explaining why so many in London can't fathom the idea that Obama could possibly lose to McCain. The title of the article is **Barack Obama the Speechmaker is Being Rumbled.** He writes, "Traveling in Britain this week, I've been asked repeatedly by close followers of US politics if it can really be true that Barack Obama might not win. Thoughtful people cannot get their head around the idea that Mr. Obama, exciting new pilot of change, supported by Joseph Biden, experienced navigator of the swamplands of Washington politics, could possibly be defeated." At first, Baker seems inclined to build the case for Obama's candidacy, but he soon begins to tear him down line by line. Baker has decided to join the rest of the hacks and pile on. He backs up none of what he says with appropriate facts but manages to build his case by picking and choosing very vague issues—issues that, if one were to independently examine them more closely, would paint a much more favorable picture of Obama.

Baker writes, "The essential problem coming to light is a profound disconnect between the Barack Obama of the candidate's speeches and the Barack Obama who has actually been in politics for the past decade or so." One can immediately see where Baker is going here. Take what a politician says in a speech, find a piece of his legislation that specifically contradicts his words, and draw a sweeping conclusion based on it. Baker adds:

> Speechmaker Obama has built his campaign on the promise of reform, the need to change the culture of American political life, to take on the special interests that undermine government's effectiveness and erode trust in the system itself. Politician Obama rose through a Chicago machine that is notoriously the most corrupt in the country. As David Freddoso writes in a brilliantly cogent and measured book, *The Case Against Barack Obama*, the angel of deliverance from the old politics functioned like an old-time Democratic pol in Illinois. He refused repeatedly to side with those lonely voices that sought to challenge the old corrupt ways of the ruling party.

Are you suggesting that Obama favors corruption, Mr. Baker? You're being lazy! Somehow I find it difficult to believe that Obama refused to side with those lonely voices. Baker obviously doesn't understand that voting your conscience does not necessarily mean voting against your party: "Speechmaker Obama talks about an era of bipartisanship. He speaks powerfully about the destructive politics of red and blue states. Politician Obama has toed his party's line more reliably than almost any other Democrat in US politics. He has a near-perfect record of voting with his side." Remember, Mr. Baker, voting with his side means voting against Bush policies, a vote that most Americans agree with now. So when you say, "He has the most solidly left-wing voting history in the Senate," you're really saying he is solidly anti-Bush in his philosophy. Obama speaks of being a champion of transparency in government, yet from you this brings him only criticism: "His one act of bipartisanship, a transparency bill co-sponsored with a Republican senator, was backed by everybody on both sides of the aisle. He has never challenged his party's line on any issue of substance."

Dear Mr. Baker, have you ever heard of a party being on the right side of a huge majority of the issues? Why would any Democrat, at least one with an ounce of sanity, side with the Republican Party of the past eight years on any issue? We don't challenge our party line just for the sake of being able to proudly say we did. Should Obama have reached across the isle on the issue of privatizing social security? After all, he would then have been able to meet your standard of bucking your own party—right Mr. Baker?

Baker's final comments are laughable: "Here's the real problem with Mr. Obama: the jarring gap between his promises of change and his status quo performance. There are just too many contradictions between the eloquent poetry of the man's stirring rhetoric and the dull, familiar prose of his political record." Mr. Baker will probably eat every last one of these words in the near future. Too bad, for his sake, that he's now on record.

John McCain was on *The View* today. He waffled when Barbara Walters asked him if Palin had requested any earmarks. McCain said that Palin had not while she was governor. This is an absolute lie! McCain is now lying with ease and getting away with it. On CNN today, Dana Milbank offered an opinion on this whole lying episode. He joked, "Mark Twain said a lie can travel halfway round the world while the truth is putting on its shoes." Milbank at least knows that McCain is lying and has the courage to say so in a rounabout way.

The women of *The View* continued grilling McCain. They are doing the dirty work for the press. McCain was confronted about two ads he's currently running. The first is the sex education ad I've mentioned. The second covers the issue of the lipstick on a pig comment. The ad claims that Obama was definitely referring to Palin being the pig. McCain responded to the accusation by saying, "Actually they [the ads] are not lies." Barbara Walters told McCain that he had also used the lipstick on a pig line in the past, and she reminded him that Obama was not talking about Palin. McCain injected, "Senator Obama chooses his words very carefully, ok. He shouldn't have said it." McCain wanted to change the subject and get off this lying accusation. He tried to suggest that it was somehow Obama's fault that he has to put these lying ads up against him. McCain claimed, "If we had done what I asked Senator Obama to do," regarding holding town hall meetings together, "I don't think you'd see the tenor of this campaign."

Palin did her second sit-down with Charles Gibson today. She was equally unimpressive. Palin was committed to persuading the American people that she was an earmark reformer—this despite the fact that her state requested more earmarks per capita than any other state in the country this year. Jeffrey Toobin put it best. "For her to suddenly become an enemy of earmarks is insane." I've been waiting for a journalist to call all of this what it is, and "insanity" is a perfect word. Thank you, Jeffrey Toobin. Toobin is also one of the only corporate media members, along with Keith Olbermann, who is deciding to call all of these McCain-Palin claims exactly what they are: Lies! Toobin and Olbermann would have received high praise from Euripides who claimed, "A man's most valuable trait is a judicious sense of what not to believe."

DAY 20
THE PIÑATA

Obama is campaigning in Manchester, New Hampshire, today—Saturday, September 13—while McCain is in Arlington, Virginia. Both candidates are focusing their attention on the devastation that Hurricane Ike has caused. Nevertheless, this has quickly become pile on Obama season in the political world. McCain has managed to take the lead in the polls for the past week and the media is hitching its wagon to the falsely labeled "Straight Talk Express." The media is kicking Obama while they think he's down. Instead of forcefully making the case for how he is being lied about by the McCain campaign, the press is grabbing a bat and taking their own swipe at the piñata. Yes, Obama has quickly become a piñata for Republicans, some of his own supporters, and the media to take a big swing at. How did it happen? Perhaps the country expected Obama's dominance in the Primary to have taken root also in the General Election. After all, voters remember that this is a man who defeated the Clinton machine. He is only a piñata because he is mature enough to allow himself to be one for the time being. He'll take the hits, barbs, jabs, cheap shots, lies, and doubts. Why? Because he sees the big picture, and the minute he starts letting his supporters—even the ones who feel that he should do exactly as they recommend because they've given him money—tell him how to run his campaign, he's finished.

Republicans, the media, and fellow Democrats expected Obama to be up in the polls by something like twenty at this point. Because he isn't, many people are finding it quite easy to kick him while he's down. But they are misreading the tealeaves. He may already be up in the polls by a large margin. No one with a cell phone has been polled, and Obama is more patient, calculated, and intelligent than anyone we've seen in decades. He is biding his time—readying himself for the debates, and moving in for the kill. It will be up to the media to recognize the political kill when it presents itself. And it will present itself during the first debate. People are begging him to fight back. But their idea of fighting is much different from Obama's. He has said that he will not lie about his opponent. He will not meet lies with lies. But during the first debate, he will likely counter the lies with a bevy of searing facts about McCain's true record. He will have McCain on the ropes and likely put him on the canvas. The media should then count McCain out, but will instead probably help him up, ensuring that he can recover and fight in debate number two. Better for the ratings!

Given their past performance, the predictable thing for the press to be saying right now is *McCain Flies His Campaign Past Obama.* And indeed, this is the actual title of Michael Barone's article in today's *US News & World Report.* Barone writes, "John McCain was trained as a fighter pilot. In his selection of Sarah Palin, and in his convention and campaigning since, he has shown that he learned an important lesson from his fighter pilot days: He has gotten inside Barack Obama's OODA loop. That term was the invention of the great fighter pilot and military strategist

John Boyd. It's an acronym for Observe, Orient, Decide, Act."
Barone fails to mention one extremely relevant word while
assessing the lessons McCain has learned: Lying! Did McCain
learn how to do that at flight school? He hasn't gotten inside
Obama's OODA loop—he has simply tapped into his own
"McCain OODL loop." This is my acronym for Observe,
Orient, Decide, and Lie. Note to Mr. Barone: John McCain
has been making a living by lying the past few weeks. Being a
good pilot doesn't negate the immorality of lying. Spare me
the flight school jargon and stop seeing only what you want
to see, Michael Barone. There are little things called facts.

I guess the temptation to make comparisons between
shooting planes down and shooting political opponents
down was too tempting for Barone to resist. Barone writes
about Obama's failure to meet step one of the OODA loop—
Observe. He quotes Robert Coram, Boyd's biographer, about
how to outwit an opposing pilot by "operating at a faster
tempo than the enemy" in order to "get inside the mind and
decision cycle of the adversary." Barone adds, "For a fighter
pilot, that means honing in above and behind the adversary
so you can shoot him out of the sky. For a political candidate,
it means acting in such a way that the opponent's responses
again and again reinforce the points you are trying to make
and undermine his own position." McCain evidently was
acting as an ace pilot when he selected Palin as his running
mate, according to Barone:

> The Palin selection—and her performance at the
> convention and on the stump—seems to be having
> that effect. The McCain campaign shrewdly kept

the information that she was on the short list and that she was the choice to a half-dozen people, who didn't tell even their spouses. The Obama team failed to Observe.

What the Obama team failed to observe was the Jekyll & Hyde act that John McCain was readying himself to pull off. The Maverick left the building and the nation has witnessed a man become a pathological liar. So yes, the Obama team failed to observe. They were guilty of believing that McCain was honorable enough not to play dirty politics. You know—the "honor" of a fighter pilot? After all, McCain did say that he wanted to wage an honorable campaign back when he first received the nomination.

Barone goes on to show how Obama failed at part two of the OODA loop. He writes, "Then they failed to Orient. Palin, as her convention and subsequent appearances have shown, powerfully reinforces two McCain themes: She is a maverick who has taken on the leaders of her own party (as Obama never has in Chicago), and she has a record on energy of favoring drilling and exploiting American resources." Being a maverick for the sake of being a maverick can at times be foolish. Barone claims that Palin's convention appearance showed that she is a maverick. He is insulting our intelligence by concluding that a person who can read a teleprompter and deliver an e-mailed forwarded joke passes the maverick test. And her subsequent appearances have only shown her continue to repeat the same exact speech—hardly the essence of a maverick. Barone goes on to show how Obama failed the last two parts of the OODA loop—to Decide and Act:

Then team Obama and its many backers in the media failed to Decide correctly, so when they Acted they got it wrong. Their attacks on Palin tended to ricochet and hit Obama. Is she inexperienced? Well, what has Obama ever run (besides his now floundering campaign)? Robert Coram describes what can happen when one player gets inside another's OODA loop. 'If someone truly understands how to create menace and uncertainty and mistrust, then how to exploit and magnify the presence of these disconcerting elements, the loop can be vicious, a terribly destructive force, virtually unstoppable in causing panic and confusion.... The most amazing aspect of the OODA loop is that the losing side rarely understands what happened.'

John Boyd would have been a terrific political consultant. Regardless of how this election turns out, one thing is certain: The losing side will indeed understand what happened. This will have nothing to do with the brilliance of an OODA loop. If Obama wins, McCain will know that Obama managed to effectively combat the vicious lies that have been levied against him. If McCain wins, Obama will know that the country fell victim to those very lies. At this point, one can only wonder how Obama's grassroots movement is aiming to shoot McCain's game plan out of the sky.

DAY 21
LIES

Obama is in Chicago, Illinois, today—Sunday, September 14—while McCain is in Jacksonville, Florida. What do you call a false statement made with deliberate intent to deceive, an intentional untruth, a falsehood? You call it a lie. Lies are very resilient creatures. Once they're put out into the political atmosphere, they're difficult to kill. John McCain's campaign has released two specific lies into the media world that are hurting Obama: the accusation that Obama called Palin a pig, and the assertion that he is for teaching kindergarteners about sex before teaching them to read. Truth: He did not call her a pig, and he is for teaching kids how to recognize sexual predators. Nevertheless, the lies are having an effect, and McCain will likely continue them. He has deployed his surrogates, and they are now blurring the line between truth and lies. They've effectively muddied the waters, and it's as if we are no longer able to recognize the truth when it presents itself. Everyone is beginning to appear to be dishonest. The lies are now feeding on themselves and the Republicans have shown no signs of owning up to them. It has become a culture of sickness. If one is seeing success as a result of telling lies, he is unlikely to change. The ends justify the means. This is a critical moment in the campaign. Only the media can separate fact from fiction. But they have to do so with vigor—with a disdain for lies—with an angry watchdog persona. Anything less will serve only to inflate the lies and ensure they continue to permeate the media.

In today's *New York Times*, Thomas Friedman tried to push back against some of this political pollution. "Of course, we're going to need oil for many years, but instead of exalting that—with 'drill, baby, drill'—why not throw all our energy into innovating a whole new industry of clean power with the mantra 'invent, baby, invent?' That is what a party committed to 'change' would really be doing." This is rare music to my ears. Friedman continues: "As they say in Texas: 'If all you ever do is all you've ever done, then all you'll ever get is all you ever got.' [This] is symbolic of the campaign that John McCain has decided to run. It's a campaign now built on turning everything possible into a cultural wedge issue—including even energy policy, no matter how stupid it makes the voters and no matter how much it might weaken America."

If the media will begin to take its cues from Friedman, there just might be hope for this campaign to find the right track again and begin moving in a new direction. But Friedman writes for the *New York Times*. His face is not in front of the average American seven days a week like Wolf Blitzer, Anderson Cooper, Chris Matthews, etc. are. Friedman speaks to the diligent, politically savvy demographic. He makes too much sense, much like Obama. But he is one of the most respected minds in America, and his editorial today could not have come at a more critical time. He characterizes McCain correctly writing, "I respected McCain's willingness to support the troop surge in Iraq, even if it was going to cost him the Republican nomination. Now the same guy, who would not sell his soul to win his party's nomination, is ready to sell every piece of his soul to win the presidency." This assessment is sad but true. The McCain of 2000 is gone. Friedman adds, "In order to disguise the fact that the core of his campaign is to continue the same Bush policies that have led 80 percent of the country to conclude we're on the wrong track, McCain has decided to play the culture-war card." And his sidekick, Palin, is doing the bulk of the dirty work.

For any serious political historian, I could not begin to do justice to the anti-Obama one-hour *Meet the Press* that aired today by simply writing about it. One must go to the NBC archives to watch and hear it. If someone had paid Tom Brokaw (who knows?) to stick a knife in Obama's back while acting even-handed for the sake of the camera, he couldn't have done a better job of it. Every—and I say every—video or quotation he threw at both Democratic Sen. Schumer and later at Republican Rudy Giuliani were carefully chosen for their insidious, anti-Obama slant.

Brokaw began by putting up several polls. The *Newsweek* Presidential-Election Poll has the candidates tied at 46%. Rather than focusing on how these numbers represent an impressive jump for Obama to tie things back up after McCain's convention bump, Brokaw immediately jumped to this: "…but the most interesting numbers, really, as you know, come in what we call 'the internals'. " At this point Brokaw chose, out of myriad subcategories, to select the one area of the poll that has always been the weakest for Obama. He selected "Has Strong Leadership Qualities Needed to be President" to put up on the screen. He then put up Knowledgeable and Experienced Enough to Handle

Presidency. McCain led in this poll too. Brokaw proved that he came into today's show with an agenda by saying, "So many of our viewers and so many people who have been polled just don't think that he's ready to lead in a dangerous world, even after going through some twenty debates and nine months of primaries. Isn't that the single most significant challenge that he has before him?"

Next Brokaw throws up this poll: "Presidential Election Among White Women." He didn't choose to put up the poll that shows Obama leading among men. Next on his agenda was Presidential Election Among Senior Citizens, another subcategory in which McCain is leading. At this point I made a prediction: Brokaw will not show a single favorable Obama poll during the hour. He didn't. And there are many polls in which Obama leads by a large margin. He wasn't finished. He now targeted rural white men and suggested McCain was leading in that area. Just when I thought his sense of fairness might kick in, Brokaw showed a poll entitled "Shares Your Values and Principles" in which McCain is slightly ahead. He opined: "That's the kind of thing that's very hard to turn around with an effective speech. It really speaks to the discomfort a lot of people [read "and I"] have with his background and who he is." Finally, Brokaw threw this last dagger: a poll that shows McCain up by four points in the "Strongly Support Your Candidate" area. Brokaw said, "The fact is Sen. McCain got a much bigger bounce out of his convention than did Sen. Obama for all the theatrics at the football stadium."

We all witnessed the less than impressive performance of Palin with Gibson this past week. With the plethora of damaging footage Brokaw could have chosen, he picked only a snippet of Palin criticizing Obama for not choosing Clinton as his running mate. With a big smile on his face, Brokaw led into footage of Joe Biden jokingly suggesting that Hillary might have been a better choice than himself. Brokaw injected his opinion again. "I thought the test was you always pick the person who is most qualified to be your Vice Presidential candidate." He wasn't talking about McCain picking Palin. He suggested that Obama made a mistake in not picking the more qualified Clinton. Does anyone, besides Brokaw, believe six-year senator, Hillary Clinton, is better qualified to be Vice President than 36-year senator, Joe Biden?

Brokaw next managed to turn the fact that Obama had raised $66 million last month, mostly from small donors, the most in history, into a negative for Obama. That took all of Brokaw's skill and then some. He then introduced Rudy Giuliani, and without showing him any of the favorable Obama polls, Brokaw instead played edited clips of McCain saying the following: "This will be a respectful campaign. Americans want a respectful campaign…. They're tired of the attacks; they're tired of the impugning people's character and integrity. They want a respectful campaign. And I am of the firm belief that they'll get it and that they can get it if the American people demand it and reject a lot of this negative stuff that goes on." These quotes reached back to April to make McCain look like the candidate who had always been opposed to negative campaigning. Brokaw's not finished yet!

I've pretty much exhausted the conversation about McCain's sex education ad over the past week, but it won't go away. When the news media played it for free for the McCain camp all week long during work hours, it may have been seen in passing by people in doctors' offices, passengers at airports, or stay-at-home moms or dads. That wasn't enough for Tom Brokaw. Once again he put it up for Rudy Giuliani to defend as the whole world watched. There was no one there on the air—not Tom Brokaw and certainly not Rudy Giuliani—to correct the lies. Giuliani validated the perverted ad—an ad, as I've described before, filled with photos that depict Obama as a leering possible pedophile. Again, not once did Brokaw point out the fact—the undeniable fact— that the ad was an absolute lie. He simply asked Giuliani if he thought the ad was "inappropriate on the part of the McCain campaign." He let Giuliani dance. And after he was finished dancing, Brokaw immediately moved on. The effect, then, of today's program was to juxtapose a kind, gentle, grandfatherly McCain against an evil leering Obama. The visual propaganda was stark! Even though he went on to ask Giuliani if he thought he had gone too far in poking fun at Obama's having been a community organizer, and even though he intimated that perhaps the sex education ad was a "misrepresentation" of Obama, Brokaw never undid the colossal damage he had already done during the first half hour. Brokaw never showed a kind, loving, brilliant Obama during the hour—just the kind fair-campaign advocate and soft-spoken McCain. The visual propaganda is stark! Tom Brokaw masterfully took Tim Russert's powerful strategy of talking truth to power and turned it on its head.

Did Tom Brokaw watch any of the news this past Friday? The dominant story of that day was McCain's failure to

LIES

overcome the onslaught from the women of *The View.* Not
once during his show today did he mention what every major
newspaper in the country considered a pressing story—the
video evidence that McCain is now intentionally lying. As
the anti-earmark champion in Congress, McCain took on
Palin about her earmark requests. Why didn't Brokaw put
up a snippet of McCain lying when he said Palin had not
requested any earmarks? He should have made Giuliani
address this video evidence. But no! Instead, Giuliani got a
chance to add to the lie that Obama sponsored a bill about
sex and little kids. Giuliani had no problem spinning that
ad, and Brokaw completely let him off the hook. He's slick,
all right, this Tom Brokaw. In his defense, however, having
sold his soul to the corporations that took over the once
public-service oriented network news in the eighties, he has
no choice but to step into Tim Russert's seat sans a moral
compass.

John King of CNN could easily be charged with aiding
and abetting if lying without being under oath were a crime.
He had Bush's press secretary, Dana Perino, on his 11:00 am
program this morning. He let her tell one lie after another
without once correcting her. Why even have her on? He must
understand that his job is to be a moderator of the truth.
This reminds me how much the nation misses Tim Russert.

The way the media is approaching the McCain camp's
lies is to say that both camps are lying. So far I haven't heard
what exactly they're saying is an Obama campaign lie. It just
makes the media feel that they are being even-handed, I
suppose. Even-handedness is holding both sides to the same
standard of truth. It doesn't mean if you find out that one

side is lying, you have to say the other side is lying so they'll be even.

We finally heard a snippet from a Joe Biden speech. It became immediately clear that the power and effectiveness with which he spoke will be playing a major role in tilting the polls in Obama's favor. Had the media been feeding us his words rather than Palin's exclusively for the past ten days, the McCain camp's lies could have been exposed sooner. Biden made one particularly good point regarding the McCain-Palin tax policy. If you make $50,000 a year and have a $12,000 dollar health insurance policy paid by your employer, the McCain camp would tax your income at $62,000. According to Biden, this is McCain's idea of "change" regarding health insurance. He also pointed out that McCain-Palin are touting a $5,000 health insurance tax credit, but if your policy costs $12,000, that leaves the taxpayer owing $7,000. He joked, "That's a bridge to nowhere alright."

Speaking of the bridge to nowhere, Palin lied again at a campaign stop in Nevada today. She said she " told Congress 'Thanks but no thanks' on that bridge to nowhere." Even after that assertion has been thoroughly vetted and dismissed as at best misleading by fact checkers everywhere, she continues touting her anti-earmark rhetoric every day. She's either unaware of the vetting or unable to learn how to nuance her rote message or unlearn a speech once she has it down pat. The bridge to nowhere was originally designed to connect the mainland with a sparsely populated island in Alaska, an idea, which, to be honest with you, may not have been a bad one if the island began to develop. That's not the point! She can't continue, without lying, to sell herself as an anti-earmark reformer when she is on record as having campaigned for governor in favor of earmarks for this bridge. Is it a good thing that Barack Obama voted present over 100 times while he was in the Illinois State Legislature? Most critics would say no. If he now came out and made one of his major issues that he was a reformer who was against people who voted present in the Illinois State Senate, we would know he was a bald faced liar, or at the very least, not very smart. Can you imagine turning on the television tomorrow, only to find Obama at a campaign rally shouting, "I told the corrupt, good old boys network in Illinois, 'Thanks but no thanks on that option to vote present?" Then, and only then, could the media say Obama was as big a liar as Palin.

DAY 22
"THE FUNDAMENTALS OF OUR ECONOMY ARE STRONG"

Obama is campaigning in Grand Junction, Colorado, today—Monday, September 15—while McCain is in Orlando, Florida. Carly Fiorina, McCain's senior economic advisor, was David Gregory's guest today on *Race for the White House.* She was on to discuss the financial crisis that is front and center in the news today. Gregory asked her what McCain meant when he said today, "The fundamentals of our economy are strong." This was a statement that shocked America, and it is unbelievably the 22nd time McCain has uttered it. Fiorina never managed to make sense of his out-of-touch comment. The fact is that America lost $500 billion in the market today. We are officially in economic panic mode. Obama is doing his best to pin the crisis on Bush and McCain. One would think this would be an easy pin job, but the media is allowing the Republican talking heads to spin out of this, instead blaming the financial crisis on the Democratic Congress of the past two years. Republicans are suggesting that their own six-year congressional majority run had nothing to do with it. It is amazing to see them successfully make this case. But the press is giving them a platform.

There is this prevailing notion that both candidates are slinging mud at each other and that it's not just McCain who's lying. The word is out that Obama is also guilty. On MSNBC at

11:19 am, Contessa Brewer mentioned "the outright lies that are flying back and forth" between the two campaigns. This is hardly the case. Brewer is clueless in her attempt to assess the state of the race. Mark Halperin and Candy Crowley also jumped on this media talking point. Halperin told Anderson Cooper today that McCain never has been comfortable running this type of campaign. He was referring to McCain's supposed discomfort with suddenly being the leader of a dirty campaign. McCain has seemed pretty comfortable to me. He is lying with what looks like ease. He doesn't seem uncomfortable—just unprepared.

Crowley told Anderson Cooper that Obama has also been taking McCain's words out of context. She suggested that some fact check organization has proven that Obama has unfairly used McCain's previous comment about who is rich in America. McCain told Rick Warren of Saddleback Church that he considers those making five million a year to be rich. Crowley claimed that McCain was not necessarily being serious. Crowley needs to understand something. When McCain said that Palin had not requested earmarks this year, it was a lie. When Obama says that McCain said that he considers five million dollars a year the marker for determining who's rich, he is not lying. Crowley can't say that McCain didn't say those exact words. He did! Since when has the media been in the business of looking for what a candidate was actually trying to say? The press has always prided themselves on holding people accountable for what they say—not reading people's minds.

Mark Halperin then suggested that Obama was making a mistake by calling McCain out for saying that the economy was fundamentally strong. Halperin said that even Obama is not going to say that there are no fundamental elements of the economy that are strong. But Halperin muddied the waters again. McCain never said some "elements" of the economy are strong. He said—word for word—"The fundamentals of our economy are strong." This is an exact quote. There is no "elements" in that quote, Mr. Halperin. Your job is not to level the playing field. Stop bailing McCain out! McCain is lying, and Obama is using McCain's words against him. When John McCain said that we could be in Iraq for 100 years, is it my job to use my psychic abilities to determine what he means—to determine whether or not he means war or occupation? Is it my job to tell people what he was actually trying to say? Halperin and Crowley have shown tonight that even when proof is offered that McCain is flat out lying, the press will create the perception that Obama is lying, or at least misunderstanding, when he says McCain is.

Since Palin has been unwilling to give any further interviews, Anderson Cooper decided to zero in on the willing Joe Biden. Cooper said that Biden's willingness to talk to the press in the past has given him an opportunity to put his foot in his mouth—"something he is known for." Cooper then had Joe Johns do a short piece that tried to suggest that Joe Biden was prone to gaffs and possibly is a credit card crook. They provided clips of a few gaffs, but no proof of corruption. The piece had no merit. It did serve its purpose, I guess—to plant doubts in people's minds about Biden. As long as Palin continues her silence, Cooper and his colleagues will fill their time preying on Joe Biden, the distinguished statesman—and, might I add, willing interviewee.

DAY 23
I DIDN'T KNOW MCCAIN INVENTED
THE BLACKBERRY!

Obama is campaigning in Los Angeles, California, today—Tuesday, September 16—while McCain is in Vienna, Ohio. When John McCain told the American people yesterday, "The fundamentals of our economy are strong," one would have surmised that the press would have destroyed him for it. That has not been the case. This morning John McCain said that he was referring to the American workers as the fundamentals of our economy. He was obviously backtracking on the unbelievable comment he made yesterday, but no one is buying that he was referring to the American workers as the fundamentals of our economy. McCain is obviously trying to be crafty. A wise person once said, "Crafty men deal in generalizations." The media is questioning him on it, but they are also relenting. Considering the magnitude of this particular financial crisis, if any other political candidates had made this preposterous comment, it would likely be the end of their political campaigns. After all, the government had to bail out insurance giant AIG today for $85 billion.

Barack Obama gave a very detailed speech this morning on the financial crisis. He gave a six-point plan and talked in great depth about how the country can solve its financial woes. It was a nuanced speech, and reassuring. He pointed out the fact that John McCain has, for 26 years, been an opponent of government regulation. Obama said that he himself had been calling for regulation for years. McCain has magically become the regulating champion within the past 26 hours. The media knows that McCain has always been opposed to government regulation, yet they are allowing him to tout his false pro-regulation credentials. McCain is flip-flopping faster than investors are bailing out of the stock market. Why won't the media call him out for being a Johnny-come-lately? McCain also said this morning that too many CEOs are getting rich off this crisis. He failed to mention that one of his senior financial advisors, Carly Fiorina, cashed out and took an enormous severance package from the company she left. She is one of the many CEO golden parachute beneficiaries leading up to this financial crisis.

There are three new lies that should be haunting the McCain campaign: They claimed today that one of their recent campaign rallies had over twenty-thousand people in attendance. The number was actually eight thousand. Palin claimed today that her teleprompter stopped working while she was giving her speech at the convention. It has been determined today that this is not true. Third, McCain's domestic policy advisor, Douglas Holtz Eakin, said today that McCain was responsible for inventing the Blackberry phone. The press should be destroying McCain for all three lies. These are lies that didn't even have to be told in that they didn't help. McCain and his surrogates are becoming compulsive liars.

Another lie that the press is letting McCain get away with is his claim that Obama will raise taxes on the middle class. This is a proven lie. But the media is allowing surrogates to tell it with little challenge. McCain campaign's Carly Fiorina spoke to Andrea Mitchell today on MSNBC. Mitchell asked her why she had told a radio host that Palin did not have the ability to run a major corporation. Fiorina responded by saying that neither could McCain, Biden or Obama. Unbelievable! McCain's own advisor is telling the country that the man she supports can't run a corporation. How does she expect him to run a government responsible for trillions of dollars? This story quickly heated up, and the McCain camp yanked Fiorina off the air by canceling the rest of her scheduled TV appearances.

At 11:07 am on MSNBC, John Harwood was talking about Obama's continued critique of the McCain foible yesterday—the one regarding the economy being fundamentally strong. Harwood asked Elisabeth Bumiller, "Wasn't that a cheap shot" on Obama's part? Harwood clearly thinks that Obama is being unfair to McCain. Harwood didn't ask, "Was" that a cheap shot? He asked, "Wasn't" that a cheap shot. This suggests that he believes it was indeed a cheap shot. Be careful, Mr. Harwood. Don't show your hand.

Chris Matthews had Paul Begala on with him this afternoon. Begala said that McCain was showing dishonor in the campaign. Matthews immediately said, "Dishonor is a strong word." Why is Matthews so willing to defend McCain? Of course McCain is showing dishonor. I can't think of a better word to describe what he has been engaging in. Matthews went on to dismiss Obama's detailed speech on the economic crisis as "dispassionate." He used that word at 2:55 pm. He went on later in the show to say about Obama's speech: "Where's the passion? I don't see it. That was terrible!" Mr. Matthews is making this personal. To call a fantastic speech—one filled with the details our country is pining for—"terrible" is totally unacceptable coming from Matthews. If dishonor is too strong a word to use against McCain, why does Matthews feel that the word "terrible" is ok to use against Obama? Can you say "hypocrite"? Besides, we don't need passion right now from a leader. We don't need hot air—the kind you are so fantastic at blowing, Mr. Matthews. We need a smart speech with proposed policies that get to the real issues plaguing the country's financial markets. Matthews is losing his credibility by the day. On a day when John McCain has shown himself to be completely detached from the issues facing America—on a day that has seen his own advisor dismiss him as being unfit to run a corporation—you, Mr. Matthews, chose to call Barack Obama's speech "terrible." The only thing terrible today was your complete and utter inability to hold McCain, and only McCain, accountable for his mistakes. Obama is not your target. Getting at the truth is—or should be. Chris Matthews' journalistic style is becoming nothing more than pathetic. He should be ashamed of himself. While he did a decent job of critiquing John McCain's mistakes today, he just couldn't resist throwing a cheap shot at a man who is trying to communicate regarding a difficult and vital topic, a topic that doesn't lend itself to solution by "passion".

David Gregory couldn't let the day go by without throwing Obama under the bus. Again, I guess the obvious target—McCain—was too easy for Gregory to hit. Gregory was discussing Obama's claims that he has always been for regulation. Gregory said with disdain, "[Obama's] message hasn't broken through on the issue of regulation." Gregory tried everything he could to insure that McCain didn't completely drown because of his disastrous economy comment. Gregory needs to realize that even if Obama's message of regulation hasn't broken through, his is still a message of "regulation." McCain's has always been a message of deregulation. Why don't you see if Obama's message of regulation is worthy of "breaking through" by leading a discussion on it, David Gregory? Is Gregory more upset at Obama for trying to do the correct thing than he is at McCain for doing the wrong thing? *Salon's* Joan Walsh tried to defend Obama by saying that he had been talking about regulation for months. *Time* magazine's Jay Carney said, "Having a position paper is not leading in Congress." These journalists will not give it up for Obama. They believe that because he hasn't already solved the economic crisis as a senator form Illinois, he deserves to be belittled for trying. For trying! Note to the petty journalists: He is not the President—yet.

Joe Biden said this today: "I am sick and tired of this Republican garbage." I see Biden and I raise him, because I am sick and tired of this media garbage. If we find video evidence of John McCain hugging and dancing with Osama Bin Laden, will the press say that they have seen no sign that Barack Obama isn't just as willing to meet and negotiate with Bin Laden? On a day that would have seen most politicians meet their political doom and drown, the media has managed to throw enough life support to McCain to ensure his survival, and along the way, they have creatively pushed Obama overboard for no reason, at least no reason they have managed to communicate.

FOX News' Sean Hannity is quickly becoming the poster child for journalistic pornography. His work is designed to arouse the passions of his audience but has no socially redeeming value. He spent one segment of tonight's program speaking to Nancy Pelosi's daughter with no goal in mind except trying to get her to say that she feels the election of Sarah Palin would be a setback for women. To her credit, Ms. Pelosi didn't bite, but it is absolutely unconscionable that she should be subjected to this insistence that she fight a woman for Hannity's pleasure. I'll answer for Pelosi. Yes, Hannity, the election of Palin would be a setback for women because she has been chosen, not on merit but only because she is a woman. She's the secretary who can't type, but is pleasurable for sexist men, like you, to have around to stoke their cynical egos. The real setback for women was displayed by you tonight. It is the realization that disrespecting women on national television is still an acceptable practice and still a form of entertainment. Asking that the secretary—man or woman—know how to type is not a put down. Asking that a potential Vice President be qualified for the job—and not someone who abuses power—is also not a put down.

DAY 24
THE OLD BOYS' NETWORK

Obama is campaigning in Elko, Nevada, today—Wednesday, September 17—while McCain is in Grand Rapids, Michigan. "It is a multi-trillion dollar issue facing America." This from the mouth of Senate Majority Leader Harry Reid regarding the country's financial crisis this morning. The news has officially taken Palin off the front pages. Several reporters have referred to the crisis as a blessing for Obama because it has put the spotlight back on George Bush. Republicans have suddenly become proponents of regulation; McCain has become a populist, and George Bush is in hiding. One would think that having a Republican President along with a six-year Republican Congress would be enough to drive Obama way up in the polls. The press is obsessed with suggesting that Obama is having trouble connecting on the issue of the economy. What they have failed to articulate is the fact that Obama is up against two major forces: the Republican Party and the corporate media. It's not Obama's fault that the press has been unwilling to drive this point home to American voters regarding his tax proposal: If you make less than $250 thousand a year, Barack Obama is going to give you a significant tax break—and 95% of the country falls into this category. Those making more than $250 thousand will see a significant tax increase. Getting this information out to the public would certainly help Obama connect on the economic issue, but the media has done little to assist Obama in delivering this clear and concise message. Too focused on tabloid drama.

Obama is in Nevada today and a poll shows him leading there among voters between the ages of 18-29 by 60% to 35%. Why didn't Tom Brokaw show this poll last Sunday? This is a staggering number for a state that shows the candidates in a virtual tie. Why didn't Brokaw ask Giuliani why McCain is having such a terrible time connecting with these young voters? James Carville said today that he believes the race is all but over and Obama will win as a result of McCain's gaff regarding the economy being fundamentally sound. John McCain tried to convince voters in Michigan today that he was the man to lead them out of the tough economic times. He only had one problem: as he was leaving the crowd began chanting "Obama 08, Obama 08, Obama 08!" The media has shown very little of this embarrassing moment.

Illinois congressman, Rahm Emanuel, was on MSNBC earlier and talked about McCain's sudden philosophical change regarding government regulation. He said that McCain has always been a deregulator, and now that everyone is blaming the Republicans for their judgment over the last seven years, McCain is "singing from a different song book." He surely is, and the media is allowing him to. They seem to be more concerned today that Obama attended a huge fundraiser in Hollywood yesterday and got a huge hug from Barbara Streisand. Andrea Mitchell asked NBC News Washington Bureau Chief Mark Whitaker, what he thought about Obama's decision to go to Hollywood on a day that saw the market tank. Whitaker said, "Hollywood is not necessarily the best place to be." There is this notion that Obama shouldn't be allowing himself to be seen with the Hollywood big wigs. Whitaker should have suggested that McCain consistently standing next to his wife, who is worth over $100 million, is not necessarily the best place to be either.

A new *Gallup* poll shows Obama leading again, 47% to 45%. The press hasn't made a big deal about this jump. Eight days ago, September 9, McCain was leading in the same poll, 48% to 43%. September 9 was the day Bill O'Reilly aired the third part of the interview he did with Obama. Since that day, Obama has been climbing in this poll. The last time he led in this particular poll was September 5. At 2:34 pm Wolf Blitzer said, "What Sarah Palin has done is unify the party." On a day like today, this comment seemed quite out of place. What he should have said is that Americans are still laughing over the hilarious impersonation Tina Fey did of Palin this past weekend on *Saturday Night Live*. Fey was a spitting image of Palin, and by using Palin's own words, reinforced the overwhelmingly obvious fact that she is unprepared to be Vice President. Fey has managed to brand into our minds the image of Palin as a laughable figure. With one skit, Fey has undermined Plain's credibility. What Blitzer said was false. Palin hasn't unified the party. If anything, the party is in disarray because of the economy tanking. She may have unified a portion of the Republican base, but the party is completely out of whack—especially over the past 48 hours.

Obama can't get the media to stop putting hurdles out front for him to clear. Today, at 2:45 pm, Chris Matthews said, "[Obama] still has to prove that he cares deeply about what's going wrong in the country," and that he has the "tool kit" to fix it. Obama has already proven both. It is McCain who needs to prove that he has a tool kit. Doesn't Matthews think that Obama's having to watch his mother die while arguing with insurance companies provided enough incentive? He's convinced me that he cares deeply about what's going on with this country's broken healthcare system? Doesn't he think that recently paying off a mountain of school loans was enough to show that Obama cares deeply about the broken school loan system? Why does Matthews hold Obama to such a higher standard of proof of his deep feelings about the problems of the country than he holds the other three candidates? Does he think Biden and Palin care deeply? Does he think McCain cares deeply about poor people's problems? If he does, he's not saying it about anyone except Obama.

David Gregory showed a clip of Obama speaking today in Nevada. It was a very short clip that did nothing to represent anything significant that Obama had actually said. He then immediately tried to imply that McCain had been much more assertive during his speech. Gregory claimed, "McCain had a much more aggressive tone today." He said these words with a tone that suggested McCain had been more aggressive than Obama. This was definitely the implication. Gregory then had the audacity to suggest that McCain is giving a more effective response to the economic crisis. After a guest had touted Obama's plan, Gregory said, "And yet McCain is making a narrower argument." He said that McCain was making a narrower argument because he was talking about reform and taking on Wall Street. He then opined, "That's a message that resonates right now." Why is Gregory willing to make the laughable claim that reform and taking on Wall Street are narrow arguments? Both ideas are broad at best.

Gregory interviewed Clinton Labor Secretary Robert Reich today. Reich spoke broadly about the steps that will need to be taken in order to insure an economic recovery. Gregory asked, "What makes you believe that Obama has the right prescription to take on the economy?" Reich said that Obama has been in favor of regulating and "essentially you've got to regulate." He also spoke favorably about Obama's approach to taxes. Reich said, "Let's have tax cuts for average working people." One has to wonder if this was enough to finally stop Gregory from constantly showing—whether intentionally or inadvertently—his implicit contempt for Obama. *Google* CEO Eric Schmidt told Gregory that a good future President is "going to bring back some sort of optimism." I am trying to be optimistic about Gregory's future analysis of Obama's candidacy. He doesn't seem to have a problem offering favorable opinions about Palin. He showed a clip of Palin talking to a reporter today while she sipped coffee in a Michigan café. Palin vaguely spoke about her impressions of the current financial woes. She said that prices keep going up and people's pay keeps going down. Gregory added, "She's an effective spokesperson on this issue." He backed his opinion up by reminding us that Palin has five children and can therefore relate to these personal kinds of economic issues. Gregory didn't bother reminding his viewers that Obama has two children and as a result may also be an effective spokesperson on this issue.

Obama drew huge laughs today in Nevada when he talked about McCain's recent claim that he was going to take on the old boys network. Obama joked, "Old boys network? In the McCain campaign that's called a staff meeting." One reporter after another has asked if Obama had gone too far in mocking McCain. When he gets serious they suggest that he needs to lighten up. When he jokes they wonder if he's being too insensitive. He can't win with the press. When McCain suggested that the way to solve the economic downturn was to form a commission, Obama jokingly said that this isn't 9/11! We don't need a commission. He claimed that McCain had pulled out one of the oldest tricks in the book and that we need leadership, not a commission.

Obama must have gotten sick and tired of the media's refusal to show his entire detailed speeches on the economy. He released a two-minute ad that gets pretty specific. The ad also encourages viewers to go to *barackobama.com* to read his entire economic plan. I'm sure the press will be right back to calling Obama Mr. Vague tomorrow. One would think that the media would be inclined to report the suggestions of anyone who wasn't part of the Republican Party that got us into this heaping Wall Street mess. Anyone! But instead we don't have to settle for anyone. We have a brilliant senator from Illinois who is offering something completely different as a solution. Instead the media is spending time trying to figure out how Palin's e-mail account was broken into. E-mail news aside, Palin is busy trying to shake off the bad news she heard today—that Hillary Clinton cancelled her scheduled appearance at the United Nations. McCain was hoping that a Palin and Clinton photo op at the UN would go a long way toward enhancing Palin's foreign policy credentials. Was Palin planning to make this joint appearance a statement that would go a long way toward putting her on a level playing field with Clinton? Needless to say, the McCain camp is very upset at this news.

Palin did her first town hall meeting today with McCain. She was asked very specifically by a woman to clear up this perception about her not having any foreign policy experience. The woman asked for specifics. Palin looked like a deer caught in the headlights. She never answered the question. On CNN tonight, Paul Begala suggested that Palin's non-answer was actually better than the answer she gave Charles Gibson last week: that she could see Russia from her backyard. Begala said, "From my backyard I can see the moon, but that doesn't make me an astrophysicist." Begala also accused McCain of being ridiculous for suggesting that he is now the change candidate. He jokingly said that McCain saying change "is like me saying Clooney. Clooney, Clooney, Clooney!" He then asked the CNN panel if he had gotten any better looking because he uttered the name Clooney. It was funny and he was right. Just because you say it doesn't make it so. Radio host Stephanie Miller got in on the fun and said that she could see the ocean from her house and therefore wanted to be Secretary of the Navy. Begala couldn't resist talking about McCain's economy gaff. He said that Herbert Hoover was actually the first leader to talk about the fundamentals of an American economy being strong. He claimed that McCain was actually quoting Hoover who uttered the same line back in 1929. Begala read the Hoover quote and then said that we know what followed that line back in 1929. Let's hope that we're not headed for another Great Depression. Thank God for the Democratic strategists and

Saturday Night Live comedians. Maybe the details and humor they are providing will be enough to beat back the corporate media tide that is pulling Obama into an ever increasing and potentially devastating undertow.

DAY 25
"I'D FIRE HIM"—EXCEPT YOU CAN'T

Obama is campaigning in Espanola, New Mexico, today—Thursday, September 18—while McCain is in Cedar Rapids, Iowa. "You don't want to take on a mom of five who's been elected governor. She knows a little something about people and she knows a lot about politics, but this race will boil down to John McCain and Barack Obama." These comments about Palin came from former Tennessee Congressman Harold Ford, Jr. today on MSNBC. David Gregory immediately responded to Ford's comments with this: "Yeah, and in many ways, uh, will boil down even further to uh, uh, as sense about Barack Obama and whether people trust him." Gregory offered this odd dig at Obama and then immediately moved onto a different subject. It was a completely out-of-place comment that had no relevance to the issue Ford had been discussing. Gregory never told us what area of trust he was referring to. Was he talking about Obama needing to earn trust in the area of the economy, foreign affairs, security—what? He just offered the vague question of trust as an indictment against Obama.

Campbell Brown was talking to Candy Crowley this evening and claimed that "a lot of people" are saying Obama's message on the economy is "pretty fuzzy." Brown never told us who she had been talking to—who her supposed "a lot of people" are. I wonder if the people she reportedly heard from actually used the word fuzzy or was this Campbell Brown's choice adjective used to knock Obama down a few notches. On a day that saw President Bush say, "Americans can be sure we'll act to strengthen markets," we can also be sure that Brown and her corporate media colleagues will find the right negative adjectives to hit Obama in the shins with. Did Campbell Brown see Obama's two-minute ad last night? Did she go to his website and read his entire bullet-form economic plan? It was crystal clear—anything but fuzzy.

John McCain said today that if he were President he would fire the chairman of the Securities and Exchange Commission. This was his way of talking tough. He thinks that firing people instead of changing the actual policies is the way to handle a crisis. He was for firing Donald Rumsfeld after the War in Iraq began to unravel. He never suggested then that the war itself was the problem. Someone might want to suggest to McCain that our current financial crisis has less to do with the chairman of the SEC and more to do with his own 26-year, pro-deregulation record. Someone also might want to point out to him that the President doesn't have the authority to fire the chairman of the SEC. The media should be pouncing on him for this latest episode of passing the buck and taking no personal responsibility. His 26-year record has helped lead us into the greatest financial meltdown since the Great Depression, and today the Federal Reserve pumped $180 billion into money markets overseas. The Bush administration is also preparing plans to supposedly rescue more banks. Who else is McCain going to claim he would fire? Obama said today, "Well, here's what I say: In 47 days, you can fire the whole Trickle-Down, On-Your-Own,

Look-the-Other-Way crowd in Washington who have led us down this disastrous path."

A new *Time* poll shows Obama and McCain tied in the state of Florida at 48%. Obama is speaking in New Mexico today with a new *Allstate/National Journal* poll showing him leading there 49% to 42%. At 10:40 am, MSNBC showed a headline that read: **77% of Obama Ads Since the Democratic National Convention Have Been Negative. 56% of McCain Ads Since the Republican National Convention Have Been Negative.** Talk about arbitrary! What, according to MSNBC, constitutes a negative ad? It's hard to make sense of this information. Obama may be running negative ads that are based in fact, but McCain is running negative ads that are lies. If MSNBC would show us the percentage of McCain ads that include lies, this would be noteworthy information. We all know that most ads are negative anyway, but for MSNBC to choose this information to break down is biased, especially considering the fact that it presents Obama as the more negative candidate, contrary to what my own eyes and ears inform me.

Joe Biden was asked today if those making over $250 thousand should really have to pay more taxes. He said they should and that it was a way of showing patriotism. He is taking some heat from the press over this comment. Norah O'Donnell showed Biden's comment at 12:03 pm and then asked Missouri Sen. Claire McCaskill whether "a flub like that on the part of Senator Biden" will hurt. Why is O'Donnell so certain that it was a flub? She could just as easily have suggested that such strong language is actually called for and may help Obama. Joe Klein of *Time* touched on Biden's comment online today writing, "And Biden's right: in a system of progressive taxation, it is the patriotic duty of the wealthy to pay more than the middle class or the poor...and furthermore, since we're all going to be paying for the mess the Wall Street sharks made, I'd go Biden a step further: there probably should be a confiscatory shark tax for any and all executives whose companies have gone belly up and required a federal bailout."

Today, Jay Carney of *Time* discussed five new polls that his magazine just released. The polls show Obama up in Ohio and Wisconsin, McCain up in Indiana and North Carolina, and the two candidates tied in Florida. Carney said that Obama looked good in Ohio, but added, "Wisconsin is a trouble area for Obama." This may sound like an innocent comment, but it was oddly stated because Carney never offered any analysis of McCain. He focused entirely on Obama. He could just as easily have said that Florida or North Carolina were trouble spots for McCain. There is a pattern developing of journalists over-analyzing Obama's positioning in the polls. If he's up by six, they say he's barely ahead, and if he's down by one people claim it could spell real trouble for him. It is becoming laughable. I have heard no one, including Carney today, say that it is stunning to see Obama and McCain tied in Florida, but because McCain is close in Wisconsin, the press is claiming that Obama should be worried. I have heard this exact commentary today on CNN, FOX News, and MSNBC. McCain should definitely be worried about Florida, a state that he has been leading in, and one that he's expected to win. But somehow he continually manages to escape examination by the press when it comes to poll positioning, regardless of how far behind he is. If he's ahead, even by a single point, the media appears to celebrate the good news and emphasize Obama's grave danger. It's truly an oddity to watch.

McCain argued today that Obama is exploiting the financial crisis for political gain. Talk about the pot calling the kettle black. McCain just recently said that this wasn't the time to point fingers and blame others, yet didn't he just say that he would fire the SEC commissioner? Sounds like exploitation to me! He's using this crisis to throw people under the bus as we speak. Palin is claiming that her state of Alaska provides 20% of the nation's energy supply. Several fact-check organizations have cleared the record up on this lie. Alaska only supplies 3.5% of the nation's energy. This Palin inaccuracy should be major news, especially considering the fact that McCain is touting her as his potential Vice Presidential energy czar, but the press is barely touching it. McCain has also claimed that Palin knows more about energy than anyone else in the country. Wow! She does a good job of hiding her totally superior expertise.

Ron Paul made news today at 12:40 pm when he was asked if he would endorse fellow Republican McCain. He said, "I could never endorse someone who said, 'Bomb, bomb, bomb Iran.'" Michelle Obama drew huge laughs while talking about what voters should look at when deciding whom to select. She said that they should take a hard look at the issues and that voters shouldn't say, *She's cute, so I'll vote for her.* There was a long pause as the audience grasped what she was saying. The implication was that she was obviously referring to Palin. She then said, "And I'm talking about me." The audience erupted. Meanwhile, her husband was in New Mexico telling voters, "Our destiny isn't written for us—it's written by us." I hope this will be the case. One gets the feeling that Obama's destiny is being written by the press. Even Karl Rove still has enough power to steer the media in a direction that may eventually undermine Obama. One has to wonder if the press will subconsciously take their cues from him. Rove recently said that McCain was running ads that were not 100% true. Keith Olbermann used that Rove comment against Republicans, but I thought of it as mysterious bate. I trust nothing Rove says and am certain that that comment was designed to confuse Democrats. He is playing devil's advocate when he writes **Obama Needs to Sell Himself, Not Attack McCain** in today's *The Wall Street Journal*:

> The idealism and discipline that led to Mr. Obama's early primary victories has been replaced by unattractive attacks on Mr. McCain. Both campaigns have engaged in a tit-for-tat, but because Mr. Obama ran on 'turning the page' on 'old politics,' he suffers more than Mr. McCain, especially since his attacks are more fundamentally unfair. It is a mistake for Mr. Obama to spend a lot of time attacking Mr. McCain.
>
> In a revealing slip in an interview with ABC recently, Mr. Obama said, 'If we're going to ask questions about who has been promulgating negative ads that are completely unrelated to the issues at hand, I think I win that contest pretty

handily.' That he is in fact winning the contest for the most negative campaign could well spell his defeat.

So much for minunderstanding Obama's meaning. For Rove, winning at negative ads means having more; for Obama it means having fewer. Rove knows that this financial crisis is a complete loser for McCain. He knows that if Obama continues to run ads that point out McCain's terrible track record on regulation, Obama will begin to pull away. Rove knows that appealing to Obama's high mindedness is the only hope the Republicans have of avoiding the inevitable. If the shoe were on the other foot, Rove would attack Obama until the cows come home. How he loves to turn someone's integrity against them. That, for him, is the stuff glee is made of. Again, Rove knows that if Obama continues to attack McCain on the economy, the Republicans will lose. Rove is trying to run his game on the Democrats. Don't fall for it, Obama! When Obama said earlier, "John McCain can't decide whether he's Barry Goldwater or Dennis Kucinich," one had to wonder if McCain's confusion was coming as a result of a confusing message being whispered in his ear by the ever-calculating Karl Rove.

DAY 26
"SPARE US THE LECTURES"

Obama is campaigning in Coral Gables, Florida, today—Friday, September19 —while McCain is in Green Bay, Wisconsin. "My friends, this is the problem with Washington. People like Senator Obama have been too busy gaming the system and haven't ever done a thing to actually challenge the system. We've heard a lot of words from Sen. Obama over the course of this campaign. But maybe just this once he could spare us the lectures, and admit to his own poor judgment in contributing to these problems. The crisis on Wall Street started in the Washington culture of lobbying and influence peddling, and he was right square in the middle of it." These were the poetic words of John McCain this morning from Green Bay, Wisconsin. On a day that sees the country in a complete economic panic, McCain is busy blaming the entire crisis on Obama. Instead of chastising McCain, Obama said, "John McCain and I can continue to argue about our different economic agendas for next year, but we should come together now to work on what this country urgently needs this year.…. This isn't a time for fear or panic. This is a time for resolve and for leadership. I know we can steer ourselves out of this crisis. That's who we are. That's what we've always done as Americans."

A new Marist College Institute Poll shows Obama leading McCain 50% to 41% in Michigan. According to the same poll, he's up 45% to 42% in Pennsylvania, and the two are tied in Ohio. At 12:53 pm, Norah O'Donnell said, "In Ohio I would have thought that Obama would have opened up a little bit more of a lead." Out of Michigan, Ohio, and Pennsylvania, O'Donnell chose to focus on the Buckeye state. Why? She didn't bother offering the same critique of McCain being behind in Michigan. I wouldn't have thought McCain would be being blown out in this state, Mrs. O'Donnell. Focus on that.

It is well understood that the *Wall Street Journal* is conservative, but both Democrats and Republicans respect the newspaper for its credibility. As of 2007, the paper had a worldwide daily circulation of more than two million, with approximately 931 thousand paying online subscribers. That is a lot of people. It's disappointing to see the *Wall Street Journal* give Karl Rove and Rush Limbaugh a place to spew their vitriol. Rush Limbaugh is up in arms about a recent ad that Obama ran. The ad is in Spanish and links McCain to Limbaugh on the issue of immigration. A Spanish speaking man can be heard saying the following in the Obama ad: "They want us to forget the insults we've put up with . . . the intolerance . . . they made us feel marginalized in this country we love so much." This incensed Limbaugh, who claimed that Obama knew that McCain had disagreed with him on the issue of immigration. McCain has actually changed his position on immigration and pressure from Limbaugh and other conservatives was a big reason why. Limbaugh writes **Obama Is Stoking Racial Antagonism** in today's *Wall Street Journal*:

I understand the rough and tumble of politics. But Barack Obama—the supposedly post partisan, post racial candidate of hope and change—has gone where few modern candidates have gone before.

Mr. Obama's campaign is now trafficking in prejudice of its own making. And in doing so, it is playing with political dynamite. What kind of potential president would let his campaign knowingly extract two incomplete, out-of-context lines from two radio parodies and build a framework of hate around them in order to exploit racial tensions? The segregationists of the 1950s and 1960s were famous for such vile fear-mongering.... We've made much racial progress in this country. Any candidate who employs the tactics of the old segregationists is unworthy of the presidency.

The Wall Street Journal should remember that Limbaugh is the man who rolled out a parody labeling Obama "The Magic Negro." This is also the same man who was fired for racist remarks he made on *ESPN*. He said the following about Donovan McNabb, an African American NFL quarterback: "Sorry to say this, I don't think he's been that good from the get-go. I think what we've had here is a little social concern in the NFL. The media has been very desirous that black quarterbacks do well. There is a little hope invested in McNabb, and he got a lot of credit for the performance of this team that he didn't deserve. The defense carried this team." On October 2, 2003, *ESPN.com* news services reported, "In the wake of his controversial statements regarding Eagles quarterback Donovan McNabb, Rush Limbaugh has resigned from his position on ESPN's Sunday NFL Countdown pregame show." The *Wall Street Journal* also should not forget that Limbaugh imitated actor Michael J. Fox's Parkinson's symptoms and intimated that Fox had been exaggerating the effects of the disease while filming a commercial. They should not forget what *Media Matters* reported on June 21, 2004: "Radio host Rush Limbaugh lied about a recently released report by the 9/11 Commission. He falsely claimed that the report confirms Vice President Dick Cheney's claim that September 11 hijacker Mohamed Atta may have met with an Iraqi intelligence officer in April 2001. Limbaugh directly contradicted the report while purporting to summarize it." I guess the *Wall Street Journal* is less concerned about their credibility and more interested in turning their paper over to Limbaugh to use as a bully pulpit. Regardless of what Limbaugh says about the Obama ad, it rings hallow to those of us who have heard him repeatedly demean far too many Americans.

McCain gained Limbaugh's endorsement only because he caved on his original immigration position. On August 2, 2007, FOX News reported:

> Republican presidential hopeful John McCain on Thursday backed a scaled-down proposal that imposes strict rules to end illegal immigration but doesn't include a path to citizenship. The move away from a comprehensive measure is

an about-face for the Arizona senator, who had
been a leading GOP champion of a bill that
included a guest worker program and would
have legalized many of the estimated 12 million
illegal immigrants in the U.S. It failed earlier
this year….McCain's immigration position has
been a campaign liability among Republican
voters and hurt his efforts to raise money. Other
GOP presidential candidates, fellow Arizona
Republicans, and immigration opponents
throughout the country have loudly decried his
position.
Observers said McCain's switch was political. 'He
recognizes his position on the issue is killing
him,' said Steven Camarota, research director at
the Center for Immigration Studies, which favors
vigorous immigration enforcement.

As I have previously mentioned, the *Wall Street Journal* has
also been far too willing to let Karl Rove muddy the political
waters. They should remember the almost irreparable
damage this man has done to the sanctity of our legislative
branch of government. On May 13, 2008, the *Associated Press*
reported: "A House Judiciary Committee deadline passed
Monday with former White House adviser Karl Rove standing
by his refusal to testify about allegations that he pushed the
Justice Department to prosecute former Alabama Gov. Don
Siegelman." On July 10, 2008, CNN reported, "Karl Rove,
President Bush's longtime political guru, refused to obey an
order to testify before a House Judiciary Committee hearing

Thursday. Rove's lawyer asserted that Rove was 'immune' from the subpoena the committee had issued, arguing that the committee could not compel him to testify due to 'executive privilege.' *The Wall Street Journal* believes that Rove, above and beyond his executive privilege, should be given *journalistic privilege* and this does not bode well for Barack Obama. They are giving far too much power to two Right Wing men who feel that they are entirely above the law and refuse to show any respect for the Constitution of the United States. These are two men who are staunch deregulators and adherents of that old trickle down philosophy that has the nation's economy gasping for air today, not to mention a Constitution listed in critical condition for the last few years, partially because of the train wreck they each did all in their considerable power to cause.

The *Associated Press* reports today: "Struggling to stave off financial catastrophe, the Bush administration on Friday laid out a radical bailout plan with a jaw dropping price tag—a takeover of a half-trillion dollars or more in worthless mortgages and other bad dept held by tottering institutions." Both candidates are treating the crisis as a jump ball of sorts. Whoever can control this issue will likely surge forward in the polls. McCain tried to get the upper hand by rolling out a plan to address the immediate market woes today. The press is treating McCain as the responsible one for making such a quick move. They seem to be less concerned with the probability that the plan was put together entirely too fast to have any real validity. A reporter asked Obama if he was standing on the sidelines while McCain was putting forward an immediate plan. Obama said that it was going to take more than a day to put an appropriate plan together. He said, "I will refrain from presenting a more detailed blue-print of how an immediate plan might be structured until I can fully review the details of the plan proposed by the Treasury and the Federal Reserve." This responsible, Presidential-sounding language was not enough to keep the media from piling on Obama today. They have managed to paint him as an unwilling-to-take-action kind of person. I guess they like George Bush's style after all, which does not bode well for the introspective, smart, and forward- thinking Obama.

DAY 27
THE MOST LIBERAL SENATOR?

Obama is campaigning in Daytona Beach, Florida, today—Saturday, September 20—while McCain is delivering a weekly radio address from Green Bay, Wisconsin. When a person running for the Vice Presidency of the United States is caught red-handed telling a series of lies, it is time to question the judgment of any individual willing to vote for that person. Sarah Palin has been saying for two weeks now that she told Congress "Thanks but no thank on that bridge to nowhere." She has continued to also tell America that her state supplies 20% of the country's energy supply. She has continued to tell us that she fired her personal chef and continues to intimate that she sold her jet on eBay. These claims have all been proven to be complete untruths, and the media has refused to paint her for exactly what she is: a liar. It's not enough for Anderson Cooper to keep running his silly little Keeping Them Honest segment. It's also not enough for these non-confrontational fact-check organizations to come on the major news networks and say things like, *Well, we looked into that and it indeed looks like Palin is only being partially correct, and we've also looked into McCain's comments and they are factually incorrect.* This is entirely too nice and does nothing to grab the attention of most Americans, who evidently need to be hit over the head with a two-by-four in order to listen to the truth. We need someone to start running segments that include dramatic music, dark lighting, and mug shots of Palin and McCain that scare the living tar out of people. People need to be scared of individuals who will habitually lie to their faces. CNN would be within their rights to be running a segment that says, *We just want you to be completely aware that a vote for McCain-Palin is a vote for two individuals who have been caught looking you squarely in the eyes and lying.*

Whose job is it to scold Palin for the audacious lies she continues to peddle? I am finding it more and more difficult to listen to her and McCain talk in platitudes, accusing Obama for every single problem the nation faces. This financial crisis is just the latest issue they are blaming him for. McCain had been saying that Obama's problem was his limited amount of time in Washington, yet now he is claiming that Obama is part of the Washington old boys network that got us into this mess. How can the media air this without comment? McCain still hasn't apologized for lying on the *View*—not kind of fudging the facts—not waffling—not telling a half- truth. He looked Barbara Walters right in her 78-year-old face and lied. When he said that Palin had not requested any earmarks while governor, that was a lie. How is the press allowing him to get away with it? It is more than unacceptable; it's incompetence!

The *Associated Press* got in a few unprovoked jabs on Obama today. Christopher Wills writes, "For a man known as a powerful speaker, Obama has rarely wowed people in political debates. He can come across as lifeless, aloof, and windy." Wills' article is entitled **Which Obama Will Show up for Presidential Debates?** I have never considered Obama lifeless nor met anyone who does. That is entirely too strong

THE MOST LIBERAL SENATOR?

an adjective. Did Wills conduct a poll showing conclusively that Obama rarely wowed debate viewers? Almost everything Obama has said wowed people. That's why he was able to defeat the Clinton power machine. Wills wasn't finished. He interviewed a professor named Timothy O'Donnell, who claimed that Obama has only recently become polished. Wills writes, "O'Donnell says staying on offense will be the key if Obama wants to shape the discussion and reach undecided voters. The Illinois senator failed to do that in what is often mentioned as his worst performance in a major debate, an April 16 confrontation with Clinton in Philadelphia." Wills says that it was in that debate that the moderators asked him questions about his former minister, his policy on flag lapel pins, and about rural people clinging to their guns and religion. I saw the debate in Philadelphia and never considered it his worst performance. I also believe that "failed" is entirely too strong a word to use regarding Obama's supposed inability to stay on offense back on April 16. But Wills has managed to put a question in people's minds about Obama. By even asking which Obama will show up, he has cast him as something he is not: a split personality. Obama has been anything but unsteady throughout the entire primary and general elections. It is McCain whom Wills should be asking this question of. Which McCain will show up? Will it be the so-called maverick, the compulsive liar, the new ultra-conservative, the sudden pro-regulation guy, or the new, bizarre-sounding populist? We can all take comfort in the fact that in six days Obama will show up at the first debate with a calm demeanor, an honest critique of his opponent, and a classy disposition. He will be anything but lifeless, aloof, or windy—all words that completely misrepresent Obama. What Wills calls lifeless, I call Obama's introspection. What he labels aloof, I call Obama's brilliant mind at work. And what he says is windy, I choose to call the expression of broad and in-depth thought. George Bush was aloof in that he was inaccessible. He was windy because he had inadequate vocabulary and poor syntax. And if you call Bush's talking with a Southern drawl while sporting a childish smirk during some of the most serious moments in political history "full of life," I'll take Obama's sophisticated—or if you prefer "lifeless"—personality any day of the week. All of these people who don't have the intellectual capacity to follow what Obama is saying think he is not a good debater. They're the same people who think George Bush won a debate against Al Gore!

CNN's "Truth Squad" is trying to prove that Obama also has lobbyists working for him. They have determined that he has one former lobbyist on his staff compared to McCain's seven. Obama's was a supposed unpaid advisor. Wow! The "Truth Squad" is presenting this as if it's a draw. Since when have seven paid former lobbyists to one unpaid advisor been considered a draw? They also used one source to supposedly confirm McCain's description of Obama as the Senate's most liberal member. Why was CNN willing to brand Obama the most liberal member of the Senate based on information from one source? The tag is far too politically damaging for them to throw up on the screen in such a nonchalant way. Obama himself has said that this "most liberal" tag is entirely too loosely defined. Unfortunately, the segment called

"Most Liberal" that CNN ran tonight was poorly researched, painfully vague, and effectively damaging.

The Bush administration asked Congress today for the power to buy $700 billion in toxic assets. Julie Hirschfeld and Deb Riechmann of the *Associated Press* write, "The rescue plan would give Washington broad authority to purchase bad mortgage-related assets from U.S. financial institutions for the next two years. It does not specify which institutions qualify or what, if anything, the government would get in return for the unprecedented infusion." The media is still clamoring to hear whether or not Obama will endorse the Bush administration's actions. If he agrees, they'll likely say he doesn't have any ideas of his own. If he disagrees, he will be called an opportunist—bucking the system again for his own political gain—disrespectful of the hardworking men who slaved over the plan.

Today, Jonathan Alter, on *Newsweek.com,* summed up, in one paragraph of a lengthy article, the bizarre behavior that McCain has displayed this week:

> John McCain's whole campaign is based on the idea that Barack Obama is risky, untested and can't be trusted to protect the nation in a crisis. But this week it was McCain who seemed un-Presidential, as his Zigzag Express swerved back and forth across the median strip. His approach to the greatest financial crisis since 1933 was erratic and off-key. Would his presidency be any different?

Alter has been one of the few journalists to provide a breath of fresh air in the polluted media atmosphere—and a rare touch of reason. He manages to consistently tell the truth, unlike FOX News' Fred Barnes who said today that he didn't "fault Obama for being tentative" as it relates to coming out with an immediate response to the week's market crash. Barnes said it in a way that suggested that Obama was scared. Choosing to be thorough is not tentative. Mr. Barnes seems to believe that McCain was able to solve, in 24 hours, problems the brightest economists in the country haven't been able to figure out for months—how to revive our economy. McCain has changed his position on how to respond to the crisis this week more times than I can count. If Barnes is willing to call Obama tentative, he should be willing to accuse McCain of lurching. McCain's latest lie has also managed to escape the interest of the corporate media. It came in the form of a response to an Obama accusation—an accusation that was true. From Daytona Beach, Florida, Obama said, "If my opponent had his way, the millions of Floridians who rely on it would've had their Social Security tied up in the stock market this week. Millions would've watched as the market tumbled and their nest egg disappeared before their eyes." McCain responded by calling Obama's claim "a desperate attempt to gain political advantage using scare tactics and deceit." One problem: the accusation is based in fact because McCain wants to partially privatize Social Security. For McCain to accuse Obama of deceit is a lie. He's not deceiving anyone—he's telling the truth. McCain won't truthfully defend his own positions; therefore, he's lying by virtue of denying.

DAY 28
A BOX OF FRUIT LOOPS

Obama is campaigning in Charlotte, North Carolina, today—Sunday, September 21—while McCain is in Baltimore, Maryland. Thomas Jefferson said, "I believe that banking institutions are more dangerous to our liberties than standing armies." If not our liberties, Mr. Jefferson, then at least our pocketbooks. Today, the headline on the front page of the *Los Angeles Times* read: **Bailout Tab: $700,000,000,000.** This is how much the Bush administration is asking Congress for to rescue the nation's economy. This morning, on CNN's *Late Edition*, Wolf Blitzer had one economic advisor from each campaign on his program. The two gentlemen, Douglas Holtz-Eakin and Austan Goolsbee, argued over several issues. Holtz-Eakin defended McCain for staffing his campaign with lobbyists. Austan claimed that Obama had dismissed former Fannie Mae lobbyist, Jim Johnson, from his campaign months ago. This fact wasn't enough to prevent Blitzer from saying that both campaigns were equally guilty of associating with Fannie Mae and Freddie Mac lobbyists. Blitzer's accusation isn't true. John McCain's campaign manager, Rick Davis, is still working for the campaign. When the media is forced to acknowledge McCain's overwhelming negatives, they, for some reason, invariably feel compelled to concoct some negatives for Obama to even things out. Austan got in a final jab as the subject switched to the economy.

Holtz-Eakin was trying to downplay his previous comment about McCain being a creator of the Blackberry. He touted McCain's supposed detailed economic plan. Austan told viewers to go right ahead and look at McCain's plan online. He said that you could read the back of a box of Fruit Loops and find more detail.

Later on CNN's Late Edition, Carville said that some of the things McCain has done during this campaign "shakes my faith I had in him." As for Biden, I wish the media would stop shaking things up when it comes to painting him as a gaff machine. All of the networks have done segments trying to portray Biden as a man who constantly puts his foot in his mouth. But every time they run the segments, the gaffs are few and far between. They make it sound as if he has made some of the most egregious comments known to man. He hasn't! He has made maybe two comments that I'm sure he wishes he could take back, but no more than any other politician. To hear the media tell it, Biden is completely out of control and off his rocker. It's another example of the media creating their own myth then referring to it as established history.

Tom Brokaw was at it again this morning on *Meet the Press*. Toward the end of a show focused on the economy, he showed the clip of McCain blaming Obama for the cataclysmic financial meltdown. Then he showed Obama defending himself. Brokaw managed to say immediately, in closing his program, that neither one of the candidates had distinguished themselves this week. It's as if Brokaw didn't even acknowledge the catastrophic week McCain had. McCain has managed to make one mistake after another since Monday whereas Obama's biggest flaw is that he said he wanted to wait and assess the situation after he has a chance to read the proposal the Bush administration puts forth. With one deft sentence, Brokaw managed to erase all of McCain's week filled with revising history and lightening fast flip-flops. He left his viewers with his opinion that both candidates have been equally undistinguished on this multi-billion dollar, unprecedented historical issue. Thanks for rewriting history for us, Mr. Brokaw. The facts of this week indeed do show that candidate McCain distinguished himself as a person who rushes to judgment then rushes to correct himself. If McCain had publicly shot Treasury Secretary Paulson this week and Obama was present but wanted to wait until the police had completed their investigation before making public comment, Brokaw, if in his usual form, would probably sum the incident up by saying, *Both candidates were involved at the scene of a crime this week.*

An article by the *Associated Press* today entitled **Poll: Racial Views Steer Some White Dems Away From Obama** explores the possibility that race may be a deciding factor in this election. Ron Fournier and Trevor Thompson write, "Deep-seated racial misgivings could cost Barack Obama the White House if the election is close, according to an AP-Yahoo News poll that found one-third of white Democrats harbor negative views toward blacks—many calling them 'lazy,' 'violent,' responsible for their own troubles." If the press decides to give a tremendous amount of weight to this poll—more than it warrants—it could spell trouble for Obama. I say trouble because I'm of the opinion that polls may suggest to voters how they should be feeling in order to fit in with their peers.

On ABC's *This Week* today, the issue was whether the Democrats would accept the Republican bailout with no strings attached. Sam Donaldson said, "To borrow a phrase from the late gonzo journalist Hunter Thompson, 'fear and loathing,' fear will trump loathing here. And my guess is that the Democrats who already are talking bravely about let's protect the guy who's losing or the gal who's losing her home, and let's put in the stimulus, are going to fold because when the administration says on Tuesday, 'You either got to pass this by late Thursday or Friday morning or we're going over the abyss....'" Donna Brazile interrupted Donaldson adding, "But the Democrats should not rush to rubberstamp this blank check..." Donaldson injected, "How many days do you want Donna?" Brazile answered, "You know, Sam, there are 44 days left before the election. What's the rush? This is seven hundred billion taxpayer's dollars. A year ago secretary Paulson argued that the subprime crisis was not serious. Today he goes up to Capital Hill and he's raised the alarm bell, so of course it's serious, but we should not rush to rubber stamp this without getting some transparency and some accountability put into this package." Donaldson made a stupid analogy to the German invasion of Poland. I get the feeling that Donaldson has a personal stake in this. Brazil could have also said that it was only seven years ago that George Bush and company argued that unless he was authorized to invade Iraq, we face the abyss of Saddam Hussein's weapons of mass destruction.

George Will, the reliably conservative-leaning voice said, "Sam, the very people who are telling us that they know for absolute certain there is a cliff right in front of us are the same people who have told us all along that what they had done the day before would stop what is going to happen—and did happen—the next day." Donaldson quipped, "You want to take a chance?" George Will shot back, "Well, this is all a chance, Sam, because what the government is going to do with all this money is to take over opaque and damaged assets. But the heart of this crisis is that no one knows who owes how much to whom...." As the discussion got more and more heated, the only one making an ounce of sense was Brazile, who said, " Is this the last shoe that will drop?" Donaldson interrupted and sarcastically said, "Well, I don't know, Donna!" Brazile finished her sentence with, "And what other sector will put us into deeper water next week?" Donaldson, with another smart-aleck remark sarcastically retorted, "Let's just wait and see, let's just hold everything here and see if we're gonna be all right." It was at this point that Brazile seemed to be thinking about an Obama administration and how this would affect it. She said, "With $700 billion, that means the next president will have hardly any options for universal healthcare, for job creation, that's the problem here."

As the argument continued, I couldn't help but think of what McCain had actually done this week. On Monday he said, "The fundamentals of our economy are strong." Later he backtracked and said that the fundamentals he was referring to were working Americans. As the week progressed he said that we could not bail out AIG. After the government did indeed bail them out, McCain claimed that it had to be done. Then when the market crashed, he became an instant re-regulator and a hard-nosed populist.

The one thing the entire *This Week* panel should have been able to agree on was that John McCain could not be trusted to keep his word on anything, regardless of the current state of the economy. But the panel continued discussing the financial crisis. George Will made the point that there will not, in fact, be enough money with which to pay for Obama's "expensive agenda". George Stephanopoulos countered that if these new government assets from the bailout could be resold for a profit, it might be worth it. The plan, however, would give unlimited power over the American economy to the Secretary of the Treasury, with no oversight whatsoever.

The day could not pass without someone in the press taking a huge swing at Obama. In an article entitled **The Incredible Shrinking Obama,** Rex Murphy of *The Globe and Mail* gave it his best shot:

> …Mr. Obama…has a kind of welcoming emptiness. Eager acolyte or stern observer, both find it difficult not to add or project, the most flattering, even jubilant, fill-ins. The Obama candidacy, in its rocket-blast phase when he outsoared Hillary Clinton, drained the dictionaries of every superlative….
>
> There's more than a gap between the 'audacity of hope' and 'lipstick on a pig'. The mouth that spoke the first phrase should not be capable of the second. He has shrunk into a combative partisan. He crowds his own screen, leaves less space for projection. Others are not writing his narrative now. He's inscribing his own.

Wrong, Mr. Murphy! You are writing his narrative for him. The fact that your baseless article appeared on the respectable site, *Real Clear Politics*, explains why Obama is quite skillfully fighting back, as pundits such as yourself try unsuccessfully to "shrink" him.

Did John McCain learn his lesson about telling lies this week? The answer is a resounding no! On *60 Minutes* today, Scott Pelley asked McCain about the negative ads he has been running. Pelley first tried to make it sound like both campaigns had been equally dishonest, which they most certainly haven't, by saying, "I have right here, research from an independent organization—here's a stack of falsehoods that the Obama campaign has told about your campaign and here's a stack of falsehoods the McCain campaign has told about the Obama campaign, and I wonder, in making these false claims, in advertising, how that squares with the campaign you promised to run and the man you promised to be?" McCain answered, "Well, thank you Scott, but I dispute that any of the spots that we have run are not fact based. This is a tough campaign. We understand that. But I believe our ads are factual and we, on our website, can document all of the spots we've made. But the larger problem here is, I agree with you, this campaign has gotten incredibly unpleasant to say the least." Pelley interrupted with, "You're telling me that there are no errors in fact in any of your advertising?" McCain replied, "I am telling you we can back up ever single piece that we have run with facts and a record." McCain then went on to pledge that all of his future ads, like the previous ones, will be fact based. The media should, but likely won't, make this a big story tomorrow.

DAY 29
FANNIE & FREDDIE

Obama is campaigning in Green Bay, Wisconsin, today—Monday, September 22—while McCain is in Scranton, Pennsylvania. John McCain isn't taking any media heat for having defended his ads yesterday. He also isn't getting any flack this morning for having said he didn't regret his past position on deregulation. He told Scott Pelley of *60 Minutes* last night, "I think the deregulation was probably helpful to the growth of our economy." The media should be making this a top story today because after that comment, McCain has absolutely no credibility when it comes to his sudden call for regulation. The press can't let this slide. Pelley later said, "You're not an expert on the economy, Senator Obama is not an expert on the economy, so let me ask you what traits would you bring to the oval office that would help navigate this country out of the current emergency?" McCain was given an opportunity to ramble on about why he knew the economy well. The problem with Pelley's question is that he asserts that Obama is not an expert on the economy. How does he know this? Obama hasn't even been given the opportunity to prove himself as a leader on the economy yet, and it will be important for the media to refrain from branding him an economic neophyte or an expert prematurely.

A new Suffolk poll shows Obama and McCain tied in Nevada at 46%. This is surprising as Nevada consistently votes Republican. I am waiting for the media to tell us how impressive this makes Obama look in Nevada, but it's not happening. Instead, they're letting the McCain camp continue to spin information. MSNBC's Contessa Brewer had Tucker Bounds of the McCain camp on this morning at 9:47. Bounds claimed that McCain originally said he'd ask for the SEC chairman to resign if he were President. Bounds lied because McCain actually said he would fire him. Brewer never challenged Bounds on this rewritten statement.

Mitt Romney was on MSNBC at 3:00 pm today and responded to Obama's claim that McCain was a supporter of deregulation. He said, "While Barack Obama was sitting on the sidelines, John McCain was calling for new reform" as it relates to Fannie Mae and Freddie Mac. David Gregory didn't debunk the comment outright. The comment was allowed to float and will likely morph into an assumed truth if the media doesn't make clear that Obama hasn't been "sitting on the sidelines."

Austan Goolsbee, an Obama advisor, was on with Gregory. He defended Obama's history of calling for economic reform and said that the bailout should not be a blank check for Wall Street. David Gregory tried to challenge him by asking, "Who's going to be the strongest voice in his ear" when it comes to advising him on the economy?" Gregory continued: "And might he keep Secretary Paulson on...and is Paulson doing the job that needs to be done?" Austan said that Warren Buffet along with many others was advising him but that Obama himself was the main voice on the economy. Austan never said whether or not Paulson would stay on under Obama, but Gregory tried to push for an answer, almost as if he were needling him to say yes. Gregory's interview seemed to be geared toward proving that Obama couldn't possibly handle this economic situation without the help of Paulson and many others.

Chris Matthews asked Pat Buchanan today if Obama was close to taking control of the race, especially if he passes the foreign policy threshold this Friday during the debate. Buchanan jokingly said that it depends on whether or not Obama shows that he's capable and competent as opposed to some strange liberal. Matthews took this as a joke and laughed it off, but Buchanan was simply disguising his opposition to Obama with humor—humor designed to remind conservatives not to fall for Obama and remember that he's a liberal you can't trust.

When will the corporate media put an end to this Fannie Mae and Freddie Mac talk? One day McCain is accusing Obama of taking millions from them and the next Obama is tying McCain to them. But an interesting fact came out today: John McCain's campaign manager, Rick Davis, was outted by *The New York Times* for having formerly been on the payroll of Fannie and Freddie, and he was paid a reported $35 thousand a month. He ended up making two million dollars total. The fact that the *The New York Times* broke this news has the McCain camp incensed. They accused the paper of no longer being a journalistic enterprise. But the campaign never debunked the report that Davis had indeed been paid $2 million. Had a similar fact come out about his campaign manager, David Axelrod, the media would be raking Obama over the coals, McCain would be calling for Obama to fire Axelrod, and the press would deliver his message with round-the-clock coverage. I'm sure members of the press would also echo McCain's request, forcing Obama to take immediate action as his poll numbers dipped. What probably wouldn't happen, unlike the way McCain is handling the story about Rick Davis, is Obama blaming the press for reporting the story. McCain is not upset with his manager, he's upset at the press for having the temerity to do their jobs rather than being totally loyal to their corporate brothers. The fact is that McCain shouldn't have the audacity to say another word to Obama about Fannie or Freddie, but he probably will, and the press will let it slide.

The magician, David Blane, is currently trying to set a record for hanging upside down for 62 hours. Anderson Cooper just had to tell us what he thinks about Blane by saying that he was "sick of him." Cooper is sick of Blane, and I am sick of Cooper. Tonight he had Ed Rollins on his program, and Cooper said that at least McCain had come out with a list of potential people who would be advising him on the economy. Cooper also suggested that McCain was being more specific than Obama. He then added that Obama had not listed any economic advisors and asked Rollins, a Republican strategist of all things, "What has Obama misjudged here?" OBJECTION, YOUR HONOR! ANDERSON COOPER IS LEADING HIS REPUBLICAN STRATEGIST! Oh, sorry, Anderson. I temporarily forgot there is no hope for justice on your show. Rollins then proceeded to undress Obama by claiming that he should have gone up to the Capitol and met with members of Congress regarding this financial mess. Rollins said that then Obama would have looked like a leader. Cooper really set this one up for Rollins to knock out of the park, and he did just that. How dare Cooper ask such a leading question! No one but Cooper is assuming that Obama has misjudged anything. If Cooper wants to pretend he is an actual journalist, he should, at the very least, have asked Rollins "whether" Obama had misjudged anything.

McCain told Meredith Viera of the *Today* show that his economic advisor Carly Fiorina was somehow different from the other CEOs he has been lambasting for taking huge severance packages. Viera asked him how that was possible. He said that Fiorina, who took a $42-50 million severance package when she left Hewlett-Packard, was a good employee. He then rambled on but never managed to make sense of this completely hypocritical and paradoxical position regarding CEO golden parachutes.

Anderson Cooper's "Keeping them Honest" segment was misleading again tonight. Randi Kaye did a confusing piece that left the viewer feeling that possibly both campaigns are equally full of Fannie and Freddie lobbyists. She tried to equate the confirmed breaking news that McCain campaign manager Rick Davis is on Freddie Mac's payroll to unconfirmed rumors that David Axelrod got money from Cablevision. Wait a minute. Is she saying Cablevision is a part of the Wall Street meltdown along with Fannie Mae? In the same piece, Ms. Kaye shows parts of a McCain campaign ad accusing Franklin Raines, former CEO of Fannie, of being an Obama campaign advisor, a claim that both Obama and Raines say is an out-and-out lie. How is this keeping anybody honest when all it does is confuse the viewers, leaving them believing that Obama campaign manager Axelrod has been an unconfirmed yet somehow suspicious Cablevision employeee and therefore is as tainted as Rick Davis, a confirmed Freddie Mac lobbyist?

DAY 30
PLAYING THE AYERS' CARD

Obama is campaigning in Clearwater, Florida, today—Tuesday, September 23—while McCain is in Strongsville, Ohio. On FOX News this morning, Laura Bush spoke of the impending end of the Bush tenure in the White House, saying that it will be nice to get back to normal life. She described how maybe George will be grilling on the back porch while she is in the kitchen cooking. Barack Obama wrote *The Audacity of Hope*. Someone should write a book called *The Audacity of the Bushes*. For her to even mention how nice it will be to get back to normal life after the severe damage her husband has done to this country is audacious, to say the least. Larry McMurtry had it right. "Incompetents invariably make trouble for people other than themselves." Let's just recap here for a moment. While he has been President, we have suffered through the complete mishandling of 9/11, the War in Iraq, Hurricane Katrina, and now the worst financial crisis since the Great Depression. As Rachel Maddow put it, just one of these catastrophes being mishandled the way Bush did would be enough to brand any other Presidency a complete and utter disaster.

Sarah Palin has managed to finagle her way out of facing any media scrutiny over her involvement in "Troopergate." Her husband has refused to respond to a subpoena and Palin herself has taken no questions on the issue. I'm trying to imagine what life would be like right now for Michelle Obama if she were refusing to respond to a subpoena. The media would most certainly cover the story with more voracity. They covered her with voracity when she simply said something perceived to be unpatriotic. Refusing to testify in a case involving her husband's alleged abuse of power would certainly draw the ire of the media.

At 10:22 am, David Gregory discussed Palin's meetings with foreign leaders at the U.N. today. He just had to remind us that this was no different from Obama's going overseas recently to meet leaders. Gregory, of course, said it in a way that was defending Palin. There is a general feeling that these Palin meetings are a bit silly, so Gregory's tone was designed to beat back some of that speculative feedback from the media and everyday Americans regarding Palin's crash course in foreign policy. Gregory failed to mention McCain's recent visit to South America—a trip designed to shore up his expertise in the Western Hemisphere.

Lawmakers are scrambling to hammer out a financial crisis bill while holding a bailout hearing this morning on Capitol Hill. Sen. Jon Tester asked Treasury Secretary Paulson and others at the hearing why Congress was only being allowed one week to respond to this enormous financial problem. He asked why he and his colleagues hadn't been made aware of it sooner.

John McCain was busy defending Carly Fiorina again today. He said, "She is a role model for millions of young Americans. I'm proud of her record." The question I have is *Is he proud of his own?* How can he rail against CEOs and at the same time praise Fiorina, a person who thinks he—a long time senator—could not do her job? Joseph Pulitzer said in 1878, "The money power has grown so great that the issue of all issues is whether the corporation shall rule this country or the country shall again rule the corporation." It's evident that with John McCain in charge the corporations will continue to rule—not to mention the corporate media.

Today at 2:32 pm, FOX News ran a headline that read, **What Was Obama's Relationship With William Ayers?** They then did a two-minute segment trying to link Obama to Ayers in some kind of substantial way, but they categorically failed to do so. FOX News is obsessed with Obama's relationship with Ayers, but they have never been able to gain any traction on linking the two in any damaging way. They want the relationship to hurt and possibly sink Obama's campaign, but it isn't. Their coverage of Ayers is becoming completely comical because no reputable news outlet has wasted any time on the former Weather Underground member. FOX News' segment showed one of their reporters trying to get an interview with Ayers only to have him say, "No, no, no, I'm not talking to FOX News." In the segment, Obama said that Ayers is "someone who lives in my neighborhood who did something I deplore 40 years ago." Ayers and Obama sat on a college board together and have been friendly toward one another, but FOX News seems to think that they can uncover more. Maybe they are ignorant enough to believe that back when Ayers supposedly carried out some of his violent acts with The Weather Underground, Obama, as a seven-year-old, was in on the act. FOX News also ran an advertisement for Greta Van Susteren's upcoming show that asked, **Why is Obama Losing Ground?** There is not a current national poll in the country that shows him losing ground. FOX News is getting harder and harder to cover. CNN, CBS, ABC, NBC and MSNBC have all been subjected to my scrutiny, and though I have critiqued FOX News as well, I am inclined to put them in a different category altogether—the category of lowbrow news entertainment and unapologetic spin.

This afternoon, Chris Matthews asked the *Politico's* Jonathan Martin, "Is Obama too professorial—too detached" when it comes to debating? I'd like to ask Chris Matthews a few questions. Was Obama too professorial to defeat Hillary Clinton? Was he too professorial to draw two hundred thousand people to come see him in Germany? Was he too professorial to have your colleague, Pat Buchanan, say that his Denver speech was the greatest political speech he'd ever heard? Was he too detached to recognize that the War in Iraq would be a mistake? Was he too detached to inspire the most powerful grassroots uprising in American political history? If being professorial and detached leads one to the kinds of successes Obama has achieved so far, order me up some "professorial" and "detached."

Obama spoke to the media today in Florida regarding the government bailout. He said, "This is not welfare for Wall Street CEOs." He also added, "The American people should share in the upside as Wall Street recovers." Obama laid out four principles that must be met in the bailout: no CEO golden parachutes, independent oversight, taxpayers share in upside, help homeowners avoid foreclosures. Is that specific enough for the media? Probably not.

On MSNBC, Howard Dean said, "The McCain campaign has deteriorated into a dishonorable campaign." Dean then claimed that McCain was "hot headed and irascible." Dean could have quoted Paul Valery who decades ago said, "A Man who is of sound mind is one who keeps the inner madman under lock and key." McCain will have to use all of the restraint he can muster up this Friday in order to keep from blowing his top during the debate. He'll probably blow a gasket and the press will spend all of next week telling us how unfair it was for Obama to push his buttons.

The media got upset today at the McCain camp because they wouldn't allow reporters in to cover Palin's sit-downs with foreign leaders at the U.N. There was a one-hour delay before one of her meetings could take place because the press, even members of FOX News, threw a fit about not being allowed in to cover the meeting. Palin's camp finally succumbed to pressure, but only allowed the press to come in for 30 seconds to cover her talk with Henry Kissinger. It was nothing more than a photo op, and this is all just a continuation of McCain flexing his muscles and strong-arming the media. The media should be holding McCain accountable for his refusal to allow press members to interview Palin consistently, but they're not. I am waiting for one of the major networks to run a scathing story on McCain and Palin that holds them accountable and scolds them for their unwillingness to talk freely to the press. Why are they going after Obama and Biden instead of the people who are allowing no access to the press? Today, McCain gave his first press conference in over a month.

This evening on MSNBC, Andrea Mitchell talked about her early career—back when there were only three networks— prior to cable. She said that during the Reagan Presidency, a representative from each network was allowed into the private meetings with foreign leaders. She said that when cable came along, that number grew to five or six people being allowed in. As cable grew, it was decided that only one person would be allowed in to represent the entire press corp. Mitchell said that we have never been allowed "zero" people in. The position taken by the Palin camp—to not allow anyone in—is unprecedented and was met with complete anger by the press. A spokesperson for the Palin camp has since apologized for what she called a "mix-up." Mitchell said that the McCain camp would probably still keep the upper hand when it comes to getting access to Palin. She said that this policy is largely due to the fact that voters tend to take Palin's side when there is any kind of perceived feud going on between the media and Palin. If Mitchell's comment is any indication of how the greater press will respond to the Palin episode today, we can expect the media to continue treating her with kid gloves in hopes of getting that precious access.

Bush spoke at the U.N. today along with Iran's Mahmoud Ahmadinejad. The mainstream media largely ignored Bush's comments, but Ahmadinejad was front and center. He was Larry King's guest today and said, among other things, that Bush had lost a lot of opportunities to meet with him. He said that he had no preference for Obama or McCain. He was interested in what policies they wanted to pursue. He said he wanted to debate McCain and Obama in public, before the press.

He should know that the reason neither candidate wants to talk to him is because a policy he has said he would like to pursue is wiping Israel off the face of the map. King asked him if he considered himself a controversial figure. He said that he will always defend the rights of his nation. King asked, "Are you glad that the U.S. helped get rid of Sadaam Hussein?" He said that he might have been but the U.S. decided to stay in Iraq. He asked King if he would have been happy with that.

Katie Couric interviewed Joe Biden today and asked him what he thought about the ad Obama ran against McCain showing him as computer illiterate. Biden said that he didn't like the ad. The media is now trying to suggest that there may be a rift between Obama and Biden. FOX News even suggested that Clinton might be getting ready to replace Biden. Obama can't afford to have any gaffs from his surrogates, let alone his VP, because the press will pounce on him with force—something they have been reluctant to do to McCain.

Newsweek confirmed today that McCain Campaign Manager Rick Davis had worked for Freddie Mac as late as last month. As I mentioned yesterday, this is a story that should eliminate all talk coming from the McCain camp about Obama's relationship to Fannie and Freddie. The media could be asking McCain whether he plans to fire Rick Davis. If this were David Axelrod, I can just imagine Sean Hannity, Anderson Cooper, or David Gregory asking, *Isn't it a conflict of interest for Obama to keep Axelrod in charge of running his campaign, and what does this say about the type of President Obama will be, and how much credibility will he take into the Oval Office?* But with McCain no such questions are raised. None!

A new *LA Times/Bloomberg* poll shows Obama leading McCain 48% to 35% on the issue of who voters trust to get us out of this financial crisis. I can't help but look forward to Sunday's *Meet the Press*. Will Mr. Brokaw beat us over the head with this newsworthy piece of information? You can take this answer to the bank: NO!

Anderson Cooper's "Keeping Them Honest" segment was completely misleading once again tonight. Sarah Palin is campaigning on the idea that she is against earmarks. Joe Biden is not using that as a campaign issue. But the *Keeping them Honest* team tried to say that though Biden has been poking fun at Palin for her bridge comments, he himself has asked for earmarks for a bridge. Cooper's report also emphasized that both Obama and Biden had voted for the Bridge to Nowhere. What they actually voted for was a nationwide Transportation Bill that included some of Alaska's pork projects. McCain voted Not Present. Earmarks are actually what keep America's infrastructure sound. Both Obama and Biden have not been hypocritical or lying about their requests for money for infrastructure and improvement projects. Cooper could do a similar report about every member of the Senate, if he wanted to be serious. But he should remember that none of those senators are running as the Republican VP and lying about having taken over a hundred million dollars worth of earmarks. That's the issue. Once again, Cooper has equated Palin and McCain's lie with Biden's request for money for his state, a part of his job description. If Palin had been running on the boast that she has dinner with her family every single night, that would be a good thing. But if it turned out that it wasn't true, that would make her a liar. If Biden then decided to poke fun at her for telling this lie, he would be well within his rights, even

PLAYING THE AYERS' CARD

if Anderson Cooper's *Keeping Them Honest* squad uncovered the fact that Biden himself doesn't have dinner with his own family every night. If Biden hasn't told that lie, he's not dishonest. If Anderson Cooper wants to keep them honest, he might want to start with comparing apples to apples, dogs to dogs, and pigs to pigs. Anderson Cooper doesn't have the discipline to keep anyone—including himself—honest. Note to Cooper: The dinner example was just a hypothetical. Joe Biden actually does ride the train home every night to have dinner with his family. Why should I need to explain simple logic to people at the very top of American media? Could it be because the most competitive, not the most qualified, rise to the top in corporate America?

DAY 31
"I'M SUSPENDING MY CAMPAIGN!"

Obama is campaigning in Dunedin, Florida, today—Wednesday, September 24—while McCain is in New York City. President Bush is scheduled to address the nation's economic troubles tonight. This move isn't giving anyone a particular sense of security. Laura Bush told America yesterday that she was looking forward to their time in office coming to an end so that she and George could go back to Texas. It is there where she imagines George grilling while she piddles around in the kitchen. Who can blame her? Considering the fact that she shared this dream with the entire nation yesterday on FOX News, it's nice to see George taking time out of his busy schedule to address the direst financial situation in over 70 years. I mean, think about it! He spent the last eight years fucking up the whole world and now he and Laura are going to go...BARBECUE? Are you kidding me?

According to the new polls, Americans are as pissed off as I am. A new *Washington Post/ABC* national poll shows Obama leading McCain 52% to 43%. This is the largest lead Obama has had since the general election campaign began. Joe Biden gave a major foreign policy speech today from Cincinnati. It went a long way toward convincing me that he has what it takes to begin cleaning up the Bush mess. A new *Wall Street Journal* poll shows that 64% percent of voters believe Biden is qualified to be president—40% say Palin is qualified.

Obama was speaking today from Florida about the sacrifices Americans are going to have to make because of this crisis. He said that people from all walks of life are going to have to come together—black, white, Native American, gay, straight, Republican, and Democrat. As he was speaking on CNN at 11:16 am, the network cut away in order to conduct an interview with Donald Trump. CNN seems to believe that hearing Donald Trump say that "This is a great time to buy a house," which he actually said, is more important than hearing our possible future President tell us how we need to work together to overcome these difficult times. Trump went on to say, "Not picking Hillary is hurting Obama right now." Trump also said, "I think he'll [McCain] be a great President."

Joe Biden's policy on the use of coal is to focus on creating clean coal technology. FOX News did a segment of Biden' so-called gaffs. They showed one of Joe's comments to a voter that he wanted no more coal in America except clean coal. They highlighted his phrase "no more coal in America" as his gaff but left off his caveat that future coal must be clean, meaning that it must be mined and burned using new technology that is not environmentally harmful. FOX's campaign to portray Biden as a gaff machine will need to do a better job of taking him out of context if they are to prove that his comments are indeed "gaffs". No one who knows Joe Biden, and that includes the coal states, will buy that he wants "no more coal in America."

At noon today, McCain decided to suspend his campaign and return to Washington, D.C. in order to deal with the economic crisis. This is the latest in a string of impulsive and odd moves by McCain. Within a week McCain has gone from saying that America's economic fundamentals are strong to now saying he must suspend his campaign. He is instability personified. He asked Obama to join him in suspending the campaign and also postponing Friday's debate. McCain found out today that he's down by nine points in a national poll, and perhaps he sees this move as a way to regain some political traction. Obama hasn't responded to McCain's request. There are two positions taking shape regarding McCain's decision. One view is that he is afraid to debate Obama and is politicizing the financial crisis. Another view is that McCain is showing leadership and putting politics aside. Congressman Rahm Emanuel said that the Iraq War is also still going on but we're not postponing that.

CNN has just reported that Obama feels that there is no reason to suspend the campaign or postpone Friday's debate. In fact, Obama himself has just stepped to the podium and said that this is exactly the time when Americans need to hear from the person who may be President in 40 days and will inherit this mess. Obama said that he called McCain this morning to suggest that the two issue a joint statement regarding how to deal with the financial crisis. Obama was left with the impression that the two would work together on a statement and then come out later in the day to present it. Instead, McCain spoke to Obama a few hours later and then went on television immediately. It was at that point that the country heard, for the first time from either candidate, information regarding any of these events, so it appeared that McCain was driving the entire issue. At that point, McCain said that he had spoken to Obama and was working with him on a joint statement and that he had decided to suspend his campaign and ask for the debate to be postponed. McCain conveniently left out the fact that Obama was the one who initiated the call this morning. McCain made it sound as if he was the one driving this entire joint statement issue. McCain said, "I have spoken to Senator Obama and have asked him to join me" regarding suspending the campaign and heading to Washington. Until Obama clarified this situation and told the country that it was he who had called for the joint statement, we had all been led to believe, by McCain himself, that he was taking the lead and asking Obama to join him—that he was being bipartisan and above politics. This misleading senario has stood for most of the day. We have sincce found out that it was the exact opposite that happened, and Obama was the leader on this. Obama said that he is in constant communication with members on the Hill and would be willing to head to Washington if they need him. He said that a President needed to be able to do more than one thing at a time. Obama added that both candidates have big jets with their campaign slogans plastered on the sides of them, and if they are needed in Washington on Friday, they can fly there from Mississippi and back if need be.

I am waiting for one single news anchor to ask, "Why is John McCain making it look as if he's the one asking Obama to join him when it was Obama who originally called him?" It is the press' job to sort out the messiness of this—to put the "who called whom" and initiated "what...when" in the right order. Instead, the media is allowing McCain, again, to muddy the waters and create mass confusion—confusion that serves him well on a day that sees him behind by nine points nationally.

The McCain campaign is trying to sell the media on the idea that it is time to put partisanship aside. On MSNBC, McCain's economic advisor, Douglas Holtz-Eakin, said that people don't want to see the candidates side by side at a debate in the midst of a financial crisis. The debate commission has just come out and said that they intend to move forward as scheduled with the debate. This isn't stopping people like Lou Dobbs from saying this evening that by suspending his campaign, McCain "is filling a leadership void." If that isn't a ringing endorsement of McCain from the self proclaimed Mr. Independent, I don't know what is.

As this debate postponement idea is being mulled over by the press, it is becoming glaringly obvious that McCain is politicizing this financial crisis situation. The media needs to present this ruse for what it is—McCain carrying out the latest in a series of panicky ploys. The obvious political tactics that McCain is employing are being met with far too much acceptance by the mainstream media. If Obama had been the one calling for delaying the debate after just finding out that his poll numbers had dipped, the press would be claiming that he was afraid to talk to the American people during a time that requires leadership from our candidates. Republican Senator Orrin Hatch of the finance committee told Chris Matthews that McCain is willing to lose the race. He said that all of the candidates ought to come back to Washington. He said that McCain is "willing to risk being President" in order to solve this financial mess.

This afternoon, radio host Randi Rhodes, talked about an article the conservative columnist George Will wrote in the *Washington Post* regarding McCain's sudden odd behavior. Part of what Will wrote in an article entitled **McCain Loses his Head** has the media buzzing. He writes, "It is arguable that, because of his inexperience, Obama is not ready for the presidency. It is arguable that McCain, because of his boiling moralism and bottomless reservoir of certitudes, is not suited to the presidency. Unreadiness can be corrected, although perhaps at great cost, by experience. Can a dismaying temperament be fixed?"

Even in paying a slight compliment to Obama, George Will manages to incorrectly peg Obama as unready. Will, a known conservative, has a way of completely knocking Obama down while pretending to take on his fellow Republican, McCain. But Will isn't telling a single person anything they don't already know about McCain. The fact that he is a hot head is news to no one and pointing it out is not going to suddenly lead conservatives to defect—especially considering the fact that Will asks an open-ended question about whether McCain's temperament can be "fixed"—while at the same time, casually asserting that electing Obama may cost us greatly. Will is clever, and knows that McCain can survive a hit regarding his temperament, but going after Obama indirectly is the most effective way he can come off as not being to heavy-handed. Will prides himself on being a serious professional as well as a conservative, and he knows that he can't afford to take on Obama the way FOX News does. He has to be creative. If Will had asked, "Can a person who has been lying for political gain be trusted," I might be willing to believe that Will was truly introducing a new McCain to fellow conservatives and asking them to think long and hard about whether to elect him. Instead, all we were told is that McCain is erratic, certain about everything, and hot tempered. I, for one, have always known this. In the end, it's possible George Will knows that McCain is a sinking ship politically and doesn't want his conservative ideas to sink along with him.

At a time when the nation is in the midst of a financial crisis due largely to lack of regulation, it is too much to ask of us to ignore John McCain's past involvement in the Keating Five scandal. The mainstream media has completely ignored it so far. Charles Keating served five years in prison for his part in the Savings and Loan Scandal in which depositors lost $285 million. The taxpayers seized Keating's Lincoln Savings and Loan to the tune of two billion dollars. Keating's American Continental Corporation had originally purchased Lincoln in 1984. Its net worth jumped from $1.5 billion to $5.5 billion. The growth was largely due to deregulation that had taken place in the early 80s, allowing S&Ls to make highly risky investments with depositors' money. Keating had made large contributions to various senators, including McCain, and some wondered if he had then asked those senators to deregulate his industry. He was convicted of securities fraud, racketeering, and conspiracy. McCain was one of the five senators brought up on ethics charges in relation to Keating and deregulation. Of the five, McCain was also the closest personal friend of Keating. The Senate Ethics Committee reprimanded McCain for "poor judgment."

Considering the fact that our current government is in the middle of deciding whether or not to bailout Wall Street, how can a candidate who was right in the middle of one of the most expensive government bailout scandals in history be skating by without the issue even being discussed? Now that McCain is fancying himself as a new fan of regulation, one would think that the media would be touching on the Keating Five—a scandal that would remind voters of the overt hypocrisy McCain is currently displaying. Perhaps it will come up soon. I doubt it. The American people have the right to know more about the Keating Five from the media—even if, in the end, they decide to vote for McCain anyway. Which journalist will have the courage to break free from the grip McCain has on the neck of the press, and talk about it?

President Bush addressed the nation this evening. He assured us that "ultimately or nation could experience a long and painful recession" if we don't pass the bailout bill. President Bush also asked McCain and Obama to meet him in Washington tomorrow at the White House, and both candidates have agreed. The overwhelming consensus among Democrats regarding McCain's insistence on heading to Capitol Hill is that it is not necessary, and even a distraction. Democrats say they have been busy hammering out the bill and that having the candidates show up would be awkward. Sen. Chuck Schumer said it would be like an artist finishing up his painting only to have someone walk in at the last minute and insist on adding his own few strokes. Whether or not McCain intends to stick to his guns, stay on Capitol Hill, and not show up to the debate on Friday, remains to be seen.

DAY 32
"HEY JOHN...YOU NEED A RIDE TO THE AIRPORT?"

Obama is in Washington, D.C. today—Thursday, September 25—while McCain is in New York City. "Frankly, we are going to have to interrupt a negotiating session tomorrow...to troop down to the White House for a photo op." This is what Congressman Barney Frank had to say last night regarding the President's call for members of Congress to meet with him today to discuss the bailout. The media is waiting to find out if McCain will have a change of heart and decide to attend the debate Friday.

The Democrats and Republicans have reached an agreement in principal for a bailout this morning, but negotiations are still under way. The media has managed to turn McCain's decision to suspend his campaign into a question about Obama's judgment. They are asking if Obama should have put politics aside as McCain did in order to deal with the economy. During times like these it becomes glaringly obvious that the late Tim Russert is sorely missed. He was a journalist who would not have allowed McCain to get away with these kinds of shenanigans. He would have insisted that Palin sit down and speak to him on *Meet the Press* or publicly wonder why. Ever since Russert passed away, it's as if members of the media have suddenly realized that they have no adult supervision and are running wild and breaking everything in the house. We need a grownup to make the children behave themselves. Russert would not have allowed the McCain camp to present Palin only as they wish without letting the media vet her by asking hard-hitting questions on a daily basis—questions that she hasn't been prepped for. Russert would have demanded that Palin answer questions. He simply would not have stood for this.

The media is giving very little attention to an interview Katie Couric did with Palin. Couric sat down with Palin and said, "...I'm just going to ask you one more time - not to belabor the point—specific examples in his 26 years of pushing for more regulation?" Palin answered, "I'll try to find you some, and I'll bring them to ya." Why isn't this a major story? Palin is the one who originally told Couric that McCain had shown many examples of being a regulator.

At 12:37 pm, MSNBC's Norah O'Donnell said that Warren Buffet, one of Obama's economic advisors, called this an "Economic Pearl Harbor." She then asked an Obama advisor, "If this is true, why wouldn't Barack Obama suspend his campaign." McCain's ability to control the media narrative is still on full display. O'Donnell's question is perhaps valid, but the more important point to be made is that Congress has the bill virtually finished, and McCain marching in to act as if he's the one who can save the day is ridiculous. He is obviously setting himself up to be the man who put politics aside and solved the Congressional gridlock—gridlock that perhaps he himself is causing.

The media is giving McCain a bit of a hard time over an appearance he cancelled yesterday with David Letterman. McCain called Letterman to tell him that he had to leave

New York City immediately in order to head to Washington. One problem: McCain was actually cancelling in order to do an interview with Katie Couric at the same time, and Letterman soon found this out. During the taping of his own show, Letterman and Keith Olbermann, McCain's last minute fill-in, watched live coverage of McCain being prepped on the set at CBS for his interview. Olbermann and Letterman joked and the audience laughed along. Letterman yelled at the studio big screen, "Hey John, I gotta question—you need a ride to the airport?" Not only did McCain do the Couric interview, he then stayed in New York last night and attended the Clinton Global Initiative this morning. Twenty-six hours later, he has arrived in Washington. So much for immediately!

Congress is still negotiating over the bailout. The President's meeting with Obama, McCain, and other Congressional leaders just ended, and Obama spoke to the media. He said, "We need to make sure taxpayers are treated as investors.... Main Street's still hurting, the fundamentals of our economy are not strong, and when you inject presidential politics into delicate negotiations," it's not helpful. He also said that doing things in the "spotlight" right now is not helpful. People have been waiting all day to find out if the debate will happen tomorrow night. Obama said, "I believe that the most important thing John McCain and I can do tomorrow...is to go to Mississippi and debate.... My hope is that the debate goes forward, and I intend to be there." Obama said that he will stay in Washington tonight and take part in the ongoing negotiations before heading to Mississippi tomorrow. He also intimated that trying to make sure you get credit for having been the one who brokered the deal should not be the issue. He didn't say whom he was referring to, but we can all take an educated guess.

At least fifteen McCain campaign offices around the country are fully operating, several not even aware that McCain has supposedly suspended his campaign. McCain representative Tucker Bounds, must not have gotten the memo on the campaign suspension because he was on television today giving his usual talking points. No one in the media asked him why he was still talking during the so-called "suspension."

Chris Rock was on *Larry King Live* today and did a better job of putting this entire campaign drama into perspective than any surrogates or journalists have been able to. He described McCain as a boxer who is about to be knocked out but is holding on to his opponent to keep from falling. He then transitioned into the Hillary and Obama drama. He said that Bill Clinton was failing to convincingly endorse Obama and that this was understandable considering whom he's married to. He said that it was difficult to watch Palin speak because the more she talks the more you begin to feel sorry for her. Rock was on his comedic game but Larry King couldn't seem to ask him anything that didn't involve black people. He even had the nerve to ask Rock if the menu would change when Obama becomes President. Rock appeared to be somewhat uncomfortable with the barrage of race-related questions King was bombarding him with. King asked Rock if he was proud that a black man would possibly be President. Rock said that he's proud because it's this particular man but that he wouldn't be proud if Flava Flave (an African

American rapper) became President. Rock said that he hoped the disgruntled Hillary supporters, especially the ones who were Democrats, would come around and support Obama because black people have "gone down in flames with white people" in the past. Chris Rock evidently got tired of this constant emphasis on Obama's race, but he seemed to cut Larry King some slack for his generational lack of sensitivity.

During this campaign, Larry King's commitment to his format regardless of what comes up in conversation is costing the Democrats. He typically has had two representatives from each party on the screen at the same time and allows them to take turns giving their talking points. Too often he, whether intentionally or not, allows the Republican talking head to go unchallenged. Tonight, he allowed Republican Michele Bachmann basically to blame Franklin Delano Roosevelt, Jimmy Carter, and Bill Clinton for the current financial crisis we are in. King personally never challenged her nor did he provide time for one of the Democrats to specifically beat back that charge—a charge so absurd that it demands an absolute and immediate rebuttal. Even when King managed to show a lighter side by showing a comedic segment regarding the Letterman-McCain dust up, there was a bold headline on the screen that read MCCAIN STANDS UP TO LETTERMAN. Perhaps the headline was supposed to say MCCAIN STANDS UP LETTERMAN. Nevertheless, it was a headline that presented McCain as a tough guy who took on Letterman, when he actually did nothing short of lying to him. I, like Chris Rock, will give Larry King the benefit of the doubt on the headline.

Paul Begala called President Bush a "high-functioning moron" at 7:20 pm on *Anderson Cooper 360*. I'm surprised he didn't stick to calling Sarah Palin one, because the more the media shows of her interview with Katie Couric, the more embarrassing it becomes. Couric asked Palin for clarification: "You've cited Alaska's proximity to Russia as part of your foreign policy experience. What did you mean by that?" Palin answered, "That Alaska has a very narrow maritime border between a foreign country, Russia, and, on our other side, the land-boundary that we have with Canada. It's funny that a comment like that was kinda made to … I don't know, you know … reporters." Couric fed her the word she was searching for by saying, "mocked?" Palin said, "Yeah, mocked, I guess that's the word, yeah." This would have been enough in itself to ruin Palin's performance, but she had more. Couric asked, "Have you ever been involved in any negotiations, for example, with the Russians?" Palin answered, "We have trade missions back and forth, we do. It's very important when you consider even national security issues with Russia. As Putin rears his head and comes into the air space of the United States of America, where do they go? It's Alaska. It's just right over the border. It is from Alaska that we send those out to make sure that an eye is being kept on this very powerful nation, Russia, because they are right there, they are right next to our state."

The more Palin begins to speak to the media, the more she mirrors George Bush in policy and ineptitude. She actually appears to be losing her confidence—perhaps a false confidence, born out of the positive response she garnered when she first took the stage at the convention.

Couric asked, "You don't think the United States is within its rights to express its position to Israel? And if that means second-guessing or discussing an option?" Palin said, "No, abso ... we need to express our rights and our concerns and ..." Couric interrupted, "But you said never second guess them." Palin then gave this startling answer:

> We don't have to second-guess what their efforts would be if they believe ... that it is in their country and their allies, including us, all of our best interests to fight against a regime, especially Iran, who would seek to wipe them off the face of the earth. It is obvious to me who the good guys are in this one and who the bad guys are. The bad guys are the ones who say Israel is a stinking corpse and should be wiped off the face of the earth. That's not a good guy who is saying that. Now, one who would seek to protect the good guys in this, the leaders of Israel and her friends, her allies, including the United States, in my world, those are the good guys.

Don't children use words like "good guys" and "bad guys?" If the media doesn't use this disastrous interview against the McCain camp, they should all be accused of stealing rather than earning their paychecks or of being puppets of a Republican-run press. I can't help but wonder if McCain will decide to remove Palin from the ticket. This is a person who will be a heartbeat away from the Presidency. Why do I keep expecting reason in this unreasonable political climate?

An article by William Kristol of the *Weekly Standard* entitled **A Presidential McCain**: *McCain's Bold Move Could Reframe the Election—and Win It* hit the press today. Kristol manages to present McCain as a hero:

> ...This year, for the first time in U.S. history, both major party nominees for president are sitting senators. The winner may be the one who can convince some portion of the electorate that he's less 'senatorial,' and more 'presidential,' than the other...That's why McCain's action Wednesday—announcing he would come back to Washington to try to broker a deal to save our financial system—could prove so important. The rescue package that was so poorly crafted and defended by the Bush administration seemed to be sliding toward defeat. The presidential candidates were on the sidelines, carping and opining and commenting. But one of them, John McCain, intervened suddenly and boldly, taking a risk in order to change the situation, and to rearrange the landscape.

Kristol fails to mention the fact that McCain managed to sit through an entire one hour meeting with Obama, the President, Vice President, and leaders of Congress, without adding anything substantial. According to several media outlets, Obama had to eventually call on him to add something to the conversation. Senate Majority Leader Harry Reid said that McCain was virtually silent during the entire meeting. This hardly sounds like Kristol's description of a bold man taking risks and rearranging the landscape. The only thing he's rearranging is David Letterman's guest lineup. Kristol then writes:

> ... As for the question of Friday night's debate, which some in the media seem to think more important than saving the financial system—if the negotiations are still going on in D.C., McCain should offer to send Palin to debate Obama! Or he can take a break from the meetings, fly down at the last minute himself, and turn a boring foreign policy debate, in which he and Obama would repeat well-rehearsed arguments, into a discussion about leadership and decisiveness. And if the negotiations are clearly on a path to success, then McCain can say he can now afford to leave D.C., fly down, and the debate would become a victory lap for McCain....The media, being talkers and debaters, love debates, overestimate their importance, and are underestimating the possible effect of McCain's dramatic action. In the debate itself, McCain should mock the media's greater concern for gabbing than solving our economic problems, and should associate Obama with such a talk-heavy media-type approach to politics. If the race is between an energetic executive and an indecisive talker, the energetic executive should win.

Is this the same executive that Carly Fiorina said couldn't even run Hewlett Packard? Suggesting that Palin debate Obama takes away any credibility that Kristol had. Has he seen Palin's interview with Couric? And you, Kristol, are the biggest "talker" in the media that you refer to. You refer to McCain's action as "dramatic." You are correct, but it is painfully dramatic and offers nothing more than the same unpredictability that comes out of your mouth. Actually, I take that back—you are far too predictable and painfully ignorant. The most unfortunate thing about this article is that too many people will read it. The complete and utter disrespect Kristol has for Obama would be far more understandable if it were being spouted from the mouth of a cunning five-year-old. Or is the childish article by Kristol a part of the McCain campaign's childish game plan? It sounds as if Kristol and the McCain-Palin campaign's talking point for the week is this: *McCain, acting Presidential, snubs liberal media and petty debate, selflessly postponing his own hopes for victory—all this to ride heroically into Washington and save the government from collapse.* If so, it might have worked in the hands of better players.

DAY 33
WHAT THE HECK, I'LL SHOW UP AND DEBATE YOU!

Obama and McCain are in Oxford, Mississippi, today—Friday, September 26. "My administration continues to work with Congress on a rescue plan... We are going to get a package passed." This is part of what President Bush said this morning at 6:35 am. No agreement has been reached on the bailout and John McCain is still claiming that he will not attend the debate tonight. Obama has said that he will take part in negotiations this morning and will then head to the University of Mississippi for the debate. A headline in this morning's *Los Angeles Times* reads, **Who'd Win a One-Man Debate?** The entire nation is asking this question as the public holds out hope that the debate will indeed take place tonight. As of now, it depends on the success of the on-going Congressional negotiations. Democrats are suggesting that Republicans on the Hill are the ones holding this plan up. They are also suggesting that a deal was coming together before McCain showed up in Washington and that since then, House Republicans have completely backed away from the table. Democrats are blaming McCain for this breakdown in talks, but the media is refusing to completely sign on to this narrative.

The word "stunt" was used by Sen. Claire McCaskill to describe John McCain's decision to suspend his campaign.

This morning, Sen.Chuck Schumer said, "We need to respectfully tell McCain to get out of town—he's not helping." Sen. Harry Reid said, "The insertion of presidential politics has not been helpful." Democrats are puzzled by the fact that the bill they are ready to move forward on was actually presented by the President himself—surprising considering that it's Republicans who are holding it up. Democrats want strong bi-partisan support for the bill.

"John McCain Will Attend Tonight's Presidential Debate." This headline hit the airwaves this morning at 8:28 am. One can't help but think that his threat to cancel has only raised the stakes for him to perform well as an even larger number of Americans will now want to view the debate. His actions have drawn more attention to tonight's event. There is also pressure for McCain to perform well in this particular debate because it features an issue, foreign policy, which is his supposed strong suit. If Obama had pulled this stunt, the press would probably be far more critical of him and would likely be claiming that it speaks to his inexperience and could likely be a sign of the things to come in an Obama administration. They would be asking if Americans could trust Obama. This episode has only further cemented the fact that McCain can do anything he wants and still survive the lukewarm heat from the media. Now that McCain has decided to grace us with his presence in Mississippi, it will be fascinating to see how the press does pre- and post-analysis of the debate.

In yesterday's edition of the *Los Angeles Times,* Rosa Brooks reminded us again of a topic that our media is choosing to ignore. Part of what she writes in **Keating Five Ring a Bell?** is worth noting:

> Once upon a time, a politician took campaign contributions and favors from a friendly constituent who happened to run a savings and loan association. The contributions were generous. They came to about $200,000 in today's dollars, and on top of that there were several free vacations for the politician and his family, along with private jet trips and other perks. The politician voted repeatedly against congressional efforts to tighten regulation of S&Ls, and in 1987, when he learned that his constituent's S&L was the target of a federal investigation, he met with regulators in an effort to get them to back off. That politician was John McCain, and that generous friend was Charles Keating.

At 3:16 pm Mike Galanos of *CNN Headline News* felt compelled to bring up the issue of Obama being aloof when it comes to the debates. Again with the aloof comment! At 3:30 pm, CNN's Brian Todd said, "Obama will have to counter perceptions that he's aloof." The press is bringing up the issues of aloofness and race quite a bit leading up to the debate. On MSNBC, John Grisham told David Gregory, "I think the race is close because of his race."

At 4:24 pm, MSNBC's Andrea Mitchell must have forgotten that Tucker Bounds of the McCain camp along with Nancy Pfotenhauer were making the rounds on the networks yesterday—hardly the actions representative of a campaign that has been suspended. Instead of saying that she herself was certain the McCain camp hadn't suspended their campaign, Mitchell said, "The Obama folks say that he never did stop the campaign, but that's a debate that's along the margins." There is no possible way that Mitchell believes that this is a "debate that's along the margins." She knows better! How can she say this when she knows that McCain had his surrogates out talking and his campaign offices open? MSNBC itself has been reporting these facts. Rachel Maddow did an entire segment yesterday on this very issue.

With about fifteen minutes until the debate begins, the networks are getting their last minute opinions out. At 5:47 pm, CNN's David Gergen suggested that McCain had more of a sense of humor than Obama and that could serve him well. This is obviously an arguable point. At 5:52 pm CNN reported that *The Wall Street Journal* made an error in running an ad before the debate even started that read, "McCain Wins Debate." The ad ran earlier today, before McCain even confirmed that he was coming to the debate. The tension has reached its apex, and it is time for the debate to begin. With the horrific week that McCain has had, along with the bailout in Washington still up in the air, it should be riveting.

The debate in Mississippi just ended and the media is giving mixed reviews. Chris Matthews offered this right out of the box: "Let's bring in MSNBC political analysts Pat Buchanan and Eugene Robinson. Pat, I think you had a very interesting point tonight and that is that we don't know who won this debate until we know how the, to put it bluntly, the white working class guy, the regular working stiff out there responds. I do think Barack Obama could have done a hell of a better job tonight talking about the world in which that guy and that woman find themselves right now economically…" Buchanan responded with, "You know, where was the passion and fire that he should have brought to this?…I do think Barack Obama did something tonight that he had to do. And that is those folks out there that say, 'is this guy some whacko, is he, all his left wing friends. He's got all these—What kind of guy is he?'" Matthews then turned to Eugene Robinson, who happens to be African American,and asked this doozy: "Gene, did it surprise you that he was so un-ethnic tonight—that he never once talked about the condition of African Americans in this country?" Matthews is of the belief that only African Americans can answer questions about African Americans. I guess he went to the same school of questioning as Larry King and Bill Maher. Maher had Chris Rock on HBO's *Real Time* tonight, and just about every question he asked Rock centered on black issues. Note to the media and all talk show hosts: Chris Rock is not the spokesperson for black people. And neither is any other black celebrity. This kind of naivety in questioning African American celebrities is becoming the norm and is quite embarrassing. Black people are qualified to talk about white people also. Please give it a try.

Now that the candidates have exited the stage in Mississippi, the Republican talking heads are saying McCain won, and Democrats are saying that Obama won. Obama talked more substantively about the issues and looked McCain in the eye repeatedly. The media is of the general opinion that Obama said that he agreed with McCain too often. The most glaring element of the debate was the lack of discussion about the bailout that is being negotiated in Washington and the fact that McCain never once looked at Obama. There are mixed views about whether McCain's refusal to look at Obama showed pettiness. Some are saying that it was designed to show that he doesn't feel like Obama deserves to be on the same stage with him and is certainly not ready to be President. Chris Matthews was very hard on McCain for his refusal to acknowledge Obama. After the debate, Donna Brazile on CNN said, "John McCain needed a game changer, and he didn't get that." CNN's Leslie Sanchez said, "Barrack Obama was somewhat on the offensive." Campbell Brown said, "McCain was excellent tonight on foreign policy—clearly." Here are some of the more entertaining exchanges that took place during the debate that was hosted by Jim Lehrer:

> **OBAMA:** …I just want to make this point, Jim. John, it's been your President who you said you agreed with 90 percent of the time who presided over this increase in spending. This orgy of spending and enormous deficits—you voted for almost all of his budgets. So to stand here and after eight years say that you're going to lead on controlling spending and, you know, balancing our tax cuts so that they help middle class families when over the last eight years that hasn't happened I think just is, you know, kind of hard to swallow.
>
> **LEHRER:** Quick response to Senator Obama.
>
> **MCCAIN:** It's well known that I have not been elected Miss Congeniality in the United States

Senate nor with the administration. I have opposed the president on spending, on climate change, on torture of prisoner, on - on Guantanamo Bay. On a—on the way that the Iraq War was conducted. I have a long record and the American people know me very well and that is independent and a maverick of the Senate and I'm happy to say that I've got a partner that's a good maverick along with me now.

As the debate shifted to the issue of foreign policy, Obama showed a strong command of this issue, which is considered McCain's strength. The first 30 minutes of the debate were rather dull, but the exchanges heated up. McCain continued his refusal to acknowledge Obama and the two became more confrontational.

MCCAIN: The next president of the United States is not going to have to address the issue as to whether we went into Iraq or not. The next president of the United States is going to have to decide how we leave, when we leave, and what we leave behind. That's the decision of the next president of the United States. Senator Obama said the surge could not work, said it would increase sectarian violence, said it was doomed to failure. Recently on a television program, he said it exceed our wildest expectations. But yet, after conceding that, he still says that he would oppose the surge if he had to decide that again today.

Incredibly, incredibly Senator Obama didn't go to Iraq for 900 days and never…

LEHRER: …Well, let's go at some of these things…

MCCAIN: … Senator Obama is the chairperson of a committee that oversights NATO that's in Afghanistan. To this day, he has never had a hearing…

LEHRER: What about that point?

MCCAIN: I mean…it's remarkable.

LEHRER: All right. What about that point?

OBAMA: Which point? He raised a whole bunch of them.

LEHRER: I know, OK, let's go to the latter point and we'll back up. The point about your not having been…

OBAMA: Look, I'm very proud of my vice presidential selection, Joe Biden, who is the chairman of the Senate Foreign Relations Committee, and as he explains, and as John well knows, the issues of Afghanistan, the issues of Iraq, critical issues like that, don't go through my subcommittee because they're done as a committee as a whole. But that's Senate inside baseball. But let's get back to the core issue here. Senator McCain is absolutely right that the violence has been reduced as a consequence of the extraordinary sacrifice of our troops and our military families. They have done a brilliant job, and General Petraeus has done a brilliant job.

54

But understand, that was a tactic designed to contain the damage of the previous four years of mismanagement of this war. And so John likes—John, you like to pretend like the war started in 2007. You talk about the surge. The war started in 2003, and at the time when the war started, you said it was going to be quick and easy. You said we knew where the weapons of mass destruction were. You were wrong. You said that we were going to be greeted as liberators. You were wrong. You said that there was no history of violence between Shiite and Sunni. And you were wrong. And so my question is...

LEHRER: Senator Obama...

OBAMA: ...of judgment, of whether or not—if the question is who is best-equipped as the next president to make good decisions about how we use our military, how we make sure that we are prepared and ready for the next conflict, then I think we can take a look at our judgment."

LEHRER: I have got a lot on the plate here...

MCCAIN: I'm afraid Senator Obama doesn't understand the difference between a tactic and a strategy. But the important—I'd like to tell you, two Fourths of July ago I was in Baghdad. General Petraeus invited Senator Lindsey Graham and me to attend a ceremony where 688 brave young Americans, whose enlistment had expired, were reenlisting to stay and fight for Iraqi freedom and American freedom. I was honored to be there.

I was honored to speak to those troops. And you know, afterwards, we spent a lot of time with them. And you know what they said to us? They said, let us win. They said, let us win. We don't want our kids coming back here. And this strategy, and this general, they are winning. Senator Obama refuses to acknowledge that we are winning in Iraq.

OBAMA: That's not true.

Most analysts are of the opinion that Obama got the better of McCain during that exchange. The debate then focused on Pakistan and Afghanistan. The two candidates have a fundamental disagreement about that area, and Obama believes that is where our military focus should be.

McCAIN: ...So it's not just the addition of troops that matters. It's a strategy that will succeed. And Pakistan is a very important element in this. And I know how to work with him. And I guarantee you I would not publicly state that I'm going to attack them.

OBAMA: Nobody talked about attacking Pakistan. Here's what I said. And if John wants to disagree with this, he can let me know, that, if the United States has al Qaeda, bin Laden, top-level lieutenants in our sights, and Pakistan is unable or unwilling to act, then we should take them out. Now, I think that's the right strategy; I think that's the right policy. And, John, I—you're absolutely right that presidents have to be prudent in what they say. But, you know, coming from you, who, you know, in the past has threatened extinction for North Korea and, you know, sung songs about bombing Iran, I don't know, you know, how credible that is. I think this is the right strategy…

Several post debate polls have been released and the consensus is that Obama won. FOX's Fred Barnes said, "McCain put him on the defensive a lot." Also on FOX, Nina Easton of Fortune Magazine said, " I thought it was a really good night for John McCain…. The first thirty-five minutes I counted seven or eight attacks. He just went after Obama…It seemed to have knocked Obama off balance. He really had trouble getting his sea legs again…just in terms of style, John McCain comes off as very clear, direct, you know, 'I looked at Putin and saw K.G.B. in his eyes.' There's just still something bland and policy speak about Barack Obama that I don't think does really well in these settings. I know people use the word cool, but I just find it policy speak and rounded edges and not direct." Bill Kristol then said, "Yeah I actually agree with Nina…I didn't think it was close. There were eight rounds of questioning and if you were grading this as a boxing match I would have given Obama the first round and McCain every other round with maybe one or two of them tied…McCain got under Obama's skin…He got him visibly irritated…frustrated…He didn't counterpunch." FOX's Chris Wallace interviewed Senator Lindsey Graham who said, "I quite frankly thought that it was pretty astounding….No, no

Senator Obama, you don't understand. You're not just naïve my friend, you're dangerous." Wallace didn't even respond to the words Graham used. Calling Obama dangerous is entirely over the top.

After the debate, MSNBC's Norah O'Donnell immediately said, "McCain had a rough week but I think he had a good night." Pat Buchanan added, "John McCain clearly won this battle on points." The media seems to be holding back on giving any really scathing commentary either direction as polls continue to come in. Even Pat Buchanan, noticing the poll results that show Obama winning, has changed his tune a bit about being so certain of McCain's victory. The polls are making the press hold back on offering their certainty of anything. Tomorrow will likely bring a more clear-minded analysis of tonight as the current, palpable energy will have subsided and the partisan rhetoric will be juxtaposed against definitive poll results.

DAY 34
LOOK AT ME WHEN I'M TALKING
TO YOU!

Obama is campaigning in Greensboro, North Carolina, today—Saturday, September 27—while McCain is in Arlington, Virginia. "You know, what surprises me is that Sen. Obama, who voted to increase taxes on people making $42 thousand a year or more is now concerned about the middle class. If he's worried about the middle class, he needs to control government spending and stop proposing to raise people's taxes 'cause that will kill job growth and that's what I think people in my neighborhood care about—is whether we're gonna have a job." At 11:23 am, this is what Republican Congresswoman Heather Wilson said on FOX News this morning. This talking point went unchallenged. At some point, either the Obama camp or the media is going to have to put an end to the inaccurate talking point that Obama wants to raise taxes on the middle class.

John McCain's refusal to acknowledge Obama last night has people talking. His stubbornness and almost self-righteousness made for a debate that was difficult to watch at times. Obama would have been well within his rights to say the following: *With all due respect Sen. McCain, both of us are U.S. senators, and each of us is garnering at least 45% of the vote. I am choosing to show you, and those millions who support you, the respect you deserve, by looking you in the face while we debate.*

I would kindly ask that you give me and my millions of supporters, along with the millions of undecided independents, the same respect, by having the decency to look at me as we debate the issues that affect the millions of Americans who intend to vote for one of us in the coming months.

McCain use of the word "naïve" in reference to Obama during last night's debate didn't fit. Even as Obama made points that were based in fact and completely coherent, McCain would often say that Obama just didn't get it. But the fact is that he, McCain, did "get it," and his repeated use of the phrase made him look over rehearsed—like he was told to say "Obama doesn't get it" by his team, and he just repeated it like a programmed robot. Depending on which candidate you're for, it could certainly be argued who had the more effective night. Today, in her article, **The First Debate,** *Forbes.com's* Suzanne Garment writes:

> It is the morning after the first presidential debate. Tens of millions of people are delivering themselves of opinions about which senator won, and tens of thousands of them are actually getting paid for it. The instant opinions are almost wholly filtered through the lens of whom the opiner wants to win the election. However, it is clear that a big winner has been us, the public discourse, the country. Yes, the foregoing sounds incredibly sappy; but it is probably the most important judgment that can be made about any political contest.... Because Obama's rhetorical self-control was well-known, McCain's ability to deliver a consistent message

seemed more striking—but, then, maybe I am just the victim of some McCain spokesman's rhetoric of diminished expectations.

The media is also in agreement that last night's debate was critical in showing whether or not Obama was able to pass a threshold test and come across as strong enough to be President. The consensus is that he passed that test convincingly. Unfortunately, throughout this campaign, the media tends to move with the wind, and Obama has not been able to solidify his image with the press. They'll say that he is strong enough today and that all of the talk about him not being ready is out the window, and tomorrow they will claim that he has as much to prove as the painfully uninformed Palin. Palin's ignorance will likely present itself even more at next Thursday's debate in St. Louis against Biden. There's not an honest Republican in America who could say with a straight face that Palin's performance with Couric doesn't have them terrified. Biden should be licking his chops over the opportunity to debate the grossly uninformed Palin. In an op-ed yesterday, entitled **Palin's Words Raise Red Flags**, Bob Herbert of *The New York Times* worries about Palin's qualifications to take high office:

> The country is understandably focused on the financial crisis. But there is another serious issue in front of us that is not getting nearly enough attention, and that's whether Sarah Palin is qualified to be vice president—or, if the situation were to arise, president of the United States.

… The idea that the voters of the United States might install someone in the vice president's office who is too unprepared or too intellectually insecure to appear on, say, *Meet the Press* or "Face the Nation" is mind-boggling.

… If it turns out that she has just had a few bad interviews because she was nervous or whatever, additional scrutiny will serve her well.

If, on the other hand, it becomes clear that her performance, so far, is an accurate reflection of her qualifications, it would behoove John McCain and the Republican Party to put the country first—as Mr. McCain loves to say—and find a replacement for Ms. Palin on the ticket.

Today, Democrats have enough votes on their own to get the bailout bill passed but they don't want to move forward without it being bi-partisan because of the fallout that may ensue politically. Democrats don't want to own it. There is hope that the bill can get passed tomorrow. Lou Dobbs is trying to tie both candidates to the financial crisis and downplayed their debate performances with: "The American people didn't win last night…These two men were running from leadership rather than asserting it." Robert Zimmerman told Dobbs, "It's premature to say who won." Ed Rollins then said, "McCain proved at 72 that he wasn't an old man." I'm not quite sure how he proved that.

On FOX News at 6:11 pm, Karl Rove claimed that it is wrong to say that Democrats always want to regulate and Republicans don't. Does Rove read political history books—at least ones that aren't written by right-wing ideologues? Rove also claimed that McCain will get more credit than Obama for the bailout bill passing because he will be credited with bringing House Republicans together. Doesn't Rove know that there are some of us out here who saw this silly little stunt from the beginning—House Republicans acting stubborn and confused, only to have the Maverick fly into town to save the day? Rove added, "Fannie and Freddie are the contagions that spread to the rest of the market." He along with many other Republicans is trying like hell to blame this entire financial meltdown on Fannie and Freddie. They obviously believe that Democrats can be linked to these two giants by constantly bringing up former Fannie Mae CEO, Franklin Raines. Republicans are trying to get as much mileage as possible out of linking him to Obama, but they conveniently fail to mention the other corporations that are completely tied to Republican wrongdoing. After all, they are the party of deregulation. Democrats would be wise to stop allowing Rove and the like to make them own Fannie and Freddie. They would also be wise to point out, in no uncertain terms, the fact that Raines has never been involved in advising Obama.

McCain often says, "We came here to change Washington and Washington changed us." This is a statement that should raise the eyebrows of the press. They should be asking McCain how it has changed him and if it has, how can he claim to be the change candidate? How does the fact that he allowed Washington to change him demonstrate independence or strength? He should be claiming that Washington has not changed him. This statement, which he also made last night, is one that Obama can, and should, exploit. It links him to the past and shows that he is admitting to being a part of the very problem that has led to the worst financial catastrophe in decades. Again, the press is just letting the statement slide.

At 9:29 pm, Nancy Pelosi and Harry Reid gave a statement on the bailout negotiations. Reid said, "I have to say the breakthrough came about an hour ago." This seemed to signify the possibility that a deal had been reached. But then Reid added, "We think that we should have an announcement sometime tomorrow." Secretary Paulson then spoke adding, "We've still got more to do to finalize it, but I think we're there."

DAY 35
$700 BILLION

Obama is campaigning in Detroit, Michigan, today—Sunday, September 28—while McCain is in Arlington, Virginia. In this morning's *Los Angeles Times*, Todd Gitlin, writes an op-ed entitled **Race for President Builds Characters.** The problem with the article is that the title should be *We in the Press Like to Mischaracterize the Candidates.* By the time Gitlin finishes his article, he has McCain as tall and heroic as Paul Bunyan and Obama as short and mysterious as an African Pygmy:

> … The true campaign is the deep campaign, the subsurface campaign, which concerns not just what the candidates say but who they are and what they represent—what they *symbolize*.
> … Senator John McCain is relatively familiar. He is the leathery man of the West, of exactly the sort who has entranced the Republican Party for almost half a century now. It is the role that Barry Goldwater, Ronald Reagan, and George W. Bush played before him.
> … Mythically, therefore, Obama is elusive, Protean, a shape-shifter who, when not beloved, arouses suspicion. Perhaps he is that object of envy and derision, a 'celebrity,' as the McCain campaign suggested, but he's also an egghead.

He's the professor—but one who can sink the shot from beyond the three-point circle. He too has a sidekick, but, if you judge by their resumes, it is as if Robin has chosen Batman. One thing is clear: He is not a man of the ranch. Personifying a welter of archetypes, he thrills some, confounds others and jams circuits. Some people ask, 'Who is this guy?' … So that's the clash. McCain, the known quantity, the maverick turned lawman, fiery when called on to fight, an icon of the old known American story of standing tall, holding firm, protecting God's country against the stealthy foe. Obama is the new kid on the block, the immigrant's child, the recruit, fervent but still preternaturally calm, embodying some complicated future that we haven't yet mapped, let alone experienced. He is impure—the walking, talking melting pot in person. In his person, the next America is still taking shape.

Gitlin manages to do what too many well-educated, politically astute journalists so easily do—he mischaracterizes Obama. And Mr. Gitlin, a professor of journalism at Columbia University, Obama's alma mater, may even be inclined to vote for Obama. He writes that Obama arouses suspicion but fails to point out that it is a suspicion largely created by the illegitimate brand of journalism coming out of FOX News and Rush Limbaugh radio. Are those his sources? Nothing about Obama himself creates these suspicions. Yes, Obama is smart, but calling him an egghead has a negative connotation.

As a matter of fact, all of the words Mr. Gitlin uses to describe McCain in the article have a positive connotation. Granted, Gitlin says he's revealing a myth, but he's also helping to further the myth by using positive words and phrases only in relation to McCain: *leathery man of the west, rugged individualist, plain spoken, straight talking, self-sufficient, warrior in command, warrior turned lawman, known quantity, Maverick turned law man, fiery, icon, standing tall, holding firm, and protecting God's country.*

The words and phrases he uses in reference to the Obama myth are negative: *arrogant, scrambled, outsider, city slicker, suspect, lone ranger closer to the color of Tonto, elusive, shape-shifter, arouses suspicion, egghead, stealthy foe, immigrant's child, complicated future, and impure.* I'm not saying that Gitlin intended to create a negative image of Obama, but my idea of an Obama myth is much more positive than this. Oh, and by the way, Obama is not the son of an immigrant, but rather the son of a brilliant Harvard economics major, who studied in this country on a student visa.

A new *Gallup* poll shows Obama up by eight points nationally. The tendency has been for the McCain camp to change gears quickly and make a big splash any time Obama makes a positive move in the polls, so I expect to see some fireworks in the coming days. Obama can thank the American people for the break he's getting from the press. As soon as the debate ended the other night, the media's first reaction was to paint McCain as the winner. It wasn't until the polls started coming in, showing that Obama had won, that the press backed off and called it a draw. There's not a pundit on the air who lacks an opinion about what

Obama did or didn't accomplish Friday night. Some say he missed an opportunity to tie McCain to Bush. Others claim he started off very tentative. Today, CNN's Alex Castellanos claimed that Obama "looked like he was trying to remember his flashcards." Gloria Borger disagreed. Obama's stature has certainly grown since the debate, and Republicans have been forced to respect him. He passed the *mano y mano* test.

When John McCain was asked this morning why he didn't look at Obama, he said that he never looks at his opponents during a debate. He takes notes and looks at the moderator. His excuse was unconvincing. It will be interesting to see if he chooses not to look at Obama during the next debate. There are some who believe that Obama should have demanded more respect. Maureen Dowd of *The New York Times* wrote yesterday, "Given the past week, the debate should have been a cinch for Obama. But, just as in the primaries, he willfully refuses to accept what debates are about. It's not a lecture hall; it's a joust. It's not how cerebral you are. It's how visceral you are. You need memorable, sharp, forceful and witty lines." Dowd needs to take heed of what Obama has been saying. He is creating a different brand of political theater—one that doesn't lend itself to playing games. Unlike Dowd, Obama doesn't equate debating to jousting. She says that Obama refuses to accept what debates are about, but she obviously doesn't understand what winning is about, because the last time I checked, Obama beat Clinton. Perhaps Dowd feels that it was Clinton who was able to accept what debates are about. A lot of good that did her! Dowd can have Clinton's and McCain's debate skill-set and I'll take Obama's—a skill-set that allowed him to defeat Clinton and one that is proving capable of taking down McCain. I also found Dowd's choice for a title, **Sound, but No Fury,** a bit too dramatic. All of the polls show that his performance had enough fury to win him the debate in rather convincing fashion.

Today in Detroit, Joe Biden said that on Friday at the debate we saw a man in John McCain "who is literally out of touch with America. He lacks the judgment to be President of the United States." Biden is chomping at the bit to take on Palin this coming Thursday, only four days from now. There has never been a bigger underdog than Palin in a Vice Presidential debate. The key is for Biden not to be so dominant that it makes voters feel sorry for her. The problem is that he is so much more qualified and knowledgeable, that by virtue of opening his mouth he will make people feel sorry for her. It's a mismatch; she's way in over her head. I think the nation already feels collectively sad for her, and, in a way, we wish McCain would rescue her before she completely implodes in front of the world.

Today on ABC's *This Week*, Obama economic advisor Robert Reich said, "The top one percent is now taking home almost twenty percent of national income. In 1980 the top one percent was taking home eight percent of national income. We have not seen this degree of economic concentration since 1928, so there's not adequate purchasing power in the middle class." He said that the next President will need to focus more on investment in education and infrastructure rather than spending on new programs.

Tom Brokaw interviewed Bill Clinton today on *Meet the Press*. I just want the record to show that, even though Clinton gave a good, supportive speech at the convention, he still looks a bit pained when talking about Obama. Clinton has said in the past that he admired McCain and that he was a great man. Brokaw asked Clinton, "Would you use the same words for [Obama] that you have used for Senator McCain—that you admire him and that he's a great man?" Instead of simply saying yes, Clinton danced around like a jealous baseball veteran who can't give it up for the young up-and-coming star. It is obvious that Clinton has an issue with Obama. He masks it with his clever little words, but it's painful to watch him try to muster up the courage to simply say what the rest of us already know about Obama—that he's smart, sharp, charismatic. All he had to do was answer Brokaw's question specifically and say that he admires Obama and thinks he's as great a man. That would have helped Obama politically. Someone needs to remind Clinton that McCain, the man he speaks so glowingly of, is the same man who made fun of his daughter Chelsea and who casually allowed a woman to refer to Hillary as a "bitch."

At 9:05 pm, Julie Hirschfeld Davis of the *Associated Press* wrote, "Congressional leaders and the White House agreed Sunday to a $700 billion rescue of the ailing financial industry after lawmakers insisted on sharing spending controls with the Bush administration. The biggest U.S. bailout in history won the tentative support of both presidential candidates and goes to the House for a vote Monday." Nancy Pelosi said, "We sent a message to Wall Street Sunday. The party is over." Once the bailout bill is voted on, the Presidential campaign will likely heat up again and the McCain camp will try to get back to their smear tactics, especially considering the lead Obama is showing today in the polls. I wonder what McCain has up his sleeve!

DAY 36
PELOSI HURT OUR FEELINGS

Obama is campaigning in Denver, Colorado, today—Monday, September 29—while McCain is in Columbus, Ohio. The financial bailout bill has failed to pass in the House of Representatives. In one morning, I saw and heard more bipartisan speeches than I've ever before heard from representatives up for election. Nancy Pelosi, all the Democrats, and all the Republicans who spoke regarding the bill to bail out Wall Street, whether speaking in favor or against the bill, were speaking without blame or partisanship. When the bill failed, the Republicans, some of whom had just spoken with bipartisanship and who had just minutes before complimented Speaker Pelosi for her leadership, immediately spoke as a group that the reason the bill failed was Nancy Pelosi's partisan speech. I heard her speech. It was not partisan. It was scathing toward the administration and Wall Street players who had asked for $700,000,000,000 with no strings attached. Now the House Republicans' game seems to be "Kill the messenger". Rep. Cantor of Virginia blamed no one for the failure of the bill except Speaker Pelosi for her inability to lead. He held up a copy of Pelosi's speech and said that he was holding in his hands the reason the bill didn't pass. Cantor said that Pelosi injected partisanship into her speech and that caused the bill to fail. Let me get this right! Cantor excused hurting the entire country because of a supposedly insensitive speech? Mr. Cantor should be ashamed!

On MSNBC, Chris Matthews blamed John McCain for not being able to lead Republicans toward a resolution in their caucus. Immediately following failure of the House to pass the bill, McCain blamed Barack Obama for "watching from the sidelines". As Chris Matthews continued to blame Republicans for not corralling enough votes, MSNBC's Contessa Brewer tried to challenge him by saying, "There were Democrats that were not following their leadership too." Brewer at times tries to provide balance by pulling out her Republican card.

Speaker Pelosi then spoke regarding the failed bill. She once again reiterated her insistence that the Democratic caucus had delivered their vote for the bill. Again, she emphasized the bipartisan nature of the agreement that resulted in the bill as presented for the vote. "The crisis is not going away," she said. Majority Leader Steny Hoyer said that the Democrats had delivered 60% of their caucus. Rep. Barney Frank added that if the Republicans who voted against the bill are right, and that Secretary Paulson has indeed exaggerated the peril to the overall economy, he'll be happy to forget about it and go home. Upset at some who voted against the bill because of what they perceived to be Pelosi's partisan tone, Frank joked, "Give me those twelve people's names and I will go talk uncharacteristically nicely to them, and tell them what wonderful people they are and maybe they will now think about the country." He added, "Because somebody hurt their feelings, they decided to punish the country." Nancy Pelosi said, "Thank you all for your interest.

Stay tuned. We are here to protect the taxpayer." It is now up to the media to decide whether or not to spin this in the favor of one of the candidates.

At 3:44 pm, Wolf Blitzer was talking about the upcoming Vice Presidential debate and made the case that Joe Biden doesn't always say "the smartest" things. Blitzer was referring to the previous Democratic debates that he had moderated. At 3:45 pm, Lou Dobbs told Blitzer that Biden had made "so many more mistakes" than Palin. MSNBC's David Gregory showed Palin telling a crowd today that she was looking forward to debating Biden. She said that she had never met Biden, but had been listening to him speak all the way back since she was in the second grade. Gregory then laughingly added, "She is very good with a zinger." David Gregory needs to spend more time listening to zingers that are actually funny. He was far too easily impressed with Palin's line and seemed to be reveling in the fact that she had made a dig at Biden. I doubt he would have laughed if Biden had been the one joking about Palin.

The media is already setting the bar very low for Palin this Thursday by rhetorically asking if her poor performance with Couric has somehow lowered expectations. CNN's Jeffrey Toobin argued that it is a mistake to allow Palin to skate by with only having to not make any mistakes. He feels that she should be held to the same standard as Biden because both of them are running for Vice President. John McCain himself is still coddling Palin. The two of them sat down with CBS's Katie Couric today. Couric asked her about a recent conversation she had with a voter about Pakistan:

Katie Couric: Over the weekend, Governor Palin, you said the U.S. should absolutely launch cross-border attacks from Afghanistan into Pakistan to, quote, 'stop the terrorists from coming any further in.' Now, that's almost the exact position that Barack Obama has taken and that you, Senator McCain, have criticized as something you do not say out loud. So, Governor Palin, are you two on the same page on this?

Sarah Palin: We had a great discussion with President Zardari as we talked about what it is that America can and should be doing together to make sure that the terrorists do not cross borders and do not ultimately put themselves in a position of attacking America again or her allies. And we will do what we have to do to secure the United States of America and her allies.

Couric: Is that something you shouldn't say out loud, Senator McCain?

John McCain: Of course not. But, look, I understand this day and age of 'gotcha' journalism. Is that a pizza place? In a conversation with someone who you didn't hear … the question very well, you don't know the context of the conversation, grab a phrase. Governor Palin and I agree that you don't announce that you're going to attack another country …

Couric: Are you sorry you said it?

McCain: … and the fact …

Couric: Governor?

McCain: Wait a minute. Before you say, 'Is she sorry she said it,' this was a 'gotcha' sound bite that, look …

Couric: It wasn't a 'gotcha.' She was talking to a voter.

McCain: No, she was in a conversation with a group of people and talking back and forth. And … I'll let Governor Palin speak for herself.

The women of America should be appalled at the way John McCain jumped in and spoke for Palin. Since when is a voter asking a Vice Presidential candidate a question in a café considered gotcha journalism? Unless a journalist asks it, it can't be gotcha journalism. It would have to be "gotcha café customer questioning." And that is laughable! This whole McCain-Palin situation is becoming embarrassing. How far is he going to take this approach to protecting her? I have never witnessed a Presidential candidate make more mistakes during a campaign than McCain. I am waiting for the media to give commentary on how he treated Palin like a child and chose to speak for her. Does he not think she can speak for herself? And when McCain interrupted Couric, he seemed a bit angry that she had even asked Palin if she was sorry she said what she said. McCain needs to suspend his campaign and take a few days off. Only this time he needs to really do it and not even announce it. He desperately needs to regroup, because right now everything he says can and will be used against him.

The *Associated Press'* David Espo writes today, "Lagging in the polls, Republican presidential candidate John McCain unleashed a blistering attack Monday on his Democratic rival, saying the race comes down to a simple question: 'Country first or Obama first?'" One question for McCain: Is Obama not part of the "country"? John McCain should be taking a beating for mistakenly saying earlier today that the bailout bill had passed. He said it in an almost boastful way, only to find out two hours later that the bill had failed. At that point he blamed Sen. Obama for injecting partisanship into the situation, which caused the bill to fail. He blamed Obama! But, in his very next sentence—VERY NEXT SENTENCE— he said that now is not the time to point fingers or place blame. Unbelievable! He said two completely opposite things in two sentences. McCain had earlier claimed that his call for a White House summit meeting Thursday and his visit with House Republicans beforehand had helped pave the way for the bill's passage. He told this to a crowd in Columbus, Ohio. What a terrible mistake! It requires a scolding from the media, but McCain isn't getting one. They reserve that type of unending scrutiny for Obama. The press should now tie McCain to the bill's failure. If he was the man who flew into town to broker a deal, why didn't more Republicans vote for the bailout? One would think that a Presidential candidate would wait for the result of a vote before clumsily bragging about his influence over it.

Barack Obama spoke in Denver today and told a crowd that he "read the other day that Sen. McCain likes to gamble." Obama added, "He likes to roll those dice. And that's ok. I enjoy a little friendly game of poker myself every now and then. But one thing I know is this—we can't afford to gamble on four more years of the same disastrous economic policies we've had for the last eight."

At 7:44 pm, CNN's Ed Rollins said of Palin: "This is a smart woman who's got an extraordinary record as a governor." David Gergen claimed that Palin was "a very talented woman who may have lost her confidence." Looks like the media is doing its best to keep this smart, talented woman from drowning. "Very talented" is a little too strong Mr. Gergen. But, I agree that she has lost her confidence. Gergen then said, "If you want to play in the big leagues, you've gotta hit big league pitching." The question is, will Palin get big league pitching thrown at her Thursday night from PBS's Gwen Ifill? I have a feeling she will.

On FOX News, Karl Rove told Bill O'Reilly that Pelosi's speech today "was five minutes of the most vicious, partisan rhetoric.... I was appalled by this.... It hurt a lot." It is completely obvious that Rove and the Republicans are upset that the bill didn't pass and that their ploy didn't work. They guessed that the Democrats would overwhelmingly vote for it. Then they figured they could go home and tell their Republican constituents that they overwhelmingly voted against it. But the Democrats stuck to the original deal of only providing enough votes for a bi-partisan passage. The Republicans miscalculated on their belief that they could lie on Sunday by telling Pelosi that she could rest assured that Republicans would deliver the number of votes necessary for the bill to pass in a bi-partisan fashion on Monday. But the Republicans obviously never intended to deliver enough votes. Their gamble backfired and now they look petty, as if the only reason they didn't supply more votes is because their feelings were hurt by Pelosi's speech. CNN's David Gergen blamed Republicans saying, "Let there be no doubt; it was the House Republicans who derailed this. This was one of the worst mistakes I've ever seen Congress make."

Republicans have a lot of egg on their faces today. Even Mitt Romney went on NBC's *Today* show this morning and bragged about McCain's ability to lead the way in getting this bill passed. Oops! Karl Roves knows that he and McCain never intended for House Republicans to give enough votes for the bill to be bipartisan. They figured that one-third of the House Republican vote would be enough for passage, and then McCain could still falsely claim that he was the one to get a bi-partisan bill through. Karl Rove should be more concerned about how his party's failure to keep their promise has hurt the economy today. The DOW suffered the biggest one-day point drop in history at 777 points down. Tomorrow, John McCain will probably claim that he is the one who killed the bailout bill by calling House Republicans at the last minute to tell them not to support it. And if he does, the media, if true to form, will let him get away with it.

With Obama up by eight points in the Gallup poll nationally and McCain melting down, Sean Hannity is in full attack mode. He is now trying to tie Obama to voter fraud, of all things. Apparently, Obama, as an attorney, represented a voter registration group called ACORN years ago. Hannity is claiming that this group is linked to voter fraud. Tonight, Hannity said, "It seems like every time I turn around, Barack Obama is tied to radicals." That's strange! I was just thinking that every time I turn around, Hannity is trying every trick in the book, unsuccessfully, to tie Obama to radicals. If this ridiculous comment is any indication of the things to come from FOX News this week, the Obama camp should prepare for the worst attacks they've seen during the entire campaign so far.

DAY 37
COURIC'S HARDBALL QUESTIONS—NOT!

Obama is campaigning in Reno, Nevada, today—Tuesday, September 30—while McCain is in Des Moines, Iowa. "Congress must act." These were the orders of President Bush this morning as he addressed the nation. Congress' failure to pass the bailout bill was the subject of his speech. John McCain said this morning, "Inaction is not an option." Obama said that we've got to put the economic fire out first and then worry about those people who left the stove on.

On MSNBC this morning, Tamron Hall asked Kate Zernike of *The New York Times* if either McCain or Obama are "taking responsibility for what went wrong?" Zernike said that both candidates would have taken credit for the bailout bill if it had passed. She said that we saw how McCain tried to do just that yesterday before finding out that it had failed. Zernike failed to mention that Obama never tried to take credit for it yesterday, and I doubt he would have tried to take credit for it at all if it had passed. She, along with far too many members of the press, is too willing to equate Obama's steadiness to McCain's erratic behavior. They make the mistake of assuming that because they are petty, other people are too. Just because McCain is royally screwing up, doesn't mean we have to hypothesize and imagine ways to make Obama look equally ridiculous. Zernike should have simply said that McCain tried to take credit for the bill, but

Obama didn't. Stop trying to act like you're in the business of predicting what might have happened if the bill had passed. Obama has never tried to take credit for something he didn't do, yet McCain does so every day. We usually determine what people might do by assessing what they always do. Since when does Obama do anything that McCain does? If McCain tried to take credit for something, Obama would likely do the exact opposite. That has been his pattern of behavior. Did Obama go to Mississippi during the hurricane, like McCain? No! Did he rush back to Washington when McCain did? No! Did he suspend his campaign when McCain did? No! Zernike should stick to the facts that are in front of her, not the ones floating around in her head that she dreamt up last night.

This morning at 9:45 am, FOX News' Gregg Jarrett asked, "Is ACORN trying to steal the election for Obama in Ohio?" FOX News is going to throw ACORN at Obama until it sticks. If CNN and MSNBC start to discuss it, then Obama should begin to worry. Perhaps they'll have the common sense to ignore it and let theACORN story live and die in the arms of FOX News.

Mona Charen of the *National Review* writes today in the article **ACORN, Obama, and the Mortgage Mess** about ACORN's connection to Obama. ACORN stands for the Association of Community Organizations for Reform Now. Charen has very little good to say about the organization:

> … ACORN does many things under the umbrella of 'community organizing.' They agitate for higher minimum wages, attempt to thwart school reform, try to unionize welfare workers (that

is, those welfare recipients who are obliged to work in exchange for benefits) and organize voter registration efforts (always for Democrats, of course). Because they are on the side of righteousness and justice, they aren't especially fastidious about their methods …

… ACORN members have been prosecuted for voter fraud in a number of states. Their philosophy seems to be that everyone deserves the right to vote, whether legal or illegal, living or dead …

… ACORN attracted Barack Obama in his youthful community organizing days…. Obama was not just sympathetic—he was an ACORN fellow traveler.

Between what Charen writes and FOX News spews, one has to wonder what level the Right is willing to stoop to. Charen must have loved Giuliani's and Palin's convention speeches. After all, they reveled in poking fun at community organizers too. I'm sure this is just the first of many stories to come from Charen on ACORN. She'll do her best to aid Sean Hannity and FOX News in their quest to make ACORN heavier. Then they'll try to wrap it around Obama's neck and drown him with it. Until some legitimate negative news surfaces about ACORN, I'll assume they are decent, concerned citizens, given Hannity's hatred of them.

Former House Majority Leader Tom DeLay told Chris Matthews today, "This Congress has got to be the most incompetent Congress in my career." DeLay said that Pelosi doesn't understand the economic situation. Matthews told

DeLay, "Pelosi shouldn't have given a political speech ... She gave them a permission slip to leave." No, not really, Mr. Matthews! Unless you're equating them to children!

Joe Scarborough filled in for David Gregory today. McCain economic advisor Douglas Holtz-Eakin told him that McCain "suspended his campaign. He put his country first." He then said, "Senator Obama has two, maybe three, positions on every issue." Scarborough didn't even respond to that ridiculous assertion. It went unchallenged. Instead, Scarborough asserted, "A lot of people on Wall Street are wondering what [Obama's] position is" on the bailout. I guess Scarborough went down there and asked them today. This "a lot of people" phrase sure gets thrown around a great deal when the media is talking about Obama.

John McCain said this morning that he intended to be bipartisan and not point fingers in order to get the bailout plan finished. He then immediately ran an ad that blamed Obama for the failure of the bailout. Real bipartisanship! At the same time, the Republican Party also ran an ad that assumed the bill had passed but that they had been against it. Talk about getting caught red-handed! Between McCain taking credit for the bill's passage, Mitt Romney praising McCain for leading the way on the bill's passage, Republicans blaming Pelosi for hurting their feelings, McCain swearing not to place blame on anyone, McCain blaming Obama for the bill's failure, the Republican party running an ad touting their resistance to a passing bill, and all of Palin's disastrous gaffs, I am finding it hard to keep my sanity. It's unhealthy—getting inside these Republicans' thought processes!

Palin's downward spiral picked up even more steam today. Couric asked her what newspapers she reads and she couldn't name a single one. She actually said, "All of them." That's a lot of newspapers. Hope she recycles! There are also reports coming out that when Palin was asked on camera to name a Supreme Court decision other than *Roe vs. Wade* that she disagrees with, there was nothing but silence. CBS is reportedly going to air the auspicious moment tomorrow. THIS IS GETTING ABSOLUTELY UNBELIEVABLE AND HARD FOR ME TO CONTINUE WRITING ABOUT. IF I WERE PITCHING THIS MCCAIN-PALIN DRAMA TO HOLLYWOOD EXECUTIVES, THEY WOULD LAUGH AT THE ABSURDITY OF IT AND PROBABLY KICK ME OUT OF THE ROOM. For a potential Vice President not to know and discuss a single Supreme Court decision is scary. I am officially scared! Between McCain acting schizophrenic and Palin continuing to demonstrate nothing higher than a fifth-grade education level, it is time for America to collectively worry. It is also being reported that Palin recently said that humans lived with dinosaurs. Media video showed her practicing for the debate today at McCain's Arizona ranch. She was doing a mock debate in front of a creek and, reportedly, struggled so much that Republican insiders themselves are very worried.

There is talk that some members of the Republican Party are asking for Palin to be removed from the ticket. The media is also continuing to ask if Palin's performance is lowering expectations so much that the debate can only work in her favor as long as she completes her sentences, a task, given past performance, she may not be up to. At 6:42 pm, Rachel

Maddow asked, "Does Sarah Palin maybe win here because expectations are going to be so low?" More and more members of the press are piling on Palin. CNN's Fareed Zacharia said, "Picking Palin was irresponsible of McCain." A former Bush speechwriter said, "Palin is not up to being President." *Salon's* Joan Walsh added, "Palin would be a menace as commander-in-chief." Thursday night's debate moderator, Gwen Ifill, fell down today and broke her ankle. Unfortunately for Palin, Ifill still intends to show up and play hurt.

DAY 38
BLAME IT ON THE MODERATOR

Obama is campaigning in La Crosse, Wisconsin, today—Wednesday, October 1—while McCain is in Independence, Misouri. "I won't allow the bailout to become a Wall Street welfare program," said Obama this morning before heading to Washington to vote on the bailout. Joe Biden and John McCain are also scheduled to be in Washington to vote. Biden will then head to St. Louis for tomorrow's vice Presidential debate. Debate moderator Gwen Ifill is under some scrutiny today for a book she is writing that features Obama as one of the central characters. This book has conservatives up in arms and many of them are calling for her removal. Michelle Malkin of the *New York Post* writes extensively about the controversy today. The article, **A Debate 'Moderator' in the Tank for Obama,** presents Gwen Ifill as completely partisan:

> My dictionary defines 'moderator' as the nonpartisan presiding officer of a town meeting.' On Thursday, PBS anchor Gwen Ifill will serve as moderator for the first and only vice presidential debate. The stakes are high. The Commission on Presidential Debates, with the assent of the two campaigns, decided not to impose any guidelines on her duties or questions. But there is nothing

'moderate' about where Ifill stands on Barack Obama. She's so far in the tank for the Democratic presidential candidate, her oxygen delivery line is running out.

John McCain said earlier today that having Ifill moderate isn't helpful, but he thinks she is a professional journalist who will be fair. Democrats should expect nothing less from conservatives, as they are likely to use every possible issue imaginable over the next few weeks to try to gain an advantage now that Obama seems to be pulling ahead. A Quinnipiac poll released today has him up in Florida, Ohio, and Pennsylvania. A CNN poll has him up in Missouri, Wisconsin, Virginia, and Nevada. This is devastating news to Republicans. Malkin continues her pan of the so-called liberal media:

> In an imaginary world where liberal journalists are held to the same standards as everyone else, Ifill would be required to make a full disclosure at the start of the debate. She would be required to turn to the cameras and tell the national audience that she has a book coming out on Jan. 20, 2009—a date that just happens to coincide with the inauguration of the next president of the United States. The title of Ifill's book? 'The Breakthrough: Politics and Race in the Age of Obama.' Nonpartisan my foot.

The funny aspect of this breaking news today is that anyone who was paying attention should have known about

Ifill's book since July when that information was made available to the public. The book features more black politicians than just Obama, but I guess Republicans see this as a way to ensure that they have cover for tomorrow in case Palin tanks. If she does, they will likely say that it was all Ifill's fault. Malkin is not going to let up on Ifill:

> Like Obama, Ifill, who is black, is quick to play the race card at the first sign of criticism. In an interview with the Washington Post a few weeks ago, she carped: '[N]o one's ever assumed a white reporter can't cover a white candidate.'
> It's not the color of your skin, sweetie. It's the color of your politics. Perhaps Ifill will be able to conceal it this week. But if the 'stunning' 'Breakthrough' she's rooting for comes to pass on Jan. 20, 2009, nobody will be fooled.

Regardless of how much mileage the press gets out of this Ifill-Obama conflict-of-interest story, Palin still has to show up tomorrow and debate Biden. And even thought the press is suggesting that Biden go easy on Palin tomorrow yet not be condescending, I think he should actually go right at her. If Biden will simply treat her like any other candidate and talk about the issues with his depth of knowledge, Palin's lack of knowledge will be glaring. This is not a time in history for niceties. We owe it to the country to vet our candidates completely, regardless of gender. Considering the fact that Palin's inability to name a Supreme Court decision that she disagreed with other than *Roe vs. Wade* is all over the news today, it is a perfect time for Biden to eliminate her completely tomorrow night. The latest exchange between Couric and Palin could be a game-ender if the media loops it as they did when Obama's former pastor, Reverend Wright, was caught on tape. Couric asked:

> **Couric:** What other Supreme Court decisions do you disagree with?
>
> **Palin:** Mmmm … Well, let's see … There's [deep breath] of course in, the great history of America there have been rulings that um … there's never going to be absolute consensus by every American, and, um, there are those issues again like *Roe v. Wade* where I believe are best held on a state level and addressed there so … you know … going through the history of America, there would be others, but, um…
>
> **Couric:** Can you think of any?
>
> **Palin:** Well, I would think of any, again, that could best be dealt with on a more local level. Maybe I would take issue with! But, um, you know as a mayor and then as a governor, and even as a vice president, if I'm so privileged, to serve, would be in a position of changing those things, but in supporting the law of the land as it, as it, reads today.

If anyone on the face of the earth can read the above statement, regardless of your political affiliation, and decipher what she is saying, you ought to be in the business of code breaking. To imagine Palin as a viable Vice President requires a willing suspension of disbelief.

The Senate now has enough votes to pass the financial bailout bill. Obama spoke earlier on the floor. McCain said nothing. The question now is can they get it through the House? Now that the Senate has done its job, McCain will hit the campaign trail again, and his fellow Republicans want him to ratchet up the attacks. Mike Allen and Jonathan Martin write in *Politico.com* today that "John McCain's recent polls, combined with a barrage of negative news coverage during the financial crisis, has leading Republican activists around the country worrying about his prospects and urging his campaign to become much more aggressive against Barack Obama in the remaining month before Election Day."

In the past, when McCain has gone on the attack, the media has given him far too much leeway, allowing the lies to gain traction. Allen and Martin's article, **Nervous GOP Urges McCain to Attack,** provides further insight into what we can expect:

> A flurry of new polls shows Barack Obama gaining in several battleground states – most notably Florida, Pennsylvania and swing states throughout the West. Officials worry early voting, which is under way in important states such as Ohio, is likely to favor Obama in this toxic political climate. Several state GOP chairmen in interviews urged the McCain campaign to be more aggressive in hitting Obama's vulnerabilities, such as his past

relationship with the Rev. Jeremiah Wright and
other problematic associations from Chicago.

… GOP officials also believe that a sustained attack
on Obama's ties to his former pastor, the Rev.
Jeremiah Wright, scandal-stained businessman
Tony Rezko and former radical war protester
William Ayers could sway undecided voters.

At 6:30 pm on CNN, Kellyanne Conway said that Palin is "at
least presiding over an eleven million dollar budget of Alaska
and has an 82% approval rating," unlike Obama. Conway
needs to brush up on her facts before spreading them to the
nation on CNN. Palin's Alaska approval rating is now 68%,
not 82%. This is a fact! Conway believes that simply presiding
over a budget is worth more than "competently" presiding
over a budget or any other political entity for that matter.
Any living, breathing person can preside over a budget. Palin
is certainly proving that. The key is competency!

At 6:33 pm on CNN, Karen Hughes said that Biden
made the most significant gaff when he said that Franklin D.
Roosevelt got on television when the stock market crashed in
1929. Hoover was in office in 1929 when the market crashed
and Hughes and other conservatives are going to town with
this Biden gaff. But, I don't think it is as significant a gaff
as Hughes suggests. Palin is making multiple gaffs everyday.
Hughes then laughably added, "[Palin] is choosing her words
carefully." Apparently she is not choosing them carefully
enough. And the order she puts those carefully-chosen words
in—what language does that syntax come from?

Barney Frank told Anderson Cooper tonight that the Republicans had control of Congress from 1995 to 2006. He tried to explain to Cooper that the Republicans never passed any regulatory bills against Fannie and Freddie. Frank tried to further point out to Anderson Cooper that if he had the type of control over Fannie and Freddie that Cooper seemed to be suggesting, he would have single handedly stopped the Iraq War bill and many other Republican-led bills. He said that within four months of the Democrats taking control of Congress, they stiffened regulations on Fannie and Freddie. Cooper didn't seem to be grasping the concept of the Democrats not having control of Congress for twelve years. It's as if Anderson Cooper and the rest of the media can't simply accept the reality that McCain is a mess, Palin is embarrassing, and the Republican-led Congress, along with Bush, is responsible for the financial disaster that's taking place. It's not that difficult to understand. We don't have to blame both Parties, Mr. Cooper. "Keeping them Honest" doesn't mean, "Making unequal things balanced."

DAY 39
FOX NEWS—"FAIR AND BALANCED" MY ASS!

Obama is campaigning in East Lansing, Michigan, today—Thursday, October 2—while McCain is in Denver, Colorado. This morning, MSNBC showed two clips, one of Biden telling rich Americans to be patriotic by paying their taxes and the other showing Palin struggling to name a Supreme Court decision that she disagrees with. They made it look like these were equal mistakes. But the news of the day continues to be Gwen Ifill's role in tonight's debate. Republicans are insistent on giving Palin an "out" if things don't go well. They can always say that Ifill was unfair and biased. I wonder if the media will be make a big deal out of the fact that Tom Brokaw, who is the moderator of the next Presidential debate, is on record saying that he is friendly with the McCain campaign?

FOX News is also trying to discredit the speech Obama gave on the Senate floor yesterday. Brit Hume referred to the fact that Obama is in the Senate today, a place he hasn't been much lately, but added, "nor, of course, has John McCain [been] of late as both are campaigning for president." Hume says that Obama is saying "the same thing McCain has been saying—*Let's step up to the plate and pass this economic rescue measure.*" Hume continued until he had gotten in his talking point: "It is hard to tell how Obama's remarks were taken.

Bernie Sanders, who is a socialist who was sitting behind him—he looked like he was bored to tears. I guess Obama is not nearly far enough left to suit him, but who knows?" Brit Hume should see me watching his continuous droll attacks without any sign of balance. I'm not just "bored to tears," I'm terrified for the future of journalism.

CNN's Candy Crowley noted the obvious about Palin today by claiming that the VP candidate has had an "extremely unsteady" performance over the past couple of weeks. How about incompetent? But Crowley can be given a bit of a pass when compared with what's coming out of a "Fair and Balanced" segment on FOX News. Meghann Kelly, in speaking with Frederico Pena, said that the Obama camp is saying that Palin is a very good debater. She asked Pena if that's "how the Obama camp is gonna spin it?" What does that mean? She then sent him this loaded opinion to respond to: "Joe Biden has been exaggerating, some would say out and out lying." Again, in the segment she said that Biden had played "fast and loose with the facts." Bill Hammer later threw his guest Tracey Schmitt, a Palin debate coach, a soft ball to discuss. He said that some people have been saying that the McCain camp has been protecting Sarah Palin from the media. "Is that fair, Tracy?" He means is it fair to say that. How can it not be fair to say that when the public has not been able to assess Palin's competency to fill the job except through speeches and handpicked, sympathetic news anchors and pundits? FOX is not done yet, however. They allowed Tracey Schmitt and Karl Rove to throw around attacks against Obama. Rove begins by asserting that "there are persistent doubts about Obama." They go over various polls, all of which show Obama quickly gaining ground over McCain, after which Schmitt says, "However, there are still persistent doubts about Obama, isn't that right, Karl?" Excuse me, aren't these the exact words Rove used to start off this segment? Rove than tries to spin Biden the same way he has just been spinning the polls. He tries to further the planted opinion that Biden is a gaff machine. "Biden needs to be extremely careful to avoid gaffs after the stream of them lately." He then reiterates the so-called gaffs, which to me do not seem like gaffs at all. But if Rove says so. Isn't that why the American public has believed lies to be facts for the past eight years—because Rove says to? If Rove's spin has not caught you on the conscious side, there was this headline on the screen to wiggle into your subconscious: BIDEN NEEDS TO AVOID SEXISM.

At 2:15 pm on MSNBC, Chris Matthews said that Obama needs to stop talking like Adlai Stevenson and start talking like a regular guy. Moments later he referred to Palin as "a very appealing person." Wow! At 3:07 pm, David Gregory felt like taking some heat off Palin. He injected this opinion following the clip of Palin struggling to think of any Supreme Court decisions that she disagreed with other than *Roe v Wade*: "I think a lot of political figures would have struggled with that question." Actually, I don't think another person running for Vice President, in the history of the United States, would have struggled with that question, Mr. Gregory. But, nice try!

At 5:32 pm on CNN, Anderson Cooper seemed puzzled by the lead Obama is building in the national polls. He persistently asked, "How strong is the support" for Obama, and can't it shift? Yes, Anderson, Obama is leading, and despite your efforts to keep the race close, he is pulling away. I know it pains you to see this happening, but if you work hard enough, I'm sure you can run more "Keeping Them Honest" segments and tighten the race back up.

At 5:47 pm on CNN, Jeffrey Toobin said that Palin's comments to Couric were "incompetent." Bravo, Jeffrey Toobin! Gloria Borger disagreed with him and stood up for Palin. Then John King stood up for her as well. He said that we've all had bad moments on live television, and if Palin can do well tonight, there are a lot of voters out there who will follow her—just as they followed Ross Perot.

As the debate is about to begin, the McCain campaign has decided to pull out of Michigan. Obama has a ten-point lead in the state, and the McCain camp feels that it's no longer winnable. They will pour all of their resources into Pennsylvania instead, as it is a blue state that they feel they can still win. Michigan is a blue state that they hoped they could try to steal. They're retreating.

The Vice Presidential debate has just ended and the media is already saying that Palin did surprisingly better than expected. My own opinion is that she failed to answer any of the questions. At one point she actually said, "I may not answer the questions the way you and the moderator want me to...." Ifill didn't respond, but I was stunned that a candidate would actually admit that they intended not to answer questions. Politicians are known for not answering the question put to them, but few admit it before they segue into their talking point. But Palin stayed true to her word and preceded not to answer many of the questions Ifill threw her way during the ninety-minute debate. Palin managed to attack Obama with one lie after another, and she managed to read her index cards effectively, but Ifill never asked any follow-up questions. Palin has shown that she struggles with those. I am insulted that Ifill would allow a candidate to get away with not answering questions. When Palin agreed to debate, she was agreeing at least to attempt to address the issues presented for discussion, not to simply regurgitate talking points.

Campbell Brown said, "Palin did what she needed to do, which was to be reassuring...He [Biden] lost people a little bit when he got into the Senate speak." "She stopped the bleeding," said Andrea Mitchell. Mitchell also felt that Palin might not have answered the questions that were asked but that she still stopped the bleeding. Chris Matthews felt that "her energy level was much better than Biden's. At 8:23 on CNN, John King showed a poll that asked which candidate seemed more like a typical politician. Over 70% said Biden. That's a terrible, loaded question. Of course the answer would be Biden! He's much older—he's been in the Senate for 36 years. A CNN poll shows that Biden won the debate 51% to 36%, but that didn't stop Joe Lieberman from saying, on FOX News, that Palin was "brilliant tonight." CNN's Ed Rollins said that Palin had not helped McCain tonight in that she had not effectively attacked Obama nor distanced the McCain-Palin ticket from Bush but that she seemed to be trying to help herself. He feels that Palin may be thinking of becoming a Presidential candidate in 2012 as a result of tonight's performance.

DAY 40
POP POLITICS

Obama is campaigning in Abington, Pennsylvania, today—Friday, October 3—while McCain is in Pueblo, Colorado. It appears that America has gotten a good night's sleep because Palin is being accused by voters of not answering questions last night, which is, of course, the correct analysis, despite how the media is spinning it. When Palin tried to be flirty and give her homespun phrases, the audience responded negatively, based on CNN's dial testing analysis. Every time Palin tried to be cute, the CNN dial testing line dipped considerably. It looks as if the country has finally figured out the McCain-Palin shtick and is no longer buying it, but that hasn't stopped the media from continuing to help the Republicans try to sell it. One Republican surrogate after another is on television this morning telling us how dynamic Palin was last night.

Today's big news is the passing of the bailout bill by the House. Bush signed the bill. Now that it has been passed and Palin has completed her one and only debate, the media can get back to focusing on the top of the ticket. There is talk that McCain intends to muddy up the waters again in the coming days, and this probably means a heavy dose of talk about Reverend Wright, community organizing, sex education, William Ayers the radical, Tony Rezco the crook, and whatever else the McCain camp can throw at the wall in hopes that it will stick.

One of the major ways that the media hurts Obama is by allowing surrogates to come on television and spin the facts. Susan Molinari was a guest of David Gregory who said that Palin was "absolutely brilliant" at connecting Joe Biden to all of the negative things he had said about Obama during the primary. Without Molinari's input, no one on earth would associate Palin with brilliance. John Harwood said Palin was "charming". David Gregory asked the panel if Palin's winking was too much. Joan Walsh joked that she didn't feel that Palin was winking at her personally.

Gwen Ifill asked the candidates last night if there was anything they had promised that would now have to be cut as a result of the bailout. Biden mentioned some items that would have to be cut, but Palin amazingly said that there was nothing she would have to scale back on. The media should be demanding a clarification from the McCain camp today for that comment. Of course, they are going to have to make some cuts after the government has just spent $700 billion.

David Gregory showed a clip of the debate in which Palin was saying how she was obviously a Washington outsider because she didn't understand the way that Joe Biden talked. She then accused Joe Biden of wanting to lose the war by saying, "Your plan is a white flag of surrender in Iraq." This childish little comment came directly after Biden had given a very astute summary of the situation in Iraq. After Gregory showed the clip, he said, with a big goofy grin on his face that Palin had a "likeable" way of getting in there and turning the knife, etc. I literally wanted to jump in the television and start choking him. Joan Walsh must have agreed with me because she said that the comments were rather "unlikeable." But neither Walsh nor Gregory assessed the clip accurately. Palin's facial expression, tone, posture, inflection, gleeful malice, and overt lie was unbearable. During the debate, Biden got emotional when telling the story about his sons almost dying in a car accident. He said that he knew what it was like to wonder if a child is going to make it. As he said it, he got choked up. It seemed like a natural moment for Palin to be sensitive, understanding, and bi-partisan, but instead she just transitioned right into talking about John McCain being a maverick. It was as if Palin had no feelings. I think the rest of the world was connecting with Biden and trying to imagine what it must have been like for him to lose a wife and child, only to be left with two young sons to raise. It was a powerful story and makes one feel certain that Biden is a man who can handle a crisis that may come his way. He certainly handled that crisis better than most people would have. Larry King must have had a different view of Biden's display of emotion. He asked his guest today if Biden's emotional moment was "hokey." I simply can't understand why King asked this question. Of course it wasn't "hokey"! It was real—and relevant.

There are too many distorted comments Palin made last night for me to cover, but it is safe to say that she has successfully managed to take the integrity of over 220 years of America's political process and turn it on its ear. I have never heard any candidate talk the way she did during a debate. In five weeks, she has dumbed down Presidential politics, with the help of the media, more than any thoughtful person could have imagined. At this very moment, and history will show just how true this is, the Republican party—and the press—should feel it their duty to say in one unified voice, *This is the most embarrassing political figure ever to take the stage, and we all ought to be ashamed of ourselves for allowing it to happen. But we are so desperate to be players in the show that we'll allow any Tom, Dick, or Harry, regardless of their intellectual capacity or ancient social views, to use a cute little smile, wink, or platitude to undermine the seriousness of the political process.* As a matter of fact, the media played a role in resuscitating what was an otherwise unviable political candidate in Palin. The media continues to hurt Obama albeit not by targeting him specifically the way they did earlier in the campaign but rather by being the judges that keep the McCain-Palin ticket in the game. Journalists should be the ones holding the bar in its place, but instead they've allowed Palin to lower it to a level that suits her competence thus allowing her to conceivably become the most unqualified Vice President—possibly President—in history. American Idol and other reality shows seem to be serving as the blueprint from which serious journalists are drawing inspiration. The problem here is that the voter has no opportunity to vote the first rounders—you know, the ones that can't sing—off the ticket. If Palin were in a pool of one hundred singing VP hopefuls, she would have been voted off immediately. Instead we—America—may have her singing for us around the world with a voice that has foreign leaders covering their ears or laughing behind her back. Welcome to American Idol politics brought to you by the Republican party and the corporate media! The last so-called winner they gave us who couldn't sing a lick was George W. Bush. I've been covering my ears for eight years.

The fact that Tom Brokaw is moderating the next debate should have Democrats worried. One of the questions Brokaw should ask McCain is, *What did your running mate mean when she said that she looked forward to the Vice President having a bigger role in the Senate?* Palin seems to believe that the Vice President can do more than the Constitution allows. She gave every indication that she intends to expand the Vice President's duties. When Ifill asked her about her role as VP, Palin looked down at her notes and appeared quite nervous. She obviously has no clue about the Vice President's role.

"How about Sarah Palin last night?" This is what John McCain asked a crowd in Pueblo, Colorado today. The audience erupted. McCain wasn't the only one singing Palin's praises. Today, the *Wall Street Journal's* Peggy Noonan writes, "The whole debate was about Sarah Palin. She is not a person of thought but of action. Interviews are about thinking, about reflecting, marshaling data and integrating it into an answer. Debates are more active, more propelled—they are thrust and parry. They are for campaigners. She is a campaigner. Her syntax did not hold, but her magnetism did. At one point she literally winked at the nation…. As far as Mrs. Palin was concerned, Gwen Ifill was not there, and Joe Biden was not there. Sarah and the camera were there." I strongly disagree with Noonan's assessment. Biden was there and he was treating the serious institution of political debating with the respect that our forefathers would have been proud of. Palin was also there, but she was taking up space that would have been better filled by an individual with the mental capacity to answer questions with conviction and clarity. And the magnetism that Noonan speaks of would be better put to use on the stage of *American Idol*. Noonan has fallen victim to "pop politics."

Howard Fineman of *Newsweek* seemed to disagree with Noonan because he called Palin a "useful prop" on MSNBC today. Fineman is managing to keep his wits about him, and he doesn't appear anxious to take Simon Cowell's place as a pop artist judge. He understands his role as a serious journalist, and winking at him is not enough to excite him into writing blindly about a woman who is certainly unqualified to be a Vice President. Rich Lowry wrote this very odd, and sexual, bit of information in today's *National Review* about Palin:

> A very wise TV executive once told me that the key to TV is projecting through the screen. It's one of the keys to the success of, say, a Bill O'Reilly, who comes through the screen and grabs you by the throat. Palin too projects through the screen like crazy. I'm sure I'm not the only male in America who, when Palin dropped her first wink, set up a little straighter on the couch and said, 'Hey, I think she just winked at me.' And her smile! By the end, when she clearly knew she was doing well, it was so sparkling it was almost mesmerizing. It sent little starbursts through the screen and ricocheting around the living rooms of America. This is a quality that can't be learned; it's either something you have or you don't, and man, she's got it.

At 7:13 pm, Anderson Cooper asked, "How are McCain and Obama both spinning this financial bailout?" I haven't heard Obama spinning the bailout at all. He stood on the floor of the Senate two days ago and asked his colleagues to "step up" and vote for the bill. What about that sounds like spin? Cooper also suggested that none of the members of Congress had taken responsibility. He said that he had talked to Barney Frank, a Democrat, and asked him if he was willing to take any "personal responsibility." Cooper then said that Frank told him "No, it was all the Republican's fault." Interesting how Anderson Cooper used a Democrat to make his point about no one taking responsibility. Cooper then talked about Obama's mounting lead in the polls. He asked, "Can't McCain gain any ground?" He didn't ask, "Can he?" It's as if he himself believes McCain can certainly gain ground on Obama and he can't understand why he already hasn't. Be patient, Mr. Cooper. There's still time for McCain to catch up. Then you can ask questions like, *Isn't it amazing how McCain has managed to catch up? And what in the world is Obama going to do now? Isn't it over for him?* Today was Obama's sixteenth wedding anniversary. He stopped by a Pennsylvania flower shop to grab roses for Michelle. I'm surprised Anderson Cooper didn't ask, "Don't you think Obama is pandering a bit to women by buying flowers for his wife with all of those cameras on him?"

DAY 41
O. J.—AGAIN?

Obama is campaigning in Newport News, Virginia, today—Saturday, October 4—while McCain is in Sedona, Arizona. How many times can one candidate wink during a single debate? This is a question that people are asking about Sarah Palin's debate performance Thursday night. She seemed to wink at the camera every time she was attempting to make her point. Palin is now saying that McCain should send her into Michigan along with her husband, Todd, instead of pulling out of the state while the media is saying that McCain's decision to pull out of the state is the first tell-tell sign of a possible defeat. But the media is also saying that McCain will likely turn to an even nastier brand of politics in the coming weeks.

Obama is up 51% to 43% in Florida according to a Quinnipiac poll. It's news like this that has the McCain camp scrambling. Obama is even up in the red state of Nevada. Speaking of Nevada, O.J. Simpson was found guilty on twelve counts of robbery and kidnapping in Las Vegas today. Maybe Hannity will try to tie Obama to Simpson. After all, Obama did attend Occidental College, which is in the same metropolitan area O.J.'s from. Did their paths ever cross? Hannity is probably in Brentwood investigating as we speak.

The New York Times is providing some fuel for the McCain camp that possibly will aid in linking Obama to William

Ayers. An article entitled **Obama and '60s Bomber: A Look Into Crossed Paths** hit newsstands today. Scott Shane writes, "At a tumultuous meeting of anti-Vietnam War militants at the Chicago Coliseum in 1969, Bill Ayers helped found the radical Weathermen, launching a campaign of bombings that would target the Pentagon and United States Capitol." The article itself doesn't do any damage to Obama, but the headline certainly doesn't help the Illinois Senator. So far it has been FOX News alone trying to take down Obama with the Ayers' stories, but now *The New York Times* will at least have people scratching their heads. Scott Shane may be scratching his:

> Twenty-six years later, at a lunchtime meeting about school reform in a Chicago skyscraper, Barack Obama met Mr. Ayers, by then an education professor. Their paths have crossed sporadically since then, at a coffee Mr. Ayers hosted for Mr. Obama's first run for office, on the schools project and a charitable board, and in casual encounters as Hyde Park neighbors.
>
> Their relationship has become a touchstone for opponents of Mr. Obama, the Democratic senator, in his bid for the presidency.

All the major news networks are suggesting that the McCain camp intends to change gears and go into full throttle smear mode. Sarah Palin brought up the Obama-Ayers connection today, taking her cues from *The New York Times*: "There is a lot of interest, I guess, in what I read and what I've read lately. Well, I was reading my copy of today's *New York Times,* and I was interested to read about Barack's friends from Chicago. I get to bring this up not to pick a fight, but it was there in *The New York Times,* so we are gonna talk about it." She accused him of "palling around with terrorists". Would she have made Ayers her theme if *The New York Times* had not printed the article? We'll never know. She did, however, use the paper as validation for bringing the subject up. After all, I don't think she would have quoted FOX News to the world. McCain is obviously deploying her to begin the dirty work. It is so predictable. Certain writers are suggesting ways that McCain can come back and still win the election. *Real Clear Politics* posted an article today by the *Weekly Standard's* William Kristol entitled **Can They Catch Up? Of Course.** Kristol gives a blueprint of the things to come:

> The odds are against John McCain and Sarah Palin winning this election. It's not easy to make up a 6-point deficit in the last four weeks. But it can be done.
>
> ... The positive component is pretty straightforward: McCain and Palin are common sense conservatives and proven reformers. The record of reform can be emphasized and contrasted with Obama's and Biden's records of conventional, go-along, get-along liberalism. And implicitly: If McCain and Palin are reformers and outsiders, it's not Bush's third term. More important is the negative message. The McCain campaign has to convince 51 percent of the voters

> they can't trust Barack Obama to be our next president. This has an ideological component and a character component.
>
> Character is a legitimate issue. Obama hasn't shown much in the way of leadership or political courage, and he's consorted with dubious figures. It's fair to ask whether Barack Obama is personally trustworthy enough to be president, and the McCain campaign shouldn't be intimidated from going there.

If McCain takes Kristol's advice and tries to paint Obama as untrustworthy, it will be up to the rest of the press not to create drama where there is none. *Newsweek's* Eleanor Clift's October 3rd article, **Palin Reignites the Culture War,** seems to be a first attempt at creating the very drama I speak of. She says, "Her everywoman act plays well, and the GOP may try again to target Obama as elitist." I am not as certain that her everywoman act played as well as Ms. Clift suggests. I actually think that more and more women in America are getting sick and tired of Palin. Clift adds, "Biden looked on with a mixture of awe and horror as she did her every-woman show, winking at the camera, celebrating hockey moms and giving a shout-out to her brother's third-grade class." Is she serious? Biden never looked on with "awe" and most certainly didn't give any looks of "horror." I also don't believe that Palin did an "every-woman" show. If winking flirtatiously, refusing to answer questions, and telling lies, is what Clift believes constitutes an "every-woman show," I wonder if she thinks very highly of women?

Clift quotes Yuval Levin with the *Ethics and Public Policy Center*, noting that Levin is "speaking from the perspective of the right when she says, 'Even though McCain comes from a military aristocracy and married an heiress and Obama's family was on food stamps for a time, Republicans can still make the elitist label stick on Obama.'" If Levin is "speaking from the perspective of the right," she is certainly glad that *Newsweek's* Clift considers her opinion newsworthy. It is only this very small, right-leaning group that considers Obama an elitist.

Today on CNN, Amy Holmes took issue with Obama's suggestion that America's standing in the world has changed. She disagrees with his assertion that America is no longer looked upon with the same amount of respect. Holmes said that Obama is completely wrong to suggest such a thing. She disagreed with the idea that people around the world no longer see America as a "beacon of freedom." She asked, "Do you think it's actually true that people no longer want to come to this country?" As a matter of record, Ms. Holmes, Obama never said that people no longer want to come to this country. During my own recent trips to Paris, Venice, and Morocco, I discovered Mr. Obama's claims to be true. Many people in those parts of the world cannot believe that we voted for George Bush a second time. Holmes needs to do more traveling. And if she did so with her ears open, she would certainly discover that Obama is more popular overseas than he is in America. Europe will actually be stunned if we don't elect Obama. This is a fact that Holmes would probably refuse to believe, even if every person in London told her so. She would find one Londoner, who liked McCain, and she would come back to the States and say on CNN, *I talked to a woman overseas, and she still thinks of America as the greatest place on earth. She also loves John McCain.* Message to Amy Holmes: Whether you are willing to accept it or not, America's standing in the world has been severely damaged over the last eight years. Wake up! And if you want to hold onto one shred of your credibility, if you have any, give Obama his due when he speaks the truth, even if you are told to present yourself as a brainwashed, right wing nut. Just because you worked as a speechwriter for a Republican, doesn't mean you have to follow the party like an obstinate, narrow-minded, bullheaded, and groveling adolescent.

DAY 42
THANK YOU, TINA FEY

Obama is campaigning in Asheville, North Carolina, today—Sunday, October 5—while McCain is in Sedona, Arizona. It has been two days since the VP debate, and there has been little if any talk about Joe Biden's excellent performance. The media has been largely focused on Palin's good, bad, or adequate performance. It is important to note that Joe Biden showed a tremendous amount of discipline during those ninety minutes. There were several key moments when Palin was definitely trying to goad Biden into being defensive or condescending. He did neither. At one point, Palin actually said, "Say it ain't so, Joe." She then accused him of using Bush's name before every statement he made. Biden just smiled and didn't respond. Biden also gave very thorough answers that, under other circumstances and against a more able opponent, would have elicited a similarly detailed response. But Palin was able to say silly little folksy charmers like "you betcha" and "Joe six-pack" to finagle her way out of having to actually say something substantial. Just before the debate started and the candidates walked onto the stage, Palin leaned into Biden and asked, "Is it ok if I call you Joe?" Biden said it was fine. We soon found out why she had asked that. It was only so she could say the rehearsed line—"Say it ain't so, Joe!" In a skit on Saturday Night Live last night, Tina Fey played Palin and asked, "Is it ok if I call you Joe?" The actor playing Biden said, "Yes," and then Fey replied, "Good because I've worked on some zingers where I refer to you as Joe." She nailed the absurdity of Palin's performance better than anyone in the media has managed to do.

Sarah Palin has made the phrase "Joe six-pack" popular during her run for high office. She claims to be trying to appeal to those Joes and hockey moms across America. But I am puzzled by her desire to appeal to guys who like finishing off six-packs of beer. "Joe Six-Pack" is probably a guy who drinks too much, gets in his car, and drives drunk. I would think that the politically active MADD (Mothers Against Drunk Driving) and conservative Christians, who preach that drinking is a sin, would be against Joe. Isn't Sarah Palin an evangelical Christian? Is drinking alcohol part of Palin's family values? Do you think she might get tossed out of the evangelical church for promoting a sin?

John Voight, on FOX News, at 5:26 pm said, "[Obama's] affiliation with Ayers is always pushed to the side." Voight evidently is teaming up with Palin to sling mud for the next four weeks. Angelina's father failed to mention, however, that the media has brought Ayers to the center of the table, gnawed on that bone searching for meat, and then—and only then—"pushed [it] to the side" and even off the table. If they want to pick up this old, cold bone and put it back on the table to gnaw on some more, I say *Go for it if you're that desperately hungry.* During the debate, Palin accused Biden of looking backwards by talking about Bush. She is now hypocritically asking people to look backwards and try to tie Obama to a 1960s radical like Ayers. The desperation is palpable if not palatable. Sean Hannity, tonight on FOX News, did an entire show entitled, "Obama & Friends: History of Radicalism." The first so-called radical he tied Obama to was Rev. Wright. I can imagine interviews that could take place this week in response to Sean Hannity's breakthrough documentary on radicalism. NOTE TO SEAN HANNITY: These are pretend.

CNN REPORTER: Sen. Obama, FOX News is suggesting that you know Rev. Wright. Would you care to respond?"

OBAMA: Well, yes I would. Look. What planet were you on when I told the world that he is no longer my pastor and hasn't been for several months?

CNN REPORTER: You did that?

OBAMA: Yes

CNN REPORTER: Oh, right. Been there done that. Then I won't make a fool of myself anymore and ask you about it. Do you promise not to tell my boss?

OBAMA: I promise. Next question?

Next interview:

MSNBC REPORTER: I know that we should be asking you questions about the second Great Depression that may be looming, but in response to Hannity's report Sunday, I must ask, did you help William Ayers by driving the get-away vehicle from the Pentagon when you were eight years old?

OBAMA: *Look…it's true, I did learn to drive—some would say ride—when I was eight years old, but it was a Spiderman bicycle.*

MSNBC REPORTER: *Just a follow-up—before any of the respectable journalists show up—is it true that you rode your bicycle in a radical fashion?*

OBAMA: *Well, now, yes…that's true. I did like to pop a wheelie from time to time.*

MSNBC REPORTER: *Just one more follow-up. Did you say "pop"?*

OBAMA: *Next question.*

Next interview:

C-SPAN REPORTER: *Is it true that you wrote a thesis at Columbia University that no one can find now? And isn't it also true that that paper was radical?*

OBAMA: *Yeah. I FED-EXed it to Osama bin Laden, but he thought it was too radical and sent it back. I thought that since it was too radical for him, I would trash it.*

C-SPAN REPORTER: *IS ANY OF THAT ACTUALLY TRUE?*

OBAMA: *No. Next question.*

Next interview:

PBS REPORTER: *There has been some suggestion on the part of Sean Hannity that you were radically tied to the radical voter registration group ACORN. First of all,* is there any truth to the rumor that the R in ACORN stands for radical? Just kidding. Please respond.

OBAMA: *Yes, it is true that I was associated with them and that I did represent them when I was practicing law.*

PBS REPORTER: *But what's radical about that?*

OBAMA: *Look…I'll come clean on this one, there are rumors that many of those recently-franchised voters, thanks to the help of ACORN, cast their ballots for George W. Bush…hence the totally un-American and irrational, radical behavior. That is a little too radical for me. One more question.*

Next interview:

CBS REPORTER: *Is it true that when you decided that running for the Presidency was in your future, you figured it would be a good idea to buddy up to a future convicted felon named Rezko?*

OBAMA: *I was just getting into the political arena and had run into Sen. John McCain. He told me that his friendship with Keating had radically set him apart from the pack and put his face on the cover of many a magazine. He's been running for President ever since.*

CBS REPORTER: *Is it true that saying things that actually make sense are code words for elitism, meaning that you are among the IQ elite? And is it true that when you applied for Harvard Law they told you they were accepting only the elite? Also, is it true that you actually think the American people are looking for that quality* *too and you're offering your services to work for them, but realize that in that respect your candidacy represents a really radical change from the present administration— a radical change that has sent the likes of Sean Hannity into an intellectual tailspin?*

OBAMA: *Yes!*

As he was campaigning in Asheville, North Carolina, today, Obama responded to Palin's accusation that he was "palling around with terrorists." He said, "Senator McCain and his operatives are gambling that he can distract you with smears rather than talk to you about substance. They'd rather try to tear our campaign down than lift this country up." Obama had the crowd in the palm of his hand as he continued. "It's what you do when you're out of touch, out of ideas and running out of time." He then jokingly said, "We're not going to let John McCain distract us. We're not going to let him hoodwink ya, and bamboozle ya, we're not going to let him run the okie-doke on ya."

But the McCain campaign is hitting back and not backing down. Spokesman Tucker Bounds said, "The last four weeks of this election will be about whether the American people are willing to turn our economy and national security over to Barack Obama, a man with little record, questionable judgment, and ties to radical figures like unrepentant terrorist William Ayers." Joe Lieberman on FOX News today said that the issue of Ayers is "fair game."

Considering the fact that the corporate media has decided to give voice to these claims of radical associations, it is important to note where Obama stands in the polls. Today could very well be the last day he holds such a lead because the media is going to provide a stage from which the McCain camp can get out their talking points. And the press wants a ballgame. They want this thing close. In both the Rasmussen and Gallup polls today, Obama has a seven-point lead nationally. Think about it! With 29 days left until the election, Obama leads by seven nationally. He leads by ten in Pennsylvania, eighteen in Minnesota, seven in Ohio, four in Nevada, ten in Michigan, nine in Virginia, four in Florida, sixteen in Iowa, one in Colorado, and eight in New Mexico. Leading in these states at this stage is remarkable, but the McCain camp's strategy of illuminating Ayers and the press' willingness to assist them will likely destroy these poll numbers. Today is Sunday. It will be up to Obama to defeat McCain in the debate Tuesday night, and perhaps bring up the Keating Five. But, will the media make Keating seem as villainous as Reverend Wright or William Ayers? We shall see.

In the *Washington Post* today, Michael Abramowitz writes, "GOP vice presidential nominee Sarah Palin opened a new assault on Barack Obama on Saturday, accusing the Democratic presidential nominee of being 'someone who sees America as imperfect enough to pal around with terrorists.'" The *Washington Post* article is entitled **Palin Seizes On Obama's Ayers Ties.** The article actually credits *The New York Times* for being the source from which Palin drew her comments. Thank you *New York Times*! Palin would have been reluctant to reference FOX News as her only source during her speech but perhaps felt empowered by the reputable

Times. It's important for the record to show that McCain's first reference to Ayers came yesterday from the mouth of Palin via *The New York Times.* The paper never should have given the Obama-Ayers relationship one drop of ink unless and until they had evidence of some nefarious plot between the two.

On *Meet the Press,* David Gregory said something to the panel that was striking: "The McCain campaign wants to do something else and make it about *Who is this guy, really?* It's the mystery part of this. In 2004, what they did to John Kerry was say that he was weak and that he was a flip-flopper. You know, tough stuff but not as bad as what they want to do here. I spoke to a McCain advisor who said this is about character, this is to prove that Obama is a liar. That he lies to you about Ayers. That he lies to you about our record. He lies to you about his position on taxes." Yeah, right, David Gregory. The Rove machine didn't try to ruin John Kerry's character and make him into a war hero turned laughing stock who lied about his service? Gregory is fooling no one by his slick deceitful source reference. When he says "a McCain advisor" told me such-and-such, it rings hollow. It unquestionably comes across as his own desired talking point—a way of getting back at the Obama campaign, which actually did catch the McCain campaign in a series of lies and finally called them on it. It is Gregory who is saying that Obama is lying and that he is a "mysterious" character. I have never heard Gregory say that he'd spoken to an Obama advisor who told him that McCain was lying. Obama advisors have probably told him such things. Gregory just chooses not to share it with the rest of us. It's the Brokaw method of journalism: sift through a thousand random stories then pick the one that does the most damage to your political opponent to share with the world. These sources never have a name.

At one point during the program, Chuck Todd was showing the electoral map to Brokaw. Brokaw said, "Chuck, a very senior Republican was startled the other day when he called me and said, 'What in the world is going on in Florida—why are we in trouble there?'" I wonder why a very senior Republican is calling Brokaw? Why not a very senior Democrat? Brokaw also read part of William Kristol's **Can They Catch Up** article from yesterday's *Weekly Standard*. When William Kristol is being highlighted on *Meet the Press*, it's time to worry.

DAY 43
THREATENING CROWDS

Obama is campaigning in Asheville, North Carolina, today—Monday, October 6—while McCain is in Albuquerque, New Mexico. The DOW hit a record one-day drop of 782 points today. But even with this disastrous news, a McCain campaign spokesman said that if their camp continues to talk about the economy, they will lose the Presidential race. Obama said that the American people have already been losing, and the notion that the McCain campaign wants to turn the page on discussing the economy is hard to believe. Obama said that he intends to keep talking about the economy and wants to do so at tomorrow's debate. The notion that McCain would see discussing the economy as a losing proposition boggles the mind. He would rather talk about William Ayers. He is truly playing the desperate card.

Andrea Mitchell showed a clip of Palin referencing William Ayers and then a clip from Obama's new thirteen-minute web video that features McCain's involvement in the Keating Five. Obama has decided to meet smear with smear, and he obviously had no choice. At 10:16 am, after she had showed the clips, Mitchell said, "Doesn't this seem like a detour perhaps on both sides? … It's twenty years old, the Keating Five." Obama spokeswoman, Stephanie Cutter tried to defend Obama's use of the new video. Mitchell then said, "The Ethics Committee report … said that John McCain did not break any Senate rules." She then played another clip of Palin speaking today and saying, "Barack Obama says that Ayers was just someone in the neighborhood. That's less than truthful." Mitchell asked Cutter, "Is this damaging to you guys?" It's damaging only if you keep showing it, Andrea Mitchell.

Kirsten Powers of FOX News, a supposed Democratic strategist, acted as if she was defending Obama by claiming that the McCain campaign was overplaying the Ayers-Obama connection. She then said that it was also being underplayed by the Obama campaign. Powers said that for the Obama campaign to say he didn't even know Ayers is not believable. I don't recall Obama suggesting that he never knew Ayers, but Kirsten Powers must know that in order for her to keep her job at FOX, she can't solely jab McCain. FOX News' "Democratic representatives" have a habit of making subtle digs at Obama.

All of the networks are doing a balancing act, trying to give equal airtime to both Ayers and Keating. The Ayers story doesn't seem to be gaining any traction. But that isn't stopping McCain. In New Mexico today, he said, "For a guy who authored two memoirs, he's not exactly an open book … In short, who is the real Barack Obama?" A person in the audience yelled, "A terrorist!" No one in the press has asked why McCain hasn't denounced that comment. He actually ignored it and just continued on with his speech. Today in Clearwater, Florida, as Palin was preaching to her Republican choir and talking about Obama's ties to domestic terrorists, a person in the crowd shouted, "Kill him," in reference to Obama. The Secret Service is investigating who actually said that, but neither Palin nor McCain have apologized for that horrific comment. She, like McCain, just went right on talking.

McCain is also running an ad today that asks, "Who is the real Barack Obama?" This sounds like a familiar theme. A police officer introducing Palin today referred to Obama as "Barack Hussein Obama." The press is suggesting that Obama might want to retaliate by pointing out that Palin's husband was a member of a party that wanted to secede from the United States. Palin also had a pastor from Kenya pray for her at church in an attempt to protect her from witches. Obama has refused to involve himself in smearing Palin or McCain with anything other than the Keating issue.

At 7:16 pm, CNN showed Palin saying, "I'm just afraid that this is not a man who sees America the way that you and I see this great country." Anderson Cooper said that the Obama camp is clearly trying to play down Obama's relationship with Ayers, but the McCain camp is trying to play it up. Cooper then asked, "So what is the truth?" The truth is that we are sick and tired of CNN talking about an issue that was beaten to death during the Democratic primary. And it was you, Mr. Cooper, who played a huge role in posing questions about Obama's associations with so-called radicals.

CNN reported tonight that Obama and Ayers' paths crossed at an Annenberg Grant project. The report suggested that Annenberg Challenge gave money to "radical community organization" groups. CNN also reported that under Obama's chairmanship, Annenberg Project gave money to several organizations and that Bernadine Dorn, Alison Palmer, and Obama were all at Bill Ayers' home to raise money. Why did CNN run a whole piece—now—on William Ayers? CNN is saying that the McCain camp is trying to hang the "judgment peg" on Obama with this strategy.

David Gergen suggested that most Americans will penalize any candidate who doesn't remain focused on the economic disaster. Gergen feels that Obama is in danger of getting down in the mud with them if he is not careful. He said that it's not the media's fault that the two candidates are not able to talk about the economy. If David Gergen is suggesting that had Obama given a serious economic speech today, he and Anderson Cooper wouldn't be talking about William Ayers right this moment, it isn't true. Nothing could stop them from talking about Ayers. Nothing! Obama did talk about the economy today. But *Anderson Cooper 360* is not a news show. It's an analysis of whatever they want to talk about, and they chose to discuss this Ayers subject? STOP TALKING ABOUT IT!

Candy Crowley said that the McCain camp has to keep casting those doubts about Obama. Do they have to, Candy? Is this a rule for electing our leader? Or is it just the common knowledge that you and other Machiavellian analysts have adopted. On MSNBC, Chuck Todd said that McCain is trying to make the case that "he's change too" but that "he's just change that you're more familiar with." Todd is correct in his analysis, perhaps, but I wonder if he just offered up a slogan that McCain can put on his posters. You know—think about it. "JOHN MCCAIN-THE CHANGE YOU'RE FAMILIAR WITH."

It is noteworthy that Sarah Palin, a person who is hurling the most ridiculous comments imaginable at Obama, is being covered around the clock today. Our media has sunk so low. For them to allow this country, which is going through so much financial pain, to be subjected again to the same ludicrous accusations that Obama defended himself against in the primary is going too far. Our government is broken, the economy is in shambles, people are losing their homes by the minute, students can't get college loans, unemployment is rising, gas prices are through the roof, millions of Americans are without healthcare, seniors are worried about Medicare, people are having to put off retirement, some in the South are recovering from hurricanes, we're involved in two wars, Darfur needs our help, Bin Laden is on the loose, Global Warming continues to threaten, we're dependent on foreign oil—yet with all of this to deal with, our media is utterly consumed with analyzing video footage of Sarah Palin saying that Barack Obama is friends with William Ayers and Jeremiah Wright. The press has a disease and the cure has yet to be discovered. The best thing they could offer America today is this sound bite from Palin: "[Obama] launched his political career in the living room of a domestic terrorist." Where is this talk of Obama as terrorist heading?

DAY 44
"THAT ONE"

Obama and McCain are in Nashville, Tennessee, today—Tuesday, October 7. Tonight's debate is being showcased as a critical moment in the election for the McCain campaign. Poll after poll shows that voters believe the Obama-Biden ticket has out performed the McCain-Palin duo in the debates. McCain has been talking for months about his preference for the town hall format. Well, tonight he will get his chance to perform in that type of environment. The media is bouncing around the question of whether or not McCain should take an audience member's question and then immediately pivot into talking about Ayers, Wright, or any other controversial figure he can link to Obama.

An *NBC/Wall Street Journal* poll showed that 77% of those asked feel that the country is on the wrong track. The McCain campaign feels that they are the answer to this problem. McCain senior advisor Nicolle Wallace told Wolf Blitzer today that "John McCain is the only person who sounded the alarm about Fannie and Freddie." She went on to tell Blitzer, "Barack Obama promises to raise taxes on small businesses." Does Wallace know what she's saying is a complete lie? Blitzer asked Wallace when Sarah Palin was going to have a news conference. Wallace dodged the question by saying, "Her priority is talking to the American people … Her life is an open book … She does interviews every day out there." Wallace took a defensive attitude with Blitzer, but she managed to get her talking points out there and was able to completely distort Obama's plan on taxes. She should never have been allowed to say that Obama wants to raise taxes on small businesses. The overwhelming majority of small businesses do not make more than $250 thousand a year, and Obama's policy is not to raise taxes on those earning less than that. Period!

Doris Kearns Goodwin was on MSNBC at 1:48 pm. She was talking about tonight's debate and responded to the notion that McCain needs to be tougher with Obama. She said, "It's harder to attack character in this type of format." Goodwin said that tone is more important than words tonight and that people will have no patience for attacks. Switching from Goodwin to FOX News guest Lynn Forester De Rothschild was like going from heaven to hell in a matter of seconds. De Rothschild, a former Hillary Clinton supporter, is backing McCain. She was on FOX News to continue tying Obama to Reverend Wright. She was told that the Obama camp intends to respond forcefully to any attacks linking him to so-called radicals. De Rothschild said, "I'm not afraid of [the Obama camp]." This is the same woman, herself a multi-million dollar heiress, who called Obama an elitist.

Chris Matthews had Obama campaign manager David Axelrod on his show today and asked why Obama hung around with Ayers. Axelrod said that they were just on a couple of boards together. Matthews asked if McCain was trying to "create a shroud of mystery around Barack Obama." Axelrod replied, "You oughta ask [the McCain camp] about that." Matthews asked if the Obama camp was doing a good enough job tying McCain to Bush and then told Axelrod, "There's definitely a difference in tone and attitude between Bush and McCain." Matthews had to get his opinion in there. He then added, "According to *The New York Times*, you're out to make [McCain] cranky." Matthews is all over the board with these questions but he answers most of his own questions without managing to draw Axelrod into his game. Axelrod stayed above the spin and stuck to the issue of the economy.

Chris Matthews asked if six points was a solid lead for Obama (He's up 49% to 43% today). The *Politico's* Roger Simon pointed out, "We don't know what the race factor is." He was referring to the "Bradley Effect," which is a term used to describe what happens when white voters tell pollsters that they intend to vote for the black candidate but then don't when they are in the privacy of the booth.

At 2:34 pm, Karl Rove of FOX News said that whom you're associated with does matter and that the Obama camp has accepted that notion because they are using that tactic against McCain by bringing up Keating. Rove said, "[Obama] has a pattern of misstating his relationships." In this segment, they mentioned the "two scandals" the candidates are involved in—Ayers and Keating. No one bothered to point out that Barack Obama has not been involved in an Ayers scandal (Ayers' activities happened 40 years ago) but that John McCain was a leading player in the thick of the Keating Five Scandal. Once again the media has managed to equate information that is not in any way equal.

At 2:45 pm, David Gregory allowed McCain senior advisor Nicolle Wallace to tell one lie after another without challenge. He gave her a free five-minute platform to launch an attack ad against Obama. She accused Obama of being a liar time and again, then said, "I'd lie too if I had a record like Barack Obama." Gregory said nothing. He then introduced Valerie Jarrett, an Obama senior advisor. Gregory summarized Wallace's contentions, then let Jarrett respond. During this response, Gregory did jump in and took issue with what Obama has been doing. He reminded Jarrett of the Ayers association. Remember, Gregory did not remind Nicolle Wallace about Keating nor did he review what that scandal involved. Jarrett was left to defend Obama rather than attack McCain. David definitely did not treat the two candidates evenhandedly. Again and again he put up negative quotes about Obama and required Jarrett to defend against them. She did, however, manage to continue the policy-driven tone of the Obama campaign. David Gregory allowed the Republican spokesperson to take the offense while he demanded that the Democratic one stay on defense. Later in his show, Gregory asked Pat Buchanan what the candidates should do during tonight's debate. Buchanan said, "McCain could say 'Barack Obama is not telling you the truth. It's a pattern with you, Barack Obama.'" Gregory's response was a simple, quiet, "Yeah".

It is difficult to move on from David Gregory's program because he dedicated the majority of it to discussing what McCain needs to do tonight. He referenced Nicolle Wallace throughout the hour. He allowed Pat Buchanan to get out his opinions for a good five minutes with little interruption. Buchanan said that Obama needed to show white guys that he was "tough" and would fight back but then added, "He's not good at it. He's a nice guy. He's faculty lounge." Gregory didn't have anyone on to counter the overwhelmingly conservative Buchanan, and with the debate only two hours away, this show reeks of Republican bias.

At 4:11 pm, Lou Dobbs' program had a headline that read, "Up Next: Obama's Radical Ties." Dobbs, interviewing a panel of three, said, regarding Obama's ties to Ayers, "It turns out we're seeing a far more extensive relationship." No lead-up, nor follow-up that actually proved this assertion to be true. Dobbs didn't seem to care about bringing up the Keating Five—at all! Keith Olbermann, on the other hand, pointed out some very interesting facts about McCain and Palin—facts that are far more disturbing than those surrounding the Obama-Ayers connection. John McCain's name was on the letterhead of an organization called the US Counsel For World Freedom, a notoriously dangerous right-wing group. Olbermann also referred to other McCain and Palin ties to organizations and individuals who have either flaunted their anti-Semitism and, in Palin's case, anti-Americanism or who openly helped arm America's enemies, including fighters who later became known as the Taliban and included Osama bin Laden. With the media's pervasive streaming today of the McCain-Palin campaign's theme of tying Obama to "domestic terrorists", Olbermann was the sole voice on the TV media to emphasize McCain's real vulnerability in the guilt-by-association narrative. The Obama campaign hasn't even brought up any of these associations, other than Keating—yet!

The second Presidential debate has concluded in Nashville, and the CNN post debate poll shows that Obama won by a considerable margin of 54% to 30%. McCain decided not to bring up Ayers during the debate, but he did say something that has the media buzzing. At one point he was referring to a bill that had been sponsored by Bush and Cheney and loaded full of "goodies" and other pork projects. He asked the audience, "Do you know who voted for it?" He then pointed at Obama and surprisingly said, "That One." He was referring to Obama, but it was quite odd, and there are many who are claiming that using that phrase has racial undertones. Jeffrey Toobin of CNN said, "I thought that was a moment that people will remember." Paul Begala called it "a sneering, snarky sort of thing." Whatever it was, it will probably get lots of press coverage tomorrow.

FOX News ignored the CNN post-debate poll and conducted their own text- message poll. Of course, McCain won that 80% to 20%. They had former Senator Fred Thompson on saying that Ayers should have been brought up. MSNBC's Pat Buchanan felt the same way. James Carville of CNN pulled no punches about the performance, adding, "I thought Obama won the debate. It wasn't a tie. Obama won the debate." Even the conservative Bill Bennett said of McCain, "He didn't break through enough." But Bennett also commented about a moment when Obama chastised McCain for singing "Bomb, bomb, bomb, Iran." Bennett said that McCain originally sang that in front of some fellow military veterans. He added, "People can understand that as a joke." Uh … not me, Mr. Bennett! There's nothing funny about it. McCain actually made this little "joke" it at a rally in April of 2007. According to Gothe, both Bennett and McCain are of questionable character. Gothe observed that "Men show their characters in nothing more clearly than in what they think laughable." For me, raining bombs on people's heads is never a hoot. Even Bennett's fellow conservative Alex Costellanos scored the debate in Obama's favor saying, "A status quo debate probably goes to the guy who's ahead."

McCain is being ridiculed a bit for having left the debate stage sooner than Obama, who stayed around and shook hands for awhile. It will be interesting to see how McCain and Palin decide to attack now that they've seen these debate polls. Tomorrow will likely bring a new smear narrative, and Palin will be back again spouting false talking points. It's time for the media to put this embarrassing governor into a more defensive position. They should make her spend the next four weeks defending every single one of these questionable associations that she and her husband have. They should be relentless and not make Obama do their dirty work. They didn't need Hillary to provide them with fodder on Reverend Wright—they only needed a lead from Sean Hannity. Now it's time for them to take their lead from Keith Olbermann and send the governor back to Alaska in shame—or at least having to denounce some of their former associations.

DAY 45
ERRATIC

Obama is campaigning in Indianapolis, Indiana, today—Wednesday, October 8—while McCain is in Bethlehem, Pennsylvania. "You know, back in 1980, Ronald Reagan asked the electorate whether you were better off than you were four years ago. At the pace things are going right now, you're going to have to ask whether you're better off than you were four weeks ago." This is what Obama told a crowd of twenty thousand in Indianapolis this morning. In Pennsylvania, a person introducing John McCain and Sarah Palin referred to Obama again as, "Barack *Hussein* Obama." And again, neither McCain nor Palin took issue with the dig at Obama's middle name. A new national Gallup tracking poll shows Obama leading 52% to 41%—Obama's largest lead to date. Even with news of this lead, however, the media seems quite content with focusing on Sarah Palin. Mike Barnicle said this of her on MSNBC: "A lot of people like her. There's a lot to like there." He later added that Palin is a "natural communicator."

The McCain camp is calling Obama's campaign the "fussiest campaign in American history." It's their talking point for today, coming in response to the hits McCain is taking for calling Obama "That one." Here is how the comment came about last night during the debate:

BROKAW: Should we fund a Manhattan-like project that develops a nuclear bomb to deal with global energy and alternative energy or should we fund 100,000 garages across America, the kind of industry and innovation that developed Silicon Valley?

MCCAIN: I think pure research and development investment on the part of the United States government is certainly appropriate. I think once it gets into productive stages, that we ought to, obviously, turn it over to the private sector.

By the way, my friends, I know you grow a little weary with this back-and-forth. It was an energy bill on the floor of the Senate loaded down with goodies, billions for the oil companies, and it was sponsored by Bush and Cheney.

You know who voted for it? You might never know. **That one.** You know who voted against it? Me. I have fought time after time against these pork barrel—these bills that come to the floor and they have all kinds of goodies and all kinds of things in them for everybody and they buy off the votes.

I vote against them, my friends. I vote against them. But the point is, also, on oil drilling, oil drilling offshore now is vital so that we can bridge the gap. We can bridge the gap between imported oil, which is a national security issue, as well as any other, and it will reduce the price of a barrel of oil, because when people know there's a greater supply, then the cost of that will go down.

That's fundamental economics. We've got to drill offshore, my friends, and we've got to do it now, and we can do it.

And as far as nuclear power is concerned, again, look at the record. Sen. Obama has approved storage and reprocessing of spent nuclear fuel.

And I'll stop, Tom, and you didn't even wave. Thanks.

BROKAW: Thank you very much, Senator.

Yes, thanks, Tom, for letting McCain refer to Obama as "That One" without questioning what he meant, then allowing him to continue rambling along without the kind of time constraint you put on every Obama response.

"What is McCain's path to victory?" This was the pressing question that MSNBC's Mika Brzezinski asked today. She also said that the choice of Palin seems to have been "brilliant". She was filling in for David Gregory on *Race for the White House*. At one point she said to Obama supporter Claire McCaskill, "Certainly people are looking for answers—I don't think they're looking for a friend in their next President—I think they're looking at someone who can guide us through this economic crisis and I wonder if Barack Obama needs to do more to explain exactly how—even John McCain talked about the foreclosure situation and put out some ideas last night. Barack Obama—it seems to me—some could argue—is resting on his laurels and letting this situation take care of itself—monitoring this situation—keeping out of it because it's politically safe to do so. Is that leadership?" McCaskill didn't get upset. She just calmly explained how McCain is being "erratic," but then Brzezinski cut her off and said, "Ah ah ah! That's the campaign word. I've heard that all across the board. Come on now!" McCaskill decided to say instead that McCain was "jumping all over the place." She said, "He is not 'steady on the tiller' like he said last night. Anything but!" Brzezinski said, "Ok, but when you see parallels in strategies that the campaigns put out and the words being used by similar campaign folks, I gotta call you on it, but ok, jumping all over the place works as well."

Today's *Race for the White House* seemed completely geared toward figuring out a way for McCain to catch up with Obama. On a day that shows Obama up by eleven, one would think that Brzezinski could have spent more time talking about how strong Obama is looking with 27 days left. Instead, she accused him of "resting on his laurels," and she propped up McCain by claiming that he "put out some ideas last night." Since when has the media stopped surrogates from getting out their talking points? For her to stop McCaskill from saying "erratic" sounded, quite frankly, a bit desperate of Brzezinski. She should have spent more time analyzing the "That one" comment.

During last night's debate, McCain, surrounded by a Nashville audience of mostly white voters, along with a white moderator, turned to an African American candidate and referred to him as "That one". Let's pretend for a minute. Suppose the debate had been held in Harlem, New York, with an audience that was—say— 80% African American and was also being moderated by an African American. Suppose that under those conditions, Barack Obama had questioned who was guilty of wrong-doing, had turned to John McCain, pointed at him, then said, "That one." Then suppose that after allowing Obama to continue to deliver a few more accusatory comments, the African American moderator kindly said, "Thank you very much, Sen. Obama." This senario would have drawn the ire of so many Americans. Such insolence would likely have ended Obama's candidacy, and the media would have crucified him for it. They wouldn't be asking "if" the comment was offensive, as they are today. They would have been asserting that the remark was indeed offensive and the moderator biased. But today, the media has slowly let McCain's comment fade away.

Anderson Cooper tried to point out how the McCain campaign is trying to link Obama to Ayers. His choice of words leading into the segment was interesting. He said, "Critics are trying to paint [Obama] as less than 100% American." What critics have used these words? Cooper managed to put the latest McCain-Palin nonsense into words that not even they themselves have managed to dream up. *"Less than 100% American?"* I have never heard those words used in describing Obama. Anderson Cooper has a unique—and detrimental— way of paraphrasing. He, along with the rest of the media, is showing us how the McCain campaign is asking who the real Barack Obama is. I can recall this same question being posed by the media 45 days ago at the Democratic National Convention. The *"Who is Barack Obama?"* question was written by the media, and now McCain has simply adopted it and put it back in play. Forty-five days ago at the convention,

David Gregory said this: "To know Barack Obama is to be comfortable with—what?" Remember that?

Maureen Dowd wrote **Mud Pies For 'That One'** in today's *The New York Times*. She finds it difficult to believe that John McCain is not " disgusted with himself for using the tactics perfected by the same crowd that used these tactics to derail him in 2000." She finds him to be "curmudgeonly, even hostile, toward the press—the group he used to spend hours with every day and jokingly describe as his base." As for Palin, Dowd says, "The woman is sounding more Cheney than Cheney." Dowd quotes Palin questioning Obama's qualifications to be President because of his "relationship with the former Weatherman William Ayers". Dowd points out that Palin told William Kristol that she questions Obama's ties with Rev. Wright. Dowd then quotes Palin wondering "why that association isn't discussed more".

DAY 46
"SAY IT TO MY FACE!"

Obama is campaigning in Dayton, Ohio, today—Thursday, October 9—while McCain is in Waukesha, Wisconsin. Yesterday, during ABC's Charles Gibson's interview with Obama, Gibson stated, "What John McCain has unloaded on you in the last seventy-two—ninety-six—hours, as has Sarah Palin—McCain saying essentially 'We don't know who Barack Obama is—where he came from. I'm an open book, he's not.'" Gibson then asked, "Were you surprised that he didn't bring it up last night at the debate and use that line of attack?" Obama answered, "Well, I am surprised that, you know, we've been seeing some pretty over the top attacks coming out of the McCain campaign over the last several days—that he wasn't willing to say it to my face. The notion that people don't know who I am is a little hard to swallow. I've been running for President for the last two years. I've campaigned in 49 states." The only state Obama hasn't visited is Palin's Alaska!

An article by Dorothy Rabinowitz in today's *Wall Street Journal* is entitled **News Flash: The Media Back Obama: *Its Activist Role Has Been the Single Constant in this Eternal Election.*** Rabinowitz says, "The single constant in the eternal election remains the media, whose activist role no one will seriously dispute." I agree with Rabinowitz on this point, but she quickly loses me. She writes, "To point out the prevailing (with honorable exceptions) double standard of reporting so favorable to Mr. Obama by now feels superfluous—much like talking about the weather. The same holds true for all those reports pointing to Mr. Obama's heroic status outside the United States—not to mention the cascade of press analyses warning that if he fails to win election, the cause will surely be racism."

I would like to refer Rabinowitz to Day One of this book for some real examples of media bias. Three points for her to consider: 1) The media's reporting has been anything but favorable to Obama, 2) Reporting about Obama's "heroic" status outside the United states is like saying *Baywatch's* David Hasselhoff is more popular as a singer in Europe than he is in the States—it's just a fact! and 3) Suggesting, on a day when America is watching the McCain camp once again inject "*Who is Barack Obama?*" into the race, the suggestion that race will not be a factor if Obama loses is flat out ignorant.

Rabinowitz goes on to say, "None of this means that the media's role will go unremembered—who will forget MSNBC news, voice of the Obama campaign? Never has a presidential election produced more fodder for the making and breaking—or tainting—of reputations." Rabinowitz's television must not pick up FOX News. She contined:

> That first debate brought the usual legions of commentators—among them CNN foreign correspondent Christiane Amanpour. John McCain, she pointed out, had stumbled over Ahmadinejad's name, and as he was supposed to be the expert on foreign policy, it made her

giggle. 'That's not fair—people make mistakes all the time,' Anderson Cooper shot back. But Ms. Amanpour, whose capacity for sustained levels of bombast is one of the wonders of the world, was having none of it.

Funny—I thought it was Anderson Cooper's comment that showed an intense bias. Boy, did he jump in to defend McCain!

Rabinowitz, not having sat in Rev. Wright's church for twenty years nor having been a part of the political culture of the South Side of Chicago, nevertheless finds it within her perview to evaluate Obama's motivation for making his speech on race:

> ... Sen. Obama is not responsible for the political culture, but he is in good part its product. Which is perhaps how it happened that in his 20 years in the church of Rev. Jeremiah Wright—passionate proponent of the view of America as the world's leading agent of evil and injustice—he found nothing strange or alienating. To the contrary, when Rev. Wright's screeds began rolling out on televisions all over the country, Mr. Obama's first response was to mount a militant defense and charge that Rev. Wright had been taken out of context, 'cut into snippets.' This he continued to do until it became untenable. Then came the subject-changing speech on race. Such defining moments tell more than all the talk of Sen.

Obama's association with the bomb-planting humanist, William Ayers ...

Unless she doesn't consider *The Wall Street Journal* part of the media, her strong opinions about Jeremiah Wright and William Ayers make her a hypocrite, especially considering the fact that she is a member of *The Wall Street Journal's* editorial board. And if she feels that the Wright story is a primary example of how the media has shown favoritism toward Obama, why did she use the words "News Flash" in her title? That story most certainly is not news. It's been shoved down our throats for almost a year—hardly a "news flash".

Today, MSNBC's Contessa Brewer showed the copy of *Newsweek* with Palin on the front cover. Brewer said that she thought it was unfair not to retouch the photo because there were stray hairs showing around her lip, as well as other imperfections. Brewer claimed that she herself was a person who was "right down the middle" politically. Yeah right! For her to be spending even one second on such a ridiculous story with the economy in the shape it's in tells us all we need to know about where Brewer stands politically. I didn't know that Obama had freckles, but the last picture of him on the cover of *Time* certainly showed that he does. Did Brewer throw a fit over that cover? NO! Republican strategist Andrea Tantaros appears more disturbed than anyone about the *Newsweek* cover of Palin. Is she feeling some vulnerability about her own looks? She wrote this on FOX News online yesterday:

The left's blatant bias has crept from within its pages onto the cover shot. The latest *Newsweek* shows a magnified, purposely un-retouched photo of Sarah Palin that highlights every imperfection on her beautiful face. Women will understand this. We're talking unwanted facial hair, wrinkles and un-extracted pores. Heck, we all have them. We just don't expect them to be showcased on the cover of a national magazine, especially when we are running for the position of second in command of the United States.—Calling it unflattering is an understatement. Trust me.

At noon, CNN presented this headline: "Is it Race? Skin Deep Differences Color the Campaign." CNN then did a segment on a Florida sheriff, Mike Scott, who called Obama "Barack *Hussein* Obama." The sheriff is now being investigated. The segment showed a blogger asking, "What would that sheriff do if a house were on fire but had an Obama sign in the front yard?" Good question!

After the debate this past Tuesday, David Gergen said that it was too early to determine if Obama had the election wrapped up because, "Barack Obama's black." CNN is highlighting that comment today. Gergen went on to explain how Obama's being black could cost him as much as six points in the polls. CNN is pivoting today and putting the issue of race front and center. They are putting the "Bradley Effect" on the table. The effect of CNN spreading the "Bradley Effect" word is perhaps to explain away and therefore dampen the growing excitement among the electorate about what many are beginning to feel is a done deal for Obama.

Over the past few days, one could have made the argument that Palin's comments have racial undertones, but it is CNN, unfortunately, that is bringing race to the front burner today. It's as if they have decided to give people who can't think of anything except race—hopefully a decided minority in the mix—a platform from which to speak. Rick Sanchez possibly has good intentions in trying to delve into racial politics during the noon hour, but in doing so, he is launching his own perhaps detrimental campaign. He had three African American men on his show—Rufus Montgomery, Michael McNeely, and Austin King—who were not going to vote for Obama. He presented this information as somehow shocking news, as if all African Americans are expected to fall in line behind Obama automatically. The three men are Republicans. Given the fact that the Obama campaign's explicit policy is to avoid race as an issue, CNN's decision to zero in on it is a tactic diametrically opposed to the Obama camp's wishes. They have done for the McCain camp what the McCain camp itself is afraid to do, and that is to use the actual word "race". Will this be a one-hour CNN segment, or are they launching a new campaign that will play out over the next 25 days? So far Rick Sanchez has accomplished two things in running this segment: 1) let undecided African Americans know that it's ok to vote against Obama and 2) let closeted white racists know that they can feel okay about being on a bandwagon of people who say one thing to the pollsters but do another thing in the voting booth. Toward the end of his show, Sanchez was forced to pivot back to the overriding issue of the day: the Wall Street plunge. The Dow has dropped below 9,000 for the first time since 2003.

Anderson Cooper definitely needs someone to keep him honest. Tonight, Drew Griffin of his "Keeping Them Honest" team did one of the sloppiest reports I have ever seen presented as journalism. The charge he brought up was regarding possible fraud committed by ACORN. Griffin implies throughtout the segment that ACORN is involved in "fraud". He becomes confused during the segment about whether it is an individual ACORN worker's registration fraud or ACORN itself trying to commit voter fraud. This is an important distinction to make. As a viewer, I feel as if Cooper's piece is quickly and intentionally passing a verdict while being loose with the facts. Early in the segment, Griffin, while talking to an unidentified female, says, "There's been no fraud yet because people haven't voted yet, right?" The unidentified female answers, "Correct. We'll find out on Election Day." Griffin responds, "But it certainly sets up a potential." So, at this point, Griffin has established that there can not possibly be voter fraud—yet. But later in the segment Cooper says, "Drew, Senator McCain is calling for an investigation. Is what's happening in Indiana a crime?" Griffin answers, "It absolutely is a crime. That was a fraud, somebody who filled out those forms. And I looked at them, Anderson. They're obviously a fraud." Hmmm. I thought it couldn't be fraud until Election Day. What type of fraud, Mr. Griffin? I thought that there was potential for fraud. During this segment, Cooper put up a picture of Obama and tried to connect him directly with ACORN. The problem with the report is that the people alledging fraud stated they were not handwriting experts yet they claimed they knew for a fact that signatures on the voter registration forms were forgeries. Even Griffin acknowledged that he is not a handwriting expert. Yet he knows a crime has been committed. Since when do journalists report something as definitely fraud based on such flimsy evidence?

If there is voter fraud going on, I'm the first to want it stopped, but Cooper and Griffin are the ones who committed fraud by fraudulently reporting that fraud is occurring without evidence of fraud from experts. (I'm finding myself using the term almost as frequently as they did during the segment.) Griffin also made the point that Obama had donated money to ACORN. I kept waiting for verifiable evidence. It didn't happen. Cooper's crack investigative team did go to several ACORN headquarters. The fact that the offices were empty made ACORN seem even more suspicious, like scam artists having left town in the middle of the night. It didn't cross Cooper's or his sleuth's minds that possibly the deadline for voter registration was passed and ACORN had closed up shop. Cooper's team put together senarios that conceivably could be fraud on the part of an individual, but that is not evidence—certainly not against Obama as they insinuated.

Cooper tried again today to keep the campaigns even. With McCain's campaign getting out of control with comments like "terrorist" and "kill him" being hurled at their rallies, Cooper had the audacity to tell David Gergen that both campaigns were "throwing hand grenades." Anderson Cooper has a lot of nerve! He offered no examples of vitriol coming from the Obama side, but a whole slew of them from the McCain side. How is this both sides *throwing hand grenades*? Cooper's own words were the grenades he threw at Obama's campaign.

Paul Begala tried to defend Obama against Cooper. He said, "Let's not pretend that this is equal amounts of rage and anger here." He said that Obama has been cool and that no one at his rallies was shouting, "Kill him". He agreed that both candidates are launching attack ads but said that Obama's attacks are nowhere near as dirty as those of McCain. Gergen tried to tell Cooper that he was worried about McCain's rallies inciting actual violence. Cooper seemed stunned by that possibility. He said, "Really"? Almost everyone watching McCain's campaign rallies can see a mob mentality developing—almost everyone, that is, except Cooper. Once again, in his defense, Cooper may just be trying to present unbiased reporting. His problem lies in not knowing how to be unbiased. If he reports negative information about one camp he thinks he must make up something negative about the other camp to even things out. The network should require more of Cooper!

Todd Palin decided to respond to his subpoena regarding Troopergate. He is answering questions in writing. The media has certainly put this story on the back burner in favor of the more sensationalized Ayers stories. Today, Chris Matthews said that the McCain campaign was "trying to de-Americanize the guy [Obama]" by bringing up his middle name and talking about terrorism and radicals. Pat Buchanan said of the McCain campaign: "They're trying to say that this is not a mainstream American." Are "they" trying to say it or are you, Mr. Buchanan?

DAY 47
"HE'S ARAB"

Obama is campaigning in Chillicothe, Ohio, today—Friday, October 10—while McCain is in La Crosse, Wisconsin. "It's not hard to rile up a crowd by stoking anger and division," said Obama this morning. John McCain's campaign has finally been forced to deal with the very anger that Obama is speaking of. At a rally today, a woman in the audience, with McCain at her side, held the microphone and called Obama an "Arab". McCain took the microphone away and said, "No ma'm! No ma'm!" He told her that Obama was a "decent family man" and a "citizen". Moments earlier, a gentleman in the audience had said that he feared for his unborn child if Obama becomes President. McCain took the microphone from him and said that Obama was a "decent person" and that people didn't need to be "scared" if he becomes President. With that comment, people in the audience began to boo. It soon became apparent that McCain had lost control of them and, in a broader sense, his entire campaign. It was encouraging to see McCain correct both of these misguided audience members, but it is he and his running mate who have stoked the anger. It now may be too late for them to rein that anger in. McCain also could have pointed out that there is nothing wrong with being an Arab. He should have reminded the racist woman of the thousands of Arab Americans that add to the fabric of the United States. When did the word "terrorist" become synonymous with Muslim—become synonymous with Arab—become synonymous with brown skin—become synonymous with anyone who isn't white? Who am I kidding? That day was 9/11.

Palin told her audience this week that she wasn't being negative in talking about the Obama-Ayers connection—that she was just telling the truth. Now McCain is scrambling to alter that so-called truth in order to dampen the fires of anger burning throughout their audiences. It is becoming evident that Palin is little more than a demagogue.

Chris Matthews spent one segment of his program today pointing out that the McCain campaign is stirring up their audiences by making references to Obama being connected to domestic terrorists, etc. But Matthews had an odd smirk on his face for most of the segment, and on a day that sees the campaign getting ugly—so ugly, in fact, that many are fearful of the violence that may be brewing—the smirk was damaging. There is a racial element to the fear in the air, and Matthews needed to treat the issue more seriously. He was correct in accusing the campaign of stirring up anger, but he had the odd smirk on his face and even mentioned the word "immigrant" in discussing Obama. Matthews said, "Big surprise. A guy is born with a Swahili name. Let's go to Richard here. This is really subtle politics. The guy is born as an American immigrant, which is what we like in this country. He comes to the country as an immigrant with an African father, raised in difficult circumstances… It's an immigrant story, OK?" What the hell is Matthews talking about? Obama was born in the United States. If this isn't media assault, I don't know what is. I cannot believe what I'm hearing!

The last thing a bunch of riled up, anti-immigrant Republicans need to be hearing from Matthews today is a reference to Obama as an immigrant. First of all, Obama's father was not an immigrant; he was a foreign student who moved back to Africa. And Obama himself isn't an immigrant, so to whom was Mathews referring? He has completely lost any grasp of the facts surrounding this issue.

It seems painfully difficult for Matthews to understand and articulate Obama's biography. He always makes it sound "odd" and "mysterious." It isn't a difficult biography to explain. He was born in Honolulu, Hawaii, lived in Indonesia for a few years with his mother, moved back to Hawaii (an American state) to live with his grandparents, and then went to college. Why does Matthews struggle to deliver the simplicity of this story? It's almost as if he wants it to sound confusing. He should try making it as simple as possible over the next few weeks to make up for his previous misstatements. Maybe that would calm some people down.

Over the past few weeks, Matthews has rhetorically asked what the McCain campaign is trying to imply about Obama with the references to Muslim and Ayers and terrorism? He keeps saying that they are trying to make Obama "mysterious." Matthews has used that word repeatedly, and it needs to stop. He is acting as if only he has figured out how McCain and Palin are trying to paint Obama as this mysterious, foreign-sounding guy, assuming the rest of us aren't already aware of McCain's tactics. We know what they're doing, Mr. Matthews. Why do you struggle to articulate their game plan? Just say you know what they're doing and leave it at that. Your willingness to discuss their game only serves to fan the flames. You continue to ask, "What are they doing? Aren't they trying to paint Obama as this mysterious guy who hangs out with terrorists? Isn't that what they're doing? I think that's it. I know that's what they're doing!" We already know that. Dramatizing their game plan may help some get the picture, but it's getting old.

During a time like this, the late Tim Russert is sorely missed. We needed him here to point out the very serious nature of what has taken place today. Each day this week, the comments have gotten worse at the McCain-Palin rallies. Unless a respected voice in the media, as Russert was, decides to step forward with the message the country needs to quell the hate that's brewing, something bad is going to happen. Matthews must get serious. Perhaps Bill Clinton can step up and be the calming influence the nation needs. The country is in need of a sobering, calming voice, not the politically sarcastic and almost joking message Matthews is delivering.

Republican strategist Andrea Tantaros was at it again today. She went on FOX News and ranted about the Palin *Newsweek* cover. As I said before, she really must have an inferiority complex when it comes to her own looks to be so obsessed with this topic. She just had to get this off her chest:

> This cover is a clear slap in the face at Sarah Palin. Why? Because it's unretouched. It highlights every imperfection that every human being has, but we're talking unwanted facial hair, pores, wrinkles—this is a gross slap in the face to Sarah Palin after *Newsweek* has done so many favorable

covers of Barack Obama that make him look Presidential—that are clearly retouched—he looks flawless. This is a slap in the face and the biggest reason it's a slap is because the title says 'She's one of the folks' and in parenthesis it says 'and that's the problem'.

Any woman who would look at this cover or if this were me or if this were you—if this camera would zoom in on me right now—the viewers—it ain't pretty. And I tell you what; I'd be pretty upset. To put her on this cover—any woman that sees this cover would be shocked and horrified. She's a gorgeous woman, but this was a clear slap in the face.

Andrea Tantaros, I hope you don't think you've hit on the game-changing issue for the McCain campaign. If so, sit down, girl, 'cause we need to talk. What you should be "pretty upset" about is FOX News putting you on camera ranting about such idiotic, "unretouched" valley girl-like slang. FOX News has given you a "clear slap in the face" to allow any knowledgeable viewer, male or female—especially female—to see how petty and inarticulate you are. You should expect your career to tank after that interview, just as Sarah Palin's began to tank, not because she's not "pretty" enough on *Newsweek's* cover, but because, like you, she opened her mouth and let the country know how unqualified she is for her job.

Doris Kearns Goodwin, returning us to the more serious side of the news, told Rachel Maddow today that Sarah Palin was the "chief stoker" of the rising anger among McCain-Palin supporters. CNN's Campbell Brown did an entire show called "Race in the Race" in which a panel discussed how Obama's ethnicity is affecting voters. Her program was interrupted by breaking news about "Troopergate". Sarah Palin was found guilty of abusing her power as governor by trying to have her former brother-in-law fired as a state trooper. Now the McCain campaign is having to deal with three major issues: 1) being behind by ten points in today's National Gallup poll. 2) angry rally crowds, and 3) a Vice Presidential candidate found guilty of abusing her power and betraying the public's trust. Palin has been claiming for weeks that Obama is untrustworthy. How will she be able to deliver this message with an ounce of credibility now? The media should hold this verdict over her head by reminding viewers of today's verdict the minute she brings up the issue of trust. According to the report, Palin didn't break a specific law, but abuse of power is usually enough to end a politician's career

DAY 48
"BLIND AMBITION"

Obama is campaigning in Philadelphia, Pennsylvania, today—Saturday, October 11—while McCain is in Johnstown, Pennsylvania. Tivo is a wonderful thing! This morning, I was able to watch last night's edition of *Larry King Live* during which King showed a portion of McCain's new attack ad about Obama. The ad is called "Blind Ambition". Again, the media is airing McCain's dirty work for him:

> **Narrator:** Obama's blind ambition! When convenient he worked with terrorist Bill Ayers. When discovered, he lied. Obama! Blind ambition—bad judgment! Congressional liberals fought for risky sub-prime loans. Congressional liberals fought against more regulation. Then the housing market collapsed, costing you billions. In crisis we need leadership, not bad judgment.
> **John McCain:** I'm John McCain and I approve this message.

Saying that Obama worked with a terrorist "when convenient" is a lie. Through the ad, McCain is making it sound as if Obama took part in terrorist acts along with Ayers. Larry King should not have shown the ad. It accuses Obama of lying about being involved with terrorist activity.

The ad goes entirely too far. At the very least, before showing it, King should have spent time discrediting it. Instead, after the fact, he has a panel argue for and against its validity, as if facts are a matter of opinion. Evidently all Republicans and Democrats are allowed to do on these panels is state their opinions regarding lies—some in favor of the lies, others opposed. Discrediting this ad doesn't take a panel—it takes a reputable journalist looking into the camera and telling the American people that it is a flat out lie. That's what the credibility Larry King has spent years earning is supposed to be used for. Once he aired the ad, the damage was done.

Asked by a reporter in Pennsylvania if yesterday's charges were true, Palin replied: "No, and if you read the report you will see that there was nothing unlawful or unethical about it. You have to read the report." The media needs to hold Palin accountable for being charged with abusing her power. We know that she is going to focus on the fact that she didn't break the law, but that shouldn't fly with the press. She abused her power and she betrayed the public's trust. One journalist after another should remind her of that fact on a daily basis.

Obama told a crowd in Philadelphia today: "Now, I want to acknowledge that Sen. McCain tried to tone down the rhetoric yesterday in his town hall meeting, and I appreciate his reminder that we can disagree while still being respectful of each other." He went on to say, "I have said it before and I'll say it again—Sen. McCain has served this country with honor and he deserves our thanks for that." I hope Obama is ready for the Ayers attacks that are going to be thrown at him by McCain during Wednesday's debate. He has three days to prepare for the onslaught, and he will likely have some of his own ammunition. Regardless of what happens over the course of the next three weeks, Obama apparently believes that he will need to make one final plea to the voters before Election Day. He has been negotiating with the major news networks to buy a half-hour segment the week before the election. It is a multi-million dollar proposition. He is still in negotiations with ABC.

John McCain is taking a bit of a beating for his proposal regarding the mortgage crisis. He wants to spend $300 billion to buy up bad mortgages. The "McCain Resurgence Plan" would replace the mortgages with manageable, fixed-rate mortgages. His initial plan called for mortgage companies to absorb at least some of the cost of renegotiating the mortgages. But now his campaign says the government would pick up the full tab. McCain is hoping that the proposal will affect the polls. Here are some of today's numbers, both nationally and state by state:

> Rasmussen/Oregon – Obama up by 11
> Gallup/National – Obama up by 9
> Rasmussen/National – Obama up by 7
> Reuters/National – Obama up by 4
> Newsweek/National – Obama up by 11
> SurveyUSA/Iowa – Obama up by 13
> SurveyUSA/Alabama – McCain up by 27
> Research 2000/Florida – Obama up by 5
> Morning Call Tracking/Pennsylvania –
> Obama up by 12

"The Bradley Effect" is being discussed more today than it has been throughout the race so far. There is still a strong belief that people who say they intend to vote for Obama will actually pull the lever for McCain come election day. But as long as the race issue is being highlighted without condemnation by the media, those who harbor racist feelings will know that they are being acknowledged as an acceptable demographic for the completely unacceptable views that they hold.

DAY 49
CASTRO WEIGHS IN

Obama is campaigning in Toledo, Ohio, today—Sunday, October 12—while McCain is in Arlington, Virginia. Congressman John Lewis is taking some heat for these comments about the McCain campaign: "What I am seeing reminds me too much of another destructive period in American history. Sen. McCain and Gov. Palin are sowing the seeds of hatred and division, and there is no need for this hostility in our political discourse." He went further: "George Wallace never threw a bomb. He never fired a gun, but he created the climate and the conditions that encouraged vicious attacks against innocent Americans who were simply trying to exercise their constitutional rights. Because of this atmosphere of hate, four little girls were killed on Sunday morning when a church was bombed in Birmingham, Alabama."

The comments didn't sit well with John McCain who fired back by saying: "Congressman John Lewis' comments represent a character attack against Governor Sarah Palin and me that is shocking and beyond the pale." I guess John McCain hasn't seen his own recent attack ad, which is really "beyond the pale." What will have to happen for McCain to understand what Lewis is trying to say? Obama has already been called an Arab, a terrorist, a Muslim, "That one", and a radical. A person has shouted "Kill him" at a rally and Palin said nothing in response. Maybe Lewis thinks that the "Kill him" comment was enough to warrant bringing up George Wallace. Someone at a recent McCain rally was holding a stuffed monkey that had an Obama tee-shirt on. It seems reasonable to think that someone saying the "n" word is highly likely at one of these future rallies. John Lewis is simply trying to warn McCain about what is brewing. No one thinks that McCain is George Wallace reincarnated, but racism is racism, and inciting violence is inciting violence. McCain needs to be proactive and stop the escalating racist remarks and innuendos.

Governor Jon Corzine of New Jersey was a guest on *Meet the Press* today. He was talking about the Obama-Ayers connection and defending Obama for having served on the same board in Chicago with Ayers. Corzine told Tom Brokaw: "Somebody sits on a board where somebody else is on the board—by the way, it's Walter Annenberg's board on school reform and [Annenberg] picked Mr. Ayers, not Barack Obama. They happened to be on the same board. So that's the classic guilt by association. It's really futile." Brokaw interrupted and said, "What about John Lewis and guilt by association—linking [McCain] with George Wallace?" Once again, it's Brokaw to the defense of McCain!

At 8:16 am, Tom Brokaw showed McCain's "Blind Ambition" attack ad. I guess Brokaw didn't understand the *Saturday Night Live* skit this past week that portrayed him as being unfair to Obama. In the skit, every time Obama began to speak, the actor playing Brokaw would say, "Time's up!" It was striking how, during the last debate, Brokaw reminded Obama about the time limit almost every time he spoke.

Brokaw rarely gave the same reminder to McCain. At one point, Obama even told Brokaw, "I'm just trying to keep up with Sen. McCain." It could be said that Brokaw also tried to benefit McCain by the kinds of questions he chose to close out the debate. Selection of questions, by his own admission, was Brokaw's role. Why, then, did he choose questions related overwhelmingly to foreign policy, the area that polls show is John McCain's only real area of strength, for the last 30 minutes of the debate? The debate was supposed to cover the economy.

Debra Saunders in today's *The San Francisco Chronicle* wrote **Playing the Race Card**. In the article she brings up the degree to which race will accompany voters into the voting booths on Election Day. I never knew the race card was gone from the table, but Saunders must think it disappeared for a while:

> The race card is back. After Tuesday night's debate, Washington party-crossover dean David Gergen announced it was 'too early' to declare victory for Democrat Barack Obama, not because the election is a month away, but because 'Obama is black…'
>
> … Of course, racism exists in America and there are white voters who will not vote for a black candidate, but there are also many white voters who would love to see an African-American in the White House. Gallup analyst Jeff Jones crunched the numbers and concluded that while 6 percent of voters say they are less likely to vote for Obama

because of his race, 9 percent say they are more likely to vote for Obama because of his race. So do you think that if Obama wins with a margin of three points or less that newspapers will run stories that assert that Obama won because he was black? Of course not...

Sarah Palin is willing to focus on that racist six percent that Debra Saunders writes about. Palin continues to play to the hateful feelings this demographic harbors toward Obama. Even after being found guilty of betraying the public's trust, Palin blasted Obama's support for abortion rights yesterday as "absolutely radical." Again, she managed to get her talking point out and utter the word "radical." This woman has no shame. She was booed while dropping the puck at a professional hockey game between the Philadelphia Flyers and the New York Rangers—booed for a solid two minutes. Perhaps this episode will teach her to show a little humility, but I strongly doubt it. She acted as if she didn't hear the boos raining down on her and her poor young daughter. It was a sad sight to see, but she managed to drop the puck and scurry off the ice before anyone got hurt. She definitely doesn't seem to be popular in the city of brotherly love. Philadelphia is apparently mad at the country's most famous hockey mom for some reason. Maybe it's her refusal to stop calling Obama a radical.

Bravo Wolf Blitzer! At 9:35 am, he said that John McCain should have gone a step further when the woman at the rally this week called Obama an Arab. Blitzer said that McCain should have told her that there is nothing wrong with being an Arab or a Muslim. He said that both candidates need to make this point from now on whenever the issue comes up. Blitzer's comment came just after Gloria Borger said that the last thing the Obama campaign should be doing is injecting race into the campaign. She was referring to John Lewis' comment. Borger needs to be reminded that it is the McCain campaign that has injected race into the campaign—they've just done it in a more underhanded way. John Lewis isn't injecting race into anything. He's trying to stop race from becoming the dominant issue. Perhaps he feels that comparing McCain to a known racist is the only way to get him to stop before emotions boil over and cause someone to get hurt.

Even Fidel Castro weighed in on the race issue surrounding Obama today. He said that it was a "pure miracle" that Obama has not been assassinated. He accused the United States of being marked by "profound racism", adding that "[m]illions of whites cannot reconcile in their minds with the idea that a black man with his wife and children would move into the White House, which is called just like that - White". Castro also got in a dig at Sarah Palin, who he said, "knew nothing at all about anything". Hopefully the media won't allow the McCain campaign to link Obama to Castro now. That's the last thing Obama needs.

DAY 50
"OBAMA BIN LYIN'"

Obama is campaigning in Toledo, Ohio, today—Monday, October 13—while McCain is in Virginia Beach, Virginia. "Well, I'm very, very pleased to be cleared of any legal wrongdoing ... any hint of any kind of unethical activity there," Palin said Saturday. Her comments are getting airtime today, her sense of denial considered an oddity. Palin has forgotten that she was found to have violated Alaska's ethics statute. She went on to say: "Todd did what the state's Department of Law web site tells anyone to do if they have a concern about a state trooper. And that's you go to the commissioner and you express your concern." Palin is digging a deeper hole for herself, forcing the media to point out her lies. She added, "Todd did what anyone would have done given this state trooper's very, very troubling behavior and his dangerous threats against our family. So again, nothing to apologize there with Todd's actions and again very pleased to be cleared of any legal wrongdoing." Palin was asked whether she thought she had done anything wrong, given the report's finding that she abused her power. She said, "Not at all and I'll tell ya ... I think that you're always going to ruffle feathers as you do what you believe is in the best interest of the people whom you are serving. In this case I knew that I had to have the right people in the right position at the right time in this cabinet to best serve Alaskans, and Walt Monegan was not the right person at the right time to meet the goals that we had set out in our administration."

A 3:43 pm, David Gregory chose to show a poll done by *The Denver Post* in which Obama and McCain are tied at 44%. There are more than enough polls that show Obama with a substantial lead in surprising states like Virginia and North Carolina, but Gregory picked Colorado to analyze. He had Senator Ken Salazar from Colorado on, and he asked him about the general question concerning the comfort level with Obama. He presented the Colorado poll as a surprise, meaning that McCain has surprisingly managed to tie things up. The fact is that Colorado was always expected to go to McCain. The real surprise that Gregory should focus on is the closeness of the polls in West Virginia. Clinton hammered Obama there and McCain is an overwhelming favorite in the state. The fact that Obama is leading in Virginia is also astonishing. Today, Paul Begala of CNN said that Virginia was a state that wouldn't have allowed Obama's parents to get married when they did.

Next, Gregory interviewed Mike Duhaime, a McCain spokesman and asked him what McCain needs to do to win the remaining toss-up states. So let me get this straight, David Gregory. On this segment, the Democratic senator has to answer questions about voter discomfort with Obama while the Republican spokesperson has to give suggestions to help his guy catch up in the polls. For some reason, this approach does not seem even-handed to me.

At 3:54 pm, Gregory showed two signs held by McCain supporters at a rally, both of which read "Obama bin Lyin'". He then allowed Duhaime to dismiss them as not representative of the real McCain. Unless you are one of the few hundred people who were at the rally where those signs were being held up, you would never have seen them unless television programs, in this case, *Race for the White House*, showed them. Gregory closed out his show with Jesse Jackson to speak for Obama and to talk about the issue of race in the campaign. Gregory is no fool. Anyone who is politically savvy understands that showing Jesse Jackson, whom I haven't seen on television for weeks, is a negative cue for anyone with a propensity to be racist. Voters who might be thinking about putting their racist feelings aside will likely forget all about doing so with the sight of Jesse Jackson. It's sad, but true. Whether we like it or not, the media has painted Jackson as a black person to fear, and Jackson himself didn't help matters when he was caught off camera a while back on FOX News saying that he wanted to "cut [Obama's] nuts off." Again, Gregory's propaganda techniques are skillful and subtle.

In an upstate New York county, hundreds of voters have been sent absentee ballots on which they could vote for "Barack Osama." The absentee ballots sent to voters in Rensselaer County identified the two presidential candidates as "Barack Osama" and "John McCain." Today, a Virginia GOP chairman said that Obama and Bin Laden "both have friends who bombed the Pentagon". Yes, the rhetoric is getting worse by the minute. But at least the DOW had an historic one-day jump.

Today could very well mark the beginning of a media shift in how they intend to cover Obama for the next 22 days, with apparently a more positive bent developing toward Obama. Several factors contribute to my assumption:

1) Obama continues to maintain a strong national lead of eleven points according to *Newsweek*.

2) John McCain himself said today, "The national media has written us off." He must be noticing that the media is no longer totally in his corner. Welcome to Obama's world!

3) The ultra-conservative *National Review's* William Kristol is beginning to show signs of giving up on McCain by suggesting that McCain should "fire his campaign".

4) Several prominent Republicans, including Florida Governor Charlie Crist and Mitt Romney, appear to be jumping ship.

5) The highly-respected Civil Rights leader John Lewis has spoken out and said, for the record, how he feels about the racist tone of McCain's campaign, and the media is perhaps afraid of endorsing racism.

6) Sarah Palin was found guilty of abusing her power and has become a national embarrassment.

7) Those polled overwhelmingly chose Obama and Biden as the winners of their respective debates, and as a result, the media was forced to do favorable post-debate analyses of them.

8) Tom Brokaw pivoted today on *Hardball With Chris Matthews* when he acknowledged that McCain was unprepared for his debate question about whom he would name as Secretary of the Treasury. McCain had oddly said, "Not you, Tom,"

when asked the question by Brokaw last Tuesday night.

9) At a time when the country is desperately looking for help, Obama was ready with his detailed four-point economic relief plan which includes job creation, relief to families, relief to homeowners, and responding to the financial crisis.

I can think of two sports analogies that can be made here. One involves the actual dual that is taking place between Obama and McCain. Consider it like a tennis match between two greats. Both players are engaged in what appears to be a very competitive match, and the score is relatively close. But one player, in this case Obama, is standing in one spot and sending shots toward McCain without having to break much of a sweat. Meanwhile, the other player, McCain, is diving all over the court and running himself ragged simply to hit the ball back over the net. The players are certainly involved in a long volley, but one is spending much more energy and, as a result, is being dominated. The other sports analogy involves the media and the Obama campaign. The game begins with two reputable teams engaging in a much anticipated football game. The sportscasters are obviously for the McCain team. The first half gives them ample opportunity to rally round their team, but with team Obama scoring left and right, it's becoming more difficult for them to make their case. They are forced to acknowledge what's happening on the field. And what exactly is happening on the field at this point? The superiority and effective game plan of team Obama and the fumbling nature of team McCain is forcing the sportscasters to feel the inevitability of the impending blowout. In the game of politics, however, the media has been known to take the game into their own hands.

The most troubling news of the day came from Rev. Arnold Conrad, past pastor of Grace Evangelical Free Church in Davenport, Iowa. He prayed the following at a McCain rally in Davenport yesterday:

> I would also pray, Lord, that your reputation is involved in all that happens between now and November, because there are millions of people around this world praying to their god—whether it's Hindu, Buddha, Allah—that his opponent wins, for a variety of reasons.
>
> And, Lord, I pray that you would guard your own reputation, because they're going to think that their god is bigger than you, if that happens. So I pray that you will step forward and honor your own name with all that happens between now and Election Day.

To say that this prayer was disturbing would be an understatement, but it would also be an understatement to say that Palin is getting away with lying to the American people. She was found guilty of abusing her power. This is a fact. But when she was asked about it she said, "Well, I'm very, very pleased to be cleared of any legal wrongdoing ... any hint of any kind of unethical activity there." No kind of unethical activity? Are you kidding me? She looked right into the camera and said that to the American people. The media isn't framing this lie very well. They are showing her tell the lie, and they are pointing out that she did indeed abuse her power, but they are not using the word "lie". Actually, Rachel Maddow did use that word on her program today, but she is in the minority. She called Palin a "liar". Palin didn't just lie, though, she did it without batting an eye and she did it with a smile on her face—and in the face of widespread public information to the contrary! She proved during the debate that she didn't have a clear understanding of foreign or domestic policy, and now she is making it clear that her grasp of the law leaves a great deal to be desired. This is a woman who, as Sheryl Crow said on CNN today, "doesn't seem to know what she doesn't know." She also doesn't know that by continuing to lie about what she has already been found guilty of is a continuation of abusing her power. She thinks that because she is a Vice Presidential candidate, she is somehow above having to be honest and held accountable. This is a woman whom the media has completely let off of the hook. In so doing, they are continuing to hurt the Obama candidacy.

Palin's actions show that she has no respect for the law. A legislative panel, the majority of them Republicans, said that she was guilty of something, yet Palin is basically telling them that she doesn't have to respect their findings. She is acting like George Bush, Karl Rove, Dick Cheney and the rest of that "above the law" gang of neocons. The media must put enough pressure on her to show, at least publically, respect for the law and to demonstrate some sign of contrition for abusing her power. But maybe she, like McCain, can't acknowledge a reality when it's staring her right in the face. Think about it! McCain found out that he was down by eleven points in the national polls today, yet he said, "My friends, we've got them just where we want them." Really? Does McCain know something we don't?

DAY 51
"'NOTHING TO LOSE"

Obama is campaigning in Oregon, Ohio, today—Tuesday, October 14—while McCain is in Blue Bell, Pennsylvania. At 9:40 am, MSNBC showed a *Quinnipiac* poll that has Obama leading in Colorado by nine points. Makes me wonder if David Gregory will analyze this poll today. Actually, I don't wonder this because the poll favors Obama. How could a poll yesterday have the two candidates tied in Colorado but Obama up by nine in a different poll today? This is odd.

ACORN is being treated like a Republican piñata as of late. The McCain camp is trying to make the organization symbolize something dark and ugly and also linked to Obama. The fact of the matter is that some ACORN employees may be guilty of registration fraud, not voter fraud. Obama himself told reporters today that ACORN may have hired workers who signed up people in order to simply get paid—as workers' jobs depend on the number of voters they register. This problem would make sense considering the fact that one ACORN worker signed up members of the Dallas Cowboys. Obama jokingly said that he seriously doubted if Cowboy quarterback Tony Romo would be showing up to vote in the state of Ohio. Point taken!

John McCain himself was at an event in 2006 that was co-sponsored by ACORN members. He seems to have forgotten the fact that he told his audience at that event, "What makes

America special is what's in this room tonight." Obama said that he and the U.S. Justice Department represented ACORN some thirteen years ago in their attempt to enforce the motor voter registration law. This is the so-called nefarious connection the McCain camp is trying to make between Obama and ACORN. I guess he'll be going after the U.S. Justice Department next in that they also wanted to enforce the law that allowed voters to register when and where they got their driver's licenses. The reality is that the McCain campaign is scared of ACORN because they've registered 1.3 million new voters that will likely vote for Democrats. At 9:45 am on MSNBC, Contessa Brewer suggested that voter fraud is taking place in tossup states and those leaning toward Obama. Really? Only in those states? Must be Obama and ACORN plotting to steal the election! This is subtly becoming a racist issue because every time the networks show ACORN, we see African American's signing up voters. Combine this with the attempt to link Obama to ACORN and so-called voter fraud in states that favor Obama, and you have good old-fashioned racism. Ooh, those bad people who want to enforce and promote the Voting Rights Act of 1968 rather those good, patriotic Americans who set up barriers on the streets in predominantly black neighborhoods on Election Day 2000!

A new CBS/*New York Times* national poll has just come out, and it shows Obama leading McCain 53% to 39%. This poll should give the McCain camp pause, but it will likely incite more violent language at the McCain-Palin rallies. Today, in Scranton, Pennsylvania, while Palin was speaking about Obama, once again a supporter shouted, "Kill him".

Neither McCain nor Palin has spoken out against these "Kill him" comments. John Lewis warned them. Instead of taking Lewis' advice, McCain told the press today that Lewis' comments were the worst he's heard in his entire political career and that Obama should have immediately denounced Lewis' comments. McCain said that Lewis had linked him to segregation and bombing churches.

McCain went on record today regarding the issue of bringing up Ayers at tomorrow's debate. He said that Obama's challenging him last week to bring up Ayers to his face has "probably ensured that it will come up this time." I guess it never occurred to McCain that Obama challenged him to say it to his face because he wanted him to do exactly that— say it to his face.

On MSNBC at 2:13 pm, Congresswoman Janice Schakowsky of Illinois said that Sarah Palin is trying to "other-ize" [Obama] when she claims that he doesn't see the world as "we" do. Schakowsky pointed out that America is a very diverse place and to use the word "we" suggests that Obama is different.

Tomorrow night's debate will be McCain's last chance to bring up William Ayers to Obama's face. The media is trying to predict whether McCain will actually summon up the nerve to do so himself or leave it to the moderator, Bob Schieffer, to do it. There is also pressure on McCain to perform well because of what he said Sunday to his campaign staff at his Arlington, Virginia, headquarters: "After I whip his you-know-what in this debate, we're going to be going out 24/7." His staff began to laugh and applaud. McCain immediately added: "I want to emphasize again, I respect Sen. Obama.

We will conduct a respectful race, and we will make sure that everybody else does, too." Let me get this right. He respects him but he tells people he is going to "whip his you-know-what"? That's a new kind of respect, I guess.

At 3:37 pm on MSNBC, Pat Buchanan said, "It is very hard for me to see how McCain turns it around." Could even Buchanan be pivoting toward Obama in an attempt to catch the bandwagon before it leaves town? Is this part of the media shift toward the frontrunner?

Lou Dobbs said, "I noticed the Obama campaign using the word 'erratic' a lot. What is that code for?" The Obama campaign has been referring to McCain's behavior as erratic for the past few weeks. Maybe Lou Dobbs will come to realize, like the rest of us, that erratic means erratic. It isn't code for anything. I'm thinking and thinking and can't imagine what the word could be code for. Old? I've never referred to or heard anyone refer to old people as being erratic.

In discussing the heated nature of the campaign, Sarah Palin told Rush Limbaugh today that she's "got nothing to lose in this." She may have FOX News to lose if she isn't careful. During *On the Record With Greta Van Susteren*, there was breaking news flashing on the screen. It read: "New Polls Show Sarah Palin's Support is Slipping." Is that breaking news? I guess if it was a poll conducted by FOX News, and the results weren't overwhelmingly favorable for Palin, it was indeed breaking news—perhaps shocking news to them. Maybe her favorabilities have dipped because she keeps saying that just once she'd like to hear Sen. Obama say that he wants to win the war.

Anderson Cooper told David Gergen tonight, when speaking about the accusations being levied against ACORN, that Sarah Palin "keeps saying it's voter fraud—it's not voter fraud—it's registration fraud." Cooper made sure to make this distinction tonight. Someone needs to remind Cooper that he did an entire "Keeping them Honest" segment this past Thursday that never made this distinction. How soon he forgets! Did Cooper's boss at CNN call him on the carpet about that ACORN report? Did Obama's camp get in touch with him? At least he got it right tonight. Too bad millions of viewers who saw Thursday's segment may have missed tonight's correction. What a crime!

David Gergen told Anderson Cooper that Obama has to do more than "sit on his lead". He said, "I think there's been too much of that." He was referring to tomorrow night's debate, but Obama putting out an economic recovery plan this week hardly constitutes "sitting on a lead". One poll shows Obama up by fourteen nationally today. As long as he's moving up in the polls, that's not sitting on a lead, that's increasing your lead.

DAY 52
"I AM NOT PRESIDENT BUSH"

Obama and McCain are in Hempstead, New York, today—Wednesday, October 15. Health problems are a dominant theme in the political world today. Former First Lady Nancy Reagan has been hospitalized with a broken pelvis and Vice President Dick Cheney is preparing to have outpatient surgery for an irregular heartbeat—this as the two Presidential candidates make their way toward Hofstra University for tonight's third and final showdown.

At 10:12 am, Robert Gibbs of the Obama campaign was Andrea Mitchell's guest on MSNBC. Mitchell asked him what the Obama camp means when they refer to McCain as erratic. Gibbs said, "When I say erratic, I mean erratic." Mitchell also pointed out that Nicolle Wallace of the McCain campaign stated earlier this morning that the Obama campaign has spent more money on negative ads than anyone in history. Obama may be spending more money on ads, but there is a difference between negative ads and lying ads. The nature of most campaign ads has been and will possibly always be negative. But ads filled with lies cannot simply be put into the negative ad category where the McCain camp has consistently tried to put them. The media has also consistently allowed McCain's campaign to squirm out of having to face any serious censure for their attacks filled with lies.

On August 29, the day after Obama delivered his acceptance speech in Denver and before the present economic crisis hit, the national Gallup daily tracking poll showed Obama at 49% and McCain at 41%. But now the media seems to have forgotten that. His current lead is being attributed exclusively to the economic woes. The media suggestion is that it isn't Obama's strategy or progressive youth ground movement that has him in the lead—it is simply the bad economy. It isn't Obama's ability to effectively tie McCain to President Bush on the War in Iraq and a host of other issues—it's only the economy. It isn't Biden's domination of Palin during their one debate—it's merely the economy. It isn't Obama's clear victories in both Presidential debates—it's that darn economy. It isn't the lurching from one issue to another that McCain has displayed over the past 52 days or his failed attempt to tie Obama to a Sixties radical or Palin's complete display of incompetence—it's the simple issue of the economy. Actually, it isn't only the economy that has Obama in the lead. It is his consistent message of hope and change, his steady hand, his original position against the Iraq War, and, yes, his handling of the economic crisis.

Today, David Gregory asked Mika Brzezinski if there would be some "blowback" if it begins to be perceived that Obama is "buying the election". If it were as simple as buying an election, a billionaire like Mike Bloomberg would be vying for the Presidency right now. Besides, Obama is buying his ads with small checks from the largest army of disgruntled voters in American history. If he didn't spend this money, he would be negligent as a candidate. And if he hadn't raised this much money, the media would be saying he's ineffective at fundraising. He can't win!

Bill Ayers. Bill Ayers. Bill Ayers. The media won't stop talking about Bill Ayers. Obama has answered every question put to him on the pervasive issue of Bill Ayers. I can't imagine how he could say more: it's a relatively distant relationship, lives in the neighborhood, Chicago evidently finds him a respectable citizen, college professor, did detestable things 40 years ago when Obama was 8. If tonight's debate comes up with more dirt on Bill Ayers, we will see whether Obama still comes out as totally, unequivocally clean as he has done over and over again since the April 16 debate with Hillary Clinton. This line of questioning will then need a good judge to say to the prosecutors: "That question's been asked and answered. Go to another line of questioning, please."

The debate just ended and the media seems to believe that McCain had his best performance. Bill Bennett of CNN suggested that McCain clearly won the debate. David Gergen said that Obama lost the first 30 minutes but then did better toward the end. Andrea Mitchell said, "I think that this debate went to John McCain." Rick Davis, McCain's campaign manager, stated on CNN, "I thought that Obama looked very defensive." Sean Hannity was practically drooling after the debate. He said, "You know, [McCain] didn't use my line. My line would have been, 'You can't fight terrorism, Sen.Obama, when you're friends with, sit on a board with, give speeches with, start your career at, and blurb the book of a terrorist.' That would have been my line." Geraldine Ferraro sharply responded with: "That's why you're usually sitting in this seat instead of as a Presidential candidate." Bravo Geraldine!

Wait a minute! Stop the positive McCain analysis. The American people have just spoken, and they have stopped the media dead in their tracks. The press was ready to give an endless list of reasons as to why McCain had been the aggressor while Obama had been completely flat, but the CNN post debate poll just came in showing that Obama won in a landslide—58% to 31%—a stunning number! The CBS post-debate results show an even bigger win for Obama at 53% to 22%. These poll numbers have the media in a state of shock. They should have saved their comments until after these polls. Just as the media was beginning to sing the praises of McCain, commentators like Republicans Amy Holmes and Leslie Sanchez of CNN were forced to acknowledge that Obama won. It looked painful for them to admit. But it was these debate polls that forced their hands. The American people have spoken, and they didn't believe that Obama was "flat" as was being suggested. They didn't want a Hollywood performance, and unlike the press, they weren't impressed with McCain's angry, aggressive disposition, his disrespect for Obama, or his decision to bring up the issue of Bill Ayers. The American people didn't buy it when McCain told Obama, "Sen. Obama, I am not President Bush". They didn't like the fact that McCain questioned Obama during the debate for not having denounced Civil Rights legend John Lewis' comments about George Wallace:

> **McCain**: One of them happened just the other day, when a man I admire and respect—I've written about him—Congressman John Lewis, an American hero, made allegations that Sarah

Palin and I were somehow associated with the worst chapter in American history, Segregation, deaths of children in church bombings, George Wallace. That, to me, was so hurtful.

And, Sen. Obama, you didn't repudiate those remarks. Every time there's been an out-of-bounds remark made by a Republican, no matter where they are, I have repudiated them. I hope that Sen. Obama will repudiate those remarks that were made by Congressman John Lewis, very unfair and totally inappropriate.

Obama: I mean, look, if we want to talk about Congressman Lewis, who is an American hero, he, unprompted by my campaign, without my campaign's awareness, made a statement that he was troubled with what he was hearing at some of the rallies that your running mate was holding, in which all the Republican reports indicated were shouting, when my name came up, things like 'terrorist' and 'kill him,' and that you're running mate didn't mention, didn't stop, didn't say 'Hold on a second, that's kind of out of line.' And I think Congressman Lewis' point was that we have to be careful about how we deal with our supporters.

McCain: Let me just say categorically I'm proud of the people that come to our rallies. Whenever you get a large rally of 10,000, 15,000, 20,000 people, you're going to have some fringe peoples. You know that. And I've—and we've always said that

> that's not appropriate. … And I'm not going to stand for somebody saying that because someone yelled something at a rally—there's a lot of things that have been yelled at your rallies, Sen. Obama, that I'm not happy about either.

John McCain has a lot of nerve to say, "Every time there's been an out-of-bounds remark made by a Republican, no matter where they are, I have repudiated them." He has done anything but repudiate them. When people on two separate occasions shouted, "Kill him," McCain never brought it up at another rally. He could have opened his speech at the very next rally and repudiated the comments before he began. When he was in New Mexico and someone shouted "terrorist," McCain certainly heard it because he gave a very surprised look as soon as the word rang out. He raised his eyebrows. It was obvious that he heard the remark. Why didn't he say right then and there: "We will have none of that?" He could have added: "If you are going to shout those types of inflammatory remarks, you are going to be escorted out of here immediately. And I'll cancel this entire rally if it persists."

McCain could have taken that opportunity to pick up new supporters. What person in America wouldn't have respected McCain for standing up to some crazy, hateful lunatic? Instead, McCain compared the "Kill him" comments to words coming out of the Obama rallies. Unbelievable! Why isn't the media pointing out this blatant lie? The press knows that there hasn't been a single comment comparable to "Kill him" at an Obama rally. If someone shouted "Kill him" in reference to McCain at an Obama event, Obama would certainly nip it in the bud right then and there. He has shown as much lately for people saying far less—like booing McCain. Recently Obama told some booing individuals, "We don't need that! We just need you to vote." McCain can say anything he wants while the press just pretends it didn't occur. They'd rather focus on a silly line like, "I am not President Bush." The press is so impressed that McCain could say those magic little words that mean absolutely nothing. He certainly isn't President Bush because I'm not so sure Bush would have allowed "Kill him" to be shouted at his rallies. A savvy candidate could hire a good Hollywood scriptwriter to win an election by having him write titillating words for the candidate to say, thereby having the press constantly on a string and salivating over those manufactured words being read from a teleprompter. The press treats clever words spoken by those who are usually boring as if they're pure gold. McCain has behaved erraticly for the past month, but he utters one line and the media is doing summersaults. Should Sarah Palin ever say something intelligent, the press will likely become worshipful and completely in awe of her.

The post-debate polls also suggest that voters didn't appreciate McCain accusing Obama of wanting to "share the wealth," nor did they like his grumpy demeanor. Did McCain stop to realize, before he made fun of Obama's off-the-cuff remark about "spreading the wealth," that many Americans are having a hard time buying gas and groceries—some practically starving—during this economic crunch? This is not the time to make fun of lending a helping hand, especially when you are the candidate with more homes than you can count.

McCain needed to smile more during the debate. Roger Simon of *Politico* said on MSNBC: "[McCain] was so negative throughout the debate." He was right. Another aspect of the debate that the American people didn't enjoy was when John McCain belittled the issue of a woman's health as it relates to abortion. On MSNBC, Howard Fineman of *Newsweek* said that making fun of a woman's "health" in the abortion issue sounded "cruel". McCain had used his fingers to put quotation marks around the word "health". Here is how that issue played out at Hofstra:

> **Obama:** With respect to partial-birth abortion, I am completely supportive of a ban on late-term abortions, partial-birth or otherwise, as long as there's an exception for the mother's health and life, and this [bill] did not contain that exception.
>
> **McCain**: Just again, the example of the eloquence of Sen. Obama. His 'health' for the mother. You know, that's been stretched by the pro-abortion movement in America to mean almost anything. That's the extreme pro-abortion position, quote, 'health.'

I will be curious to see how the women of America respond to McCain's insensitive words. Chris Matthews felt that this particular moment in the debate would cost McCain with women. CNN showed the debate with a split screen, thus allowing viewers to watch the facial expressions of the candidates throughout. Each time Obama would speak,

McCain had an odd look of anger on his face. There were times when it looked as if he wanted to hit Obama. His eyes were wide open and he was constantly taking deep dramatic breaths that were being picked up by his microphone. Of the two candidates, McCain tended to interrupt Obama more often. He spent the entire 90 minutes trying to goad Obama into an argument. Obama never once took the bait. This calm may have even frustrated his supporters—it most certainly frustrated McCain. There were times during the debate when it seemed like Obama was being beaten up— when it felt like he should be hitting back, but he kept his cool—more so than probably any other politician could have managed under the same circumstances. It was almost as if Obama had decided before the debate not to engage McCain, regardless of how ugly the tone got. Obama seemed to be channeling Gandhi or Martin Luther King Jr., in that his demeanor was one that reflected a nonviolent approach. No matter how many dogs they sicced on Dr. King's followers during the Civil Rights Movement or how powerful the water from the hoses became, there was no retaliation by the victims during that hateful period. Tonight, Obama's unruffled disposition was resolute, and he followed the game plan to a tee. His calmness through this latest storm served him well, and the American people rewarded him handsomely in the polls.

DAY 53
JOE THE PLUMBER

Obama is campaigning in Londonderry, New Hampshire, today—Thursday, October 16—while McCain is in Downingtown, Pennsylvania. The media focus today is still on last night's debate and John McCain's odd facial expressions. For those viewers that watched on CNN, they had the luxury of being amused by 90 minutes of some of the most creative facial reactions in Presidential debate history. They were the only network that showed a split screen. It's as if McCain didn't realize that he was on camera while Obama was speaking.

On a day when the nation found out that Madonna is divorcing Guy Richie and Sarah Palin announced that she will be appearing on *Saturday Night Live* this weekend, another person is stealing the limelight. He has become an overnight sensation as a result of McCain's decision to bring him up last night during the debate. He is Joe Wurzelbacher, aka, "Joe the Plumber," a 34-year-old plumber from Ohio. A few days ago at a rope line during a rally, Joe approached Obama and the two had an intense exchange over taxes. Joe claimed that his plumbing business was going to be taxed too heavily if Obama were elected, and he insisted on the Illinois senator explaining to him how that was fair. The story came and went, but last night, McCain invoked Joe's name and made him famous. The two candidates ended up talking about Joe throughout the night. After the debate, reporters flooded Joe's Ohio home. He told them that he hadn't decided whom he was going to vote for and that he was "going to bed". This is just the latest example of how the media is willing to cling to the most irrelevant subjects and completely blow them out of proportion. Joe the Plumber would do the country a tremendous favor by simply going away, but perhaps he can't because it's the press that won't leave him alone. The press is even suggesting that Joe might swing the election in McCain's favor if the American people take a strong enough liking to him, a point evidently not missed on the McCain campaign. Some are claiming that Americans may truly be able to relate to Joe much like they earlier had related with Sarah Palin. Again, this is the Presidential campaign, not *American Idol.*

This morning, however, Joe is again front and center. As it turns out, Joe the Plumber may work in the plumbing business, but he is not a licensed plumber. Turns out he misrepresented himself a bit. He also does not have nearly enough money to buy a plumbing business, something Joe told Obama he intended to do. Joe's just dreaming of all this, and he makes nowhere near the $250,000 income he would need to meet the bracket that Obama plans to tax. Joe would, indeed, qualify for tax relief rather than a tax increase under Obama's plan. He is quickly becoming a laughing stock. But not to the McCain campaign! They can't stop praising him. Perhaps McCain should have spent a little more time vetting the unlicensed plumber before he decided to make his entire tax platform geared toward him during a debate that the entire world was watching. This is turning out to be the latest in a long line of McCain flubs.

Congressman Jack Murtha is apologizing today for calling the people of Western Pennsylvania "redneck". Whether some are racists or not remains to be seen, but in this political world of "watch what you say," his apology comes as no surprise. Another event that has the media all whipped up is the annual Al Smith dinner that is taking place in New York City today. Obama's and McCain's task at the dinner will be to poke fun at one another. It is a light-hearted, fun event. It comes at a time when America is not in the mood for jokes, so when Larry King chose to break into his show in order to show the two candidates roasting people, it felt odd. The timing is inappropriate as people are losing their homes and the markets are in the toilet. But politicians will be politicians! Perhaps Obama felt like he could use the event to deflate some of the damaging remarks the McCain camp has made—you know, make fun of what Republicans are depending on in order to win—like Bill Ayers. Obama did have them rolling in the aisles with some of his act:

> **Obama:** There is no other crowd in the America that I'd rather be palling around with right now.
> (LAUGHTER)
> ...And while the collapse of the housing market has been tough on every single homeowner, I think we all need to recognize that this crisis has been eight times harder on John McCain.
> ...Who is Barack Obama? Contrary to the rumors that you've heard, I was not born in a manger. I

was actually born on Krypton and sent here by my father Jor-el to save the planet earth.

Many of you—many of you know that I got my name Barack from my father. What you may not know is Barack is actually Swahili for 'that one.' And I got my middle name from somebody who obviously didn't think I'd ever run for President.

…I know Senator McCain agrees that some of the rumors out there are getting a bit crazy. I mean, Rupert the other day, FOX News actually accused me of fathering two African-American children in wedlock.

…But at least, we've moved past the days when the main criticism coming from the McCain campaign was that I'm some kind of celebrity. I have to admit that that really hurt. I got so angry about it, I punched a paparazzi in the face on my way out of Spagos. I'm serious. I even spilled my soy chai latte all over my Tshi-tzu. It was really embarrassing.

Obama went on to say some kind words about the late Tim Russert. He spoke of how Russert loved this particular dinner and how much he is sorely missed. He certainly is. And if he were alive to see what the media is up to these days, he'd probably be outraged. While Larry King cut to the dinner to show Obama speaking, his guest was Bill Maher. Maher suggested that it was unfair for Obama to say such serious things at the end of his speech, the idea being that the dinner is supposed to be for fun only. Maher failed to realize that it was Obama who brought up Tim Russert and that that moment lent itself to making some heartfelt, serious points. As I've said before, Obama can't win. If he had brought up Russert and continued with the jokes, he would have been labeled insensitive and as lacking timing.

Obama is gaining ground in polls in several Red states today, specifically Virginia, North Carolina, Nevada, and Georgia. Maybe this improvement has something to do with the DOW going up 400 points. Perhaps the voters see a correlation between Obama's third debate win and this "feel good" market jump. But Obama told his supporters earlier that there were two words they should remember: "New Hampshire". He reminded them that he was up in the polls there during the Primary and ended up getting "spanked".

In 2004, after the final Presidential debate, a *USA Today Gallup* poll showed that John Kerry beat George Bush 53% to 39%. That proves that winning a final debate doesn't necessarily carry much weight. Kerry had to deal with the "Swift Boat" attacks, and Obama is defending himself against the Ayers issue. John McCain's attempt to link Obama to Bill Ayers last night wasn't effective. McCain appeared awkward and reluctant to broach the issue, but he gave it his best attempt:

> **McCain:** Yes, real quick. Mr. Ayers, I don't care about an old washed-up terrorist. But as Sen. Clinton said in her debates with you, we need to know the full extent of that relationship.
> We need to know the full extent of Sen. Obama's relationship with ACORN, who is now on the verge of maybe perpetrating one of the greatest frauds

in voter history in this country, maybe destroying the fabric of democracy. The same front outfit organization that your campaign gave $832,000 for "lighting and site selection." So all of these things need to be examined, of course.

Schieffer: All right. I'm going to let you respond and we'll extend this for a moment.

Obama: Bob, I think it's going to be important to just—I'll respond to these two particular allegations that Sen. McCain has made and that have gotten a lot of attention.

In fact, Mr. Ayers has become the centerpiece of Sen. McCain's campaign over the last two or three weeks. This has been their primary focus. So let's get the record straight. Bill Ayers is a professor of education in Chicago.

Forty years ago, when I was eight years old, he engaged in despicable acts with a radical domestic group. I have roundly condemned those acts. Ten years ago he served and I served on a school reform board that was funded by one of Ronald Reagan's former ambassadors and close friends, Mr. Annenberg.

Other members on that board were the presidents of the University of Illinois, the president of Northwestern University, who happens to be a Republican, the president of The Chicago Tribune, a Republican- leaning newspaper.

Mr. Ayers is not involved in my campaign. He has never been involved in this campaign. And he

will not advise me in the White House. So that's
Mr. Ayers.

Obama has a new ad up today that uses McCain's own
words about not being President Bush. The media can't stop
talking about how effective that moment was for McCain.
They are asking why he didn't say that he wasn't Bush much
earlier in the campaign. No one has stopped to realize that
delivering a line doesn't prove what you actually believe.
Some speechwriter wrote a line, and McCain delivered it
effectively. Wow! Now let's all take a look at his voting record.
He voted with Bush 90% of the time. Last night's "I'm not
President Bush" moment won over the press:

> **Obama**: When President Bush came into office,
> we had a budget surplus and the national debt
> was a little over $5 trillion. It has doubled over
> the last eight years. And we are now looking at a
> deficit of well over half a trillion dollars. So one
> of the things that I think we have to recognize
> is, pursuing the same kinds of policies that we
> pursued over the last eight years is not going to
> bring down the deficit. And, frankly, Sen. McCain
> voted for four out of five of President Bush's
> budgets. We've got to take this in a new direction.
> That's what I propose as President.
> **Schieffer:** Do either of you think you can balance
> the budget in four years? You have said previously
> you thought you could, Sen. McCain.
> **McCain:** Sure I do. And let me tell you...

Schieffer: You can still do that?

McCain: Yes. Sen. Obama, I am not President Bush. If you wanted to run against President Bush, you should have run four years ago. I'm going to give a new direction to this economy in this country.

After the debate, Andrea Mitchell said, "I thought that that was the best line of the debate." And it was just that—a line. The reality is that people in Hollywood, where I sit today, and those in the media, like Mitchell, enjoy theatrics and are swayed or impressed by "lines" and dramatic moments. But people in Middle America don't respond to theatrics necessarily. This point was proven in the post-debate polls. Most Americans just want to be talked to in plain language, and they want the issues that matter to them to be clearly articulated. Obama did that last night without responding with his own well-rehearsed "line".

DAY 54
THE "L" WORD

Obama is campaigning in Roanoke, Virginia, today—Friday, October 17—while McCain is in Miami, Florida. On CNN, at 11:44 am, anchorwoman Kyra Phillips suggested that Obama should take ten million dollars of the money he has raised and put it toward helping people with their mortgages, etc. She asked a guest whether Obama could do that. Her comment was totally bizarre, and her tone had an "I'm disappointed in Obama" sound to it. She was acting like Obama was wasting money on ads. He has spent $110 million in the month of October so far. He is spending $4.5 million per day, and McCain is spending $1.5 million. As I mentioned before, Obama is spending "the people's" money. Voters are giving him five, ten, fifteen, twenty dollars per donation, which he is then using to fend off the onslaught of lying ads that are coming from McCain. Voters are giving money to him so that he can win the election. He can then turn around and help people with the big issues facing the nation. I'm surprised that an anchor, again, in this case Kyra Phillips, is injecting her unsolicited opinion into the political race. Keep your opinion to yourself when it comes to how Obama should spend the voter's money. Tim Russert, where are you? We need you.

Kyra Phillips revealed her feelings again just moments later. Joe Biden had been on the Ellen DeGeneres show and threw balls at a dunk tank in which the actress Julia Louis Dreyfus was sitting. Biden managed to hit the target and into the water went Dreyfus. It's "Breast Cancer Awareness Month," so every time a guest comes on *Ellen* and agrees to be dunked, the show donates ten thousand dollars toward breast cancer research. But apparently these facts escaped CNN's Kyra Phillips. She said of Biden, with a subtle sound of annoyance: "I'm still not sure why he dunked her and what the purpose of that was." Phillips just had to throw in her snide remark. She's clueless about the entire point of Ellen's dunk tank. Stick to reading the teleprompter. No more giving financial advice to Obama, and leave the "still not sure" comments for the preshow production meetings that you have before you go on the air at CNN—or did you miss that meeting this morning? It's during those meetings that you could find out the answers to your "still not sure" questions. Hello! Phillips' colleague Campbell Brown is suggesting that Obama give his campaign money to certain charities. Which CNN anchor will be next to give Obama financial advice?

The Wall Street Journal tried today to scare voters into voting for McCain. They tried to beat back some of the Obama momentum in an opinion piece entitled **A Liberal Supermajority: Get Ready for 'Change' We Haven't Seen Since 1965, or 1933.** The journal suggests, "If the current polls hold, Barack Obama will win the White House on November 4 and Democrats will consolidate their Congressional majorities, probably with a filibuster-proof Senate or very close to it." The piece also claims, "Without the ability to filibuster, the Senate would become like the House, able to pass whatever the majority wants." Finally, *The*

Wall Street Journal made one last plea to voters thinking about pulling the lever for Obama:

> In both 1933 and 1965, liberal majorities imposed vast expansions of government that have never been repealed, and the current financial panic may give today's left another pretext to return to those heydays of welfare-state liberalism. Americans voting for 'change' should know they may get far more than they ever imagined.

Actually, those who are voting for "change" could do no worse than what we've seen over the last eight years. Today's "left" appears to be the only group with any progressive ideas. *The Wall Street Journal* should try to refrain from reminding voters of 1933, the year Roosevelt took office, ushering in the New Deal and rescuing the country from the Great Depression. That's not the best way to make your anti-liberal argument. And 1965 is probably another bad example considering it was the year after the Civil Rights Act—an act that outlawed racial segregation in public places and employment. God forbid something as groundbreaking, positive, and humane as the Civil Rights Act take place again under an Obama administration. That would be America at its worst—right, all of you folks at *The Wall Street Journal*? But this "left" must have an appeal because the media is beginning to throw the "L" word around today, and that doesn't stand for "left". Yes, whether Obama likes it or not, and he doesn't, the press is beginning to discuss an Obama "landslide."

The Republicans are resorting to old tactics that many Americans moved past months ago. But it isn't stopping Cindy McCain from saying today: "And, yes, I always have been proud of my country." Bay Buchanan of CNN told Campbell Brown that this was a legitimate issue to bring up because of Michelle Obama's previous comments about being proud of her country for the first time. They have got to be kidding! The desperation Cindy McCain and Buchanan reveal in reaching all the way back to the beginning of the Primary is stifling any hope of an interesting, not to mention important, discussion of issues. You're really reaching, ladies.

John McCain said today, "Senator Obama said that he wanted to spread your wealth around. ...When politicians talk about taking your money and spreading it around, you better hold on to your wallet." This drew huge rounds of applause. It takes nerve for a man with eleven homes to tell jokes about spreading the wealth around. McCain and Palin are trying to accuse Obama of taking everyone's money in order to dole it out to the needy. Has McCain been paying attention to the news? He repeats the very things he is being made fun of for. He and Palin are embracing the joke. Their campaign is quickly becoming a caricature of itself. It is a full-fledged comedy show. Maybe that's why Palin is in the mood to take to the comedic stage this weekend. When asked about appearing on *Saturday Night Live* tomorrow, Palin said, "I'm excited for tomorrow night. I have no idea what to expect." She should expect to be made fun of, and if she thinks that appearing on the program is going to lighten the Tina Fey blows, she's kidding herself.

Representative Michele Bachmann of Minnesota was on MSNBC's *Hardball* today. She cited Obama's ties to Jeremiah A. Wright, Jr. and William Ayers. Of Obama, Bachmann told Matthews, "I'm very concerned that he may have anti-American views. That's what the American people are concerned about. That's why they want to know what his answers are. That's why Joe the Plumber has figured so highly in the last few days... What I would say...what I would say is that the news media should do a penetrating expose and take a look. I wish they would. I wish the American media would take a great look at the views of the people in Congress and find out, are they pro-America or anti-America? I think people would be...would love to see an expose like that." So would this media expose be called the House Un-American Congressional Activities Committee? Sen. Joe McCarthy would be proud.

At some point the media is going to have to ask Bachmann and other Republicans if they intend to go ahead and accuse Obama of treason. Have they no shame? They have proven that they are willing to take an "all of the above approach" when it comes to linking Obama to every scary Tom, Dick, and Harry that ever walked the face of the earth.

Meanwhile, Obama's transition team recently held a large organizational meeting in Virginia. This is part of an accelerated effort to plan for a possible new administration. Under the direction of John Podesta, a former White House chief of staff under Bill Clinton, the transition effort includes a dozen separate groups divided into different areas of responsibility. Cassandra Butts, a longtime associate of Obama, is in charge of the group dedicated to personnel for a new administration. Obama appears to be moving forward while the media and McCain continue to squabble over Ayers, ACORN, Arabs, advertising, anti-Americanism, Rev. Wright, community organizing, and any other irrelevant topic they can intoxicate themselves with. The media and McCain can then go on television with highs resembling addicts on speed. They can rattle off talking points with their eyes popping and adrenaline pumping. It's as if the media and the Republicans are in constant need of a quick fix—like druggies pining for another hit. Their bag of Ayers is empty and they are going through withdrawals. What's next? Maybe they'll all take a big hit of Socialism.

John McCain should have found a plumber who actually makes over $250 thousand a year. Joe the Plumber isn't cutting the mustard on his own as a celebrity, but those like Sean Hannity are running to his rescue. Today, Hannity said, "I think to attack this man who asked a simple question, that if he starts a business, you know, and to mock him and let the crowd mock him and to let the media investigate him, you know, didn't pay back taxes, this is so fundamentally despicable. Why can't you as a Democrat say, You know what? Leave Joe, the Plumber alone. He's out there swinging a wrench for twelve hours a day, probably six or seven days a week. Do you think it's unfair what's happening to him?"

I'll answer this question for Hannity with an emphatic *NO*! Hannity continued trying to stick up for Joe. He said, "They were mocking—I don't know any plumber that makes $250 thosand a year. The guy wants to own his own business." Earth to Hannity! This is Presidential politics, the big leagues. He will be "mocked" as long as he sticks his neck out and says outlandish things. When Obama asked a crowd if they knew any plumbers that make over $250 thousand a year, a solid "No" rang out. Those are just the facts. Alan Colmes then told Hannity: "Biden and Obama were not mocking Joe the Plumber. They were mocking John McCain—Excuse me. They were mocking John McCain and his use of Joe the Plumber and trying to hold this guy up. John McCain vetted Joe the Plumber about as well as he vetted Sarah Palin. That's what the problem is." The only response Hannity could give was: "That's a cheap shot against Sarah Palin." The truth hurts, Mr. Hannity. Now, go rescue a different Joe. How about "Joe Six-pack?"

DAY 55
ROBO-CALLS

Obama is campaigning in St. Louis, Missouri, today—Saturday, October 18—while McCain is in Woodbridge, Virginia. I saw the movie "W" last night during a visit to San Francisco. I am in the Bay area in search of a publisher for this book—<u>71 Days.</u> No luck so far! But I must say, having spent the last 54 days writing in Los Angeles, San Francisco seems to be much more politically engaged in the current election. Anyway, the Oliver Stone movie was entertaining. Considering the fact that Colin Powell intends to announce who he will endorse this Sunday on *Meet the Press*, I found Jeffrey Wright's portrayal of him particularly interesting. Wright, a fantastic actor, played Powell as a conflicted individual. Throughout the movie, Powell seemed to be struggling with Bush's decision to go to war in Iraq. In the end, he endorsed the decision, and that cost him in the eyes of America. But today he remains a respected national figure. He is the one remaining member of the Bush Administration who still curries favor with the American people. McCain would love to have his endorsement. On August 9, 2007, CNN reported that Powell actually donated money to McCain's campaign. McCain spokeswoman Jill Hazelbaker told CNN back then that, "The Senator appreciates the support of General Powell."

One hundred thousand people showed up to hear Obama in St. Louis today. But this news isn't the focal point. A story dominating networks today involves Republican "robo-calls" that are being sent out to prospective voters. These phone calls are designed to suggest that Obama has been involved in terrorism. This is a despicable last-ditch attempt by Republicans that will split the country in half whether it's successful or not. If the robo-calls work, and Obama is not elected, over half of the country will incorrectly believe that he has been involved in terrorism, while if he is elected, half of America will believe that our President is a terrorist. The Republicans are sinking to a new low and are playing with fire. The robo-calls describe all of the activities that Ayers was allegedly involved in during the Sixties. Could this robo-call do some serious damage?

> **Voice:** Hello! I'm calling for John McCain and the RNC because you need to know that Barack Obama has worked closely with domestic terrorist, Bill Ayers, whose organization bombed the U.S. Capitol, the Pentagon, a judge's home, and killed Americans. And Democrats will enact an extreme leftist agenda if they take control of Washington. Barack Obama and his Democratic allies lack the judgment to lead our country. This call was paid for by 'McCain-Palin 2008' and the Republican National Committee at (202)– 863-8500.

The media is showing no sense of moral outrage over this attempt to tie Obama directly to terrorist activity. It's unconscionable for the press not to step in and thoroughly correct the record on this. And they need to do it with authority—not let it float out there for days on end. The media is failing the American people. They keep referring to fact-check organizations—as if they are enough. Fact-check groups mean little when it comes to correcting the record for 300 million Americans, most of whom get their "facts" from television news. When did fact-check groups become en vogue? The media is, has, and will always be, the only meaningful FACT-CHECK ENTITY. I have seen this robo-call message played on CNN, but I haven't heard it denounced as a lie. Networks can't play this filth and then let Republican talking heads insult our collective intelligence by arguing over its validity, while Democrats pull their hair out trying to discredit it. As I've said before, lies (now being sent out in robo-calls) shouldn't be argued about between the two parties. There is no argument to be had. This call simply shouldn't have been aired.

Too often, we hear our media referred to as "the liberal media." I completely disagree with this label. In many respects, the present-day media is inherently conservative, regardless of their liberal label. Think about it. Every time Palin, McCain, or any other right-winger says something that shocks the rest of us, the media barely bats an eye. As we speak, Obama is being accused of being a terrorist, and the Republicans are getting away with it. If the Democrats were suggesting that McCain is a terrorist, the press would drop their mouths wide open and have a look of shock on their faces. My own take is that Democrats tend to be decent, fair, and more often than not, straightforward on the issues. They rarely say outlandish things as the folks who go on FOX News say. In a sense, the media is immune to and inured of the vitriol the Republicans spew, so when Palin says that Obama is "palling around with terrorists," the media doesn't blink. But when Obama, who is a rational person, says "lipstick on a pig," the media almost has convulsions. When decent people say seemingly mean things, it gets headlines.

And this kind of bias has happened consistently throughout this year's election. John McCain has arguably run the worst campaign in history, but he is *Teflon Man*. If Obama had been as erratic as McCain, this election would be an open and shut case. McCain would be up by twenty points in the polls. But this is the current political climate in America—where a black man still has to walk on water just to stay even. Just to stay in the game, he has to be Tiger Woods-like—not just be good but also rather thoroughly thrash the competition. Woods didn't start his professional career by simply winning a tournament. *History.com* reveals this of Woods' first professional win: "On April 13, 1997, Woods, then 21, won his first Masters at Augusta National in Georgia. Woods' 72-hole score of 18-under-par 270 was the lowest in the tournament history and shattered a record of 271 shared by Jack Nicklaus and Raymond Floyd. Additionally, Woods, who defeated Tom Kite by a record-setting margin of 12 stokes..." Woods practically did walk on water that day. This kind of supernatural performance is what the media expects of Obama—what he's faced with. For now! Perhaps if he becomes President, he will have become a man, rather than a black man, who, by definition in our culture, must be perfect to succeed.

I wonder how the media would be dealing with Michelle Obama if it were a known fact that she once belonged to the Alaska Independence Party? They certainly aren't raking Todd Palin over the coals for having been a card-carrying member. Where's the media on this? Why haven't they been running loops of that Party's founder, Joc Vogler, saying such stunning things as, "The fires of hell are frozen glaciers compared to my hatred for the American government?" Vogler, made the comments in 1991, in an interview that's now housed at the Oral History Program in the Rasmuson Library at the University of Alaska, Fairbanks. These are words that CNN should be plastering all over television screens. Vogler also said, "And I won't be buried under [America's] damn flag. I'll be buried in Dawson. And when Alaska is an independent nation, they can bring my bones home." Though the media has made slight mention of them, these comments aren't disturbing enough to wrestle the media's attention away from William Ayers. Instead, Todd Palin has escaped without having to deal with an ounce of scrutiny from the press. Someday, historians may ask why.

In West Chester, Ohio today, Sarah Palin said Obama is "kinda fuzzying up his connection to ACORN." She said that ACORN was involved in "rampant" voter fraud. Palin said, "As for ACORN and voter fraud, they're under federal investigation." I suppose she has temporarily forgotten that she too was under investigation in her state and found wanting in the area of integrity. Palin is playing this ACORN hand as if she knows it can't miss. Radio host Roger Hedgecock told listeners today that ACORN is a threat because they want to register voters on the same day that they allow them to vote.

What a horrible thing! You mean someone could register to vote today and then actually vote—today? Hedgecock thinks that this will favor Democrats and make it virtually impossible for Republicans to win future elections. Why is it that voters having access to the polls helps Democrats? Something to think about!

Hedgecock also claimed that Obama is lying when he says that 95% of Americans aren't going to have their taxes affected under him. He claims that 30% of Americans don't even pay taxes so Obama is lying. Very clever! I would think that those who don't pay taxes are automatically being excluded from the discussion by either McCain or Obama, but nice try. Hedgecock also said that the media was "in the tank" for Obama. He hasn't been paying attention. Let me get this right. They're so far in the tank for him that they've ignored the Alaska Independence Party—right? The funniest comment Hedgecock made involved Bill O'Reilly. He told his faithful following that O'Reilly is being intimidated by what he perceives to be Obama's impending win. I couldn't believe that Hedgecock was dissing O'Reilly. This proves that the Right Wing is starting to feed on itself.

Hedgecock's real zinger against Obama was his disgust with the fact that Obama has finally broken the record for ad spending in a Presidential race. You're right, Mr. Hedgecock! How dare he spend the people's money defending himself against claims that he is a terrorist! How dare he stand up to people like you!

DAY 56
MICKEY MOUSE CAN'T VOTE

Obama is campaigning in Fayetteville, North Carolina, today—Sunday, October 19—while McCain is in Columbus, Ohio. Sarah Palin's appearance on *Saturday Night Live* last night should have no impact on the state of the race. She barely said a word, and it was Tina Fey who stole the spotlight again. Besides, talk of Palin's performance is being upstaged by the news that Colin Powell has endorsed Obama this morning on *Meet the Press*. Conservatives are already making the endorsement about race. Pat Buchanan told Chris Matthews that he attributed Powell's endorsement of Obama to skin color. Buchanan feels that if Obama were the same person with white skin, Powell would have backed McCain. Matthews reminded Buchanan that none of us should pretend we can read what a person's motives are. Rush Limbaugh told *Politico*, "Secretary Powell says his endorsement is not about race... OK, fine. I am now researching his past endorsements to see if I can find all the inexperienced, very liberal, white candidates he has endorsed. I'll let you know what I come up with."

The media can spin Powell's motives all they want, but it doesn't change this fact: Powell's endorsement is powerful. For weeks now, Americans have been inundated with silly talking heads, childish ads, and partisan strategists. Powell's voice was soothing to the ears. The authority with which he spoke today helped to calm the political storm. His is a voice that commands respect, regardless of political affiliation. This morning, Americans listened to Powell tell us why he decided to endorse the Illinois senator. He said, "In the case of Mr. McCain, I found that he was a little unsure as to how to deal with the economic problems that we were having and almost every day there was a different approach to the problem. And that concerned me, sensing that he didn't have a complete grasp of the economic problems that we had. And I was also concerned at the selection of Governor Palin. She's a very distinguished woman, and she's to be admired; but at the same time, now that we have had a chance to watch her for some seven weeks, I don't believe she's ready to be President of the United States, which is the job of the Vice President."

Listening to Powell speak, I found myself predicting how McCain and Palin would find a way to downplay the significance of his endorsement—that they would claim to have never expected to receive Powell's support. Still, Powell's words to Brokaw were eloquent, and they affirmed what millions of Americans have been feeling for months. We needed someone of his stature to sieze the moment. He spoke to Brokaw for nearly an hour, but a few of the thoughts he conveyed are the very essence of this historic campaign:

> ...On the Obama side, I watched Mr. Obama and I
> watched him during this seven-week period. And
> he displayed a steadiness, an intellectual curiosity,
> a depth of knowledge and an approach to looking
> at problems like this and picking a Vice President

that, I think, is ready to be President on day one. And also, in not just jumping in and changing every day, but showing intellectual vigor…

…And I've also been disappointed, frankly, by some of the approaches that Sen. McCain has taken recently, or his campaign ads, on issues that are not really central to the problems that the American people are worried about. This Bill Ayers situation that's been going on for weeks became something of a central point of the campaign. But Mr. McCain says that he's a washed-out terrorist. Well, then, why do we keep talking about him? And why do we have these robo-calls going on around the country trying to suggest that, because of this very, very limited relationship that Sen. Obama has had with Mr. Ayers, somehow, Mr. Obama is tainted. What they're trying to connect him to is some kind of terrorist feelings. And I think that's inappropriate…. But I think this goes too far…. And the party has moved even further to the right, and Governor Palin has indicated a further rightward shift. I would have difficulty with two more conservative appointments to the Supreme Court…

…I'm also troubled by, not what Sen. McCain says, but what members of the party say. And it is permitted to be said such things as, "Well, you know that Mr. Obama is a Muslim." Well, the correct answer is, he is not a Muslim, he's a Christian.

He's always been a Christian. But the really right answer is, what if he is? Is there something wrong with being a Muslim in this country? The answer's no, that's not America. Is there something wrong with some seven-year-old Muslim-American kid believing that he or she could be President? Yet, I have heard senior members of my own party drop the suggestion, 'He's a Muslim and he might be associated with terrorists.' This is not the way we should be doing it in America…

…I think [Obama] is a transformational figure. He is a new generation coming into the world— onto the world stage, onto the American stage, and for that reason I'll be voting for Sen. Barack Obama.

The media is now in the process of spinning this endorsement. I'm sure we will hear things like: *Does it hurt McCain? How does it help Obama? It's a nice endorsement, but it doesn't change the fact that Obama raised a record $150 million last month,* and on and on and on. But again, listen up, media! The American people are funding Obama's campaign. It's a movement that doesn't involve you—the press. You have little influence over it, and this bothers you. It's called a grassroots movement, and you can't spin it.

Obama responded to the endorsement in Fayetteville, North Carolina: "This morning, a great soldier, a great statesman, and a great American has endorsed our campaign to change America. I have been honored to have the benefit of his wisdom and counsel from time to time over the last few years, but today, I am beyond honored and deeply humbled to have the support of General Colin Powell." John McCain's response to Powell's endorsement didn't surprise me. On FOX News this morning, he told Chris Wallace, "Well, I've always admired and respected General Powell. We're longtime friends. This doesn't come as a surprise." McCain, having gotten the Powel endorsement off the table post haste, turned to this week's talking points:

> **WALLACE:** In your radio address yesterday, you raised the "S" word, socialism.
> **MCCAIN:** Sure.
> **WALLACE:** But you did it indirectly, so let me ask you for some straight talk. Do you think that Sen. Obama is a socialist? Do you think that his plans are socialism?
> **MCCAIN:** I think his plans are redistribution of the wealth. He said it himself, 'We need to spread the wealth around.' Now, that's one of...
> **WALLACE:** Is that socialism?
> **MCCAIN:** That's one of the tenets of socialism. But it's more the liberal left, which he's always been on. He's always been in the left lane of American politics. That's why he voted 94 times against any tax cuts or for tax increases. That's why he voted for the Democratic resolution, budget resolution, that would impose taxes on—raise taxes on some individual who makes $42,000 a year. That's why he has the most liberal voting record in the United States Senate.

So now McCain is heading for the socialist accusation. But he and other Republicans are also pushing the voter fraud issue to no end. The complaints about ACORN live on. Republican officials are even reminding voters that ACORN registered Mickey Mouse this summer in Florida. Orange County officials in the state claim that they rejected his application. Mickey Mouse may have registered, but Mickey Mouse can't vote. This is an example of registration fraud—not voter fraud. Who's next, Snoopy?

Nevertheless, Republicans, led by John McCain, are alleging widespread voter fraud. The Democrats and Barack Obama say the controversy is ridiculous and is just political mudslinging. ACORN is a grassroots community group that has led civil rights causes since it formed in 1970. This year, ACORN hired more than 13,000 part-time workers. The workers then went into 21 states to sign up voters in poor neighborhoods. These neighborhoods are mostly made up of minorities. But for McCain to say that ACORN is engaging in voter fraud that could be "destroying the fabric of democracy" is ludicrous. Mickey Mouse and the rest of his Disney friends are simply phony registrants. McCain just knows that record numbers of people have registered to vote. These numbers scare him silly because he knows that record numbers favor Democrats. Don't blame Mickey Mouse.

By legal definition, to commit voter fraud an individual might arrive at the polls, present himself as someone other than who he is, vote for that person, then perhaps go to another polling place and vote for another person. If the person was claiming to be Mickey Mouse, first of all, his name probably would not be on the rolls, but if it was, people at the voting place would probably have been to Disneyland or seen it on TV and would know the person—eh, mouse—there was not the real Mickey Mouse. If the mouse engaging in this fraud were caught, he or she could go to prison according to state laws. But on Friday, during a campaign appearance, Palin told a crowd in Cincinnati, "You deserve to know.... This group needs to learn that you here in Ohio won't let them turn the Buckeye State into the ACORN State." She keeps trying to be funny, but voter fraud is actually quite rare. According to a 2007 report by the nonpartisan *Brennan Center for Justice* at the New York University School of Law, "It is more likely that an individual will be struck by lightning than he will impersonate another voter at the polls."

But this isn't stopping FOX News. Every time the network shows ACORN members, they focus on the African American workers. They use footage that shows workers engaging in activities that have nothing to do with registering voters. FOX News apparently is taping the workers while they are on a lunch break or talking on their cell phones. Did FOX go to a high school quad area to film during the lunch hour? It's FOX News' attempt to make ACORN look like a hip-hop group or some other stereotypical African American organization. They tend to show ACORN teenagers in red t-shirts engaging in non-serious behavior, like listening to their headphones or blowing bubbles with their gum. It's ridiculous, and it's FOX News playing to racial fears. It's obvious.

DAY 57
"REAL AMERICA"

Obama is campaigning in Orlando, Florida, today—
Monday, October 20—while McCain is in Yardley,
Pennsylvania. The Obama campaign should be a bit worried
about a comment Joe Biden made at an event in Seattle
yesterday:

> Mark my words. It will not be six months before
> the world tests Barack Obama like they did John
> Kennedy. The world is looking. We're about to
> elect a brilliant 47-year-old senator President of
> the United States of America. Remember, I said
> it standing here. If you don't remember anything
> else I said ... Watch, we're going to have an
> international crisis, a generated crisis, to test the
> mettle of this guy.

The McCain campaign is already seizing on these
comments. It was probably a bad time for Biden to stir up fear,
but McCain and Palin are suggesting that electing Obama
will ensure a crisis that America cannot afford. The media
should be reminded that McCain supporter, Joe Lieberman,
actually said something similar back in June on *Face the
Nation*: "Our enemies will test the new President early," said
Lieberman to Bob Schieffer. He added, "Remember that the

truck bombing of the World Trade Center happened in the first year of the Clinton administration. 9/11 happened in the first year of the Bush administration." The media should run footage of this Lieberman comment before they go haywire over this Biden episode. But we'll see over the next few days how much mileage the Republicans can get out of it.

Rush Limbaugh, as usual, made some outlandish remarks today and the mainstream news networks are airing them. The media is managing to turn the ideological views of a Right Wing nut like Limbaugh into news that everyday Americans are privy to. I have never listened to Rush Limbaugh's show. Ever! But today I heard him on MSNBC, FOX News, and CNN. Why is something that Limbaugh says suddenly surprising to the mainstream media? I gather from what I read that he always says outlandish things. But to air his divisive words just two weeks before the election strikes me as unfair to the Obama campaign. Some might say it exposes Limbaugh and makes people more likely to vote Obama, but I say it validates Limbaugh's hateful points of view. It gives him a broader audience, and even I must admit that Limbaugh has the power to influence. He's a persuasive personality. Today, he reached millions more because Anderson Cooper played his comments at 7:16 pm: "This was all about Powell and race, nothing about the nation and its welfare. He said it's not about race. And I say, OK, show me all of the inexperienced white liberals you have endorsed, if it's not about race." Cooper didn't play the entirety of Limbaugh's points, but looking at them, one wonders why any of Limbaugh's so-called insight into the mind of a black man—and black liberals in general—caught CNN's eye and led them to believe it was the kind of argument worthy of promoting. Limbaugh went much farther on his radio show:

> If Powell had endorsed McCain, you know what would have happened? Donna Brazile, the other black elites in the Democratic Party would never have forgiven him. Of course everyone's having a tizzy... [Powell] evolved over time into a calculating Washington insider who speaks incessantly to the media ... He did great damage to the Bush administration. It stuns me how Gen. Powell and others can back someone whose judgment has been so poor ... they are positioning themselves to perhaps get positions in an Obama administration.
>
> Now back to Gen. Powell: I just want to button this up ... It was totally about race. The Powell ... endorsement—totally about race. People have forgotten, but I have not, ladies and gentlemen. Colin Powell publicly broke with the administration over affirmative action, specifically affirmative action cases that were before the Supreme Court in 2003 ... He is pro-affirmative action, he is also pro-abortion ... I think he's still saying he's a Republican after all this, after endorsing Obama.

A story that should be getting more coverage involves some comments that Palin made in North Carolina this past Thursday. The *Washington Post's* Juliet Eilperin broke the news about Palin's comments. At a North Carolina fundraiser Palin raised the issue of who is and who is not a real American:

> We believe that the best of America is in these small towns that we get to visit, and in these wonderful little pockets of what I call the real America, being here with all of you hard-working very patriotic, um, very, um, pro-America areas of this great nation. This is where we find the kindness and the goodness and the courage of everyday Americans. Those who are running our factories and teaching our kids and growing our food and are fighting our wars for us. Those who are protecting us in uniform. Those who are protecting the virtues of freedom.

If Obama had been at a fundraiser in Harlem this past Thursday and referred to his audience as "Real America," his campaign would likely be over. As I've alluded to before, media leeway for McCain and Palin is miles longer than for Obama. McCain and Palin can't be given enough rope to hang themselves in the eyes of the media—that's been proven. They can say whatever, however, whenever. How else explain the closeness in the polls? Now Palin appears to be on a mission to split the country in half. What is "real America"? The notion that someone who supports Obama is not a real American is disturbing, to say the least.

The media is trying to get good mileage out of Joe the Plumber. He is giving interviews on all the main news networks, and Lou Dobbs is even comparing him to Colin

Powell. Tonight, Dobbs asked which endorsement was more powerful—Colin Powell's or Joe the Plumber's. The words **Powell or Plumber** were presented as Dobbs' headline. This takes the cake. We are now comparing one of America's most decorated generals—a man who has been in the forefront of American life, has served as Secretary of State, has seen American armed forces through war—to a plumber that no one knew a week ago. We're back again to *American Idol* politics.

Obama has cancelled all campaign events this Thursday and Friday to visit his ailing grandmother in Hawaii. The press is already pondering whether his decision to leave the campaign trail will hurt him in the polls. It will if they continue to let Palin's comments about Obama being a socialist and his supporters being un-American slide by as curiosities. It will if they continue to permit McCain to suggest that Obama was involved in terrorist activity without digging deeper. McCain's comments regarding this Obama-as-terrorist issue on FOX News yesterday are barely making waves today. He talked to Chris Wallace about some of his campaign tactics:

> **WALLACE:** Senator, one tactic that you've been using in these final days is robo-calls, automated telephone calls into people's homes, and let's listen to one of them. Here it is.
> (BEGIN AUDIO CLIP)
> **NARRATOR:** You need to know that Barack Obama has worked closely with domestic terrorist Bill Ayers, whose organization bombed the U.S.

Capitol, the Pentagon, a judge's home and killed Americans.

(END AUDIO CLIP)

WALLACE: Senator, back in 2000...

MCCAIN: That is absolutely true.

WALLACE: Can I ask the question?

MCCAIN: No, no. But before you do, that is absolutely true. And I don't care about Mr. Ayers, an old—and his wife, who was on the top 10 most wanted list. I care about everybody knowing the relationship between the two of them. That's legitimate.

Sen. Obama and Bill Ayers served on a board of the Woods Foundation and they gave $230,000 to ACORN. What's that all about? He said that he was just a guy in the neighborhood. He wasn't just a guy in the neighborhood. We know—we need to know the full extent of that relationship. That is an accurate robo-call.

WALLACE: But Senator, back—if I may, back in 2000 when you were the target of robo-calls, you called these hate calls and you said...

MCCAIN: They worked.

WALLACE: ... and you said the following, "I promise you, I have never and will never have anything to do with that kind of political tactic."

Now you've hired the same guy who did the robo-calls against you to—reportedly, to do the robo-calls against Obama, and the Republican Senator Susan Collins, the co-chair of your campaign in

Maine, has asked you to stop the robo-calls. Will you do that?

MCCAIN: Of course not. These are legitimate and truthful, and they are far different than the phone calls that were made about my family and about certain aspects that—things that this is—this is dramatically different, and either you haven't—didn't see those things in 2000...

WALLACE: No, I saw them.

MCCAIN: ... or you don't know the difference between that and what is a legitimate issue, and that is Sen. Obama being truthful with the American people. But let me tell you what else I think you should be talking about and the American people should be talking about. In the debate the other night, I asked Sen. Obama to repudiate a statement made by John Lewis...

The Civil Rights legend, John Lewis, didn't compare McCain to George Wallace—he compared the rhetoric coming from the McCain campaign to that of George Wallace. But, McCain doesn't seem to understand this simple fact. And just once I would like to see a reporter ask John McCain why he hasn't developed an agenda of his own. All he seems to do is talk about Obama and his former ties to this or that. It is getting old. Does he even have a message? I keep wondering what he is offering in the way of ideas. Who cares about Ayers, Wright, ACORN, socialism, or his hurt feelings over a comment about John Lewis? I want to know what McCain stands for. He changes his message on a daily basis.

DAY 58
BARACK KARL MARX HUSSEIN OBAMA

Obama is campaigning in Lake Worth, Florida, today—Tuesday, October 21—while McCain is in Moon Township, Pennsylvania. Palin is being scrutinized for something other than Troopergate today. She charged the state of Alaska for her children to travel with her, including to events where they were not invited but later amended expense reports to specify that they were on official business. In all, Palin has charged the state $21,012 for her three daughters' 64 one-way and twelve round-trip commercial flights since she took office in December 2006. In some other cases, she has charged the state for hotel rooms for the girls. The soap opera continues.

In the *Los Angeles Times* today, Jonah Goldberg has an opinion piece called **The Media vs. Joe the Plumber.** He is the latest in a long line of writers to suggest that Obama is teetering on socialism, though he doesn't come right out and say it. Goldberg selects references to *fairness, neighborliness*—even *community, church, and soul*—as indicators of the Obamas' economic philosophy.

> We've listened to Michelle Obama promise that her husband will make Americans 'work' in his effort to fix our 'broken souls.' We've heard the candidate himself say that we should agree to

439

> higher taxes in the name of 'neighborliness,' and that he'd raise the capital gains tax—even if it demonstrably lowered revenues—'for the purposes of fairness.' His 'tax cut' for 95% of Americans is in large part a middle-class dole. He will cut checks to millions who pay no income tax at all and call it a tax cut.... In short, Obama's explanation to Joe the Plumber that we need to 'spread the wealth around' is a sincere and significant expression of his worldview, with roots stretching back to his church and his days as a community organizer."

Karl Marx introduced socialism in the 19th century, but according to the new Republican tactic, Obama is in lock step as a 21st-century follower. Karl Marx himself said, "The meaning of peace is the absence of opposition to socialism." I suppose that, to some, these are scary words indeed. Sarah Palin and John McCain haven't called Obama a socialist—yet—but I keep waiting for one of them to tell a rally audience that Obama's actual name is "Barack Karl Marx Hussein Obama." I'm sure the crowd will erupt and start chanting the name. It's getting silly.

Today, Palin spoke to CNN's Drew Griffin about Obama and socialism. She said, "I'm not going to call him a socialist but as Joe the Plumber has suggested, in fact, he came right out and said it, it sounds like socialism to him and he speaks for so many Americans who are quite concerned now after hearing finally what Barack Obama's true intentions are with his tax and economic plan." Palin is just using Joe the

Plumber to do what she considers her dirty work for her. Earlier today she told CNN's Glenn Beck: "We cannot flirt with this, and now is not the time to experiment with, as Joe the Plumber calls it, socialism."

Palin is doing everything but calling Obama a socialist herself. She made sure to tell CNN's Griffin what she thought about Biden's suggestion that Obama would be tested when he takes office:

> **PALIN**: Well, who knows what Joe Biden was talking about? All you have to do is, though, is look back at Obama's foreign policy agenda, and you can assume what some of those scenarios may be, as he considers sitting down and talking to Ahmadinejad or Fidel Castro or Kim Jong Il, some of these dictators, without preconditions being met, essentially validating some of what those dictators have been engaged in. That could be one of the scenarios that Joe Biden is talking about, is, as a result of that, that proclamation that he would meet without preconditions being met first, that could be a scenario that results in a testing of our country. And the four or five other scenarios that he is talking about, I don't know. I hope that Joe Biden will explain it.
>
> **GRIFFIN**: Does Joe Biden get a pass?
>
> **PALIN**: Ask—Drew, you need to ask your colleagues and I guess your bosses or whoever is—whoever is in charge of all of this, why does Joe Biden get a pass on such a thing? Can you

imagine if I would have said such a thing? No, I think that we would be hounded and held accountable for, what in the world did you mean by that, V.P presidential candidate? Why would you say that, that, mark my words, this nation will undergo international crisis if you elect Barack Obama? If I would have said that, you guys would have clobbered me.

Actually, you, Mrs. Palin, have said far too much that warranted being "clobbered" for, and the media has given you a pass. Biden's comments, all this talk of socialism, and the current economic corruption remind me of something Abraham Lincoln said in 1865. *Oh!—Mrs. Palin, Lincoln was our 16th President. He won the Civil War and is credited with ending Slavery.* Palin would be wise to pay close attention to his words:

> I see in the near future a crisis approaching that unnerves me and causes me to tremble for the safety of my country; corporations have been enthroned, an era of corruption in High Places will follow, and the Money Power of the Country will endeavor to prolong its reign by working upon the prejudices of the People, until the wealth is aggregated in a few hands, and the Republic is destroyed. I feel at this moment more anxiety for the safety of my country than ever before, even in the midst of war.

As Palin continues to deny calling Obama a socialist, those interested in knowing the facts need only look back at some of her remarks from the past few days. This past Friday she said, "Sen. Obama said that he wants to spread the wealth and he wants government to take your money and decide how to best to redistribute it according to his priorities...Joe [the Plumber] suggested that sounded a little bit like socialism." This past Sunday she said, "Friends, now is no time to experiment with socialism. To me our opponent's plan sounds more like big government, which is the problem." And yesterday, she added, "There are socialist principles to [Obama's tax plan], yes." This rambling sounds as if Palin is accusing Obama of being a Marxist, but members of the media refuse to accuse Palin of such. After her interview with CNN, *Time's* Mark Halperin said, "Palin declines to call Obama 'socialist.'" Oh contrare! She hardly "declined," Mr. Halperin. At 8:52 pm on CNN, Bay Buchanan finally said what others in her party have been afraid to say. She stated, "Barack Obama is a socialist." Does she even know what socialism is? In fairness to Sarah Palin, she probably isn't expected to know what Obama's or anyone else's economic views are. After all, her speeches are written for her. And McCain and the Republican spokespeople are hammering away on the socialist, communist talking points this week.

DAY 59
SHOP, BABY, SHOP

Obama is campaigning in Richmond, Virginia, today—Wednesday, October 22—while McCain is in Cincinnati, Ohio. Republican Rep. Michele Bachmann says she regrets using the term "anti-American" while discussing Barack Obama's views, a remark that could threaten her re-election bid. The only reason she regrets it is because her job is on the line as a result of such an idiotic comment. Her Democratic opponent has raised a record $750 thousand since the infamous comment. I guess she had forgotten that her Congressional seat was not guaranteed. She will likely lose as a result of her ignorance.

A new NBC/WSJ Poll shows Obama leading 52% to 42%. Obama leads by twelve points among Independents. According to this poll, when asked who would be better at improving the economy, 49% picked Obama—28% McCain. The poll shows that 49% of voters have an unfavorable opinion of Palin. That is too high for comfort.

Talk of a "Bradley Effect" is still in the air, but I believe it could be an "Obama Effect," meaning those saying they will vote for McCain will actually pull the lever for Obama. Many voters may not want to admit, in public, their intentions of voting for the black Illinois Senator. We only have thirteen days until we can all find out if the "Bradley Effect" is still alive and well. I doubt it is.

Today, Senator Orrin Hatch of Utah told Andrea Mitchell: "I have never seen the mainstream media as much in the tank as they are for Barack Obama… They've had six months of gaga." Mitchell tried to push back, but Hatch managed to take over the segment and seemingly intimidated her. Usually, when powerful Republicans are this aggressive, the media cow down and cave instead of continuing to insist on the real news.

Today, Obama asked the press: "Was John McCain a socialist back in 2000 when he opposed the Bush tax cuts?" Republicans and Democrats can continue to argue back and forth until blue in the face, but it doesn't change the fact that Wall Street tumbled again today. The major indexes fell more than four percent, including the Dow Jones Industrial Average, which finished off its lows with a loss of 515 points.

Sarah Palin continues to utter words that boggle the mind. The media is beginning to scrutinize her for some comments she made on Monday while in Colorado. Palin taped an interview with Denver NBC affiliate KUSA. At the end of the interview, she was asked to participate in the station's "Questions from the Third Grade" series, in which candidates have fielded questions from local elementary school students. A student, Brandon Garcia, asked Palin, "What does the Vice President do?'" Palin responded: "That's something that Piper would ask me, as a second grader, also," referencing her seven-year-old daughter. Palin then gave this disturbing answer: "A Vice President has a really great job because not only are they there to support the President's agenda, they're there like the team member, the teammate to the President," Palin continued. "But also, they're in charge of the United States Senate, so if they want to, they can really get in there with the senators and make a lot of good policy changes that will make life better for Brandon and his family and his classroom. And it's a great job and I look forward to having that job." Today, Chris Matthews put McCain senior adviser Nancy Pfotenhauer through the ringer. Matthews asked her to explain Palin's complete misunderstanding of the Vice President's role. Pfotenhauer seemed to struggle at giving a clear explanation of the VP's duties as well. But she did so with an annoying smile throughout the segment. She did manage to say, "I am not a Constitutional scholar." McCain might want to tell his senior adviser that she doesn't have to be a scholar—just know some junior high school basics—then pass them on to Sarah Palin. Matthews nailed both Palin and Pfotenhauer today. In all likelihood, he has now successfully derailed Michele Bachman's re-election bid—The RNC is pulling money from her campaign in Minnesota at this very moment—and he has now completely exposed Palin's misunderstanding of the VP role. He has rightfully exposed Pfotenhauer as Constitutionally ill informed. Shouldn't a Presidential candidate's senior adviser know the basic tenets of the Constitution?

Michele Bachman actually tried to defend the disastrous appearance she made on *Hardball* Friday. As I mentioned earlier, Bachmann says she regrets using the term "anti-American" while discussing Barack Obama's views. Bachmann told the *St. Cloud Times* yesterday that she "made a big mistake" by going on MSNBC's *Hardball* last week and that she would like to "take back" the statement about Obama. During an interview with the *St. Cloud Times'* editorial board, she said: "I should not have used that phrase." Bachmann said that while she didn't question Obama's patriotism, "I'm very concerned about Barack Obama's views. I don't believe that socialism is a good thing for America." Again with the socialism talk! Bachmann's contradictions are dizzying. All of these statements were made at a St. Cloud Rotary Club in front of about 100. Bachmann said that she had never seen *Hardball* before and that she walked into a trap. Yeah right! She also claimed that she wasn't the one who brought up the words "anti-American". Sure, blame it on Matthews. What a cop out! She should have stopped at "I made a big mistake," but she didn't. *Now stop talking! You are giving Sarah Palin a run for her money.*

Palin said that the press would "clobber" her if she had said what Biden did regarding an impending international crisis, but the fact that she is getting away with this description of the Vice President's role suggests otherwise. Truth be told, while the Vice President does serve as president of the Senate according to the U.S. Constitution, the Vice President's role is limited to casting tie-breaking votes. The media should be informing Palin that Article I of the Constitution states that "The Vice President of the United States shall be President of the Senate, but shall have no vote, unless they be equally divided."

The Republican National Committee has spent more than $150,000 to clothe and accessorize Palin. I guess they didn't like the duds America's favorite hockey mom was sporting. According to financial disclosure records, the accessorizing began in early September and included bills from Saks Fifth Avenue in St. Louis and New York for a combined $49,425.74.

The records also document a couple of huge shopping trips to Neiman Marcus in Minneapolis, including one $75,062.63 spree in early September. The RNC also spent $4,716.49 on hair and makeup. Today, Larry King asked what this gross amount of spending has to do with "issues". It wouldn't have anything to do with issues except that McCain has spent months trying to paint Obama as the elitist.

McCain likes to say that he knows how to capture Bin Laden. Where's the press on this unbelievable claim? If he knows how, why doesn't the media demand that he get it done—now! If he doesn't win the election, is he going to then tell us that we all have to suffer now because he's not going to reveal his secrets about where Bin Laden is? Is this a vote for me or else scenario? McCain has been making this "I know how to capture him" claim for far too long. On July 25, 2008, he told CNN's Wolf Blitzer:

> I'm not going to telegraph a lot of the things that I'm going to do because then it might compromise our ability to do so. But, look, I know the area, I have been there, I know wars, I know how to win wars, and I know how to improve our capabilities so that we will capture Osama bin Laden—or put it this way, bring him to justice…We will do it, I know how to do it.

In May of 2007 McCain said, "We will do whatever is necessary. We will track him down. We will capture him. We will bring him to justice, and I will follow him to the gates of Hell." If given the opportunity, I would stick a microphone in

McCain's face every single day and ask him if he's "captured" Bin Laden yet. His promise to bring the 9/11 mastermind to justice is one that requires a strong enough media to hold his feet to the fire. We hardly have that in our press. They rarely even bring it up.

Today, Wolf Blitzer interviewed McCain again. The subject came up of Biden's comments about the likelihood that Obama will be tested on the international stage within the first few months of his Presidency. McCain made an issue of how Obama will not be up to the challenge of an international test of will. Blitzer asked if he believed that any new President would be tested as Biden suggested. McCain replied that he had been tested. When Blitzer pressed the question, McCain again knowingly said, "Trust me, I've been tested." This would have been the time for Blitzer to step up and call McCain on this POW issue. Being tested in a POW camp, horrible as it must have been for an individual soldier in time of war, is not the same as being tested to make a wise leadership decision on the international crisis stage. But, no, everyone gives McCain a pass, as he knows they will, on this issue. That's why he uses it every time—I repeat, every time, and they are legion—he is on the spot and can't answer a question. Blitzer caved in on this one and should have pressed McCain much further. How has he been tested as the President of the United States? Answer: He hasn't. No one has until they actually sit in that Oval Office.

Obama responded to the media's criticism of Biden's prediction by meeting with top foreign affairs experts today. This is an important sign because it goes right to the heart of leadership style. Obama didn't respond to the

McCain criticism by calling him names. He didn't take this opportunity to change the subject and call McCain a neocon, warmonger, or a fascist-like capitalist. Those are tactics used by McCain and Palin. When caught in a pickle—resort to name-calling.

Palin has had more disastrous events during her brief run as VP than anyone in history. Her entire campaign is a soap opera. In the media's defense—who could cover it all? But one of these episodes would have disqualified Obama or Biden. Therefore, the fact that Palin has survived this long and is at all a relevant and viable political figure, still leaves a scar on the media. Let's recall these "Days of our Lives": 1) Troopergate, 2) misrepresented Bridge to Nowhere, 3) lied about selling jet on eBay, 4) didn't know Bush doctrine, 5) 17-year-old daughter pregnant, 6) inquired about banning books from library, 7) left Wasilla millions in debt, 8) couldn't name a paper she reads, 9) disastrous interview with Couric, 10) became Tina Fey's muse, 11) associated with Alaska Independence Party, 12) blessed by a witch doctor, 13) asked the question *What exactly does the VP do?* 14) claimed seeing Russia from her porch as foreign expertise, 15) claimed air space in which Putin can rear his head, 16) $150 thousand in clothes, 17) charged the state for children's travel and per diem for working at home, 19) made fun of community organizers, 20) found guilty of abuse of power.

You may ask what more could the media do? To that I say, *Watch one of the most historic speeches ever given on the issue of race in America by Barack Obama on Tuesday, March 18, 2008.* That speech is called "A More Perfect Union". The *New York*

Times' editorial, **Barack Obama's Speech on Race,** put that moment in historical perspective back on March 18:

> Inaugural addresses by Abraham Lincoln and Franklin D. Roosevelt come to mind, as does John F. Kennedy's 1960 speech on religion, with its enduring vision of the separation between church and state. Senator Barack Obama, who has not faced such tests of character this year, faced one on Tuesday. It is hard to imagine how he could have handled it better.

Obama was forced to give that ground breaking speech in order to save his political career after all the networks ran endless loops of Reverend Wright's comments. Endless loops! As I've mentioned before, CNN would have to show—over and over and over—the Alaska Independence Party's founder, Joe Vogler, shouting hateful, anti-American comments. They would have to air the witch doctor praying for Palin—over and over and over—for days on end—in order to match that media assault on Obama during the Primary. Had he not been able to rise to the occasion and deliver that speech, on that day, with that mastery, the media was ready to stick a fork in him by continuing the loops. Period! When will the media force Palin to give a magnificent speech like Obama's to save herself? Answer: She couldn't if her life depended on it, and the media won't require it of her.

DAY 60
PEW... THIS STINKS

Obama is campaigning in Indianapolis, Indiana, today—Thursday, October 23—while McCain is in Ormond Beach, Florida. The *Los Angeles Times* ran an article today entitled **McCain Found to Get More Bad Press.** James Rainey writes, "Media coverage of the Presidential race has not always been glowing for Barack Obama, but it has clearly been negative for John McCain, according to a survey of newspaper, Internet, and television news since the political conventions." *Pew Research Center's Project for Excellence in Journalism* did the study.

On FOX News this morning, Bill Sammon suggested that the media has been completely supportive of Obama. He said, "It's a bias that is insidious... You've got anchormen talking about thrills up their legs." He was referencing a past remark that Chris Matthews had made about an Obama speech. I will send Bill Sammon a free copy of this book so that he can see how "completely supportive" the media has been of Obama. *Pew Research* posted an article yesterday, October 22, entitled **Most Voters Say News Media Wants Obama to Win.** The article states:

> Voters overwhelmingly believe that the media wants Barack Obama to win the presidential election. By a margin of 70%-9%, Americans

say most journalists want to see Obama, not John McCain, win on Nov. 4. Another 8% say journalists don't favor either candidate, and 13% say they don't know which candidate most reporters support.

I am not quite sure how valid this report is. Whether or not a voter thinks the media wants Obama to win is irrelevant because it's just a voter's guess. I have been writing about the media for 60 days now and feel that the press has been overwhelmingly damaging to Obama. And I have evidence. But given all the evidence I have, I still wouldn't tell a pollster that I think the media wants McCain to win. I would be guessing. I have shown how Tom Brokaw and David Gregory have done some inappropriate reporting, but I can't say whom they want to win the election. *Pew's* article noted what voters in the past have thought about the media and its favoritism of particular candidates:

> ...At this stage of the 2004 campaign, 50% of voters said most journalists wanted to see John Kerry win the election, while 22% said most journalists favored George Bush. In October 2000, 47% of voters said journalists wanted to see Al Gore win and 23% said most journalists wanted Bush to win. In 1996, 59% said journalists were pulling for Bill Clinton.

The question that should be asked is this: Why did *Pew* take it upon itself to do this particular media bias research question at this particular point in the game? They know from previous polls that the electorate believes journalists are biased in favor of Democratic candidates. They probably know that as investigative journalists pull up negative information regarding a candidate, that story will "make the news," thereby creating the perception that the media is focusing on, and therefore biased in favor of, the candidate who is not responsible for doing the damaging deed. The research does not take into account that journalists may appear to the public to be biased because they are reporting all this Republican dirt and not so much Democratic dirt. The *Pew* research does not look into why most of the dirt is Republican. Are the Democrats less dirty? If not, why does the truly biased reporting find so little—Ayers, for example—and try so desperately yet ineffectively to make it stick. If there is real dirt, why can't they find it? One answer as to why *Pew* did this particular poll is the fact that they partner with the American Enterprise Institute and the Heritage Foundation, both Right Wing policy advocates.

Pew found that last week "almost two-thirds (64%) of the public heard a lot about 'Joe the plumber' and another one-in-four heard a little about him." The media didn't drive that story—McCain and Palin did. When it was discovered that Joe had been less than honest about his status as a licensed plumber and his intentions to buy a business, the media simply revealed it. Exposing someone for lying is not the same as creating an image that may or may not be true. An example would be McCain's mere suggestion that Obama was linked to terrorism. The media's simply covering that innuendo is an example of a story being driven by the press. Revealing that Joe the Plumber doesn't have a license is just basic 101 reporting. But an average voter might still consider that biased reporting that favors Obama. It's not. *Pew* added:

> Discussions tied to 'Joe' made for one of the most widely heard about events of the campaign, comparable to the percentage who heard a lot about McCain's decision to temporarily suspend his campaign last month (65%) and Obama's visit to the Middle East and Europe in late July (62%). According to Pew's Campaign Coverage Index, "Joe the Plumber" was the third biggest campaign storyline last week, accounting for 8% of all campaign related news.

The best line of the day goes to Keith Olbermann who said: "Senator [McCain], Joe the Plumber is going into the toilet and he's taking you with him." Tonight at 6:15 pm, Larry King played Rush Limbaugh's rant from the other day—the one about Powell's endorsement being about race. I don't know why King feels that Limbaugh's rant is worth bringing up again. He should have been showing the insensitive comments Republican strategist Brad Blakeman made today on MSNBC about Obama's grandmother. As Obama is on his way to Hawaii, Blakeman felt the need to take a swipe at him. He was responding to a question about how John McCain could square his opposition to wasteful spending with Palin's $150 thousand wardrobe spree. He said that the real outrage is Barack Obama "taking a 767 campaign plane to go visit Grandma." He added, "Forget about the energy that is wasted, what about the hundreds of thousands of dollars to take a private trip when this guy should be humping his bags on a commercial plane or taking a smaller plane." Blakeman then made this final dig: "Taking a 767 of campaign money from people who could least afford it is more of an outrage in my opinion." I suppose Blakeman doesn't believe the poor have a right to—and know how to— place their tiny bits of money in the only investment they trust to do them any good, including a final visit to a loved one. Blakeman's sensitivity is so touching. What a lovely human being. I can't think of anyone I'd rather be than Blakeman's grandmother. She is an awfully lucky woman to have such a kind grandson.

This entire Blakeman episode escaped most of the media. Keith Olbermann managed to expose it, but it went unnoticed for the most part. Where are Anderson Cooper, Larry King, David Gregory, Sean Hannity, Rush Limbaugh, Campbell Brown, etc. on the insensitivity of this Blakeman outburst? If McCain were visiting his bed-ridden mother on his campaign jet, and Democratic strategist Paul Begala had said McCain was wasting his contributors' money on such things, Republicans would be throwing a fit and demanding that the media cover it. *How dare Barack Obama supporters make fun of old, sick women!* they would say. It would mean a lack of family values. At rallies, Palin would be saying, *To all you mothers out there, who are struggling with you health, Sen. Obama wouldn't want your son to come visit you. That's not what real America is about. We like to get in there and help out our families, unlike those Democrats who don't believe in family, or the media who support them and probably never visit their mothers. We intend to have a victory in all of our wars, so our sons can come home and visit their mothers.*

But seriously, Blakeman's comments should have made for a bigger story. First of all, the campaign planes are equipped to protect a potential President, including Secret Service accommodations, medical emergency provisions, and press corps space. Campaign pilots are trained to handle potential threats and possibly make emergency landings. Obama's traveling on commercial airlines at this point would be a logistical nightmare, not only for the Presidential candidate and his entourage, but also for ordinary citizens who are flying for personal or business matters. But the press pointed out none of these facts. They were too busy asking whether his trip to visit his grandmother will negatively impact his campaign. They were too busy defending themselves against the Republican accusation of their being in the tank for Obama—probably reacting to *Pew's* research. And they were too busy covering the first leg of McCain's Joe the Plummer bus tour.

With Obama off the trail, CNN's David Gergen commented on how there were no real issues being talked about today. Gergen suggested that Obama's absence left the media with nothing substantive to talk about. The media day consisted of showing John McCain at a rally where he seemed to be saying hello to Joe the Plumbers here, there, and everywhere. McCain didn't mention Sarah the Shopper. He did mention George the-lame-duck-drag-on-my-ticket Bush in *The Washington Times* interview **EXCLUSIVE: McCain Lambastes Bush**:

We just let things get completely out of hand. Spending, the conduct of the war in Iraq for years, growth in the size of government, larger than any time since the Great Society, laying a $10 trillion debt on future generations of America, owing $500 billion to China, obviously, failure to both enforce and modernize the [financial] regulatory agencies that were designed for the 1930s and certainly not for the 21st century, failure to address the issue of climate change seriously.

Let me get this right. He's taking responsibility, along with Bush, by saying "we," yet he still expects Americans to vote for him? He said "we" but it sounded more like his way of throwing George Bush under his Joe the Plumber tour bus. We'll see how long that bus tour lasts. I have the feeling Joe the Plumber's days are numbered and he'll soon be a distant memory like good old Joe Six-pack. Maybe the two of them can share a beer.

DAY 61
BACKWARDS "B"

Obama is in Honolulu, Hawaii, today—Friday, October 24—while McCain is in Durango, Colorado. On a day when Obama is visiting his grandmother, questions are emerging about the credibility of the account given by a McCain supporter and volunteer who claimed to have been disfigured during a mugging in Pittsburgh on Wednesday. Ashley Todd told police that she was attacked at around 9 pm Wednesday night. According to Ashley, the attacker became so enraged when he saw her McCain bumper sticker that he carved the letter "B" into her cheek. The implication is that the "B" stands for "Barack Obama." But the "B" is backwards, as if she had carved it while looking in the mirror. Police are now saying that Todd made the entire story up. She originally described her attacker as an African American male. Why this story was all over the mainstream media before the facts were known is beyond me. The press should have held off on reporting it until they had more evidence. Instead, many news outlets ran with the story, then found out it was a hoax, and are now scrambling to make sure we all know the truth. This just shows how sloppy our media has become. My questions are *How many black men were questioned as a result of the media letting this lie be spread all over the country? How did this negative story affect Obama's support? How many people heard the original story but will never hear the correction?* Again, the media dropped the ball on this one. And the McCain campaign's hands are not clean on this. Actor Tim Robbins told Bill Maher today that when Ashley Todd first reported the incident to police, McCain's campaign was calling stations trying to get the story out. Sounds a bit Karl Rovian to me. Joe Garofoli of the *San Francisco Chronicle* echoed Robbins' comments, writing today: "Talking Points Memo said the McCain campaign's Pennsylvania communications director told PA reporters an 'incendiary' version of the story 'well before the facts of the case were known or established—and even told reporters outright that the 'B' carved into the victim's cheek stood for 'Barack,' according to multiple sources familiar with the discussions."

The fact that Matt Drudge was the one who ran with this story initially in an attempt to play to racial fears should have been enough to keep the media from running with the story, but it wasn't. Drudge ran with Todd's claim that a 6'4" black male in dark jeans and a black tank top held her up at the ATM. His headline read: **SHOCK: MCCAIN VOLUNTEER ATTACKED AND MUTILATED IN PITTSBURGH... 'B' CARVED INTO 20-YEAR OLD WOMAN'S FACE... DEVELOPING...** According to a police report, Todd said the robber put a knife to her neck and demanded money. She said she gave him $60. She also claimed that he put his hand up her blouse and fondled her. That was enough to convince Drudge. This is just the latest example of what happens when a campaign spends weeks stoking up anger and playing to racial fears. Individuals like Ashley Todd, who are mentally unstable (as she has since admitted) take things too far. Todd had been stoked up by the McCain camp, and

Palin has been fanning the flames for weeks. It has been reported that McCain and Palin originally called Ashley Todd to offer their condolences. They should have called her and said that they were sorry for having asked, *Who is the real Barack Obama?* Palin should have apologized to Ashley Todd for saying this about Obama: *I'm afraid this is a man who sees America as imperfect enough to work with a former domestic terrorist who targeted his own country.* But, I wouldn't be so quick to jump to the conclusion that the girl is just mentally disturbed. If she had gotten away with this, it would have been a black eye on the Obama campaign, and the wingers on the radio would still be having a field day rather than scurrying about trying to cover their butts for what they've already said.

Todd also told police that the robber then noticed the McCain bumper sticker on her car, punched her in the back of the head, knocked her down, and continued to punch and kick her while threatening to teach her a lesson. *You are going to be a Barack supporter,* she recalled the robber saying before he sat on her chest, pinning both her hands down with his knees and scratching the letter "B" on the right side of her face using what she believed to be a very dull knife. Then the robber fled, she said in the police report. This claim was enough to convince Drudge, but he soon had to offer the "Drudge Retort". Wow! Matt Drudge is driving the mainstream media agenda. In all fairness, some networks, like CNN, didn't run with the initial story. But according to CNN's Rick Sanchez, those that did latch on to it early include FOX News, the *Pittsburgh Post Gazette, Newsday,* and radio talk show host Hugh Hewitt. Fox News' Executive Vice President, John Moody, wrote on the network's website:

> If Ms. Todd's allegations are proven accurate, some voters may revisit their support for Senator Obama, not because they are racists (with due respect to Rep. John Murtha), but because they feel they do not know enough about the Democratic nominee. If the incident turns out to be a hoax, Senator McCain's quest for the presidency is over, forever linked to race-baiting.

Mr. Moody, why in heaven's name would voters "revisit their support for Senator Obama" because of this story, which has absolutely nothing to do with Obama, whether true or not? Now the story has been exposed as a hoax. This means that FOX News is saying that McCain is "forever linked to race-baiting". It's time for Republicans to officially worry. A lot!

It's probably a good thing that Obama is off the trail and in Hawaii so that he doesn't have to answer questions about Ashley Todd. Palin isn't having to answer questions about it either because she is testifying before an independent investigator today regarding abuse of power allegations against her. Palin's attorney, Thomas Van Flein, told reporters in St. Louis, where her deposition is being held before a lawyer from the Alaska Personnel Board: "She's been looking forward to this day." Somehow I find that hard to believe.

Anderson Cooper showed a poll tonight revealing that 70 percent of those asked said that race was not an important factor in their vote. He then proceeded to discuss the Bradley Effect and other race related issues. If 70 percent say it's not an issue, when will Cooper let this go? Instead, he showed a clip of Reverend Wright's past comments about Hillary Clinton never being called a "nigga". This is the first clip of Reverend Wright that I have seen CNN, or any other network, show since the General Election started. It aired at 7:43 pm and possibly opened up the floodgates. If so, it's only right that the floodgates should be opened on Anderson Cooper's show on CNN because he showed it more than anyone during the Primary. Let the record show: *It wasn't John McCain who introduced Wright into this campaign—it was Anderson Cooper. Period!*

DAY 62
SHOO, FLY, SHOO

Obama is campaigning in Las Vegas, Nevada, today—Saturday, October 25—while McCain is in Albuquerque, New Mexico. Obama widened his lead over McCain in most national polls and surveys of key states over the course of this week. He is up eight points over McCain in an average of sixteen polls taken during the last week, according to *RealClearPolitics.com*. The Gallup Daily election tracking poll shows Obama up seven points in its national survey. The CBS/ *New York Times* and ABC/*Washington Post* polls put Obama up thirteen points and nine points respectively, while the latest *Newsweek* poll shows Obama leading McCain by twelve points. In North Carolina, which has voted for the Republican candidate in nine of the last ten elections, Obama and McCain are in a virtual dead heat. In Virginia, four recent polls put Obama in the lead, by an average margin of seven points. In Colorado, which went to Republican President George W. Bush in 2004, Obama has taken a twelve-point lead over McCain, according to a *Rocky Mountain News*/CBS4 News poll released late yesterday. The *RealClearPolitics.com* average of four Colorado polls shows Obama ahead by seven points. Obama has solidified support in the upper Midwest states of Minnesota, Wisconsin, and Michigan—all of which reliably vote for Democratic presidential candidates—while tying McCain in Indiana, a state that hasn't favored a Democrat since 1964. Obama leads by eleven points in Pennsylvania, six points in Ohio, and two in Florida, according to the *Realclearpolitics.com* average of polls in those states.

Today, Palin should be coming under fire for something she said yesterday in Pittsburgh, but so far she's gotten a pass. In the speech, Palin cited the need to do more for children with disabilities such as autism: "You've heard about some of these pet projects. They really don't make a whole lot of sense and sometimes these dollars go to projects that have little or nothing to do with the public good. Things like fruit fly research in Paris, France. I kid you not."

On September 10, 2007, *Science Daily* reported some fascinating findings in an article: **Specific Brain Protein Required For Nerve Cell Connections To Form and Function.** Palin might want to pay close attention to what was reported:

> Now scientists at the University of North Carolina at Chapel Hill School of Medicine have shown that a protein called neurexin is required for these nerve cell connections to form and function correctly.
>
> The discovery, made in Drosophila **fruit flies** may lead to advances in understanding **autism** spectrum disorders, as recently, human neurexins have been identified as a genetic risk factor for autism.
>
> 'This finding now gives us the opportunity to see what job neurexin performs within the cell, so that we can gain a better insight into what can

go wrong in the nervous system when neurexin function is lost' said Dr. Manzoor Bhat, associate professor of cell and molecular physiology in the UNC School of Medicine and senior author of the study.

The media could be blitzing Palin for this completely uneducated, insensitive response to what could be a breakthrough in an area she claims to be especially interested in, but it was a one-day story and is fizzling out by the minute. A story that is getting more coverage involves an apparent rift that's brewing between Palin and some of McCain's campaign reps. An unnamed McCain insider is saying that Palin seems to be more and more concerned with preserving her own political future for a possible run in 2012. There are no specific comments coming out of the McCain camp, but all the networks are describing the situation as tense. Perhaps the poll numbers are playing on the nerves of both McCain and Palin.

There is obviously something playing on McCain's stability evidenced by some strange words he had for a crowd in western Pennsylvania this past Tuesday. It was a gaffe that could probably go down as the worst in this campaign. McCain was trying to respond to some comments that Congressman John Murtha made about western Pennsylvania being a "racist area." McCain said, "You know, I think you may have noticed that Sen. Obama's supporters have been saying some pretty nasty things about western Pennsylvania lately. And you know, I couldn't agree with them more. I couldn't disagree with you. I couldn't agree with you more than the fact that western Pennsylvania is the most patriotic, most God-loving, most patriotic part of America, and this is a great part of the country."

I couldn't help but think back to 2004 when Howard Dean screamed while speaking to his Iowa supporters. The media made sure that he was officially eliminated for that gaffe. When what Dean said is truly examined, it's odd that his flub cost him so much. I remember him, with an extreme frown on his face and with a growl, yelling: "You know something? Not only are we going to New Hampshire—we're going to South Carolina, and Oklahoma, and Arizona, and North Dakota, and New Mexico, and we're going to California, and Texas, and New York, and we're going to South Dakota, and Oregon, and Washington, and Michigan, and then we're going to Washington D.C. to take back the White House. YEAH!"

It was that "yeah" that took Dean down along with some strong assistance from the media—the kind of assistance that the press isn't giving to McCain for his complete gaffe in western Pennsylvania. When you combine this gaffe with the one he made on October 8 when he said, "Across this country, this is the agenda I have set before my fellow prisoners. And the same standards of clarity and candor must now be applied to my opponent." When he said "my fellow prisoners" it seemed to be excused by the media, but perhaps it said quite a bit more about his state of mind. Howard Dean's state of mind was certainly scrutinized by a much less forgiving press.

DAY 63
"THE MOST TRUSTED NAME IN NEWS"

Obama is campaigning in Denver, Colorado, today—Sunday, October 26—while McCain is in Cedar Falls, Iowa. CNN is reporting this morning that a new e-mail has been sent to Jewish voters in Pennsylvania which makes some strong accusations against Obama. CNN is just now picking the story up, but Jim Rutenberg actually wrote about the false e-mail in the *New York Times Politics Blog* Friday, October 24: "A new e-mail making the rounds among Jewish voters in Pennsylvania this week falsely alleged that Mr. Obama 'taught members of Acorn to commit voter registration fraud,' and equated a vote for Sen. Barack Obama with the 'tragic mistake' of their Jewish ancestors, who 'ignored the warning signs in the 1930's and 1940's.'"

Usually, when someone makes references to the Holocaust, you know they have reached the bottom of their barrel. What's next? Previous attack e-mails against Obama have been anonymous or from some group outside of the campaign, but this one was sponsored by the Pennsylvania Republican Party's "Victory 2008" committee. This e-mail, according to Jim Rutenberg, "was signed by several prominent McCain supporters in the state: Mitchell L. Morgan, a top fund-raiser; Hon. Sandra Schwartz Newman, a member of Mr. McCain's national task-force monitoring Election Day voting, and I. Michael Coslov, a steel industry executive."

These tactics will probably get worse as we count down the final nine days remaining until Election Day.

Comedian D.L. Hughley is a funny person, and I respect his work. But I was a bit suspicious when CNN gave him his own show just nine days before the election. Why? Because his show was filled with some of the most damaging stereotypical black humor imaginable. And the timing couldn't be worse. His show originally aired last night, but it was re-aired today. During one particular segment, Hughley is interviewing an African-American man who is dressed up like a pimp. He goes by the name of "Freddie Mac—The baddest dude on Wall Street". Hughley is obviously trying to poke fun at the Fannie and Freddie debacle. The pimp is dressed in a yellow suit, purple tie and hat, and a cheetah-looking overcoat. What is CNN's slogan?—"The Most Trusted Name in News." Can I trust them not to exploit racial stereotypes? Can I trust them not to offend me? Can I trust them not to be FOX News-like—ever? These snippets from D.L. Hughley's show suggest that the answer is a resounding "No":

> **Hughley:** Welcome to the show, Freddie. Now, would you prefer to be called Freddie or Mr. Mac?
>
> **Pimp Freddie:** Well, you can refer to me as Freddie, the mac daddy of federal home financing.
>
> **Hughley:** Ok, Freddie, as the nations second largest mortgage buyer, you've been accused of costing taxpayers tens of billions of dollars through the shady accounting. How do you respond to these serious allegations?

Pimp Freddie: Well I have a message for these candidates who's tryin' to ruin my reputation—shut ya mouth bitches! [Remember this is CNN.]

Hughley: Wait a minute. All of the experts are saying your greedy actions are responsible for the financial crisis.

Pimp Freddie: That wasn't me. That was my sister Fannie Mae, man. Or as I like to call her—Fannie Mae or Fannie may not—it depends on how much money you got. (laughs)

This on CNN! Unbelievable! For CNN to allow this type of racially inflammatory material to air this close to an election involving a black man who has done everything imaginable to avoid race as an issue, begs the question: Is CNN up to something? At this very moment, the blogosphere is lighting up with comments from viewers who found Hughley's show offensive. The skit can be seen on *You Tube* and is entitled "Freddie Mac Talks to CNN." A *You Tube* blogger under the name "divadee5" responded to this skit, and I have the same question: "Why isn't this on Comedy Central?" The blogger added, "I am also suspicious of CNN's motives." Again, I agree.

The Obama campaign could not be happy with CNN over this news. FOX News, not CNN, is the network that tends to give racially insensitive material a place to reside. I wasn't surprised back on May 31, 2008, when Harriet Christian, a Hillary Clinton supporter, made some racist remarks and then was rewarded by appearing on FOX News with Neil Cavuto. Yep! Good old Neil Cavuto thought that she should come on his show. I guess because Ms. Christian insulted Obama with her comments, FOX News thought that they would aid the assault against the Illinois senator by allowing her to grace their studio with her racist presence. Harriet Christian originally made her remarks after she was removed from the DNC special meeting on May 31. Upset by being forced to leave the event, Christian screamed at reporters:

> The Democrats are throwing the election away—for what?—an inadequate black male—who would not have been running had it not been a white woman that was running for President. And I'm not going to shut my mouth anymore. I can be called white, but you can't be called black. That's not my America... I'm no second-class citizen. And goddamn the Democrats... Our Democratic party threw us down the tubes... And they think we won't turn and vote for McCain? Well, I got news for all of you. McCain will be the next President of the United States.

He may well be, given the fact that Fox NEWS gives a nut like Christian a platform and CNN is now giving air time to blacksploitation with D. L. Hughley dragging up old school race comedy—comedy that, in this case, is not even funny, that uses foul language during Prime Time, and that is possibly more damaging to Obama's chances than the Willie Horton ad of the 1988 Reagan campaign.

In Colorado today, Obama enjoyed his largest U.S. crowd to date, with local police estimating that well over 100,000 people packed Denver's Civic Center Park and spread all the way to the steps of the state Capitol. In Cedar Falls, Iowa, McCain spoke in front of a much smaller audience, roughly 2,000 people, and poked fun at Obama: "He's measuring the drapes. ... I prefer to let voters have their say. What America needs now is someone who will finish the race before starting the victory lap." Before speaking to the Cedar Falls crowd, McCain was on *Meet the Press*. He spoke of Palin, saying, "I don't defend her. I praise her. She is exactly what Washington needs... Do Sarah Palin and I disagree on specific issues? Yeah, because we're both mavericks." He responded to the polls that show him trailing in the race: "We're going to win it, and it's going to be tight, and we're going to be up late" on election night. McCain then told Tom Brokaw: "The fact is I am not George Bush. Do we share a common philosophy of the Republican Party? Of course." Obama later told his Denver audience, "I guess that was John McCain finally giving us a little straight talk, and owning up to the fact that he and George Bush actually have a whole lot in common."

The *Anchorage (Alaska) Daily News* endorsed Obama yesterday. Palin can't even win over her own local newspaper, though the endorsement takes aim more at McCain than Palin:

> Gov. Palin's nomination clearly alters the landscape for Alaskans as we survey this race for the presidency, but it does not overwhelm all other judgment. The election, after all is said and done, is not about Sarah Palin, and our sober view is that her running mate, Sen. John McCain,

is the wrong choice for president at this critical time for our nation. Sen. Barack Obama, the Democratic nominee, brings far more promise to the office. In a time of grave economic crisis, he displays thoughtful analysis, enlists wise counsel and operates with a cool, steady hand. The same cannot be said of Sen. McCain.

Michael S. Malone, one of the nation's best known technology writers, wrote an online opinion column for ABC News Friday, October 24 entitled **Media's Presidential Bias and Decline.** He feels that the media is "playing a very, very dangerous game" and that the "sheer bias in the print and television coverage of this election campaign is not just bewildering, but appalling." I agree with him on that point, but he soon convinced me that he and I think about the subject quite differently. Malone says, "What I object to (and I think most other Americans do as well) is the lack of equivalent hardball coverage of the other side—or worse, actively serving as attack dogs for the presidential ticket of Sens. Barack Obama, D-Ill., and Joe Biden, D-Del." If Mr. Malone is going to write opinion pieces about the media, he needs to watch more television and read more papers. Has he seen the "hardball coverage" of one Mr. William Ayers? The media was McCain's "attack dog" on that attempted character assassination. Malone then adds: "Why, for example, to quote the lawyer for Republican presidential nominee Sen. John McCain, R-AZ, haven't we seen an interview with Sen. Obama's grad school drug dealer—when we know all about Mrs. McCain's addiction? Are Bill Ayers and Tony Rezko that hard to interview? All those phony voter registrations that hard to scrutinize? And why are Sen. Biden's endless gaffes almost always covered up, or rationalized, by the traditional media?" Oh contraire, Mr. Malone! Networks have been playing Biden's gaffe about a potential Obama-induced international crisis for days on end—*ad nauseam!*

DAY 64
DIVA

Obama is campaigning in Canton, Ohio, today—Monday, October 27—while McCain is in Dayton, Ohio. Federal agents have broken up a plot to assassinate Obama. Apparently, two neo-Nazi skinheads were planning to shoot or decapitate 102 black people in Tennessee. They intended to target a predominantly African-American high school. Their goal was to carry out a national killing spree with Obama serving as their last target. These types of plots continuing to emerge are just another reminder that McCain and Palin waited far too long to tamp down their rhetoric about Obama's so-called ties to domestic terrorists and radical ideas. How did McCain and Palin think that young, violent people would respond to their implying that Obama was a possible terrorist? Perhaps these skinheads—who are current, viable domestic terrorists—thought that they were doing the country a favor by stopping a terrorist like Obama from potentially bombing the Pentagon or White House. Why would this be so far fetched in their minds considering that both a potential President and Vice President spent a month suggesting that Obama was a threat to America? Remember this robo-call? "Hello! I'm calling for John McCain and the RNC because you need to know that Barack Obama has worked closely with domestic terrorist, Bill Ayers, whose organization bombed the U.S. Capitol, the Pentagon, a judge's home, and killed

Americans." In these two young men's minds, their leaders, McCain and Palin, have personally called them to arms daily, for weeks on end. These are teenage young men who are obviously susceptible to persuasion because they have already joined a fringe organization, so why wouldn't they be even more susceptible to persuasion from an even more powerful leader—John McCain.

CNN's David Gergen has previously said that this kind of talk at rallies can lead to violence. It seems to me that McCain and Palin's crossed the line from "free speech" when they started yelling "fire" at a crowded rally. Let's just be glad that their incitement to violence hasn't led to anyone's death—yet. But, it was other people's good judgment, not McCain's and Palin's, that forced them to tamp down their outrageous rhetoric. When people shouted, "Kill him" at rallies, which even Obama addressed during the last debate, there were two young Americans out there who took that advice to heart. Today's cooperate journalists, very few of whom have a patriotic moral compass like that of sorely missed Tim Russert, have either nonchalantly reported on or fanned the flames of the violent-sounding attacks leveled against Barack Obama. There were weeks when the media provided a stage and amplification for people to stoke up a mob mentality.

Sen. Ted Stevens, representing Alaska for the past 40 years, was convicted on seven counts of corruption charges Monday. The jury found him guilty of accepting thousands of dollars in home renovations and gifts from an oil executive and then lying about it. Stevens set the stage for an appeal when he said, "I will fight this unjust verdict with every ounce of energy I have." Since Palin has had some relationship with

Stevens, it remains to be seen how his conviction will affect her race for the Vice Presidency. It will have an effect on the Senate if he fails to get reelected. At one point in his Senatorial campaign, he had a significant lead. Just before his conviction, he was trailing his opponent.

Several McCain advisers have suggested to CNN that they are becoming increasingly frustrated with what one aide described as Palin "going rogue". "She is a diva. She takes no advice from anyone," said this McCain adviser. "She does not have any relationships of trust with any of us, her family, or anyone else." The advisor added, "Also, she is playing for her own future and sees herself as the next leader of the party. Remember: Divas trust only unto themselves, as they see themselves as the beginning and end of all wisdom." All major networks addressed this story today, but FOX News made an attempt to accuse various people of picking on Palin. Greta Van Susteren seems particularly focused on the idea that Palin has been a target for people to take cheap shots at. Greta should try sticking to the facts—that McCain campaign advisors are the ones taking shots at FOX News' beloved Palin. Deal with Republican mistakes in a more objective and professional manner, please!

This past Friday, October 24, Joe Biden did an interview with Barbara West of WFTV Orlando. She is an anchor. I repeat—she is an anchor. All of West's questions were loaded, and it became immediately apparent that she had a Republican agenda. All I could think was *Where did West go to college for her journalism training?* Most of the networks are now running the exchange between Biden and West. So now, not only did Florida voters see the ridiculous comments, but the entire nation is privy to them. Biden couldn't believe the line of questioning and laughed at West:

> **WEST:** You may recognize this famous quote, 'from each according to his abilities, to each according to his needs.' That's from Karl Marx. How is Sen. Obama not being a Marxist if he intends to spread the wealth around?
> **BIDEN:** Are you joking? Is this a joke? … Or is that a real question? (LAUGHTER).

Biden seemed stunned by West's question. He later said, "I don't know who's writing your questions." When West asked if Sen. Barack Obama wanted to "turn America into a Socialist country like Sweden," Biden said, "I don't know anybody who thinks that except the far right-wing of the Republican Party."

Larry King had the now infamous Barbara West on his show today. He basically let her get out her talking points instead of pointing out how her questions would not pass a Journalism 101 course. If she was going to use a quote from Karl Marx in an interview, she would need to have established an objective foundation for the relevancy it. She was instead promoting her own opinions within the question. I should think she would be ripe for the picking for an old hand like Larry King. Instead, he threw her a couple of softballs and treated her as if she were a journalistic equal. The facts that she and her husband (an actual party advisor) are staunch Republicans and that her questions were from Republican talking points didn't appear to be information that struck Larry King as relevant.

As Anderson Cooper was doing a lead-in to a segment on this West story, he said, "Just ahead tonight: Joe Biden and the explosive interview you have got to see, on camera and on fire. Watch what happened between the candidate and a local TV news anchor. Judge for yourself which one of them had an agenda." Thanks, but no thanks, Anderson. It's obvious who had the agenda. How did Biden, in any way, show that he had an agenda? He didn't. Anderson Cooper did it again. It's amazing how he can take simple concepts and still manage to confuse his audience. At least Biden and the Obama camp know enough about how the press should work. They pulled Jill Biden from her scheduled appearance on West's network, as well as any future advisors or spokespeople from their campaign. This episode with West goes right to the heart of the media's assault on Obama. John McCain believes in the sanctity of unregulated markets, yet we have heard no anchor ask him if he's a follower of Hitler's brand of fascism. Of course, they haven't because he's no more a fascist than Obama is a Marxist. If an anchor asked McCain such a question, I would expect Larry King to lambast that anchor, not give her an opportunity to explain herself. She was wrong, Larry King—dead wrong. Period! For the press to spend a great deal of their day talking about how Biden should have answered the "tough" questions put to him by West is ridiculous.

The McCain campaign has spent their day blaming the media for making too big a deal about Sarah Palin's clothes.

And the media is still pondering whether or not they have indeed been unfair to Palin. David Gergen expressed his frustration over the issue to Anderson Cooper tonight. "Oh, it's just—it's absurd. It's absurd that we're sitting here … talking about her— her clothing and this and that eight days before a major national election." This West story is a much more politically relevant complaint against the media, yet Obama's camp took assertive action against the station in Florida rather than filling the airwaves with trivia.

Elisabeth Hasselbeck, co-host of "The View" tried to defend Palin today at a rally: "Instead of the issues, they are focused, fixated, on her wardrobe. This is deliberately sexist." Anderson Cooper showed Hasselbeck's comments and then weighed in: "Does she have a point?" Does Elisabeth Hasselbeck ever have a point? Palin's clothes, John Edwards' haircut—is talking about them sexist? Who cares? If their campaign contributors don't rise up in anger over how their money is spent, why should the media? Why should Hasselbeck waste the public's time with her Valley Girl inanities? Who gave her a platform? When will this lowest level of reality show news end? The McCain camp is complaining about the continuing media coverage of this issue, but their incompetent spokespeople, including Palin herself, are the only ones who keep bringing it up. This was Palin today: "Those clothes, they are not my property. Just like the lighting and the staging that everything else that the RNC purchased, I'm not taking them with me. I'm back to wearing my own clothes from my favorite consignment shop in Anchorage, Alaska."

Today, Obama told a crowd in Canton, Ohio, "Don't believe for a second this election is over. Don't think for a minute that power concedes. We have to work like our future depends on it in this last week, because it does.... In one week, we can choose hope over fear, unity over division, the promise of change over the power of the status quo." McCain, in contrast, offered this to his audience in Cleveland, Ohio:

> ...In a radio interview revealed today, [Obama] said that one of the quote – 'tragedies' of the Civil Rights Movement is that it didn't bring about a redistribution of wealth in our society. He said, and I quote, 'One of the tragedies of the Civil Rights movement was because the Civil Rights Movement became so court-focused I think that there was a tendency to lose track of the political and community organizing and activities on the ground that are able to put together the actual coalitions of power through which you bring about redistributive change.' That is what change means for Barack the Redistributor: It means taking your money and giving it to someone else...
>
> ...This election comes down to how you want your money spent. Do you want to keep it invested in your future or do you want to have it taken by the most liberal person to ever run for the presidency, and Democratic leaders who have been running Congress for the past two years, Nancy Pelosi

and Harry Reid? My friends, this is a dangerous threesome.

McCain is pulling out all the stops in his attempt to brand Obama a redistributor. Obama's actual comments from 2001 were less controversial than the media and McCain campaign are painting them. His comments are being played endlessly on CNN and FOX News. What Obama actually said was historically important, especially his comments regarding his own rights as an African-American:

> If you look at the victories and failures of the Civil Rights Movement and its litigation strategy in the court, I think where it succeeded was to invest formal rights in previously dispossessed people, so that now I would have the right to vote. I would now be able to sit at the lunch counter and order as long as I could pay for it I'd be o.k. But, the Supreme Court never ventured into the issues of redistribution of wealth, and of more basic issues such as political and economic justice in society. To that extent, as radical as I think people try to characterize the Warren Court, it wasn't that radical. It didn't break free from the essential constraints that were placed by the founding fathers in the Constitution...

In looking at the history of the civil rights of black people since slavery days, he points out that what the Warren Court did in its *Brown* decision in 1954 was not all that radical in that it never attempted to give the descendants of slavery some of the wealth that could have gotten them started toward equal footing in the country's economic arena. All it did was reaffirm some of the negative rights of citizens, in other words, the rights that government could not take away from its citizens. Given that our American government had indeed taken away the rights to life, liberty, and property (their own person) of slaves, giving their descendants only negative rights would never right the wrongs done by the institution of slavery itself. In other words, a court could decide that it had imprisoned a person unjustly for twenty years, but if it just set the person free and didn't compensate him for the loss of wages, property, family, etc., that he had lost, then it had not done him justice by just freeing him. By playing this redistributor card, McCain is actually putting a subject on the table that he probably doesn't intend to: the subject of reparations for slavery. If Todd Palin and his secessionist friends want to refight the Civil War, I think they will find a Union that wants to do more than free its disenfranchised poor people this time. McCain and Palin have opened a Pandora's box they probably will someday want to try desperately to close.

DAY 65
WACK JOB

Obama is campaigning in Chester, Pennsylvania, today—Tuesday, October 28—while McCain is in Hershey, Pennsylvania. Some of today's polls show Obama leading in several key states, and one poll has him ahead nationally by the largest margin of the general election so far—fifteen points. Even Georgia appears to be in play. Shocking news, I'm sure, to the McCain campaign. There are still seven days for these poll numbers to change:

> National/Pew Research—Obama 53%-McCain 38%
>
> Pennsylvania/Rasmussen—Obama 53%-McCain 46%
>
> Georgia/InAdv-Poll Position—McCain 48%-Obama 47%
>
> Nevada/Rasmussen—Obama 50%-McCain 46%
>
> Mississippi/Rasmussen—McCain 53%-Obama 45%
>
> Ohio/LA Times-Bloomberg—Obama 49%-McCain 40%
>
> Florida/LA Times-Bloomberg—Obama 50%-McCain 43%
>
> Colorado/Politico-InAdv—Obama 53%-McCain 45%

New Hampshire/WMUR-UNH—Obama 58%-McCain 33%

Wisconsin/Strategic Vision—Obama 50%-McCain 41%

New Jersey/Strategic Vision—Obama 53%-McCain 38%

Indiana/Research 2000—Obama 48%-McCain 47%

Montana/NBC-Mason Dixon—McCain 48%-Obama 44%

North Carolina/NBC-Mason Dixon—Obama 47%-McCain 47%

McCain is hitting Obama hard, trying to make voters question whether or not the 47-year-old senator is ready for primetime. He drew applause when he said, "I've been tested. Sen. Obama hasn't," and a standing ovation when he said, "I will bring our troops home with honor and victory and not in defeat." This idea that Obama wants to bring our troops home with anything other than honor is silly. I still haven't heard McCain, Bush, Cheney, or any other Republican explain what victory looks like.

Sarah Palin is having a grand old time naming people Joe-the-this and Joe-the-that. She seems to be doing just about whatever she wants. *Politico's* Mike Allen reported that a top McCain adviser has called Palin "a wack job." It is a bit "wack" for her to be suggesting that Sen. Stevens step down, considering that we have all recently found out her own house is quite a mess. Still, Palin said the time has come "for him to step aside." Palin also said, "Even if elected on

Tuesday, Sen. Stevens should step aside to allow a special election to give Alaskans a real choice of who will serve them in Congress." The nerve of Palin is remarkable. Her fellow maverick McCain said, "Stevens has broken his trust with the people and ... he should now step down." His nerve may be even greater than that of Palin's, considering he "broke his trust with the people" during the Keating Five scandal. As a matter of fact, though neither McCain nor Palin were found guilty of breaking the law during Keating Five and Troopergate, they both "broke their trust with the people". Why the media isn't pointing out the hypocrisy in both of their statements regarding Stevens escapes me.

Palin's hypocrisy doesn't end with the Stevens comments. She has been in lockstep with McCain in accusing Obama of wanting to spread the wealth, both now calling him a socialist. But the media has failed to pin her down on this case of blatant, audacious, or better yet—unforgivable—hypocrisy. On September 22, 2008, in an interview called **The State of Sarah Palin** with *The New Yorker's* Philip Gourevitch, Palin explained the windfall profits tax that she imposed on the oil industry in Alaska:

> And Alaska—we're set up, unlike other states in the union, where it's collectively Alaskans own the resources. So we *share in the wealth* when the development of these resources occurs. ... It's to maximize benefits for Alaskans, not an individual company, not some multinational somewhere, but for Alaskans.

Any red-blooded American, regardless of political affiliation, should find this flip-flop offensive. Palin has proven herself once and for all to be a politician who cannot, under any circumstances, be trusted. Why? Because she doesn't understand her own ironies. She has spent weeks trashing Obama for wanting to spread the wealth, essentially running on that attack. It has been her rallying cry. Putting this blatant hypocrisy into context is tantamount to trying to explain McCain's attempt to both propose a mortgage bailout and call Obama a socialist at the same time. These individuals have lost their bearings, and their gluttonous attempt to win the Presidency has rendered them void of any sense of shame. Have they no honor—no line they will not cross? Have they no sense of what they themselves have told the American people—of their own record on the very issues they accuse Obama of being dubious for endorsing? When will the press call for them to repent, just a bit, for their transgressions?

On *Larry King Live* today, former Bush Press Secretary Ari Fleischer suggested that Obama cannot be trusted when it comes to Israel. He did so without equivalent retort from anyone on the panel. King himself certainly didn't offer an effective counter. Fleischer took advantage of the platform by playing to America's fears—something he became far too familiar with under the Bush administration. That gang of fear mongers made an art out of scaring voters—and it worked! Now Fleischer is using King's popularity to seize on the American voters' fears once again. Unfortunately, he was able to say far too much, and the past eight years weren't enough to make King step in and challenge

Fleischer. Instead, King allowed Fleischer to be as bold as he wanted:

> I want to make this point, Larry, because at the first debate Barack Obama was asked to name America's three most important allies. He didn't even name Israel as one of the three most important. So when it comes to that, to turn the question around, I really worry about where Barack Obama is going to be on very important foreign policy issue. And that is America's relationship with the only democracy in the Middle East, Israel.

At what point does a journalist decide to be a patriot first? One would think that the past eight years would have been enough to make Larry King decide, once and for all, not to allow his show to be a sounding board for those who participated in lying to America about a war that should have never been waged. Of course Fleischer spins the truth. Of course he will do anything to smear Obama. King knows this. He has to know this. King also knows that Obama has said that America's relationship with Israel is "sacrosanct". I kept waiting for King to quote Obama and reiterate his "sacrosanct" comment. How much damage would an administration have to do to Larry King's country before he decided to say "enough"? How long before he demands that Fleischer and the like stop misrepresenting the truth on national television? There has to be a line—even for journalists. Sure, Mr. King, have Fleischer on your show, but make him do nothing but answer for the debacle that was the Bush administration. His comments should be limited to answering for that. That is Fleischer's legacy, and that is all it will ever be. He was part of the worst Presidency in American history—a Presidency that allowed American soldiers to die based on a lie. Fleischer helped deliver the Bush lie to America. King knows enough about history to appreciate that fact. Would King have allowed Richard Nixon or any of his accomplices, to go on his program, after they were all disgraced, and give any of them long segments of airtime to berate a Democratic candidate like Jimmy Carter? What right would any of them have had to be so bold? Larry King is an entertaining interviewer, and I rarely miss his show, but it bothers me that so many Right Wing Republicans have used his program to distort Obama's record and agenda during this election.

Fleischer's tactics should be reserved for networks with no shame, like FOX News. Speaking of FOX News, they ran a headline today that read: "LA Times Won't Release Video Of Obama With Pro-Palestinian Professor Rashid Khalidi." First Wright, then Rezco, then Ayers, and now Khalidi. Aaron Klein of *World Net Daily* writes, "The *Los Angeles Times* has been accused of deliberately suppressing a video it says it obtained of Sen. Barack Obama attending an anti-Israel event in which he delivered a glowing testimonial for an anti-Israel professor who excuses terrorism." The claim against Khalidi is FOX News' latest attempt to see if the other networks will run with a story and legitimize it. We shall see.

FOX News is also suggesting that Obama is going too far by suggesting that people take off on Election Day in order to volunteer for his campaign. Obama's Web site simply asks those who can to help out. Obama says, "We can't win this election unless every Obama supporter gets out and votes on November 4. To do that, we need a massive team of volunteers helping us. Can you take next Tuesday off from work, join the final push, and make sure that everyone who supports Barack turns out to vote?" Watching FOX News today is quite difficult. Between the breaking news that accuses Obama of everything under the sun, the rolling scroll below that is a 24-7 indictment of the Illinois senator, and the talking heads that do one show after another lambasting Obama, it's a wonder why they call themselves FOX News. They should call themselves "OBAMA News".

DAY 66
SANFORD AND SON

Obama is campaigning in Kissimmee, Florida, today—Wednesday, October 29—while McCain is in Miami, Florida. Joe Scarborough spent a great deal of his time this morning on MSNBC suggesting that Obama is buying the election. At 11:47 am, Scarborough actually said, "This election is being bought." Why MSNBC ever thought that a former Republican congressman would be a fair and balanced talk show host escapes me. His bias at times demands a channel change. He has tried, occasionally, to prove that he can see two sides of an issue, but far too often, his conservative card is displayed to his national audience.

Barack Obama put his hand over his heart today and pretended a heart attack. He was impersonating Fred Sanford from "Sanford and Son," the hit comedy from the seventies. Obama jokingly told the crowd, "Can you imagine if you had your Social Security invested in the stock market these last two weeks, these last two months? You wouldn't need Social Security. You'd be having a—you know, like Sanford and Son's 'I'm coming, Weezy.'" What Fred Sanford would actually say was "Elizabeth I'm coming to join you, honey." Weezy, the name Obama used, was from "The Jeffersons," another 70s hit. But, the line was still funny and it's a point well taken.

My feelings about FOX News have been well displayed over the past 66 days. Their approach to delivering the news is more than bias. The channel is actually a tool for the Republican Party. But even I haven't been able to bring myself to call them what one former athlete has. On the *Broadcasting & Cable.com website today*, Ben Grossman quoted former NBA great Charles Barkley, who said, "I watch CNN, they're not f***ed up like Fox." Point taken and enough said!

With six days until the election, Chris Matthews decided to have Tom DeLay, the disgraced former House Majority Leader on his show. Yesterday, I said that Larry King should have Ari Fleisher on but should at least counter his winger agenda. Today I say, *No, Chris Matthews should not give Tom DeLay a platform at all. He lost his right to a platform from which to mislead the American people when he became involved with conspiracy to circumvent Texas restrictions on campaign contributions and money laundering, forcing him from his position of leadership in Congress.* At least Matthews followed with Rep. Debbie Wasserman Schultz to counter his sleaze, but she could never, in such a short time, mop up the filthy, hate-filled philosophy that falls from DeLay's mouth every time he opens it, not to mention the years of plunder of America that DeLay enjoyed until his train of anti-American government policies wrecked and was stopped dead in its tracks. Matthews asked, "Do you think [Obama's] anti-American in his values? Delay answered, "Chris, I tagged him as a Marxist months ago...." *And the American people tagged you as a thug and crook months ago.* The minority districts in Texas that no longer enjoy representative government because of you feel the pain of your schemes. Most crooks lose their freedom instead of getting a public platform courtesy of MSNBC.

Today, in Raleigh, North Carolina, Obama joked, "I don't know what's next. By the end of the week, [McCain will] be accusing me of being a secret communist because I shared my toys in kindergarten. I shared my peanut butter and jelly sandwich." He later poked fun at Palin's insistence on calling people Joe-the-this or that. "So whether you are Suzy the Student, or Nancy the Nurse, or Tina the Teacher, or Carl the Construction Worker, if my opponent is elected, you will be worse off four years from now than you are today. Let's cut through the negative ads and the phony attacks." While the media is building anticipation for Obama's thirty-minute ad that will air tonight, McCain is countering with his own new ad, dismissing Obama's infomercial as a "TV special." McCain's ad says, "Behind the fancy speeches, grand promises, and TV special lies the truth." The ad announcer then says, "With crises at home and abroad, Barack Obama lacks the experience America needs. And it shows. His response to our economic crisis is to spend and tax our economy deeper into recession. The fact is Barack Obama's not ready yet."

At 6:50 pm, CNN had this question on the screen: IS OBAMA BUYING THE ELECTION? I am noticing a theme hear—on CNN, MSNBC and FOX News. Why are the networks trying to put the idea in voters' minds that Obama is buying the election? Remember, CNN is posing this question, not John McCain. Earlier today it was MSNBC's Joe Scarborough, not Sarah Palin, who made the accusation. It's a disturbing trend. Palin herself may not have time to worry about how much money Obama is spending on the election because a new ethics complaint has been filed against her. It's that accusation that the Alaska governor abused her power by charging the state when her children traveled with her. The complaint alleges that Palin used her official position as governor for personal gain, violating a statute of the Alaska Executive Branch Ethics Act. Her soap opera continues.

Obama's 30-minute ad is generally being considered a success. McCain is using it as an opportunity to take some swings: "When you're watching this gauzy, feel-good commercial, just remember that it was paid for with broken promises." Because the World Series is being played today, McCain took the opportunity to include baseball in a joke. "It used to be that only rain or some other act of God could delay the World Series, but I guess the network execs figured an Obama infomercial was close enough." I'm sure McCain, if given the opportunity, would delay anything to put up his own expensive infomercial. Indeed, with the help of CNN, he didn't need to do a paid infomercial because he went on with Larry King and made himself quite comfortable. It seems King has forgiven McCain for standing him up several weeks back. King asked about the amount of money Obama has raised and McCain jumped at the opportunity to blast his opponent:

> Well, whenever you have hundreds of millions of dollars undocumented in campaign contributions—these are the 'small contributions'—of course it opens itself up to question, because the one thing we need in financing of campaigns and contributions is transparency. Senator Obama has not told the American people the truth. So therefore he now

is able to buy these half hour infomercials and, frankly, is going to try to convince the American people, through his rhetoric, what his record shows that he's not.

Of course, the millions of small donors to Obama's campaign do not appreciate being called "undocumented," so it's difficult to see how this tack is going to be helpful to the McCain cause.

While McCain was talking to Larry King, Obama took the stage in Kissimmee, Florida, with former President Bill Clinton. Clinton gave his most convincing endorsement of Obama to date. It remains to be seen how the Obama-Clinton appearance will succeed with the media. It feels as if the media is not entirely happy with being by-passed in Obama's 30-minute buy. They do have the power to punish him for leaving them out of the mix.

In a just released study, **A study in Character Assassination: How the TV Networks Have Portrayed Sarah Palin as Dunce or Demon,** The *Culture and Media Institute* found that ABC, CBS and NBC are airing eighteen negative stories for every one positive story on Sarah Palin. After studying the TV news coverage of Palin from September 29 to October 12, CMI found that ABC, NBC and CBS news shows ran 69 stories about Palin. Two stories were positive, 37 were negative and 30 were neutral. I find it difficult to imagine how the media could do positive stories on Palin when almost every word that comes from her mouth is negative and mean-spirited.

In Tampa, Florida, today McCain said, "The question is whether this is a man who has what it takes to protect America from Osama bin Laden, al Qaeda, and other grave threats in the world. And he has given you no reason to answer in the affirmative." Michael Pritchard, the noted speaker and author, defined fear as "that little darkroom where negatives are developed." Unfortunately for John McCain and Sarah Palin, their entire campaign has been in that little darkroom. Where are their policies? Where the platform? All the electorate is getting from them these last days of the campaign are the fears they are so busily developing. But all have seen these tactics so many times that their effectiveness is waning, as are McCain's hopes of becoming President.

Nineteen days ago, the *Reuters/C-SAPN/Zogby* poll showed Obama with a five-point lead over McCain nationally, 48% to 43%. This poll is considered by many experts to be the most reliable. Today, *Reuters/C-SPAN/Zogby* shows Obama leading 49% to 44%—still a five-point lead. A *WMUR/UNH* poll shows Obama up by 24 points in New Hampshire. It looks like New Hampshire has made their decision. A *CNN/Time* poll has McCain leading by two in Missouri. Many believe that McCain has to win Missouri or the race is Obama's. Although he is leading in all three states, many are suggesting that Obama can lose Florida, Ohio, and Pennsylvania and still win the election. How that is possible remains to be seen. Perhaps it has something to do with the fact that some polls show Obama leading today in some key states that Bush won in 2004: Virginia, North Carolina, Colorado, and Nevada. An *Associated Press/GfK* poll actually shows Obama up by twelve in Nevada, a state that McCain expected to win.

DAY 67
"YOU'RE ALL JOE THE PLUMBERS"

Obama is campaigning in Columbia, Missouri, today—Thursday, October 30—while McCain is in Defiance, Ohio. The story of Rashid Khalidi is getting a lot of press coverage today. McCain himself acted as if he knew nothing about Mr. Khalidi when he spoke to Larry King last night. There are some interesting facts coming out about McCain's relationship with Khalidi, but it's important to take a look back at some of yesterday's interview between Larry King and McCain:

> **Larry King:** Your campaign says that they're suppressing videotape of a 2003 banquet when Barack Obama praised Palestinian activist and scholar, Rashid Khalidi. What's this all—what is this?"
>
> **McCain:** Why shouldn't they?
>
> **King:** Why would the [LA Times] suppress this?
>
> **McCain:** I have no idea. If they have the tape, they ought to make the American people aware of it, let them see it and make their own judgment. Frankly, I've been in a lot of political campaigns—a whole lot. I've never seen anything like this, where a major media outlet has information and a tape of some occasion—maybe it means nothing.

Maybe it's just a social event. I don't know. But
why should they not release it? And why shouldn't
the Obama campaign want it released?

King: Is this Palestinian some sort of terrorist?

McCain: We know that at that time, the PLO was
a terrorist organization.

KING: He was PLO?

MCCAIN: Yes. That's—that's what the allegation
is, Larry. I haven't seen the tape. So—but we
should see the tape to make it—to make the
American people make a judgment.

Larry King should have read an article, **The New
McCarthyism,** by Scott Horton of *Harper's Magazine.* The
article, released yesterday, would have provided King with a
strong counter to McCain's air of unfamiliarity with Rashid
Khalidi. Horton writes:

> ...Indeed, the McCain–Khalidi connections
> are more substantial than the phony Obama–
> Khalidi connections...The Republican party's
> congressionally funded international-networking
> organization, the International Republican
> Institute–long and ably chaired by John McCain
> and headed by McCain's close friend, the capable
> Lorne Craner–has taken an interest in West
> Bank matters. IRI funded an ambitious project,
> called the Palestine Center, that Khalidi helped
> to support. Khalidi served on the Center's board
> of directors. The goal of that project, shared

by Khalidi and McCain, was the promotion of civic consciousness and engagement and the development of democratic values in the West Bank...

Today, Keith Olbermann said that McCain actually gave Khalidi $448,000. Quite a bit of money! Somehow I don't think McCain forgets who he's involved in giving close to half a million dollars. It would have been nice if Larry King had referenced this fact instead of focusing on a video tape that the *LA Times* won't release—a tape they are not legally allowed to release. Tuesday night on FOX News' *On the Record With Greta Van Susteren*, Rudy Giuliani linked Obama to Rashid Khalidi:

> Senator Obama and Ayers, sitting on the Woods board, gave something like $70,000 or $80,000 to Khalidi's organizations that participated in giving—doing these exhibits which would, I think, tell just one side of the story in terms of the Middle East. ... But—and all that is available from public record.

Let me get this right. Giuliani has now managed to link McCain, the man he is supporting, to William Ayers. How? Because now we know that both Ayers and McCain gave money to Khalidi! And if McCain gave $448,000 to Obama's supposed $70,000, Giuliani should know that his candidate appears guilty of being even more supportive of Khalidi than Obama allegedly was. Giuliani needs to stop depending on staffers that give him partial information. He is far too uniformed. I'm still waiting for him to apologize to the community organizers of America. Ever since his Florida primary debacle, Giuliani has been a verbal train wreck.

Even Sarah Palin mentioned this supposed Obama donation to Khalidi today. No one briefed her on (or maybe no one in her camp cares anymore about telling the truth) her own running mate's sizable donation to the man she is calling a radical. Palin also said that Obama's 30-minute television ad on Wednesday sought to wrap his "closing message" before the November 4 election in warm and fuzzy commercial trappings. "He wants to soften the focus in these closing days, hoping your mind won't wander to the real challenges of national security that he is incapable of meeting," said Palin. Some of our minds don't wander so easily, Mrs. Palin. Some of our minds don't wander off into outer space when we're asked what newspapers we read. Plenty of us don't suffer from mind wandering when we're asked what the Bush Doctrine is or to name a Supreme Court decision that we disagree with. No, we will leave the mind wandering to you.

Today, in Defiance, Ohio, McCain thought that Joe the Plumber was with him on stage. He said, "Joe's with us today. Joe, where are you? Where is Joe? Is Joe here with us today? Joe, I thought you were here today." After five seconds of silence, he realized that Joe was not present. "Well," he said, "you're all Joe the Plumbers, so all of you stand up! I thank you." That was an insult to his audience. Joe the Plumber is the man who lied about considering buying a business that he couldn't afford and about not even having a plumbing license. McCain should refrain from insulting his audience so freely. The fact that Joe the Plumber is even relevant today is a testament to the sad state of our nation. We reward dishonesty because we've seen the Bush administration reward such behavior for eight years. Think about this. Joe the Plumber approached Obama on the campaign trail, and the senator decided to take the time to politely talk to him. He didn't have to do that. He was being kind—trying to communicate with an individual. And what does Joe do in return? He stabs him in the back after knowingly lying to his face about buying a plumbing business. And now he has even agreed with a man on the campaign trail who told him that an Obama Presidency would mean the end of Israel. Joe actually agreed with this nut. What does it say about our country when a guy like Joe the Plumber, who was not completely forthcoming with Obama to begin with, has now hired a publicist and signed a recording contract? Again, it's the American Idolization of our country. And McCain had the audacity to tell the entire audience today in Defiance, Ohio, that they were "all Joe the Plumber". The wheels have completely come off the Straight Talk Express, Senator McCain. Save what dignity you still have. If you don't stop this lunacy now, I have a feeling your Arizona senate seat may even be in jeopardy, because you're losing all credibility. You've spent the entire campaign, along with Palin, ridiculing, not challenging, Obama. Your honor is shot. These are the facts. History is not known to be kind to petty, dishonorable men.

The CBS-NY Times national poll shows Obama at 52% and McCain at 39%. Many are predicting an Obama victory at this point. David Gergen told Anderson Cooper today that there's about a 90% chance that Obama is going to win the election. It doesn't hurt that about 33 million people watched the Obama infomercial last night. But the attacks on Obama continue. At 7:03 pm, CNN played a negative robo-call that McCain is sending out in Arizona, a state that is suddenly in play. An *NBC/Mason-Dixon* poll shows McCain leading in his state by only four points. The robo-call tries to pin Obama to Tony Rezco, a donor and real estate developer convicted of fraud, who had business dealings with Obama. An unidentified male in the robo-call says, "Obama needs to come clean on this deal before the election, so that the voters can judge whether Obama received monetary benefits from these Rezco favors." It's time for the networks to show some discipline and stop helping McCain get his sleaze out to the American people. Again, CNN turned what was a McCain attack against Obama in Arizona into a national one. It is news that they're out there and that fact should be reported. They, however, think we need to see and hear the robo-calls. We don't!

The press is praising Bill Clinton's speech from last night. His performance was fantastic, but it's surprising that neither the media nor McCain has seized on one specific segment of Clinton's speech. It involved the issue of Obama calling people for help on the economic crisis. I'm surprised McCain isn't saying, *You see, he had to call people for help. He's not ready to lead.* But the press and McCain have missed this clever Clinton moment.:

...You know what [Obama] did? First he took a little heat for not saying much. I knew what he was doing. He talked to his advisers; he talked to my economic advisers. He called Hillary. He called me. He called Warren Buffett and he called Paul Volcker. He called all those people and—you know why?— because he knew it was complicated and before he said anything he wanted to understand...

...The second thing and this meant more to me than anything else and I haven't cleared this with him. And he may even be mad at me for saying this so close to the election but I know what else he said to his economic advisers. He said, tell me what the right thing to do is. What's the right thing for America, and don't tell me what's popular. You tell me what's right and I'll figure out how to sell it...

Even the so-called liberal media are willing to take their shots at Obama when given the opportunity. When Rachel Maddow got her chance to sit down with Obama today in Florida, she pushed him a bit on the issue of criticizing the Republican Party. Obama can't even escape from the supposed left-leaning media. Maddow said, "Senator, you criticize the Bush Administration frequently, but you almost never criticize the Republican Party itself." Obama interrupted and joked, "Much to your chagrin." Maddow then added, "Well, yeah, actually, I mean other Democrats— you will hear them talk about the GOP as the party that's been wrong on all the big stuff—creating Social Security, civil rights, the War in Iraq. But you don't really do that. Do you think there is a stark difference between the parties?" Obama answered:

> ...I'm talking to voters, and I think there are a lot of Republican voters out there—self identified—who actually think that what the Bush Administration has done has been damaging to the country, and what I'm interested in is how do we build a working majority for change? And if I start off with the premise that it's only self identified Democrats who I'm speaking to, then I'm not going to get to where we need to go. If I can describe it as not a blanket indictment of the Republican Party, but instead describe it as the Republican Party having been kidnapped by an incompetent, highly ideological subset of the Republican Party, then that means I can still reach out to a whole bunch of Republican moderates who I think are hungry for change as well.

Maddow's response: "You have the opportunity to say John McCain, George Bush, you're wrong. You also have the opportunity to say conservatism has been bad for America, but you haven't gone there either." I would not hire Maddow as my chief strategist if I were trying to win an election. Her youthful high school mentality of *my team's better than your team* is archaic. I don't want to listen to her cheer or watch her pound her chest for the next eight years if Obama wins. Those are the tactics that have been used by Republicans for the last eight years. But Obama responded by telling

Maddow, "I tell you what though, Rachel, you notice, I think we're winning right now so maybe I'm doing something right." I could be wrong, but Obama appeared a tad annoyed by Maddow's assertion. He then said, "I know you've been cruising for a bruising for awhile here and looking for a fight out there. I just think people are tired of that kind of back and forth, tit for tat, ideological approach to the problems."

He is right. She may be sorry she has been so willing to play the blame game. It's time for Democrats to listen to and try to understand what Obama is saying. He keeps talking about a "working coalition" and doesn't seem to be interested in polarizing the parties. He is of the belief that the Republican Party has been "kidnapped" by a gang of crooks. Maddow seems more interested in making the Republicans pay a price instead of first winning the White House. Obama has to win first. Dennis Kucinich is correct on most of the issues, but he couldn't get elected in America in today's climate to save his life. If you look at the most conservative person imaginable, say Newt Gingrich, he couldn't get elected either. Obama tried to explain to Maddow that that old brand of party first, say anything to get elected, and beat the other side up is old news. It's not about proving that your team is better than their team. The country needs to come together and, yes, that includes working with Republicans. But I'm sure Maddow was simply trying to please her loyal following.

DAY 68
MEATHEADS

Obama is campaigning in Des Moines, Iowa, today—Friday, October 31—while McCain is in Hanoverton, Ohio. Ronald Reagan's former Secretary of State Lawrence Eagleburger and Ken Duberstein, Reagan's former Chief of Staff, endorsed Obama today. Duberstein mentioned the lack of vetting that was done regarding Palin saying, "I think it has very much undermined the whole question of John McCain's judgment. You know what most Americans I think realized is that you don't offer a job, let alone the Vice Presidency, to a person after one job interview. Even at McDonald's you're interviewed three times before you get a job."

It's difficult to find noted Republicans who are holding fast to the McCain-Palin ticket so near to Election Day. Because of these big-name swings in Obama's direction, the media had little ammunition with which to attack Obama today. McCain is not helping them. He is sticking with the tried, but unsuccessful, strategy of attack, attack, attack. Perhaps many of these Republicans who are jumping ship grew tired of, and embarrassed with, the McCain-Palin inept campaign. Think about it. Theirs is a pathetic strategy that few can stomach for long periods. Seldom has a Presidential candidate endured more unwarranted and unsubstantiated attacks, possibly because of the length of the campaign this time, but also because—they can. Who has been there to hold their feet to the fire and demand truth, or at least some version thereof?

Today, the media seemed to enjoy showing Arnold Schwarzenegger and McCain on the stump together in Ohio. Schwarzenegger drew cheers from the crowd as he made fun of Obama's physique. He said Obama needed to put some meat on his bones, implying he is scrawny. He laughed about Obama's skinny legs and suggested he do some "squats". The California Governor also accused Obama of having "scrawny little arms". McCain, on the other hand, according to Arnold is "built like a rock". So much for lofty ideals and policy that will lead us away from the impending abyss forecast by scientists and philosophers alike. Meatheads—that's exactly what this country needs. What I needed today was to hear the rare speech from Tipper and Al Gore, but for some reason the media did not see fit to let us in on much of that. A former Mr. Universe was more important than a Nobel Prize winner. Besides, Arnold should refrain from poking fun at Obama's build. After all, if Obama were inclined to take steroids, which he is not, I'm sure he could build himself up like the admitted steroid user Schwarzenegger.

His steroid use is well documented. Back in February of 2005, the Austrian-born former actor told George Stephanopoulos: "I have no regrets about it, because at that time, it was something new that came on the market, and we went to the doctor and did it under doctors' supervision." Schwarzenegger has acknowledged taking steroids, but pointed out that they were legal at the time. "We were experimenting with it. It was a new thing. So you can't roll the clock back and say, 'Now I would change my mind on this,'" he said. Nothing like a former steroid user making fun of a man who shows the discipline not to use the juice!

Michael Moore told Keith Olbermann that it is ironic that the ground movement that seems to be winning the race can be credited to Obama's being a former community organizer, the job Republicans have been making fun of during the election. Rick Davis could have used a couple of good community organizers in his McCain campaign. It bothers me that the media never really allowed community organizers to defend their positions as valid in a democracy. I've seen a couple of news stories that attempted to investigate the life of a community organizer, but none that were powerful enough to undo the damage done at the Republican National Convention. In fact, much has been said that warrants an apology from McCain.

Speaking of rudeness—and not that this particular slight is critical, but just so the record shows—neither McCain nor Palin offered their sympathies for Obama's grandmother when America found out that she is gravely ill. Or if they did, they didn't make it public as they should have—probably wouldn't have played well with the base. A bit of common decency, however, could have gone a long way in convincing the swing voters that their ticket has a shred of feelings for Obama as a human being. Neither McCain nor Palin has condemned the remarks made by Michelle Bachmann when she called him anti-American. Why hasn't the media suggested that McCain denounce her? After all, they had no problem asking Obama to denounce Rev. Wright's anti-American remarks. So we have a blueprint. We know the media does ask these types of questions on their own volition.

McCain asked Obama to denounce John Lewis' comments regarding himself, yet he has no sense of common human feelings when it comes to vicious attacks on Obama.

McCain accused Obama—again—of measuring the drapes. I haven't heard a political cliché used more in my entire life. He also made fun of the fact that Obama has named a chief of staff. Actually, the Obama campaign mentioned Rahm Emanuel as a possible chief of staff. If Obama had not suggested a possible chief of staff, I'm sure the McCain camp would have announced theirs and criticized the Obama camp of not planning for the future.

Sarah Palin has been palling around with Greta Van Susteren, the known Right Wing FOX News operative, quite a bit lately. Greta seemed to be searching for more in-depth answers this time, though, so was forced to turn most of her attention to Palin's seven-year-old daughter Piper. Unfortunately, all she was able to elicit were a series of *I don't know's*, understandable from a seven-year-old. On their bus tour, Greta allowed Palin once again to tout her resume as an executive during her time as the mayor of Wasilla. John McCain likes to say that Palin has more executive experience than Obama and Biden put together. Neither John McCain nor the mainstream media vetted Palin on her resume claims. There may be other media reports about the job Palin uses as training for her VP run, but if so, they are buried deeply. John Stewart of *The Daily Show* sent a comedic reporter to interview the current mayor of Wasilla, Dianne M. Keller, concerning the executive duties of the mayor. The only two duties she could call to mind were staff meetings on Monday mornings and signing the checks on Thursdays. She could think of nothing else, yet when asked whether she thought her job qualified her to become the Vice President of the United States, she immediately retorted, "An unequivocal yes." For anyone interested in seeing this two-minute jaw-dropping interview, go to *You Tube* and type in "Interview With Mayor of Wasilla = Experience." Many people trying to deal with this election season have found that two comedians—John Stewart and Steven Colbert—are good sources, not only of relief from the absurdity, but also of actual information necessary for an informed electorate.

During Hannity and Colmes, FOX News' thugs came very close to assaulting Rashid Khalidi as he entered an elevator today, trying to interview him. Sean Hannity, or as Roland Martin of CNN likes to call him "Sean little ball of hate Hannity", read from a book written by Ayers that supposedly was dedicated to Sirhan Sirhan. FOX News doesn't count at this point as serious news media, but they have a large audience; therefore, Hannity's continuing onslaught of Obama terror innuendo still has time to connect with the voters. I, however, cannot take anything he says as fact, because most of it is so outlandish. He's always pulling ominous-sounding characters out of his fat ass, hoping the fact that Obama lives in the country's third largest city with them is proof of nefarious dealings. Hannity should fear being on the same show with the thugs he so happily showed pursuing Khalidi. This footage initially caught my eye because it actually looked like someone was about to be attacked. Instead, it was the professor trying to get into an elevator and away from Hannity's thugs. Since when does the likes of Sean Hannity care about the assassin of Robert F. Kennedy? If Kennedy were still alive, it would be him Hannity's thugs were pursuing. Hannity spews hatred toward people like Kennedy. How is Barack Obama different philosophically from Robert F. Kennedy? Hannity has used his power this entire election cycle to assault Obama every single day. He's obsessed. It's getting to the point where Obama's Secret Service should consider him a threat.

DAY 69
PALIN—THE BUDDING CONSTITUTIONAL SCHOLAR

Obama is campaigning in Henderson, Nevada, today—Saturday, November 1—while McCain is in New York City. Norah O'Donnell of MSNBC got the day started by spending a good 30 minutes setting the table with items that serve to undermine Obama's candidacy. Perhaps she was lobbied by a Republican and convinced to spend the Saturday before Election Tuesday hammering Obama on a slew of issues. Between 10:00 am and 10:30 am, O'Donnell mentioned the following: Schwarzenegger's comments about Obama's skinny legs, a story about Obama's aunt who is apparently in the U.S. illegally, Obama as "arrogant", Obama being mean to the press while trick-or-treating with his daughter. O'Donnell also said that Palin "has many more political skills than John Edwards". Talk about an agenda!

At exactly 10:10 am, O'Donnell asked, "Is Obama being a little arrogant?" She was referring to his decision to campaign in the red states of Nevada, Colorado, Arizona, and Virginia over the last days leading up to the election. She asked her panel if Obama was rubbing it in by visiting these states. She was also doing a lead up to the Arnold Schwarzenegger comments and said, "You're gonna wanna hear this." Actually, Norah, we don't "wanna hear this". But, apparently you do. When O'Donnell played the clip of Schwarzenegger commenting about Obama's "skinny legs", she laughed hysterically. And I don't use the word hysterically lightly. Her laugh was loud, demonstrative and quite odd. The fact that she said Palin "has many more political skills than John Edwards" is stunning. Check yourself, Norah O'Donnell! You can't be serious.

Has O'Donnell read the recent comments Palin made about the First Amendment yesterday? Palin told WMAL-AM that her criticism of Obama's associations with Rev. Jeremiah Wright and William Ayers should not be considered negative attacks. She believes that for reporters to suggest that it is going negative may constitute an attack that threatens a candidate's free speech rights under the Constitution. Is Norah O'Donnell using this interpretation of the Constitution as grounds to suggest that Palin "has many more political skills than John Edwards?" I doubt John Edwards would have made such an uniformed comment. There are those in the media who keep suggesting that Palin can learn what she needs to over the next four years in time to make her own run at the Presidency. The problem with many of the mistakes she keeps making is that they are directly related to common sense Constitutional information. First, it was her not knowing the role of the Vice President as it relates to the Senate, and now this comment to WMAL-AM yesterday:

> If [the media] convince enough voters that that is negative campaigning, for me to call Barack Obama out on his associations, then I don't know what the future of our country would be in terms of First Amendment rights and our ability

to ask questions without fear of attacks by the mainstream media.

Does Palin have any clue that freedom of the press is part of the First Amendment? Obviously not! Her ignorance pains me, and O'Donnell's praise of her adds to my agony. However, out of respect for O'Donnell's First Amendment right to bias, I'll have to suffer through it.

Today, CNN is also enjoying Schwarzenegger's "skinny legs" comment. They've been playing it all day long. Since when has an insult about a Presidential candidate's body been such fodder for members of the media to giggle over? The smallness of our press is on full display today. It reminds me of how they all took part in the joke about Obama being likened to a celebrity. Our media is far too willing to respond in the affirmative when asked to take part in belittling Sen. Obama. It reminds me of the difference between the two candidates. When crowds boo, yell "terrorist" or "Kill him" at McCain-Palin rallies, the candidates say nothing and the press doesn't call them out for their SILENCE. On the other hand, when Obama encounters rowdy supporters at rallies, he makes a point to say, "You don't need to boo—you just need to vote."

At 3:30 pm, FOX News posed a question: "Is the press already calling the election for Obama?" They are if you guys don't consider yourselves part of the press. I certainly I don't. FOX News also posed this question: "Which member of the media has had the biggest impact on the election?" My answer is Sean Hannity. He has single handedly managed to unite all Democrats and repulse Republicans enough to destroy

McCain's candidacy. Also on FOX News, Jim Pinkerton suggested that MSNBC is carrying Obama across the finish line. If this is true, Pinkerton should tell Chris Matthews that the person he is carrying across the finish line is not an immigrant, as the MSNBC host so incorrectly stated.

The *New York Post's* Kirsten Powers wrote an article today in which she complained about being kicked off the Obama bus. In the article, **A Nixonesque Move From Team Obama,** Powers writes, "Team Obama veered off message yesterday, kicking off the campaign bus reporters from three newspapers deemed unfriendly to the campaign – *The New York Post, The Dallas Morning News and The Washington Times.* This is bipartisanship?" My question to Powers is *Who should they have kicked off the bus?* No matter which three newspapers had been removed, they would have complained. Powers adds:

> The move is utterly at odds with a central part of Obama's message: the idea that he's a different kind of candidate – one who won't demonize opponents or critics, but will instead work hard to bring people together. Let's hope this isn't a harbinger of what would happen in an Obama administration.
>
> ... Reporters were bumped to make room for others from Jet and Essence, two glossy magazines targeted at African-Americans, and for a documentary unit chronicling the last days of the Obama campaign...
>
> ... All three papers endorsed McCain – was the Obama move retaliation? It seems unlikely. More

> likely, the campaign wanted to make room for
> fawning coverage – and who better to get rid of
> than papers that cover you critically?

We have Powers' take on this story, but until I hear from a more objective source, I'll take it with a grain of salt. Oh, and one question, Ms. Powers: How is it "demonizing" the press to ask them to leave the bus? I would hate to see what word you would use to describe Obama's refusal to go on *Hannity and Colmes*, a show you seem to enjoy appearing on. Would you say he's being "demonic"? Maybe he just kicked you guys off because you're not good writers. Or maybe he was doing a test to find out who would be the first one to play the race card. If so, he now has his answer.

It will be nice to see our media begin to grow up over the next four years. The country is in desperate need of civility and a sense of responsibility from all of those in the public eye. Whether we like it or not, our country takes its cues from those on television and radio. In a more sophisticated climate, I myself would not have needed to deal with the press by using what many might call partisan sarcasm. But I feel compelled to join those like Keith Olbermann, Randi Rhodes, Thom Hartmann, Arianna Huffington, and Rachel Maddow, who sprang up as a natural and critical defense against a cooperate media that has been carrying water for the far Right for eight crippling years. There is an innate responsibility that comes with being given the power to speak to millions on a regular basis through the medium of television or radio. Regardless of political affiliation, we should all agree that civility in this country must be restored, and that civility can be displayed on television and radio, particularly in how members of the press, specifically Sean Hannity and Rush Limbaugh, treat other human beings. As Obama likes to say, "We can argue and debate our positions passionately. But all of us have to summon a restored strength and grace, a civility to bridge our differences and unite in common effort—black, white, Asian, Native American, Democrat, Republican, young, old, rich, poor, gay, straight, disabled, not disabled—all of us coming together, all of us around common effort." For those unpersuaded by Obama's message, try remembering how nonpartisan we were after 9/11. Because urgency still exists on many fronts, both in America and the world, now is not the time to continue this childish battle against each other.

DAY 70
PRANKED

Obama is campaigning in Cincinnati, Ohio, today—Sunday, November 2—while McCain is in Wallingford, Pennsylvania. MSNBC political analyst Lawrence O'Donnell brought up some key information regarding the long lines that are forming across the nation for early voting. He credits the Obama campaign's enormous ground movement for this. O'Donnell said that the campaign's new mantra is "stay in line" not "get out the vote". He feels that the Obama campaign is more concerned about assuring that people stay in line for the four hours and longer that is frequently required. Lawrence O'Donnell told a story about having seen the huge lines that formed in South Africa back when Nelson Mandela was running. He remembered wondering what it would be like in America if an inspirational figure like Mandela came along. That is pretty high praise, but the early voting numbers and the overwhelming Democratic enthusiasm suggests that O'Donnell may be correct in his analysis.

Sarah Palin says she was "mildly amused" by a prank that the Masked Avengers, a Canadian radio duo notorious for prank calls to celebrities and heads of state, played on her. Saturday, the pranksters released a recording of a six-minute call with Ms. Palin, who thought she was talking with French President, Nicolas Sarkozy. Other prominent figures have been pranked, but none have actually fallen for such a ridiculous, insulting conversation with as much gullibility as Palin. The media, correctly, did not make too much of this latest Palin gaff.

McCain has been seizing on this comment Obama made in Iowa about his initial faith that he, a black man, could win in America: "On the day of the Iowa caucus, my faith in the American people was vindicated, and what you started here in Iowa has swept the nation." McCain continues to hammer Obama on this comment at his own rallies saying, "My country has never had to prove anything to me, my friends. I've always had faith in it, and I've been humbled and honored to serve it." The media has given McCain lots of airtime for his jab at Obama's—what?—lack of patriotism because he had faith that white Americans would actually vote for a black candidate for President?

Obama returned a $265 contribution to his African aunt, who continues living in Boston after her request for asylum was denied. FOX News succeeded in getting this story out as a "scandal". Sean Hannity, long working to make this the latest controversial issue, was stopped dead in his tracks when Alan Colmes reminded him about McCain having left his ex-wife and kids hanging high and dry. Hannity changed the subject pronto.

Obama told a crowd in Columbus, Ohio, today that John McCain was funny on *Saturday Night Live* last night. It was funny. The media has played it many, many times. Enough said.

The conversation kept returning to the issue of race today, as the major concern among pundits is whether the ubiquitous polls can be counted on, given Obama's race. On CNN, Dr. Cornell West suggested the reason they couldn't get past this question: "The media has an impoverished imagination about race." The power of Dr. West's words is that an individual in the media searching for answers to their conflicted positions regarding race can ponder the notion that they have an "impoverished imagination". To cure this poverty, one may be led to invest more time in stimulating their imaginations by taking baby steps outside the racial box their communities have built to protect them from the "other".

The media's—and the McCain-Palin campaign's—culpability in this subtle racism is especially evident in one specific oversight: failure to take proper note that nearly 100% of McCain-Palin rallies consist of Caucasians. If Obama's rallies, on the other hand, had been predominantly black—that would have been a big story. Again—impoverished imaginations regarding race. The McCain-Palin audience must look "normal" to most in the media. A sea of darker faces would most likely have brought to the surface that imbedded fear of the "other". A poignant moment is this campaign came on the day an individual at a Palin rally shouted, "Kill him." The poignancy is not in the obvious vulgarity of the language, but rather can more broadly be understood when one considers the environment from which these words came. The story line that our media failed to address regarding this "Kill him" issue is that violent words from an all-white audience were used against a black Presidential candidate. If Obama had been speaking to a black audience and someone had shouted "Kill McCain", those words would have been taken more seriously by the press and by the population in general. It has always been a greater crime in this country to kill a white person than a black. The populous can easily imagine Obama getting assassinated—much less so McCain.

A former Bob Dole aide, Douglas Mackinnon, offered an opinion piece in the *New York Times* today: **Media Credibility.** He begins by saying, "After the presidential election is over and the dust, animosity, glee and shock settle into something manageable, the nation will need to tackle the subject of "media bias" in a sincere and honest manner." After covering this campaign, I'm not sure it is a media bias as much as it is a misguided media. The media has simply lost track of what role it should play. Members of the press are far too comfortable being participants in the campaign itself rather than simply covering it. Mackinnon and I disagree. He writes:

> Regarding the Obama phenomenon and the media fascination with him, a senior staffer for a rival Democrat primary opponent offered up this theory to me for part of the bias. This person reasoned that the pressure within the news business to diversify and be politically correct means more minorities, women and young people are being hired. And young and ethnically diverse reporters and editors go easier on candidates who look more like them, are closer to their age or represent their ideal of a presidential candidate.

This is a skewed philosophy that lacks any historical grasp of diversity in America. If "young and ethnically diverse reporters and editors go easier on candidates who look more like them," hasn't that also been the case for the past 232 years when white Presidents looked like the white editors and reporters who were the only ones allowed to cover them? Did those white reporters and editors "go easier" on the Presidents who "looked more like them"? How long have these "young and ethnically diverse reporters," of which Mackinnon speaks, been in business? Mackinnon writes as if we have had diverse Presidential candidates, editors, and reporters throughout history from which to draw such conclusions. I'm sure all of those black editors and reporters, who barely existed when Jessie Jackson ran for President, went really easy on the former Civil Rights leader as he sought to build his Rainbow Coalition in the eighties.

Mackinnon adds, "On Friday, in an article about Mr. Obama's infomercial, Howard Kurtz, The *Washington Post* media critic, wrote: 'If the press were inclined to hammer the Democratic nominee for buying the election after blowing off public financing, the infomercial would be Exhibit A. But the press is giving him a pass on the issue.'" I'm sure if Mackinnon's old boss, Bob Dole, had been given the opportunity to have millions of small donors give him close to $800 million back in 1996, Mackinnon would have stepped in and put a stop to it in the name of campaign ethics. Yeah right!

DAY 71
HATE

Obama is campaigning in Jacksonville, Florida, today—Monday, November 3—while McCain is in Prescott, Arizona. This morning, Mike Barnicle of MSNBC suggested that if Obama loses it could very well be because the *Who is Obama?* question was a major factor. If voters are indeed still pondering that question, it could very well be a result of the latest ad the Right Wing is playing today. The ad, put out by the *National Public Trust PAC*, is playing on all of the networks non-stop. The ad is a last ditch attempt to tie Obama to the infamous Reverend Wright. The seedy aspect of the ad itself is that the words, "Hate He Could Believe In" are shown while Reverend Wright is speaking. This is obviously a play on Obama's famous "Change You Can Believe In" logo. Even the design of the ad looks identical to Obama's website, right down to the font, colors, and imagery. The words "Change" and "We" are simply replaced by the words "Hate" and "He". The ad includes pictures of Wright that show him making strained, unflattering faces. There is also a segment that shows a family picture of Barack, Michelle and their children, a wedding picture that includes Obama's mother, and finally, a framed picture of Obama and Wright. The setting is meant to look like the Obama living room. The framed pictures sit on an end table beside a couch under a lamp, suggesting a very intimate relationship between Obama and Wright. The

Right Wing saved Reverend Wright for the last day, and who knows how much they paid the networks to run it hourly. It just goes to show that if these slanderous 527s have the money, the networks will air their slime for them. That is the America we live in. Here is what the country is hearing all day today from the *National Public Trust PAC*:

> **Female Voice:** For twenty years, Barack Obama followed a preacher of hate and said nothing as Wright raged against our country.
> **Reverend Wright's Voice:** Not God Bless America—Goddamn America! … U.S. of KKK A!
> **Obama Quote:** I don't think my church is particularly controversial.
> **Female Voice:** He built his power base in Wright's church. Wright was his mentor, advisor, and close friend. For twenty years Obama never complained, until he ran for President.
> **Words on Screen:** Barack Obama—Too Radical—Too Risky
> **Female Voice:** Barack Obama! Too Radical! Too Risky!

One would have to be ignorant not to think that such an ad could sway some undecided voters toward McCain. The ad is filled with words taken out of context, and the suggestion that he "built his power base in Wright's church" is ludicrous. On the other hand, what the people who made this ad fail to realize is that many Americans—white and black—agree that America has a racist past. They also fail to realize that many evangelical Christians know of and agree with the Biblical prophet Jeremiah's warnings against countries that make the wrong decisions, the reference Rev. Wright was making. If the Right is going to play to evangelicals, they should get to know them better. With today's Gallup daily tracking poll showing Obama leading nationally, 53% to 42%, one has to wonder what effect the attack ad will have.

Barack and his sister delivered the sad news. Their grandmother passed away today in Hawaii. Her death, coming one day before the election, adds to the mystique of Obama's lonely campaign. I say lonely because he is relatively young to have lost both parents and now both grandparents. But Obama continued campaigning and 100,000 people heard him speak in Manassas, Virginia, tonight.

A story the media is just now revealing involves an interview that McCain did with a local Norfolk, Virginia, ABC affiliate last week. McCain was asked why he was not beating Barack Obama in the state, considering Virginia has voted for a Republican president in every election since 1964. McCain replied by saying, "We're doing much better, actually, there's a poll out today that shows we're within about three so we're moving up and moving up fast. And look, Joe the Bomb—uh—Joe the Plumber turned the whole thing around." McCain wasn't able to catch himself in time to avoid saying Joe the Bomb. It has been a long campaign.

John McCain kept the media up late tonight as he spoke in Prescott, Arizona, after 11 pm. As he began to speak, he appeared a bit teary-eyed. One has to wonder if these were emotions related to the thought of a possible win tomorrow, a feeling of certain defeat, certainty that this will be, as promised, his last campaign, or regretfullness about the type of campaign he has run. There is one thing for him to be sad about. As he speaks to the crowd in Prescott, the Rev. Wright 527 attack ad, which ends by saying, "Obama: Too Risky, Too Radical," is running all over the airwaves. Perhaps it is an ad he would not have approved, as perhaps many of the decisions made by his campaign are not ones he would have made without pressure from his Right Wing handlers. Was he responsible for choosing Sarah Palin? Was he coming to terms with the fact that he, though an American hero, was never truly in control of his own campaign?

ELECTION DAY
HOPE

Obama is in Chicago, Illinois, today—Tuesday, November 4—while McCain is in Phoenix, Arizona. The question that many African-Americans are being asked is *Did you ever think you would live to see this happen in your lifetime?* My answer to that, as a young man with an African-American father who didn't live to see this day, and a white mother, whom I credit with instilling in me the belief that all things are possible, is a resounding YES! Weeks before my father passed away in March of this year, I told him that Obama could be the first black President. He didn't believe it would happen and, though it did, my father wasn't alive to see it. Perhaps because my father had been born in the South in 1941 and lived through Segregation, his belief that America couldn't overcome its racism was warranted. But because I had a mother who didn't experience second-class citizenship, it was easy for her to pass that experience on to me. In fact, she probably went out of her way to do so. The fact that Barack Obama became the first African-American to be elected President of the United States today is the kind of thing I have always felt was possible. I believed that it could only happen if an extraordinary individual were to come along—a person who could address the issue of race in a way that comforted blacks and didn't make whites feel a sense of guilt about the country's history of racial ugliness. And I remember thinking, even before Obama gave the keynote address at the 2004 Democratic National Convention, that he could be the one. As he was doing a one-on-one interview during the opening day of that convention, I realized at that moment that I had never heard anyone quite like him before. I wasn't alone, because his ascension to the Presidency would begin days later when he addressed the convention crowd.

Today, millions of Americans stood in long lines to vote. Too many lines were far too long. Voters shouldn't have to wait in line for up to six hours to cast their ballot, but it happened across the country today. In the end, Obama was the victor and John McCain recognized the historical significance of the moment. He represented himself well as he spoke to a Phoenix crowd:

> Thank you. Thank you, my friends. Thank you for coming here on this beautiful Arizona evening. My friends, we have—we have come to the end of a long journey. The American people have spoken, and they have spoken clearly. A little while ago, I had the honor of calling Senator Barack Obama to congratulate him...
> (BOOING)
> Please...to congratulate him on being elected the next President of the country that we both love...
> ... I wish Godspeed to the man who was my former opponent and will be my President. And I call on all Americans, as I have often in this campaign, to not despair of our present difficulties, but to

believe, always, in the promise and greatness of America, because nothing is inevitable here. Americans never quit. We never surrender. We never hide from history. We make history. Thank you, and God bless you, and God bless America. Thank you all very much.

Palin reportedly asked to address the crowd in Phoenix, not realizing that such an act is unprecedented during a Presidential concession. She will likely claim that this is unfair treatment. She actually has claimed that she wasn't being treated fairly quite a bit throughout the campaign. She never once considered comparing her relatively soft treatment to that of Obama. Her major complaints are that the press treated her harshly regarding her pregnant daughter, Troopergate, and her many poor interview performances. She never had to deal with being called a terrorist, Marxist, Socialist, or a radical. She never had someone in her own party make references to cutting her private parts off. No one ever shouted *Kill her*. No ads were put out that hinted at her being involved in pedophilia. Her husband was never called "controversial" or described as having a "hard" presence. I don't recall hearing about any death threats regarding Palin. She was never labeled *nothing more than a celebrity* as Obama was. She never had to denounce her pastor or defend against every association she ever had in the past. She was never called an "immigrant" just because she lived in Alaska, a state that, like Hawaii, can seem foreign to many Americans. All of the complaints against Palin have involved defending herself against things that she is actually guilty of. She did allow the GOP to spend $150,000 on clothes. Her daughter did get pregnant at seventeen while unmarried. She was involved in Troopergate. She did make a fool of herself during several interviews. She is guilty of all of this. But the media assault on Obama makes Palin's treatment look like a game of tidily winks. Obama wishes his only unfair treatment from the media had come in relation to spending too much on clothes. That seems far easier to handle than trying to prove that your're not a domestic terrorist.

The media soon switched their attention to Chicago where Obama addressed a crowd of over 200,000:

> Hello, Chicago. If there is anyone out there who still doubts that America is a place where all things are possible, who still wonders if the dream of our founders is alive in our time, who still questions the power of our democracy, tonight is your answer...
>
> ...The road ahead will be long. Our climb will be steep. We may not get there in one year or even in one term. But, America, I have never been more hopeful than I am tonight that we will get there. I promise you, we as a people will get there...
>
> ...This is our chance to answer that call. This is our moment. This is our time, to put our people back to work and open doors of opportunity for our kids; to restore prosperity and promote the cause of peace; to reclaim the American dream and reaffirm that fundamental truth, that, out of many, we are one; that while we breathe, we

hope. And where we are met with cynicism and doubts and those who tell us that we can't, we will respond with that timeless creed that sums up the spirit of a people: Yes, we can. Thank you. God bless you. And may God bless the United States of America.

For the most part, members of the media are covering this historic day with a very careful and sensitive approach. Many are expressing pride in being able to cover history in the making. Let there be no doubt—this is a very emotional and powerful moment in history—for the entire country. Many who didn't vote for Obama are expressing emotion over the enormity of the event. The moment the networks announced that Obama had officially been elected the 44th President of the United States, a collective, almost palpable force of positive energy could be felt across the country. The networks took a moment to show footage of African Americans across the country exalting and almost losing themselves having been overcome with a joy that they hadn't been able to imagine. A joy that is unique to this day and has no predecessor. Though many knew that Obama would win, the shock of the actual result is unprecedented. The behavior of many African Americans appears fresh—like something that has never been seen before. Because it hasn't been! I, myself, don't know how to react. Hundreds of thoughts are racing through my mind. I keep asking myself, *What does this mean?* It means too many things to comprehend at this moment. It's as if the world got an immediate shot of adrenaline—that we all healed at the same time, even if it's just a little bit. I keep asking myself, *How would my father have reacted?* I simply don't know the answer. How would Lincoln, Douglas, Kennedy, or King have reacted?

But this book is about the media, and some are not getting caught up in the emotion. They are simply doing their jobs. After Obama addressed the crowd in Chicago, Anderson Cooper was discussing the results with Rowland Martin and Amy Holmes. Martin said, "When [Obama] calls for the American people to participate in this process, what he's saying is *Look. Don't just sit here and say it's Washington, D.C., like they're a separate entity. You are a part of this.*" Cooper shot back, "There's 47 percent of the country right now who heard that message and say, 'You know what? I don't buy it.'" Way to poop on the party, Anderson Cooper. Obama was just elected. It just happened moments ago. Your comment is completely ill-timed. The country is celebrating the most historic election in American history. They're dancing in the streets, crying, and uniting. Even Republicans are noting the historic significance of Obama's election. But, Cooper has found a way to go negative. Can't you just wait one day before dashing the hopes of millions of Americans? Just let us have at least 24 hours of celebration. Then give your unsolicited opinion.

Thursday, September 4, was perhaps the day that changed the trajectory of the election. This is definitely a theory to be further analyzed. A *Gallup* polling graph shows the beginning of Obama's rise in the polls taking place soon after his sit-down with Bill O'Reilly. The third part of the O'Reilly interview aired on September 9, and Obama began climbing in the *Gallup* poll from that day forward. There were many Democrats who were disappointed to see Obama grant an interview with Billo. It was a balsey kind of move on his part. The audience for this show was huge, keeping Obama front and center on the night of John McCain's acceptance speech. And for those Americans who watch nothing except FOX News, it was possibly their first exposure to the kind, thoughtful man they'd been led to believe was scary and evil. Most pundits credit the financial meltdown for McCain's decline in the polls. But the financial crash happened on September 15th. And if Obama's climb in the *Gallup* poll began on September 9, that was a week prior to McCain uttering, "The fundamentals of our economy are strong." Obama had already been trending upward. Yes, Obama led in this *Gallup* poll prior to McCain choosing Palin as his running mate, but the Illinois senator lost that lead on September 6 and didn't regain it again until September 16. But on September 9, the day O'Reilly aired the third part of the Obama interview, Obama began trending upward in the *Gallup* poll and ended at a high of 53% on November 4. Yes, the candidates went back and forth in this poll for months, but Obama's *no looking back* climb began on September 9. A *Gallup* daily tracking-poll-graph at *www.gallup.com/poll/107674/Interactive-Graph-Follow-General-Election.aspx* clearly shows this trend. The same graph also shows that Obama had previously been trending strongly downward since September 1. What caused Obama to begin trending upward on September 9? The answer isn't clear but will, I'm sure, be studied further. The roll our media plays in the four—or eight—years of the Obama Presidency is also a subject that should be studied closely.

ACKNOWLEDGMENTS

I would first like to thank my editor, Yuma Michaels, who worked tirelessly and put up with my frantic insistence on finishing the book in record time. Thanks also to the Overstreet family—Eddie, Joshua, Darby, Jennifer, Naomi, Sean, and Isaac.

ABOUT THE AUTHOR

Michael Jason Overstreet is an actor, screenwriter, and political activist. He lives in Los Angeles.

Made in the USA
Lexington, KY
19 December 2009